# THE CRY OF CAMEROONIANS

Echoes of Struggle and Hope: Navigating a Country's Challenges

A Book by

Dr. THERENCE ATABONG NJUAFAC

The Cry of Cameroonians

Copyright © 2024 Dr. Therence Atabong Njuafac

All rights reserved.

Except for brief quotations included in critical reviews and specific other non-commercial uses allowed by copyright law, no portion of this publication may be reproduced, distributed, or transmitted in any way, including photocopying, recording, or other mechanical or electronic methods, without the author's prior written consent. To seek permission, send an email to the author at the following address:

https://thereodons@gmail.com
https://thereodons@yahoo.com

# DEDICATION

To the brave people of Cameroon, whose words echo through the hills, mountains, and towns, wishing for justice, peace, and a better tomorrow.

To the unseen heroes—mothers, dads, teachers, and youth—who carry the weight of a nation's dreams, this book is for you.

To my beloved family, who have been my pillars of strength and my constant source of inspiration throughout this journey.

And to every Cameroonian, whether at home or in the diaspora, who continues to dream, rise, and strive for a country where respect, freedom, and wealth are not just ideas but realities—this is our joint cry, and may it never go silent.

Dr. Therence Atabong Njuafac

# FOREWORD

The history of a nation is written not only through the decisions of its leaders but also through the voices of its people. In *The Cry of Cameroonians*, Dr. Therence Atabong Njuafac offers a profound reflection on the state of Cameroon, blending the passion of an engaged citizen with the insight of an intellectual immersed in the knowledge of political and social dynamics. This book is a testimony to the resilience, aspirations, and frustrations of Cameroonians who aspire for a brighter future, one that holds promise for their well-being, unity, and progress.

In a time when the world is contending with issues of governance, identity, and human rights, Dr. Njuafac brings us on a voyage through the lived experiences of Cameroonians, revealing the deep-seated challenges that afflict the country. He paints an evocative picture of a people who, despite being wealthy in culture, heritage, and potential, find themselves caught in a cycle of political instability, economic struggles, and social unrest.

What makes this work exceptional is not only the lucidity with which it outlines these issues but also the conviction with which it calls for change. Dr. Njuafac's voice resonates with urgency, demanding that we confront the realities that have long been ignored or suppressed. This book is both a mirror and a lamp—it forces us to look critically at the state of affairs while illuminating pathways for transformation.

In reading *The Cry of Cameroonians*, one is reminded that the power to reshape a nation resides not only in the hands of those who govern but also in the collective will of its people. Dr. Njuafac's eloquence and depth of understanding offer hope—hope that the lament of Cameroonians will not go unheard, and that through fortitude, solidarity, and action, a new chapter can be written in the history of Cameroon.

For those who care profoundly about the future of this nation, and for anyone who desires to understand the intricacies of its struggles, this book is both a wake-up call and a source of inspiration. I commend Dr. Njuafac for his dedication to amplifying the voices of the voiceless and for his unwavering belief in a better destiny for Cameroon.

— [Dr. Therence Atabong Njuafac]

# PREFACE

*The Cry of Cameroonians* is a reflection of a nation's deep-seated struggles, the faith of its people, and the resilience entrenched in its culture and heritage. As a Cameroonian, I have witnessed firsthand the challenges that characterize my country's history, from political turmoil and economic adversity to social discontent and the yearning for peace and unity. This volume is created out of the collective voice of Cameroonians—a voice that resonates with grief, but also with a desire for transformation.

The journey of composing this book was not only one of intellectual endeavor but also a personal pilgrimage. In every chapter, I have sought to convey the essence of a people whose calls for justice, equity, and development remain persistent. I have endeavored to provide a balanced yet critical perspective on the realities that continue to influence Cameroon's trajectory, investigating themes that are both timely and timeless—governance, identity, human rights, and the pursuit of a brighter future.

This work is a call to action, not just for those in positions of authority but for every Cameroonian and global citizen who believes in the ideals of freedom, dignity, and collective progress. It is a reminder that we must remain steadfast in our resolve to build a nation that reflects the values we hold dear, a Cameroon that is inclusive, just, and prosperous.

As you turn the pages of *The Cry of Cameroonians*, I invite you to join me in this journey of reflection, inquiry, and ultimately, hope. May this volume serve as both a mirror and a lens—reflecting the present realities of Cameroon while offering a vision for the future.

— Dr. Therence Atabong Njuafac

# PROLOGUE

The territory of Cameroon, cradled by majestic mountains and nourished by verdant valleys, has long been a symbol of Africa's beauty and potential. Yet beneath its serene landscapes lie a tumultuous history—one marked by colonialism, political strife, and the resilience of its people. As the world turns its gaze away, diverted by its own crises, the voices of millions of Cameroonians cry out—voices yearning to be heard, to be understood, to be free.

In *The Cry of Cameroonians*, I aim to convey the agony, the hope, and the aspirations of a people who have endured years of hardship yet continue to stand erect. This book is not merely an account of events; it is a voyage through the emotional and spiritual depths of a nation in crisis. It recounts the stories of men and women whose lives have been affected by the ongoing conflict, the specter of poverty, and the quest for justice in a country where equality often seems elusive.

As a product of this nation, I have witnessed firsthand the struggles of my fellow Cameroonians. I have seen the silent weeping of mothers who fear for the future of their children, the fractured aspirations of the youth whose only desire is to live in peace, and the untold stories of those whose voices have been silenced. This lament is not only theirs—it is mine, it is ours, and it is a call for justice, for dignity, and for a brighter tomorrow.

Through the pages of this book, I invite you to walk with me through the complexities of our nation's past and present. I invite you to hear the lament that resonates from the alleyways of Bamenda to the shoreline of Limbe. It is a plea that calls for healing, reconciliation, and a collective drive toward a future where all Cameroonians can flourish.

Let this volume be a testament to the resilience of our people and a call to action for those who believe in the power of change.

# TABLE OF CONTENT

DEDICATION .................................................................................. ii
FOREWORD ................................................................................... iii
PREFACE ......................................................................................... v
PROLOGUE .................................................................................... vii
TABLE OF CONTENT .................................................................... ix
CHAPTER ONE ................................................................................ 1
INTRODUCTION ............................................................................. 1
   A. Overview of Cameroon ............................................................ 1
   B. Historical Background ............................................................. 2
      i. European Contact and Colonization .................................... 3
      ii. Partition after World War One ........................................... 4
      iii. Struggles for Independence ............................................... 6
      iv. Challenges of Post-Independence ...................................... 8
CHAPTER TWO .............................................................................. 11
POLITICAL LANDSCAPE ............................................................... 11
   A. Colonial Legacy ........................................................................ 11
   B. Post-Independence Governance ............................................. 14
   C. Democratization Efforts .......................................................... 16
CHAPTER THREE .......................................................................... 19
SOCIO-ECONOMIC CHALLENGES ............................................. 19
   3.1 Poverty and Inequality ............................................................ 22
      A. Poverty .................................................................................. 22
      B. Inequality .............................................................................. 41
   3.2 Corruption ................................................................................ 44
   3.3 Unemployment ........................................................................ 47
      A. An overview of Cameroon's unemployment rate .............. 47
      B. Impacts of Unemployment ................................................ 60

C. Addressing Unemployment Crisis........................................... 109
B. Education............................................................................. 258
CHAPTER FOUR .............................................................................. 273
HUMAN RIGHTS VIOLATIONS ....................................................... 273
4.1 Freedom of Speech and Press ................................................. 273
4.2 Arbitrary Arrests and Detentions .......................................... 280
4.3 Treatment of Minorities.......................................................... 283
   A. Political Marginalization ...................................................... 284
   B. Social and Economic Discrimination: ................................. 288
   C. Cultural Discrimination........................................................ 293
   D. Human Rights Violations and International Response....... 297
CHAPTER FIVE ................................................................................. 302
ENVIRONMENTAL CONCERNS ..................................................... 302
5.1 Deforestation .......................................................................... 302
   A. Causes of Deforerstation in Cameroon: .............................. 303
   B. Impacts of Deforestation ....................................................... 317
   C. Efforts to Combat Deforestation ......................................... 326
5.2 Wildlife Conservation............................................................. 340
   A. Biodiversity and Endangered Species .................................. 341
   B. Major Threats to Wildlife ..................................................... 347
   C. Conservation Efforts and Initiatives ................................... 351
   D. Challenges and Future Directions........................................ 356
5.3 Climate Change Impact ......................................................... 360
CHAPTER SIX................................................................................... 364
REGIONAL CONFLICTS ................................................................. 364
6.1 ANGLOPHONE CRISIS ....................................................... 364
   A. Historical Context................................................................. 364
   B. Cultural and Linguistic Division.......................................... 366
   C. Political Grievances .............................................................. 368
   D. Emergence of Secessionist Movements ............................... 370
   E. Violence and Government Crackdown ................................ 372
   F. International Response.......................................................... 374
   G. Impact on Humanity ............................................................ 376
   H. Prospects for Resolution ...................................................... 378

6.2 BORDER DISPUTES ............................................................. 381
   A. Key Border Disputes ....................................................... 382
   B. Contemporary Implications ............................................. 395
6.3 REFUGEE CRISIS ................................................................ 405
   A. Causes of the Refugee Crisis ............................................. 405
   B. Scale and Scope of the Crisis ............................................ 406
   C. Effect on Humanitarian Issues .......................................... 407
   D. Assistance and Response ................................................. 408
   E. Prospects and Difficulties ................................................ 409
CHAPTER 7 ............................................................................... 411
INTERNATIONAL RELATIONS ...................................................... 411
   7.1 RELATIONS WITH NEIGHBORING COUNTRIES ................ 411
      A. Nigeria: .................................................................... 412
      B. Chad ........................................................................ 413
      C. Central African Republic (CAR) ................................ 415
      D. Equatorial Guinea ................................................... 416
      E. Gabon ..................................................................... 418
      F. Republic of the Congo .............................................. 419
   7.2 FOREIGN AID AND INVESTMENT ..................................... 423
      A. Foreign Aid Sources ................................................. 423
      B. Impact of Foreign Aid .............................................. 426
      C. Foreign Investment .................................................. 428
   7.3 DIPLOMATIC EFFORTS ..................................................... 431
      A. Regional Diplomacy: ................................................ 432
      B. Africa's Sub-Saharan Region .................................... 434
      C. International Diplomacy .......................................... 436
      D. Economic Diplomacy .............................................. 439
      E. Peace and Security ................................................... 442
CHAPTER EIGHT ...................................................................... 447
VOICES OF CHANGE ................................................................. 447
   8.1 CIVIL SOCIETY MOVEMENTS ........................................... 447

    A. Key Organizations and Movements ........................................ 448
    B. Major Achievement ................................................................. 461
    C. Chanllenges ............................................................................. 468
    D. Future Prospects ..................................................................... 473
  8.2 YOUTH ACTIVISM ................................................................... 483
    A. Contemporary Youth Activism ............................................... 484
    B. Challenges Facing Youth Activists .......................................... 502
    C. Impact of Youth Activism ....................................................... 507
    D. Case Studies of Youth Activism ............................................. 513
  8.3 ROLE OF THE DIASPORA ...................................................... 520
    A. Economic Contributions ......................................................... 520
    B. Social and Cultural Impacts .................................................... 527
    C. Political Influence and Advocacy ........................................... 537
    D. Challenges and Opportunities ................................................ 546
CHAPTER NINE ................................................................................ 555
PROSPECTS FOR THE FUTURE ...................................................... 555
  9.1 CHALLENGES AND OPPORTUNITIES ................................. 555
    A. Challenges in Cameroon ......................................................... 555
    B. Opportunities in Cameroon .................................................... 558
    C. Strategic Directions for Progress ............................................ 560
    D. Recommendations for Change ............................................... 562
CHAPTER TEN ................................................................................. 568
CONCLUSION ................................................................................... 568
APPENDICES .................................................................................... 572

# CHAPTER ONE

# INTRODUCTION

## A. Overview of Cameroon

Cameroon, a country situated in the center of Central Africa, is a region of rich cultural diversity, magnificent natural landscapes, and a tumultuous history. With its vibrant blend of over 250 ethnic groups, each with its own distinct language, traditions, and customs, Cameroon stands as a microcosm of Africa itself. From the verdant rainforests of the south to the arid Sahel region in the north, Cameroon's geography is as varied as its people. Formerly a German colony, Cameroon was divided between France and Britain after World War I, leading to a complex colonial legacy that continues to influence its socio-political topography. Achieving independence in 1960 (for the French-controlled regions) and 1961 (for the British-administered territories), Cameroon embarked on a journey towards nation-building amidst challenges of governance, ethnic tensions, and economic development. Despite its immense natural resources including oil, timber, and agricultural products, Cameroon grapples with socio-economic disparities, political instability, and recurrent conflicts, particularly in regions like the Anglophone Northwest and Southwest. These areas have witnessed a protracted struggle for autonomy, leading to violence and displacement of civilians. In "The Cry of Cameroonians," we delve into the intricate tapestry of Cameroon's history, society, and contemporary challenges. Through the perspectives of its people, we seek to cast light on the aspirations, struggles, and resilience of Cameroonians as they navigate the complexities of nationhood and aspire for a better future.

## B. Historical Background

"The Cry of Cameroonians" is a captivating book that goes into the historical complexity and sufferings of the Cameroonian people. To create a contextual background for the story provided in the book, it's vital to investigate the historical trajectory of Cameroon. Cameroon, situated in Central Africa, has a rich and diversified history formed by many indigenous cultures and foreign influences. Prior to European colonization, the area was populated by a multiplicity of ethnic groups, each with its own unique languages, customs, and socioeconomic systems. These tribes comprised the Bantu-speaking peoples in the south, the semi-nomadic Fulani and Hausa in the north, and the indigenous Pygmies in the woods.

### i. European Contact and Colonization

The history of European contact and colonization in Cameroon's coastal regions may be traced back to the late 15th century, when Portuguese navigators first visited these coasts. In subsequent centuries, Dutch, British, and French tradesmen arrived, each putting their own particular impact on the area. However, it wasn't until the end of the nineteenth century that the tide of European influence shifted to the point of exerting colonial dominance over these areas. The introduction of German influence, which consolidated its hold on Cameroon in the late nineteenth century, was a watershed moment in this trajectory. This watershed moment was partly managed by the historic Berlin Conference of 1884-1885, which approved the division of Africa among European powers. Germany used this diplomatic meeting to stamp its colonial goals into the Cameroonian landscape. German colonialism used a multilayered infrastructure of exploitation, coercion, and administrative subjection. The plunder of indigenous resources, along with the imposition of forced labor, demonstrated the exploitative character of German colonial practices. The odious practices of forced labor not only undermined

the dignity of the indigenous people, but also took a tremendous toll on their socioeconomic fabric.
Furthermore, the imposition of colonial administration by the German state resulted in a system of governance that was fundamentally opposed to indigenous peoples' interests and ambitions. The convoluted system of colonial control, riddled with hierarchies and inequities, exacerbated the marginalization of indigenous voices, pushing them to the margins of power and influence. In one word, the arrival of European contact and subsequent colonization in Cameroon's coastal areas is a narrative of exploitation, coercion, and subjugation. The foundation of German dominance, prompted by the Berlin Conference, inaugurated an age of heinous breaches of human dignity and systematic disenfranchisement. Thus, the historical story of European contact and colonization acts as a stinging reminder of colonialism's long-lasting effects, which continue to echo in Cameroon's sociopolitical environment to this day.

### ii. Partition after World War One
Following the devastating battle of World War I, the geopolitical terrain of the world experienced a significant upheaval marked by the redrawing of national borders and the creation of international mandates to supervise the governance of formerly colonial lands. The split of Cameroon, a crucial African province that served as a window into the intricacies of post-war diplomacy and the ambitions of colonial powers, was essential to this restructuring. The

Treaty of Versailles, which was signed in 1919, marked the beginning of a new chapter in international relations after Germany's loss in World War I. The fate of Germany's colonies abroad became a top priority for the Allies. As one of Germany's colonial holdings in Africa, Cameroon was debated and divided among the winning countries, namely France and Britain. Cameroon was divided between France and Britain in line with the rules established by the League of Nations, an organization created in the wake of World War I to foster international cooperation and avert future hostilities. Territories were allocated carefully, taking into account a number of geographical, economic, and strategic variables.

As the arbitrator of post-war territorial disputes, the League of Nations awarded the majority of Cameroon to France, designating it as a League of Nations mission governed by France. This organization was thereafter referred to as French Cameroon, a name that reflected both its physical position and the administrative control that the French colonial rulers implemented. In contrast, the remainder of Cameroon was under British control by virtue of the League of Nations mandate system. Known as British Cameroons, this area was part of Britain's sphere of influence in the area, although it was under the protection of international supervision made possible by the League of Nations. Thus, the division of Cameroon exemplified the complex interactions between diplomatic talks, international legal frameworks, and colonial aspirations that typified the post-World War I period. It emphasized how imperialism is changing and how multilateral organizations are emerging to promote collective security and make it easier for former colonial areas to smoothly move into the contemporary nation-state system. Furthermore, the policies and practices of their separate colonial masters permanently altered the lives and livelihoods of Cameroon's indigenous communities, for whom the division had enormous consequences. This partition's legacy still permeates Cameroon's sociopolitical landscape today, acting as a sobering reminder of colonialism's lasting effects and the necessity of balancing aspirations for national sovereignty and self-determination with historical injustices.

### iii. Struggles for Independence

The mid-20th century is remembered in history as a turning point when passionate nationalist movements began to take root throughout Cameroon's geopolitical landscape. Driven by a passionate yearning for autonomy and release from the constraints of colonial authority, these movements formed a complex fabric distinguished by its heterogeneity with regard to racial, linguistic, and ideological connections. Among the multitude of notable individuals who profoundly influenced the trajectory of this independence movement were Ruben Um Nyobé, Félix-Roland Moumié, and Ahmadou Ahidjo. Their unwavering perseverance and unwavering determination served as beacons of hope that ultimately led Cameroon to achieve sovereignty.

The story of Cameroon's quest for autonomy revolves around the critical year 1960, when the last remnants of colonial rule started to fade and the young Republic of Cameroon emerged from the crucible of conflict, representing the hopes and dreams of its people. Under the leadership of President Ahmadou Ahidjo, Cameroon finally lifted the yoke of French colonial rule on the auspicious dawn of January 1, 1960, ushering in a new era marked by self-governance and national sovereignty. But the road to independence was not without its challenges, especially when it came to defining borders. The conclusion of a UN-sponsored plebiscite, which acted as the arbiter in the disposition of British Cameroons, coincided with Cameroon's attainment of independence. Following this plebiscite, British Cameroons were divided into Northern and Southern Cameroons, each with the authority to weave its own unique story into the larger fabric of post-colonial nationhood.

Following this plebiscite, Northern Cameroons chose to join the newly formed state of Nigeria, while Southern Cameroons chose to integrate with Cameroon, leading to the creation of the Federal Republic of Cameroon. This historic moment highlighted the intricacy of decolonization as well as the necessity of nation-building and the intricate dance of territorial sovereignty. In conclusion, Cameroon's independence struggle is a monument to the people's resilient nature, whose unwavering resolve and fortitude in the face of hardship helped to realize sovereignty and self-determination. Cameroon emerged from the crucible of colonialism, ready to write its own history, thanks to the crucible of collective action and the visionary leadership of individuals like Ahmadou Ahidjo.

### iv. Challenges of Post-Independence

Ever since achieving independence, Cameroon has had to navigate a complex web of issues including socio-political, economic, and humanitarian challenges. The persistent issues of political instability, authoritarian governance, ethnic strife, economic disparity, and human rights violations are the primary challenges to be addressed. The nation's post-independence trajectory has been significantly influenced by these interrelated concerns, which have also changed the socio-political landscape and the lives of its citizens. The persistent danger of political instability is the biggest problem Cameroon is facing. The nation has had an unpredictable political environment with shifting governments, shaky political institutions, and sporadic political upheavals. Consolidating democratic ideas has been made more difficult by the failure to create open and accountable governing structures.

Furthermore, the pervasiveness of authoritarianism taints Cameroon's political landscape. Given that President Paul Biya has been in government since 1982, his lengthy term serves as a perfect illustration of how entrenched authoritarian authority is in the country. The consolidation of power in the hands of one individual has resulted in a culture of political repression that stifles dissent and undermines the principles of participatory government. For Cameroon, ethnic conflicts represent yet another major challenge. The population of the nation is well-known for being ethnically and linguistically varied, including a wide range of groups. However, this variety has also led to strife since ethnic divides have often been used for political gain. Long-standing rivalries and historical grudges have worsened interethnic tensions, weakening social ties and impeding national cohesiveness. Economic divisions perpetuate cycles of poverty and inequality, exacerbating Cameroon's issues. Despite having an abundance of natural resources and agricultural potential, the country has structural problems, poor infrastructure, and a lack of economic diversification. The uneven distribution of money exacerbates socioeconomic inequalities by creating a larger divide between the rich elite and the underprivileged sections in society.

Furthermore, persistent abuses of human rights are undermining the fundamental freedoms and dignity of Cameroonian residents. Reports of extrajudicial killings, arbitrary detentions, and the repression of political opposition tarnish the country's human rights record. Additionally, these reports undermine trust in governmental institutions and are denounced internationally. It will be essential to advance inclusive government, bolster social cohesiveness, and defend democratic and human rights norms in order to successfully solve these complicated concerns. It requires a commitment to basic liberty protection, political change, and institutional openness. Cameroon can only begin along the path to sustainable growth and national wealth by cooperating and maintaining a strong commitment to democratic ideals in order to tackle the enormous obstacles that lie ahead.

# CHAPTER TWO

# POLITICAL LANDSCAPE

## A. Colonial Legacy

The late 19th century saw the brutal competition for Africa by European powers, which is when Cameroon's colonial history began. The nations of Germany, France, and Britain were among the conquerors fighting for dominance over the Kamerun region. Germany became the main colonial power in Cameroon after the conclusion of the Berlin Conference in 1885. Cameroonians endured cultural servitude, exploitation, and abuse under German administration. The indigenous people was deprived of its resources and autonomy by the colonial government via the imposition of severe labor laws, compulsory labor taxes, and land confiscation. In order to support the industrial aspirations of the growing German Empire, German authorities placed a high priority on economic exploitation, harvesting natural resources like rubber, palm oil, and lumber. German colonization had a significant effect on Cameroon's sociopolitical environment. German administrators imposed their own legal frameworks and bureaucratic structures, marginalizing indigenous institutions and undermining traditional forms of government. The colonial regime's use of divide-and-rule strategies planted the seeds of unrest among ethnic groups, escalating already-existing tensions and cultivating a legacy of interethnic struggle that endures to this day.

One of the most important turning points in Cameroon's colonial history was the conclusion of World War I. After Germany was defeated, the victorious Allied nations split up Kamerun in the 1919 Treaty of Versailles, with Britain and France taking up residence there. The foundation for decades of colonial exploitation and repression under French and British control was created by this split, each of which left a unique psychological mark on the people of Cameroon. Colonial policies in French Cameroun, the region of Cameroon under French administration, were similar to those of its forerunner. The "prestation," a forced labor system established by the French, compelled Cameroonians to serve on plantations and government projects for little pay. Furthermore, the French colonial government's assimilationist tactics sought to undermine native languages and cultures in favor of French language and culture as the only indicators of civilization. Similar to this, marginalization and exploitation were hallmarks of colonialism in

British Southern Cameroons. By using traditional institutions and local leaders to carry out colonial aims, the British established indirect control.

However, since British authorities continued to have final say over matters of politics and the economy, this arrangement strengthened existing power disparities and inequalities. The lengthy and complex process of Cameroon's independence movement was characterized by action, sacrifice, and opposition. French Cameroun became independent of France in 1960. British Southern Cameroons followed suit in 1961, and following a contentious vote, they joined the newly formed Republic of Cameroon. Nevertheless, neocolonial systems continued to exist, sustaining social inequality, political instability, and economic reliance, overshadowing the promise of freedom. The cries of the Cameroonian people echo through the passages of time, bearing witness to the colonial legacy that still exists on the African continent. The wounds of colonialism are deeply ingrained in the collective consciousness of the Cameroonian people, ranging from the savagery of German imperialism to the cunning schemes of French and British dominance. However, despite the remnants of injustice and exploitation, there is also resiliency and a will to take back control of one's own destiny and create a new one free from the constraints of the past. It is critical to address the colonial legacy head-on, acknowledge its inequities, and work toward a more fair and inclusive society for all Cameroonians as the country navigates the challenges of nation-building and reconciliation.

## B. Post-Independence Governance

Cameroonians have faced several governance issues throughout their turbulent march towards freedom from colonial domination. The nation struggled with nation-building, political unrest, and socioeconomic inequality in the years after independence. Though many Cameroonian citizens have found their reality to be far from the idealized visions of freedom and growth, the early years presented hope for progress and wealth. One of the main problems with Cameroon's post-independence government has been the concentration of power in the hands of a small number of people. The rights of individuals have been compromised and democratic development has been hampered by political leadership, which is often typified by authoritarian tendencies and a lack of accountability. Numerous administrations have been blamed for suppressing dissent, abusing human rights, and manipulating elections, which has left the public very unhappy.

Furthermore, regional inequality and ethnic strife have tarnished Cameroon's governing environment since the country's independence. Certain ethnic groups and geographical areas have been sidelined by the imposition of a centralized governmental system, which has fueled complaints and fostered divides within the population. Consequently, attempts to promote national cohesiveness and togetherness have been weakened, making it more difficult for the nation to realize its varied potential for shared growth. Corruption and poor economic management have made Cameroonians' post-independence problems even more severe. The majority of the population lives below the poverty line, and pervasive poverty and inequality continue despite the nation's abundant natural resources and agricultural potential. The administration of public resources has been opaque and accountable, which has impeded attempts to reduce poverty and advance sustainable development. Geopolitical interests and Cameroon's reliance on foreign assistance are two external variables that have impacted the country's post-independence administration in addition to internal issues.

Due to its advantageous position and abundant natural resources, the nation has drawn the attention of international powers, which often results in meddling in domestic matters and exacerbates already-existing governance problems. Cameroonians have persisted in raising their voices in protest and calling on their leaders to answer for their actions in spite of these obstacles. Youth, grassroots movements, and civil society groups have all been vital in promoting social justice and democratic changes. To solve the underlying problems and create a better future for all Cameroonians, the government and civil society must work together to overcome the many challenges that stand in the way of true democracy and inclusive governance. A heartbreaking reminder of the ongoing fight for justice, equality, and dignity in the post-independence age, the scream of Cameroonians echoes through the halls of power. The ambitions of the people can only be achieved by significant changes, sincere communication, and group effort, opening the door to a more affluent and inclusive Cameroon.

## C. Democratization Efforts

There has been advancement and controversy around Cameroon's attempts at democracy. Like many other African countries, Cameroon has faced difficult challenges on its path to democracy since obtaining independence in 1960. Following its independence, Cameroon was ruled by a single party, the Cameroon National Union (CNU), led by President Ahmadou Ahidjo, controlling the country's political scene. However, when democratic winds swept over Africa in the early 1990s, major changes started to occur. The 1990 National Conference, which brought together numerous political parties, civil society organizations, and individuals to debate the political future of the nation, was one of the key events in Cameroon's democracy. Opposition parties were eventually made lawful as a result of this convention, and a multi-party system was eventually implemented. President Paul Biya, who had replaced Ahidjo in 1982, won Cameroon's first multiparty presidential elections in 1992. The legitimacy of succeeding elections has been tarnished by accusations of electoral fraud and manipulation, but Biya's Cameroon People's Democratic Movement (CPDM) has remained dominant despite the advent of multiparty politics. Cameroon has also had difficulties in establishing democratic institutions and practices. Concerns include the lack of political room for alternative parties, limitations on the right to free expression and assembly, and claims of violations of human rights have continued, bringing condemnation from both local and foreign observers. Nonetheless, attempts have been made to deal with these issues. Media outlets, grassroots movements, and civil society groups have all been vital in pushing for democratic changes and keeping the government responsible. In addition, projects aiming at strengthening Cameroon's democratic government have received support and help from foreign partners.

There have been some encouraging advancements in spite of the challenges. The goal of the decentralization project, which was started in the late 1990s, was to provide local government more authority and resources while encouraging citizen engagement and governance. Improvements to the electoral procedures and the electoral legislation have also been initiated. In order to resolve the underlying socio-political tensions in Cameroon, especially in areas impacted by separatist movements and internal conflicts, there have been demands in recent years for more extensive conversation and reconciliation. In addition to political changes, addressing socioeconomic inequality, advancing inclusion, and upholding human rights are all necessary for real democracy. In summary, even though Cameroon has made progress toward democracy, there are still big obstacles to overcome. Long-term initiatives are required to strengthen democratic institutions, advance accountability and transparency, and cultivate a climate of political plurality and human rights respect. For all of its inhabitants, Cameroon can only achieve long-term democratic stability and prosperity via sincere conversation, involvement, and inclusive government.

# CHAPTER THREE

# SOCIO-ECONOMIC CHALLENGES

Cameroon, located in the center of Central Africa, serves as a demonstration of the opportunities and difficulties encountered by several countries worldwide. Cameroon has abundant natural resources, including oil and gas deposits and fertile agricultural land. It also has a diverse array of cultures and customs, making it a promising country for growth and prosperity. Nevertheless, the path to economic success is filled with challenges, with poverty and inequality being the most significant hurdles. Although Cameroon has a wealth of resources, a substantial segment of its people nevertheless struggles with poverty, missing essential provisions such as clean water, sufficient healthcare, and education. The economic inequality worsens social tensions and weakens attempts to promote unity and cohesiveness in the country. Governance is a crucial problem that contributes to Cameroon's socio-economic difficulties. Governmental institutions are plagued by corruption, incompetence, and lack of transparency, which hinders their ability to make effective policies and allocate resources. In addition, the presence of political instability and intermittent instances of violence in certain areas serve as further obstacles to advancement and discourage investment, thereby perpetuating cycles of poverty and underdevelopment.

Cameroon not only deals with governance problems but also has structural obstacles to achieving equitable economic development. These obstacles include insufficient infrastructure, restricted availability of credit and financial services for small enterprises, and discrepancies in educational possibilities, especially between urban and rural regions. These differences not only sustain economic inequality but also impede social mobility and prolong intergenerational poverty. Addressing these difficulties needs a multidimensional strategy that stresses strong governance, investment in human resources, infrastructure development, and equitable economic policy. Efforts to tackle corruption, enhance the business climate, and promote transparency are vital for restoring public faith in institutions and attracting much-needed investment.

Furthermore, investing in education and vocational training programs may equip the workforce with the skills required to compete in the global economy and foster innovation and entrepreneurship. Enhancing access to healthcare and social services, especially in neglected rural regions, is vital for increasing living standards and decreasing poverty. Moreover, fostering inclusive economic growth through targeted initiatives to support small and medium-sized enterprises, promote agriculture and sustainable natural resource management, and expand access to financial services can help uplift marginalized communities and narrow the gap between the rich and the poor. While the path ahead may be tough, Cameroon's rich cultural legacy, tenacious populace, and enormous potential offer as sources of hope and inspiration. By tackling the core causes of poverty and inequality and promoting an environment favorable to sustainable development and shared prosperity, Cameroon may overcome its socio-economic difficulties and fulfill its goals for a better future for all its inhabitants.

## 3.1 Poverty and Inequality
### A. Poverty
#### i. Income Inqualities

Income inequalities in Cameroon are a complicated problem firmly embedded into the socio-economic fabric of the nation, manifested via regional differences and socio-economic strata. At its heart, this phenomenon delineates a sharp difference between metropolitan areas, such as the bustling capital Yaoundé and the commercial metropolis Douala, and the rural hinterlands that represent a substantial percentage of the nation's geography. In major settings like Yaoundé and Douala, the economic pulse pulses with vitality, giving a wealth of chances in trade, industry, and services. Here, the skylines studded with contemporary edifices represent a lifestyle defined by access to amenities, higher-paying employment, and educational institutions. However, this affluence typically stays contained inside the metropolitan enclaves, leaving hinterlands veiled in the shadow of neglect.

Conversely, rural areas, home to a major percentage of Cameroon's population, contend with a range of issues. Access to critical services like as healthcare, education, and infrastructure is frequently restricted, creating a cycle of poverty and marginalization. The lack of proper transportation infrastructure further exacerbates this imbalance, separating rural areas from economic opportunities and crucial services. Moreover, the agricultural sector, which serves as the principal livelihood for many rural inhabitants, confronts its own set of issues. Outdated farming techniques, poor access to financing, and unpredictable weather patterns restrict agricultural production, relegating many farmers to subsistence existence. Furthermore, socio-economic discrepancies within metropolitan regions increase the abyss of inequality. While some dwellers of urban centers prosper in the areas of entrepreneurship and high-paying jobs, a considerable section of the metropolitan population grapples with informal employment, typified by poor earnings, job instability, and lack of social safety.

Education appears as a critical component sustaining wealth inequality, with access to decent education being elusive for many. Inadequate infrastructure, teacher shortages, and budgetary restrictions hamper educational achievement, restricting the socio-economic mobility of persons from vulnerable groups. Addressing economic inequality involves a broad strategy involving legislative interventions, infrastructural development, and social efforts. Investments in rural infrastructure, such as road networks and electricity projects, may bridge the urban-rural divide, stimulating economic growth and improving lives in rural regions. Similarly, measures aiming at boosting agricultural production via modern farming practices, access to capital, and market links may benefit rural populations. Additionally, boosting the school system to enable fair access to excellent education and vocational training is vital. This requires hiring and training skilled instructors, investing in educational infrastructure, and implementing targeted initiatives to serve underrepresented kids.

Furthermore, establishing an enabling climate for entrepreneurship and small enterprises, especially in rural regions, may promote economic development and offer job possibilities. This comprises giving access to financial resources, company development services, and market connections to potential entrepreneurs. Resolving income gaps in Cameroon demands comprehensive efforts targeted at supporting inclusive economic growth, equitable access to opportunities, and social development across regions and socio-economic strata. By bridging the urban-rural divide, investing in human capital, and encouraging sustainable livelihoods, Cameroon may work towards a more fair and prosperous future for all its residents.

## ii. Underemployment and Unemployment

There are continuing difficulties to Cameroon's economic stability and social cohesion that are brought about by the country's high levels of unemployment and underemployment. The problem is especially severe among the younger population of the country, which exacerbates worries about the possibilities for the future and the stability of society. Despite the fact that Cameroon has a young population that is filled with promise, the country is struggling with the difficult challenge of providing sufficient employment opportunities in order to capitalize on this demographic dividend. The widespread presence of work in the informal sector is the primary factor contributing to this predicament. Even while it provides a means of survival for many people in the absence of official work, it also perpetuates a cycle of poor productivity, small compensation, and little job security. This is despite the fact that it acts as a safety net for many people. Workers are left exposed to exploitation and insecure working circumstances because the informal sector, despite its resilience, often operates beyond the jurisdiction of legal systems.

Furthermore, the issue of unemployment is made worse by the mismatch between the skills that are required by the labor market and those that are held by those who are looking for work. Because they do not have sufficient access to excellent education and training programs, many Cameroonians are not adequately prepared to participate in an economy that is becoming more globalized and competitive. As a consequence, there is an increasing pool of talent that is not being exploited, which is a barrier to economic growth and a barrier to progress toward achieving sustainable development objectives. There have widespread repercussions across Cameroonian society as a result of the widespread unemployment and underemployment policies. Beyond economic hardship, these circumstances foster social unrest, generating animosity and despair, especially among disaffected young. The absence of significant work prospects engenders emotions of despondency and marginalization, thereby stoking social unrest and increasing existing political tensions.

Addressing the core causes of unemployment and underemployment involves a diversified strategy. Efforts to stimulate entrepreneurship, strengthen vocational training programs, and support innovation are vital to unleashing the untapped potential of Cameroon's workforce. Additionally, targeted investments in areas with high employment potential, such as agriculture, industry, and technology, may boost job growth and strengthen economic resilience. Moreover, initiatives aiming at formalizing the informal sector and enhancing labor market laws are crucial for defending the rights and well-being of workers. By encouraging fair labor standards and creating paths for upward mobility, Cameroon may build a more equitable and sustainable economy that exploits the full potential of its people resources. In essence, tackling the entrenched difficulties of unemployment and underemployment is vital for Cameroon's long-term economic and social stability. Through coordinated measures to create economic diversification, boost skills development, and enhance labor market institutions, the nation may chart a route towards a more egalitarian and bright future for all its residents.

### iii. Limited Access to Education

In Cameroon, where education is essential for reducing poverty, limited access to school is a major barrier to socioeconomic advancement. Nevertheless, the country has several obstacles that make it difficult to provide universal access to high-quality education for all of its residents. A primary hindrance is the inadequate infrastructure in schooling. Many Cameroonian schools, particularly those in rural regions, struggle with outdated infrastructure, a shortage of classrooms, and a lack of basic facilities like running water and electricity. These shortcomings in infrastructure not only jeopardize the quality of the learning environment but also discourage students—especially girls—from going to school. The educational situation is further exacerbated by the ongoing scarcity of competent educators. There is an extreme shortage of qualified teachers compared to the demand, which results in packed classrooms and worse teaching quality. The lack of instructors in isolated areas is especially severe, depriving pupils of qualified mentoring and advice that is essential to their academic growth.

In Cameroon, sociocultural constraints exacerbate the issue of educational access. The prioritization of boys' education over girls' by deeply ingrained traditions and cultural conventions frequently results in gender discrepancies in literacy and enrollment rates. Furthermore, cultural views may dissuade members of certain racial or religious communities from pursuing formal education, which would leave underprivileged populations behind in their quest for empowerment and knowledge. Because of this, a sizable segment of the populace is unable to get the necessary training and credentials in order to find productive job, which feeds the cycle of poverty. People who lack the necessary education and skills are forced into low-paying occupations or unofficial work, where they struggle to escape the bonds of economic hardship. A comprehensive strategy that includes community involvement projects, teacher training programs, infrastructure development, and legislative interventions is needed to address these issues. Expanding educational access requires inclusive initiatives that prioritize vulnerable populations and provide fair chances for everyone. Cameroon can only overcome its educational obstacles and open the door to a better, more affluent future for its people by working together.

### iv. Healthcare Challenges

Poor health outcomes contribute to the perpetuation of poverty in Cameroon. Limited access to healthcare services, particularly in distant places, exacerbates the effect of widespread illnesses such as malaria, HIV/AIDS, and TB. High healthcare expenditures further strain family finances, driving families further into poverty when confronted with medical problems.

> **Limited Access to Healthcare Infrastructure:**

The discrepancies in healthcare services between urban and rural communities in Cameroon are made worse by limited access to healthcare infrastructure. Accessing even the most basic healthcare services, such clinics, hospitals, and health centers, may be very difficult for remote areas. In addition to negatively impacting healthcare quality, this shortage places a heavy strain on both people and communities. The lack of healthcare services in rural regions forces locals to travel great distances in order to get to the closest medical facility. This trip might be difficult, particularly for those who reside in remote areas with inadequate transportation. Because of this, people often put off getting medical help until their diseases become worse, which may have a detrimental impact on their health and raise the death rate. In addition, the prompt provision of emergency medical services is hampered by the absence of a proper healthcare infrastructure in rural regions. In the absence of emergency-ready hospitals or clinics in the area, critically ill patients may have to wait a long time to get life-saving care. These delays may sometimes be deadly, underscoring the critical need for underprivileged people to have better access to medical services. Furthermore, differences in healthcare outcomes between people in urban and rural areas are partly caused by restricted access to healthcare facilities. Higher quality treatment and better health outcomes are often the result of urban regions' abundance of healthcare experts and better-equipped hospitals and medical facilities. On the other hand, the absence of basic medical resources in rural areas often leads to subpar care and worse health outcomes for locals. Comprehensive policies that prioritize enhancing healthcare delivery in rural and distant locations are necessary to address Cameroon's problem of restricted access to healthcare infrastructure. This might include making more investments in the infrastructure of the healthcare industry, such as constructing new clinics and hospitals and renovating existing ones. Moreover, initiatives to develop telemedicine services and upgrade transportation infrastructure may aid in closing the access gap to healthcare between urban and rural locations. It is imperative that local communities, non-profits, and government agencies work together to create long-term solutions that tackle the underlying reasons of inadequate access to healthcare infrastructure. Cameroon may strive toward establishing equitable healthcare results and enhancing the general health and well-being of its people by emphasizing healthcare access for all individuals.

> **Shortage of Healthcare Profesionals:** The scarcity of healthcare professionals in Cameroon is a multidimensional problem with far-reaching ramifications for the nation's healthcare system and the well-being of its people. At the core of this dilemma lies a lack of qualified experts across many medical professions, comprising physicians, nurses, specialists, and other important healthcare personnel. This scarcity of competent individuals adversely impairs the delivery of healthcare services, especially in rural regions, where the demand for medical treatment is typically most urgent. In rural parts of Cameroon, the scarcity of healthcare providers provides a strong obstacle to getting appropriate medical treatment. Numerous variables contribute to this imbalance, producing a complicated web of obstacles that hamper the recruitment and retention of healthcare personnel in these impoverished communities. One key problem is the low availability of resources and infrastructure, which may make practicing medicine in rural settings substantially more onerous compared to metropolitan locations. Inadequate facilities, antiquated technology, and a shortage of vital supplies further increase the problems experienced by healthcare workers functioning in these situations. Additionally, the discrepancy in salary between rural and urban regions acts as a substantial barrier for

healthcare personnel contemplating employment in rural locations. With lower salary and fewer incentives available in rural settings, many healthcare professionals decide to explore possibilities in more urbanized locations where remuneration and career progression prospects are believed to bc more advantageous. Consequently, rural towns are left underserved, struggle to recruit and maintain the medical competence essential to satisfy the healthcare demands of their inhabitants efficiently. Moreover, the scarcity of healthcare providers in rural regions perpetuates a cycle of insufficient healthcare service and worsened health outcomes for Cameroonians living outside large metropolitan centers. Without regular access to experienced medical workers, persons in remote regions confront difficulty in managing chronic disorders, getting preventative care, and receiving early treatment for severe illnesses and accidents. This may lead to a deterioration of health conditions, a rise in avoidable illnesses, and greater rates of morbidity and death among these communities. Addressing the scarcity of healthcare professionals in Cameroon demands a comprehensive strategy that tackles the underlying reasons leading to this problem. Efforts to improve healthcare infrastructure, broaden access to resources and vital medical supplies, and promote training and education opportunities for aspiring healthcare professionals are key components of any plan aimed at reducing the shortage. Additionally, initiatives to incentivize healthcare professionals to practice in rural areas, such as offering competitive salaries, providing loan forgiveness programs, and implementing support systems for professional development and career advancement, can help attract and retain talent in underserved regions. Furthermore, establishing cooperation between government agencies, healthcare organizations, academic institutions, and community partners is crucial for developing lasting solutions to solve the lack of healthcare workers. By working together to develop new ways and policies, stakeholders can establish a stronger and resilient healthcare workforce that is capable of fulfilling the different requirements of Cameroon's people, regardless of geographic location. Ultimately, investing in the recruitment, training, and retention of healthcare workers in rural regions is not only crucial for increasing healthcare access and outcomes but also for fostering equality and socioeconomic development throughout the nation.

> **Prevalence of Infectious Diseases:**

In Cameroon, the presence of infectious illnesses provides a complicated issue that reaches well beyond the sphere of healthcare. The burden of illnesses like malaria, HIV/AIDS, TB, and neglected tropical diseases not only affects the health and well-being of people but also inhibits the country's socio-economic growth. Malaria stands as one of the most ubiquitous health hazards in Cameroon, especially in rural regions where access to healthcare services and preventative measures like insecticide-treated bed nets remains restricted. The cyclical nature of malaria epidemics not only inflicts a severe toll on human health but also impairs agricultural output, leading to food shortages and economic instability. HIV/AIDS, although a worldwide problem, impacts Cameroon severely, with high rates of incidence among particular groups. The condition not only exacts a terrible toll on people and families but also strains healthcare systems and causes a considerable burden on the economy owing to the expenditures connected with treatment and care. Tuberculosis, while preventable and curable, continues to represent a serious issue in Cameroon, worsened by variables such as poverty, malnutrition, and restricted access to healthcare facilities. The rise of drug-resistant strains significantly complicates attempts to curb the spread of the illness and highlights the urgent need for comprehensive therapies. Neglected tropical illnesses, including ailments such as schistosomiasis, lymphatic filariasis, and soil-transmitted helminthiasis, disproportionately impact underprivileged groups in Cameroon. These illnesses not only cause physical misery but also create a cycle of poverty by affecting people' capacity to work and participate fully in society. The effect of these infectious illnesses reverberates across Cameroonian society, impeding educational achievement, lowering worker productivity, and prolonging intergenerational cycles of poverty. Furthermore, the weight of healthcare expenses involved with treating and managing chronic disorders diverts resources away from other critical services, hampering overall socio-economic growth. Addressing the complex difficulties presented by infectious illnesses in Cameroon demands a holistic strategy that incorporates not just healthcare treatments but also larger socio-economic measures. Strengthening healthcare infrastructure, boosting access to key drugs and diagnostics, promoting health education and preventative initiatives, and addressing underlying socioeconomic determinants of health are all important components of a holistic approach. Additionally, establishing cooperation between government agencies, non-governmental organizations, the corporate sector, and foreign partners is crucial to deploy resources and skills efficiently and sustainably tackle infectious illnesses in Cameroon.

> **Financial Barriers to Healthcare:**

Financial obstacles to healthcare in Cameroon are firmly established and varied, severely restricting access to vital medical treatments for a huge percentage of the population. The high healthcare expenses offer a tremendous impediment, serving as a discouragement for people and families seeking critical medical treatment. This financial strain is especially intense owing to the preponderance of out-of-pocket payments, when consumers are obliged to pay for healthcare services directly at the time of treatment. For many Cameroonians, the expense of healthcare constitutes a considerable amount of their family income, frequently pushing finances to the breaking point. In low-income homes, whose financial resources are already restricted, even little healthcare bills may have devastating implications, leading to rising poverty levels and economic instability. Moreover, the unpredictability of healthcare expenditures adds extra stress and anxiety to families already trying to make ends meet. The lack of comprehensive universal health care systems exacerbates this already severe situation. Without proper insurance or social protection systems in place, vulnerable groups, including the poor, aged, and those with chronic diseases, are especially prone to financial disaster in the case of sickness or accident. In such situations, people may skip critical medical treatment completely or postpone seeking care until their condition worsens, resulting in unneeded pain and problems. Furthermore, the absence of cheap healthcare alternatives fosters a cycle of poverty and bad health, since people are unable to receive preventative treatments or timely interventions to manage chronic disorders. This not only impairs the well-being of individuals and families but also inhibits broader community development and economic progress. Addressing these financial obstacles to healthcare needs a multidimensional strategy comprising government engagement, regulatory changes, and greater investment in healthcare infrastructure and human resources. Implementing universal health coverage schemes, extending social health insurance programs, and subsidizing healthcare expenditures for low-income populations are key measures towards providing fair access to excellent healthcare for all Cameroonians. Additionally, measures to expand basic healthcare services, promote preventive care programs, and boost health education may help reduce the financial burden on people and families while improving health outcomes and decreasing long-term healthcare expenditures. Ultimately, obtaining universal access to healthcare in Cameroon needs a coordinated commitment by government, healthcare providers, civil society, and the international community to address the core causes of financial obstacles and promote health equality for everyone.

> **Challenge in Materanal and Child Health:**

Challenges in Maternal and Child Health: Expanding on the problems in maternity and child health in Cameroon shows a complicated environment defined by chronically high rates of maternal and newborn mortality. These rates, typically considered as worrisome, underline the urgent need for comprehensive interventions targeted at addressing the underlying causes fuelling these bad consequences. One key concern is the restricted availability of vital maternal healthcare services, including prenatal care, experienced birth attendants, and obstetric services. This lack of access not only impedes the diagnosis and care of pregnancy-related problems but also raises the chance of bad outcomes following delivery. Without effective prenatal care, pregnant moms lose out on essential health monitoring, education, and treatments that may avoid or lessen possible dangers to both maternal and newborn health. Moreover, the scarcity of trained birth attendants exacerbates the issues encountered by expectant mothers. The presence of trained healthcare experts during labor is vital for guaranteeing safe births and swiftly resolving any difficulties that may emerge. However, in many parts of Cameroon, especially rural and underserved areas, the availability of qualified birth attendants remains inadequate, leaving women susceptible to avoidable maternal and newborn morbidity and death. Cultural and social issues further complicate these problems. Deep-rooted cultural attitudes and traditions may impact women's decision-making toward accessing healthcare during pregnancy and delivery. Additionally, socioeconomic inequities, including poverty, low education, and insufficient access to transportation, may operate as obstacles preventing women from getting maternity health treatments when required. These variables contribute to a cycle of poor mother and child health outcomes, perpetuating inequities and impeding progress towards improving overall health indicators.

Addressing these difficulties needs a multidimensional strategy that incorporates initiatives to improve healthcare infrastructure, boost access to key services, overcome cultural obstacles, and lessen socioeconomic inequities. By investing in comprehensive maternity and child health programs that emphasize accessibility, quality, and culturally responsive care, Cameroon may make substantial progress towards lowering maternal and infant death rates and increasing the well-being of mothers and children throughout the nation.

➤ **Healthcare Infrastructure Vulnerability to Emergencies:**
Cameroon's healthcare infrastructure suffers major vulnerabilities when faced with catastrophes, ranging from natural disasters to disease outbreaks, exerting great burden on an already vulnerable system. Firstly, natural catastrophes such as floods, landslides, and droughts pose a considerable danger to healthcare institutions and their operating capacity. Infrastructure damage arising from severe catastrophes may leave hospitals inaccessible or dysfunctional, interrupting crucial healthcare services and hindering emergency response operations. Moreover, the loss of roads and bridges might delay the movement of medical supplies, aggravating the difficulty encountered by healthcare practitioners in giving timely treatment to impacted people. Secondly, disease outbreaks,

including epidemics and pandemics, reveal the deficiencies in Cameroon's healthcare system. The spread of infectious illnesses may overwhelm healthcare facilities, resulting to shortages of crucial medical supplies, hospital beds, and healthcare professionals. Inadequate infection control procedures further worsen the problem, promoting the fast spread of infections inside hospital facilities and among the community at large. Additionally, the absence of proper readiness and response procedures magnifies the effect of catastrophes on the healthcare system. Limited resources, limited training, and fragmented coordination among important stakeholders hamper the early and efficient response to crises, increasing the length and severity of their consequences on healthcare delivery. The lack of comprehensive disaster management strategies further worsens these issues, leaving healthcare institutions ill-equipped to mitigate and handle emergency events. Furthermore, socioeconomic problems such as poverty, inequality, and inadequate access to healthcare heighten the vulnerabilities of Cameroon's healthcare infrastructure to catastrophes. Vulnerable populations, especially rural communities and disadvantaged groups, face the brunt of these issues, including hurdles to receiving needed healthcare services before, during, and after calamities. Addressing the vulnerabilities of Cameroon's healthcare infrastructure to calamities needs a multidimensional strategy that combines investment in disaster planning and response skills, strengthening of healthcare systems, and addressing underlying socioeconomic determinants of health. By building resilience and capacity at both institutional and community levels, Cameroon may better reduce the effect of crises on its healthcare system and preserve the health and well-being of its people.

A diverse strategy is needed to address these healthcare issues, one that includes funding for workforce development, healthcare infrastructure, financial protection measures, disease prevention and control programs, and maternity and child health activities. To increase healthcare access, quality, and results for all Cameroonians, cooperation between governmental and non-governmental organizations, foreign partners, and local communities is crucial.

## B. Inequality

Globally, inequality is a chronic and urgent problem that has a negative impact on society as a whole. The issue is not limited to differences in income; it also includes differences in access to opportunity, healthcare, education, and fundamental human rights. In Cameroon, inequality is a major socioeconomic problem that poses several obstacles to social cohesion, stability, and growth. The abundance of variety found in the nation's resources, geography, and culture is often eclipsed by gaps in chances for progress, access to basic services, and wealth distribution. In order to address the effects of inequality and promote inclusive development, it is essential to comprehend its causes and consequences.

In Cameroon, inequality stems mostly from historical, political, and economic issues. The socioeconomic structure of the nation is still marked by the colonial past, which concentrated money and power in the hands of a select few fortunate people. The country has had challenges in properly addressing these inequities since gaining independence, which have been made worse by elements including poor social programs, weak government, and corruption. The gap between urban and rural areas of Cameroon is one of the main signs of inequality in the country. The level of life is comparatively greater in urban areas like Douala and Yaoundé because they have better access to infrastructure, healthcare, and educational resources. In the meanwhile, many people live in rural regions, which often lack basic amenities and provide difficulties such poor access to healthcare, education, and clean water. Spatial inequality results in disadvantaged populations and impedes overall development since it sustains differences in opportunities and quality of life.

Moreover, in Cameroon, wealth disparity continues to be a major worry. Due to uneven resource distribution, a lack of good jobs, and differences in access to education and skill development, the wealthiest elite's disparity from the general populace is growing. This problem is made worse by high unemployment rates, especially for young people, which fuel social discontent and economic instability. An additional crucial component of Cameroon's socioeconomic environment is gender disparity. In spite of initiatives to advance gender parity and women's agency, discrimination against women persists in a number of domains, such as work, education, and property rights. Women's involvement in the labor and decision-making processes is often restricted by cultural norms and conventional roles, which feeds the cycle of poverty and marginalization.

Furthermore, regional and ethnic differences exacerbate Cameroon's inequality problems. Social stratification and unequal growth across various areas have been fostered by historical divides and disputes among ethnic groups. Marginalized groups, including ethnic minorities and indigenous communities, often experience the worst effects of socioeconomic inequality and face obstacles to obtaining chances for growth and resources. Comprehensive approaches that place a high priority on social justice, fair development, and inclusive growth are needed to address inequality in Cameroon. This calls for governance changes, such as actions to strengthen institutions, fight corruption, and advance accountability and transparency. Increasing human capital and closing the opportunity gap need funding for education and skill-building initiatives, especially in marginalized communities. In addition, fostering social inclusion and minimizing inequality need focused interventions to meet the unique needs of disadvantaged groups, such as women, youth, and ethnic minorities. In order to guarantee equitable access to opportunities and resources, affirmative action measures like quota systems and tailored assistance programs may be necessary. More equitable growth and shared prosperity may also be achieved by promoting sustainable economic development, diversifying the economy, and lowering reliance on extractive sectors. Leveraging technology to increase access to markets, financing, and services while embracing innovation may also aid in closing the digital divide and empowering disadvantaged groups. In the end, combating inequality in Cameroon requires cooperation with foreign partners as well as a coordinated effort by the public, commercial, and civil society sectors. Cameroon may endeavor to create a more affluent and inclusive society for all of its residents by tackling the underlying causes of inequality and putting targeted policies and programs into place.

## 3.2 Corruption

In Cameroon, corruption is still a major socioeconomic problem that has persisted for a long time, hindering the nation's progress and widening already existing divides. Corruption persists in Cameroonian society despite attempts by the government to combat it. It affects many facets of the country's life, from social cohesiveness and public service delivery to economic progress. Fundamentally, there are many ways that corruption appears in Cameroon: from small-scale bribery and theft to established networks of nepotism and cronyism inside the political and administrative structures. The negative effects of corruption on the economy are among its most harmful features. Corruption-related misappropriation of public money not only reduces the effectiveness of the public sector but also discourages foreign investment and erodes the business climate. In turn, this stunts economic progress and keeps people in poverty since money that might be used for social welfare, healthcare, infrastructure, and education is diverted by a small number of people for their own personal benefit.

Moreover, corruption weakens the rule of law and erodes public confidence in political institutions. Citizens become more cynical and indifferent to government when they believe that people in positions of authority are dishonest and operate with impunity. Wide-ranging effects of this loss of confidence may include a decline in political stability, a rise in social unrest, and a decrease in civic involvement. Furthermore, corruption makes inequality worse by sustaining privileged social structures and widening socioeconomic gaps. Those who are already marginalized or economically disadvantaged are disadvantaged when access to essential services like healthcare, education, and justice is often dependent on one's capacity to make bribes or use personal connections in a corrupt system. This leads to a vicious circle where corruption solidifies already-existing disparities, making it harder for society's most marginalized groups to escape poverty or take advantage of possibilities for growth.

Corruption in Cameroon continues despite awareness of the issue and some attempts to address it because of a number of causes. Corrupt practices are sustained in part because of inadequate supervision systems, weak institutional frameworks, and a lack of political will to impose anti-corruption laws. Moreover, social attitudes and cultural practices that accept or even encourage corruption make it more difficult to successfully resist it. A multifaceted strategy that includes institutional development, cultural shift, and legislative changes is needed to combat corruption in Cameroon. Any successful anti-corruption plan must include strengthening anti-corruption legislation and institutions, improving accountability and transparency systems, encouraging ethical leadership, and cultivating an integrity- and civic engagement-focused culture. Additionally, in order to create an atmosphere where corrupt practices are less common and possibilities for growth are more fair, it is imperative to address the core causes of corruption, which include poverty, inequality, and insufficient access to essential services. Ultimately, the government, private industry, civil society, and international community must all continue to be committed to and work together to eliminate corruption in Cameroon. Cameroon may realize its full potential for sustainable development and build a more equitable and affluent society for all of its residents by tackling corruption fully and holistically.

## 3.3 Unemployment

One of the most important socioeconomic issues facing Cameroon is unemployment, which poses a variety of difficulties for both the country and its citizens. Despite the nation's great economic potential, which is bolstered by a wealth of natural resources and a diversified labor pool, unemployment is still a problem, especially for young people.

### A. An overview of Cameroon's unemployment rate

### i. Youth Unemployment

The issue of youth unemployment in Cameroon is complex and has its roots in the socioeconomic structure of the nation. Even having a mostly young population that brings with it the potential for dynamic economic development and innovation, Cameroon finds it difficult to fully use this demographic dividend. The growing young population, which makes up around 60% of the entire population, represents both a numerical majority and a pool of unrealized potential and ambitions. This potential, however, is threatened by the lack of sufficient opportunities for meaningful involvement and productive work, which might convert what could be a demographic dividend into a socio-economic burden. The mismatch between young people's skill sets and the needs of the job market is at the core of the problem. Even though a large number of young Cameroonians get education and develop skills via official and informal channels, the economy finds it difficult to place them in jobs that fit them. This discrepancy is caused by a number of things, including flaws in the educational system, which often fails to provide students with the real-world skills that employers need. Furthermore, the pace of technological progress and the changing nature of the market have made certain skills outdated and necessitated the acquisition of new proficiencies, therefore widening the skills gap between the youthful workforce and the demands of contemporary employment.

A major contributing aspect to the challenge of young unemployment is economic considerations. Despite its diversity, Cameroon's economy suffers from structural issues including restricted private sector growth, low industrialization, and an excessive dependence on basic industries like agriculture. As a consequence, there are few employment openings, especially in industries that have the potential to employ a lot of young people. Furthermore, the informal sector, which sustains a large number of people, sometimes offers few opportunities for professional growth, job stability, or good pay, making young workers even more vulnerable. Moreover, sociocultural factors contribute to the persistence of young unemployment. For example, young women may find it difficult to enter particular professions due to traditional gender standards, which would limit their career options. Furthermore, hiring practices that are biased towards family or friends may undermine merit-based hiring, which disproportionately disadvantages young people from underprivileged backgrounds who lack the financial or social capital to find work.

Youth unemployment has far-reaching effects on society that go beyond matters of finance. High rates of young unemployment lead to social unrest, dissatisfaction, and disappointment, endangering both social cohesiveness and political stability. Furthermore, the lost human capital is a missed chance for productivity growth, innovation, and sustainable development. A comprehensive strategy that targets the underlying causes of young unemployment and promotes inclusive development and job creation is required to solve it in Cameroon. This calls for investments in skill development programs and vocational training catered to developing industries, changes to the educational system to bring curriculum in line with industry expectations, and campaigns to encourage youth-led innovation and entrepreneurship. Furthermore, improving the business climate, encouraging development driven by the private sector, and broadening the economy may increase the number of work options available to young people. Youth unemployment may be lessened and a more inclusive society can be fostered by social policies that seek to promote gender equality, eliminate prejudice, and enhance social safety nets. To put it simply, the government, business community, civil society, and international partners must work together to address structural barriers, create an environment that encourages entrepreneurship and job creation, and provide young people in Cameroon with the tools, resources, and support systems they need to succeed in the workforce and make significant contributions to the nation's development in order to fully realize the potential of the country's youthful population.

## ii. Underemployment

A widespread problem in Cameroon, underemployment takes many forms and exacerbates the country's problems with poverty and unstable economy. In addition to the depressing reality of total joblessness, a sizeable segment of the populace is entangled in insecure or informal employment. These agreements, which are marked by low pay, little work stability, and a lack of perks like health insurance or retirement plans, highlight a structural inadequacy that leaves gaps in the provision of worthwhile opportunities for long-term employment. Formal labor standards and safeguards do not apply to persons who participate in different income-generating activities in the informal sector, which is one aspect of underemployment. These unofficial businesses, which might range from small-scale farming to street selling, often function on the edges of the law, leaving employees open to abuse and without any channels of appeal in the event that their rights are violated. Workers are vulnerable to arbitrary salary cutbacks, unpredictable work schedules, and dangerous working conditions in the absence of formal contracts or legal safeguards, which feeds the cycle of economic precarity and vulnerability.

Furthermore, underemployment spreads across the formal sector, trapping a large number of people in low-paying, low-skill positions with no opportunity for advancement. These individuals are often assigned to jobs that do not fully maximize their potential, while having the necessary skills and credentials; this leads to stagnating salaries and little possibilities for professional growth. Labor markets in sectors like manufacturing, construction, and services are typified by an excess of workers compared to job vacancies. This creates fierce competition for a small number of employment possibilities and drives down salaries. Underemployment also disproportionately impacts vulnerable demographic groups, such as women, youth, and those living in rural areas. Due to ingrained gender stereotypes and discriminatory practices in the workforce, women, in particular, encounter obstacles while attempting to acquire formal job prospects. The fact that so many are forced into low-wage, informal occupations with little opportunities for growth contributes to the persistence of gender differences in involvement in the economy and income. Similar to this, young individuals just starting the workforce face major obstacles in their quest for steady, well-paying employment, which forces them into unstable contracts with little chance of long-term financial stability. Underemployment is pervasive in rural regions where agriculture is the primary source of income, and the vulnerability of rural workers and their families is exacerbated by seasonal variations in demand.

Underemployment has far-reaching effects that go beyond personal suffering; it affects all facets of society and impedes the nation's overall economic growth. Because those locked into low-paying, low-skill positions lack the incentives and possibilities for skill development and entrepreneurship, persistent underemployment stifles productivity and creativity. In addition, insufficient social safety nets make underemployed people and their families more vulnerable, which feeds poverty cycles and deprives communities of the human capital needed for long-term, sustainable development. To tackle the issue of underemployment in Cameroon, a comprehensive strategy is needed, which includes enacting policies that encourage equitable economic development, increasing the availability of high-quality education and skill development opportunities, and fortifying labor market laws to safeguard workers' rights and dignity. Policymakers can enable people to escape the cycle of underemployment and reach their full potential as engaged contributors to the nation's economic progress by creating an atmosphere that supports decent work and sustainable lifestyles.

### *iii. Urban-Rural Disparities*

Inequalities in work prospects between urban and rural areas are ingrained in the socioeconomic structures of many countries, including Cameroon. These differences have many distinct causes, including historical, geographic, and policy variables that have influenced the unequal distribution of resources and growth in various areas. The vibrant economic cities of Douala and Yaoundé in Cameroon entice job seekers from nearby rural regions with the prospect of employment and improved living conditions. But these cities' already meager infrastructure and resource bases are often strained by the flood of rural migrants, which results in congestion, subpar housing, and heightened competitiveness for the few number of open jobs. Urban unemployment rates may thus soar, especially for underrepresented groups like women and young people who often lack the training and credentials required to get formal work. On the other hand, Cameroonia's rural areas experience a very different reality, marked by underdevelopment, restricted access to essential services, and a dearth of funding for vital industries like infrastructure and agriculture. A vicious cycle of rural depopulation and urbanization is perpetuated when young people relocate to metropolitan areas in quest of better chances due to a lack of legitimate work options. Furthermore, the cyclical nature of agricultural labor adds to the instability of rural incomes, making a large number of people susceptible to food insecurity and poverty.

The differences in work prospects between urban and rural regions are not just a result of inevitable urbanization processes; rather, they are intricately linked to systemic problems such uneven access to financial, healthcare, and educational resources. The cycle of poverty and marginalization is further exacerbated by low educational achievement in rural regions, which often translates into a lack of the skills and credentials required by the contemporary labor market. In order to address these gaps between urban and rural areas, a comprehensive strategy that addresses the underlying causes of inequality rather than just providing short-term fixes is needed. In order to empower local communities to shape their own development agendas, this entails decentralizing governance structures, boosting entrepreneurship and job creation in rural areas, investing in rural infrastructure and agricultural productivity, and improving access to high-quality education and vocational training. Cameroon may realize the full potential of its human capital and achieve more equitable and sustainable economic development for all of its residents by bridging the gap between urban and rural communities.

## iv. Mismatch Between Skills and Job Market:

The mismatch between talents and the labor market is a complex issue that affects the whole employment scene in Cameroon. It all boils down to the complex interactions that exist between educational institutions, the demands of the labor market, and changing business requirements. In addition to impeding economic progress, this imbalance keeps Cameroonian workers trapped in cycles of underemployment and unemployment. First of all, graduates are often ill-prepared to handle the practical demands of modern workplaces due to the educational system's traditional emphasis on theoretical knowledge. Systemic hurdles still exist, despite significant efforts to reform curriculum and provide vocational training. Inadequate infrastructure, antiquated teaching methods, and a lack of resources make it difficult to provide students the skills they need. Because of this, many graduates have strong academic backgrounds but lack the practical skills that employers value.

Moreover, the fast progress of technology and globalization consistently alters industrial sectors, generating a constantly changing need for fresh skill sets. The skills gap is, however, made worse by the school system's lethargy and sluggish response to these developments. Emerging businesses like digital marketing, renewable energy, and information technology often struggle to locate applicants with the necessary skills, while conventional companies deal with an overabundance of graduates in subjects where demand is declining. Furthermore, the gap that exists between academics and business feeds a vicious circle of dissatisfaction for both companies and job seekers. Finding applicants with the particular knowledge and real-world experience required to spur innovation and productivity is difficult for employers. As a result, they can turn to investing in pricey training programs or recruiting foreign personnel in order to close the gap. Employers value practical skills and work experience above academic degrees, so job seekers still face obstacles to admittance even with a formal education.

It will need a coordinated effort from many parties to address this gap. In order to give priority to business collaborations, career-oriented curriculum, and experiential learning, educational institutions need to implement structural changes. Building modern facilities, encouraging internships, and supporting entrepreneurship may all contribute to the development of a workforce that is more adaptable and competent. In a similar vein, legislators are essential in ensuring that education regulations support the objectives of economic growth, providing incentives for industry-academia partnerships, and cultivating an atmosphere in business that supports innovation and job creation. Moreover, the cultivation of a culture that prioritizes continuous education and skill enhancement is crucial in closing the skills divide in Cameroon. Initiatives for ongoing professional development, apprenticeship programs, and retraining may enable people to take advantage of new possibilities and adjust to changing industry needs. In other words, resolving the mismatch between skill sets and available jobs is essential to Cameroon's social advancement and sustained economic development, not just for individual lives. A more prosperous future for all people of the country may be ensured by unlocking the potential of its human capital via the promotion of synergy across the fields of education, industry, and policy.

### v. Impact of Informal Economy

The influence of Cameroon's informal sector extends beyond data, permeating every aspect of the country's socioeconomic environment. For millions of people, it shapes their livelihoods, goals, and vulnerabilities while acting as both a lifeline and a trap. Fundamentally, the informal sector is a double-edged sword that, while providing a large number of people with work options, also traps them in a cycle of precariousness. The informal sector acts as a safety net in a nation with few official job options, especially in rural regions, by taking in excess labor and giving countless people and families a means of subsistence. For many Cameroonians, the informal economy—which includes street selling, small-scale farming, artisanal manufacturing, and domestic work—represents a crucial source of income that enables them to meet their basic needs, send their kids to school, and deal with life's obstacles. However, the absence of formalization, institutional backing, and regulation characterizes this economic ecology. Without legal safeguards, workers in the informal sector are often subjected to discrimination, exploitation, and dangerous working conditions. Individuals who lack access to social security, healthcare, or pension benefits are more susceptible to economic shocks, including changes in market pricing, natural catastrophes, or unstable political environments. Furthermore, they are vulnerable to capricious treatment by authorities or employers due to the lack of written contracts or dispute resolution procedures.

Additionally, the widespread informality impedes socioeconomic advancement and upward mobility by feeding the cycle of poverty and inequality. Informally financed company owners find it difficult to grow their companies or make investments in technology and skill development programs without access to conventional financial services or financing. Productivity stays low as a consequence, and

growth and innovation potential are inhibited. Furthermore, the dominance of the unorganized sector restricts tax revenue collection for the government, which in turn affects public spending on healthcare, education, and infrastructure—all of which are critical for long-term economic growth and social cohesion. The informal sector presents a number of difficulties that need for a multifaceted response that includes formalization and inclusive development initiatives, social protection policies, and regulatory changes. To do this, favorable conditions for small enterprises must be established, registration processes must be streamlined, finance and technical support must be easier to get, and labor rights enforcement must be reinforced. Additionally, it entails making investments in education and career training to provide people the tools they need to move into formal job sectors. Additionally, identifying common goals and creating long-lasting solutions that benefit all parties involved may be facilitated by encouraging communication and collaborations between the government, employers, labor unions, and civil society groups. Although though Cameroon's informal sector is still a significant part of the country's economy, its sustainability and inclusion depend on coordinated efforts to resolve the problems that it inevitably presents and realize its full potential as a force for growth and social advancement.

## B. Impacts of Unemployment

### i. *Economic Strain*

High unemployment rates place a heavy financial strain on the people and the state. People without jobs struggle to satisfy their fundamental necessities, endure financial instability, and may turn to illicit or unofficial means of subsistence. At the federal level, unemployment hinders the potential for economic development, lowers consumer spending, and limits tax collections, making it more difficult for the government to fund investments in infrastructure, healthcare, and education.

> **Individual Financial Insecurity:**

Personal financial instability is a complex problem that goes much beyond the short-term effects of unemployment. It includes a range of difficulties that people have when they don't have the financial security required to provide for their family and themselves. Financial instability may have a significant influence on a person's general well-being and feeling of security, in addition to the obvious effects on providing for basic requirements like food and shelter. The decline in mental health is a major effect of personal financial uncertainty. Mental health may suffer greatly from the tension and worry brought on by not knowing what one's financial situation will hold in the future. Persistent concern related to finances, taking care of family members, or managing unforeseen costs may result in long-term stress,

anxiety disorders, and even depression. Financial uncertainty may have a profound impact on one's mental health, influencing relationships, productivity at work, and general quality of life. Furthermore, people who are financially insecure are often forced to make tough trade-offs that may have long-term effects. For example, in situations when resources are few, people could put off or postpone critical medical care because of financial worries. This puts their physical health at risk, but it may also make existing diseases worse, which might result in later, more serious health problems and higher healthcare expenses. Furthermore, it might be challenging to stop the cycle of financial instability without sufficient support networks. Without access to reasonably priced education, job training programs, or stable career possibilities, people could find it difficult to get out of the poverty cycle and better their financial circumstances. As a result of this lack of upward mobility, the gap between those who are financially secure and those who are not is widened and structural inequities are sustained. Individual financial uneasiness may also have larger social repercussions, impeding development and prosperity generally and adding to economic instability. Consumer spending declines when a sizable section of the population faces financial hardship, which lowers demand for products and services. This may thereby worsen income disparity, impede the development of jobs, and impede economic progress. A comprehensive strategy is needed to address individual financial insecurity. This strategy should combine short-term measures to offer relief right away, like social safety nets and unemployment benefits, with long-term plans to advance economic opportunity, education, and workforce development. By funding programs that enable people to obtain financial literacy, pursue further education and training, and get a steady job, society may endeavor to build a more just and prosperous future for all.

> **Struggle to meet Basic Needs:**

Unable to provide for basic necessities sets off a chain reaction of problems that may have a serious negative influence on people and families. Let's examine the implications in more detail:

***Food Insecurity:*** The failure to get a stable job often results in a lack of funds for the purchase of wholesome food. Families would choose to less expensive, less nourishing choices, which might result in obesity or malnutrition. Offspring who face food hardship may face growth retardation, delayed development, and subpar intellectual outcomes.

***Housing Instability:*** It becomes harder to make ends meet when you don't have enough money for rent or a mortgage. Families may experience homelessness or congested living situations as a result of eviction or foreclosure. Instable housing compromises physical health, exposes people to more crime and violence, and interferes with children's social and educational development.

**Hygiene and Clothes:** Ordinary needs like underwear and toiletries might become prohibitively expensive extravagance. This not only compromises people's dignity and sense of self-worth, but it also puts their health at danger since poor hygiene may result in illnesses and infections.

**Healthcare Accessibility:** Having access to healthcare becomes a luxury if one does not have a steady job or enough money. Families may put off seeking medical attention, postpone necessary care, or depend only on emergency services, which are often costlier and ineffective in treating long-term illnesses. This loop of insufficient healthcare exacerbates already-existing health inequities and maintains poor health outcomes.

**Mental Health Strain:** Having unstable finances and not being able to support one's family may be very stressful. Both adults and children living in the home may experience the onset or worsening of anxiety, depression, or other mental health problems. An ongoing concern about providing for basic necessities may result in chronic stress, which further jeopardizes one's physical well-being and general standard of living.

***Intergenerational Impact:*** Children who are raised in low-income and unemployed homes are more susceptible. Adverse childhood experiences (ACEs) might be experienced by them, and they can have a lasting impact on their mental and emotional development, physical health, and socioemotional wellbeing. This keeps people in poverty and makes it more difficult for next generations to escape the grip of financial difficulty.

A multifaceted strategy is needed to address the underlying causes of unemployment and poverty, including social safety nets to assist families through difficult times financially, policies that encourage the creation of jobs, support education and skill development, and guarantee access to affordable housing and healthcare. In addition to enhancing individual well-being, funding initiatives that address economic empowerment and poverty eradication also fortify communities and promote long-term economic resilience.

➢ **Resort to Informal or Illegal Activities:**

People may find themselves in desperate situations where they feel forced to turn to unofficial or illegal activities in order to support themselves and their family when faced with the harsh realities of unemployment. Their desperation may push them in directions they otherwise would not have thought of, resulting in a variety of illegal activities that are harmful to both individuals and society at large. Engaging in illicit activities is a typical consequence of despair brought on by unemployment. People may be selling illicit commodities, including firearms, illegal narcotics, and counterfeit goods, in this underground world. By operating outside the law, they put their own safety and wellbeing at risk and aid in the growth of crime in local areas.

Participating in small-time crime is another way that this desperation manifests itself. People who are unable to obtain employment may resort to shoplifting, burglary, or stealing as a means of subsistence. Although these acts could ease financial hardship in the near term, they feed a criminal cycle that damages society's foundation and erodes community trust. Furthermore, some people could become caught up in black markets and engage in criminal activities like prostitution, gambling, or human trafficking. These exploitative businesses not only prolong human misery but also provide a boost to networks of organized crime, further fracturing communities and escalating cycles of violence and poverty. The ramifications of turning to illicit ways of obtaining income beyond the mere possibility of being apprehended and imprisoned. When someone is found doing anything illegal, they may suffer long-term legal consequences, such as having a criminal record that limits their future work options and feeds their marginalization loop. Furthermore, these actions produce social damage that spreads across society, widening gaps and escalating inequality. The prominence of unofficial and illegal activities contributes to cement unemployment and poverty rather than addressing its underlying causes, making it harder for those who are afflicted to escape the cycle of hopelessness. In order to effectively combat desperation brought on by unemployment, it is critical to address the underlying social and economic issues that force people to turn to illegal methods of subsistence. By allocating resources towards education, job training initiatives, and social support systems, communities may provide feasible substitutes for illicit activities and enable people to establish enduring livelihoods without turning to criminal activity. Furthermore, initiatives to thwart corruption, fortify legal frameworks, and advance economic progress may aid in tearing down the systems that support illicit economies and pave the way for inclusive growth and prosperity for everyone.

> **Impact on Economic Growth:**

Elevated jobless rates significantly impede economic expansion by acting as a severe barrier that impedes efficiency and reduces creativity. If a large percentage of the labor force is idle, it is a human resource that is not being used, which is like throwing money away. Such inefficiencies have a cascading effect on the economy, reducing total production of goods and services. Consider it this way: each individual who is unemployed represents a lost chance to make a positive impact on society. They can be creating novel technologies, coming up with ground-breaking fixes, or just contributing labor to the process of manufacturing. But these potentials lie dormant when they're sidelined by unemployment, creating a productivity gap in the economy. Furthermore, the effects go beyond simple underutilization. Because individuals without work have less disposable money to reinvest in the economy, high unemployment reduces consumer expenditure. This decline in demand feeds back into the economic downturn, intensifying it and prolonging the vicious cycle of stagnation. Moreover, prolonged joblessness erodes trust in the economy and discourages companies from making investments in growth or innovation. Businesses are less willing to take chances or devote resources to R&D projects when uncertainty is present. As a result, chances for revolutionary development decrease and the rate of technical improvement decreases. To put it simply, a high unemployment rate impedes both present and future economic growth. It limits the economy's ability to adapt and change by robbing it of essential expertise and resources. Reducing unemployment requires more than simply creating jobs; it also entails helping people reach their full potential and creating an atmosphere that supports long-term prosperity and economic progress.

> **Reduction in Consumer Spending:**

When consumers cut down on their purchases, consumer expenditure declines; this is often the result of economic difficulties like unemployment. This is a tendency that occurs when people and families who are struggling financially decide to put their few resources on requirements instead of non-essentials. As a result, there is a general decline in the demand for products and services, which has an impact on many different industries. When demand for their goods or services declines, businesses that depend on consumer spending are forced to reduce output. Consequently, the decrease in productivity sometimes calls for cost-cutting actions like staff reductions or shortened workdays. As a result, the already high unemployment rates often become worse, making it harder for impacted people and their families to make ends meet. The whole economy has a dampening impact as the cycle continues, with lower consumer spending causing further job losses and economic contraction. A recession or protracted stagnation may be caused by this negative feedback loop, as companies find it difficult to survive in the face of declining customer demand and increased uncertainty.

> **Limitations on Tax Income and Their Effects on the State and Community:**

High unemployment rates make it difficult for governments, both local and federal, to pay basic services since they have a substantial negative impact on tax collections. There are fewer people generating an income when unemployment is high, which means that the government receives less money from income taxes. Government finances are further strained by lower sales tax collection, which is a result of decreased consumer expenditure. These

restrictions have far-reaching effects on tax collections. Governments may find it difficult to provide the necessary funding for social welfare programs, healthcare, and education—all of which are vital for assisting disadvantaged people and advancing social well-being. The cycle of unemployment and poverty may be prolonged and social inequality can be made worse by inadequate support in these areas. In addition, insufficient tax income may make it more difficult for the government to fund infrastructure and other initiatives that promote economic expansion. This has the potential to extend times of high unemployment even longer, making conditions difficult for job seekers and growing enterprises. A diversified strategy is needed to address the limitations on tax receipts during times of high unemployment. To boost economic activity, governments may need to think about enacting specific fiscal policies, such tax breaks for companies or more funding for infrastructure projects. Furthermore, funding education and training initiatives may assist in providing people with the tools necessary to find work, which will eventually lower unemployment rates and increase tax collections. In conclusion, governments find it very difficult to collect taxes and provide basic services when unemployment rates are high. Proactive steps to boost economic development, reduce unemployment, and build a more just society are necessary to address these issues.

To summarize, the burden of high unemployment rates on the economy affects every aspect of society, affecting people individually, in their communities, and throughout the country. A comprehensive strategy is needed to address unemployment, one that combines short-term measures to ease acute suffering with long-term plans to promote job prospects and sustained economic development.

## ii. Social Consequences:

The ramifications of unemployment on society are complex and wide-ranging, beyond economic factors. This is a more thorough investigation:

> **Social Unrest and Crime:**

There is a strong correlation between high unemployment rates and rising rates of social unrest and criminal activity. The despair and desperation that people experience when they are unable to obtain job despite their best efforts might lead them to engage in illegal acts as a way of surviving. These circumstances have the potential to generate a vicious cycle in which people are compelled to engage in illegal activities due to the absence of legitimate work options. This, in turn, may contribute to the perpetuation of a bad economic climate and discourage investment, so increasing the problem of unemployment. In addition, emotions of isolation and marginalization might be brought on by unemployment experiences. It is possible for individuals to have the perception that they are not appreciated by society when they are excluded from the job market. This may lead to a decline in social cohesiveness as well as faith in institutions. It is possible for this feeling of unfairness to materialize in the form of civil unrest or protest movements, in which individuals act together to voice their discontent and call for change. These demonstrations have the potential to occasionally evolve into violent fights with authorities or with various socioeconomic groups, which further destabilizes the society.

The connection between unemployment and social unrest is a complicated one that is impacted by a number of different circumstances. These aspects include the length of time that an individual has been without work, the accessibility of social safety nets, and the degree of inequality that exists within the community. Long-term unemployment is especially deleterious since it may result in a loss of skills and employability, making it much more difficult for people to re-enter the labor because of the skills and employability they have lost. Unemployed people may turn to other methods of subsistence, some of which may be unlawful, in order to supplement their income if they do not get appropriate assistance. Economic instability and excessive unemployment may strain public services and social systems. Overburdened law enforcement and social services would fail to manage the

growing crime rates effectively, resulting to a feeling of lawlessness and insecurity within the community. This climate might be ideal for the emergence of organized crime and gang activity, which can give a sense of order and security to individuals who feel abandoned by the state.
Moreover, places with high unemployment generally suffer from poor infrastructure and lack of investment, generating urban degradation and further lowering job chances. This may lead to a concentration of poverty and crime in some communities, continuing a cycle of disadvantage and criminality. In such communities, young people, in particular, may perceive crime as a feasible alternative, influenced by the absence of role models and good options. The psychological effect of unemployment should not be underestimated. The stress and worry associated with joblessness may lead to mental health difficulties, which can, in turn, enhance the inclination for criminal activity. Desperation and despair might motivate individuals to take risks they would not otherwise contemplate, like participating in stealing, drug trafficking, or other illegal businesses. The association between high levels of unemployment and rising social discontent and crime rates is obvious via several interrelated pathways. Economic hardship may lead to criminal acts as a means of survival, while sentiments of alienation and unfairness create civic unrest. The demand on public services and the maintenance of urban deterioration further complicate attempts to break this cycle, underlining the necessity for

comprehensive policies that address unemployment, social inequality, and community support networks.

> **Political Dissatisfaction:**

Political unhappiness may be profoundly aggravated by joblessness, which frequently generates a feeling of disgust with the political system as a whole. Unemployment might encourage people to see government services and officials as disinterested or inadequate in addressing their needs. This sense of neglect or ineptitude erodes faith in public institutions, making individuals feel alienated from the democratic process. When people are jobless, they may feel that their views are not heard or respected by those in authority. This feeling of exclusion might motivate people to seek answers outside of established political structures. In their quest for solutions, individuals may lean towards extreme ideologies that promise rapid and dramatic change. This may lead to the emergence of political extremism, as individuals become more susceptible to fringe groups that threaten the existing quo. The disenchantment coming from joblessness not only affects faith in government but also presents a danger to democratic norms. As more people lose confidence in conventional political methods, the basis of democratic participation—characterized by trust, involvement, and a conviction in the effectiveness of civic institutions—begins to disintegrate. The attraction of populist politicians and extreme organizations, who typically exploit economic distress to generate support, gets greater in such settings. Ultimately, chronic unemployment may provide a fertile basis for political instability. When vast sectors of the people feel detached from the political system, it undermines the social compact and may lead to increasing civil unrest and war. This cycle of frustration and radicalization offers substantial problems to sustaining a stable and functional democracy.

> **Intergenerational Impact:**

Youth unemployment has a significant and long-lasting effect on future generations in addition to the one it affects now. Young people have several obstacles when they join the workforce during recessions, which may impede their ability to advance in their careers and maintain a stable financial future. This unstable beginning often leads to lower starting pay, less prospects for employment, and fewer opportunities for professional growth. As a result, these people could endure protracted periods of underemployment or unemployment, which would make it difficult for them to establish a steady professional path. These young people may put off important life milestones like purchasing a house, having a family, or making investments in further education while they battle to make a name for themselves in the career. Their capacity to build money and attain financial stability may be hampered by this delay, which might have long-term financial repercussions. Their ability to flourish is further reduced by the stress and uncertainty that come with having inconsistent work, which may have a detrimental effect on their physical and emotional well-being.

The effects influence not only the individual but also the larger society. Youth unemployment that doesn't go away might worsen social stratification and inequality since it can be difficult for those who started their professions during recessions to catch up to their counterparts who joined the workforce during more affluent times. This discrepancy has the potential to create a generation-long poverty cycle in which children of underemployed or jobless parents experience comparable deprivations and restricted possibilities in life. They may not have as much access to resources such as good healthcare, education, and other services, which would feed the cycle of disadvantage. Additionally, when a sizable section of the labor force is unable to make a meaningful contribution, the economy as a whole suffers. Economic development and stability may be hampered by decreased consumer spending, decreased tax receipts, and greater demand for social services, all of which put a burden on public resources. A huge opportunity for society as a whole is lost when a generation of young people who are not fully involved in the labor market loses their potential for creativity and productivity.

Therefore, addressing youth unemployment is essential for future generations' health and prosperity as well as the well-being of those who are immediately impacted. Breaking the cycle of intergenerational unemployment and poverty requires comprehensive solutions that combine measures to create jobs, policies that maintain economic stability, and programs for education and training. Society can promote greater equity and prosperity for everyone by investing in youth and making sure they have the resources and chances to thrive.

> **Loss of Identity and Self-esteem and Mental Health Issues:**

One significant and often disastrous effect of unemployment is the loss of identity and self-worth. Since many people identify themselves and their value via their work and the roles they play in their professional life, losing one's job usually results in the loss of a significant portion of one's identity. People feel wanted and appreciated when they have a job that gives them a sense of purpose and contribution. Without it, people could struggle with a lowered sense of self-worth and feel inadequate and undeserving. There may be serious effects on mental health. Feelings of hopelessness and despair are among the unpleasant emotions that are often brought on by unemployment. Worries about one's capacity to support oneself and one's family, one's financial security, and an unclear future may all contribute to anxiety that can become a lifelong companion. These worries may develop into chronic stress, which can have an impact on one's physical and emotional well-being. They are not only momentary worries. Depression is often the result of the psychological toll that comes with unemployment. Long-term unemployment may cause a persistent feeling of loss and despair that can make it difficult to find motivation or participate in everyday activities. People may distance themselves from social situations when their self-esteem declines, which exacerbates feelings of loneliness and isolation. These mental health problems are made worse by the strain of unstable finances. One's sense of worth might be further damaged by emotions of guilt and shame resulting from not being able to pay financial responsibilities. An inability to make ends meet in the absence of a reliable source of income may cause extreme emotional and psychological distress. Some people may find it impossible to bear the weight of these problems, and as a result, they may consider suicide since they are unable to see a way out of their predicament. Joblessness may cause a severe loss of identity and self-worth, which has a major negative effect on mental health. The psychological effects of unemployment are complex and include significant emotional strain, chronic stress, and a lack of purpose in life. In order to address these problems, a comprehensive strategy that combines financial aid, mental health care, and initiatives to assist people in rediscovering their sense of identity

and purpose via fulfilling work prospects is needed.
- ➢ **Stressed Social connections:**
Unemployment may cause stress in social relationships, particularly in families and communities. Frequent and heated conflicts over money and resources are often the outcome of the stress associated with financial instability. Family members who may feel the strain of running a home on a tight budget may become tense and conflictual as a result of this ongoing financial hardship. These problems are made worse by the psychological ramifications of unemployment, which include worry, sadness, and a diminished feeling of self-worth. People without jobs might feel inadequate or like failures, which can cause them to become frustrated and resentful of other people as well as themselves. Couples may find it difficult to provide emotional support to one another while managing their own pressures, which may lead to emotional strain and rifts in the marriage. Because of the increased stress and financial instability that might result in a more stressful home environment, children in these homes may also have negative effects on their emotional and psychological well-being. Moreover, people may distance themselves from social connections due to the shame attached to unemployment. They could steer clear of friends, neighborhood activities, and social gatherings due to their sentiments of humiliation and guilt over being unemployed. This retreat from social interactions may be harmful to one's mental health since there is a

strong correlation between social isolation and elevated anxiety and depression symptoms. Lack of social support may lead to a vicious cycle in which people find it more difficult to ask for assistance or locate job prospects the more alone they become. Thus, the isolation worsens not only their mental health but also their prospects of landing a new job, which feeds the vicious cycle of unemployment and social disengagement.

Community ties may also deteriorate in addition to interpersonal ones. People who are unemployed may find it more difficult to volunteer and participate in community events because they are either too busy looking for a job or don't have the energy to do so. This decline in involvement might erode ties within the community and lessen its general social cohesiveness. High unemployment rates may create a general feeling of pessimism and despair in communities, which can weaken support systems and communal spirit. The effect of unemployment is far-reaching, as seen by the pressure it places on social relationships within families and communities. It is crucial to attend to the psychological and economic needs of those impacted by unemployment.

> **Eroding Stability and Social Cohesion:** In reality, unemployment undermines the basis of social cohesiveness and stability. The implications of large segments of the population being excluded from the labor spread across

society, widening socioeconomic gaps and eroding institutional confidence. These differences show themselves in a number of ways, such economic inequality, which widens the gap between the rich and the poor. For individuals who feel left behind, this economic inequality creates a feeling of unfairness and hatred. Social division may result from the underemployed and jobless feeling alienated and cut off from the larger society. Furthermore, this fragmentation is made worse by the declining level of confidence in institutions. People who are jobless often believe that financial and political organizations are incompetent or uncaring about their situation. This idea may cause people to lose faith in political systems and become less involved in the community. The inclination to support community projects and engage in group activities declines along with a decline in confidence in these organizations, which erodes the social links that keep communities together. The capacity of society to deal with crises is significantly impacted by the erosion of social cohesiveness. A unified and cohesive community is better able to react to calamities, such as natural disasters, economic difficulties, and other crises. However, organizing group actions and promoting solidarity becomes increasingly difficult when social cohesiveness breaks down. Individuals could become increasingly self-centered and prioritize their own interests above the welfare of the group. This change undercuts mutual support and cooperative problem-solving, which are crucial for resolving crises. Moreover, it is impossible to overstate the psychological effects of unemployment. Losing a job often causes stress, worry, and feelings of inadequacy, which may deteriorate interpersonal connections and interactions in the community. The emotional toll that follows may increase feelings of loneliness and reduce social engagement. The community bonds that are essential to sustaining a stable and encouraging society are further weakened by this isolation. Unemployment deepens social divisions and undermines institutional trust, it fundamentally undermines societal stability and cohesiveness. This upheaval results in a decline in social cohesiveness, which makes it more challenging to efficiently handle group issues and manage crisis situations. To lessen its negative consequences and foster a more resilient and cohesive society, comprehensive policies and community support structures are required due to the combined economic, psychological, and social implications of unemployment.

In-depth strategies that go beyond job creation are needed to address the social effects of unemployment. Investments in social safety nets, mental health support networks, education and skill development, and initiatives to ensure inclusive growth and fair access to opportunities are all necessary. Societies should strive to promote more resilience, cohesiveness, and well-being for all members by tackling the underlying structural issues that sustain unemployment and its related social problems.

### *iii. Brain Drain:*

The occurrence of competent people looking for jobs overseas makes unemployment worse by adding to the "brain drain" impact. Frustrated with the lack of possibilities at home, a large number of highly educated and skilled Cameroonians decide to go abroad in search of better job opportunities and improved standards of life. This weakens attempts to promote local innovation and economic development and further depletes the human capital of the nation.

### Factors driving Brain Drain

> *Economic Instability*:

The problem of brain drain is mostly driven by economic uncertainty. Nations with ongoing economic difficulties, such as Cameroon, often have high unemployment rates and poor incomes. Because of these circumstances, skilled individuals feel stuck and have fewer chances, which leads many of them to look for better opportunities elsewhere. The significant wealth gap that exists between Cameroon and more developed nations is one of the main causes. Many competent people are motivated to contemplate moving abroad by the possibility of earning much greater salaries and living in better conditions. A number of variables, including purchasing power parity and currency exchange rates, exacerbate this wage difference and heighten the appeal of earning more money abroad. Furthermore, a lack of investment in vital fields like infrastructure, healthcare, and education might result from economic instability. This may further encourage skilled people to look for opportunities elsewhere by limiting their access to necessary services and professional development chances. Furthermore, a lack of economic stability often leads to future uncertainty, which includes worries about one's capacity to support oneself and one's family as well as job security. A higher standard of living and stability are what motivate many competent people to think about emigrating in order to fulfill their dreams. All things considered, economic instability—which is typified by high unemployment rates, poor incomes, and little prospects for professional growth—plays a major role in the issue of brain drain in nations like Cameroon. To lessen the effects of brain drain and promote sustainable growth, it is imperative to address these economic issues and provide a more hospitable environment for qualified individuals.

> ***Lack of opportunities:***

The paucity of major chances for career growth and professional development inside Cameroon is a key cause of brain drain. Highly educated persons typically confront restricted opportunities for applying their abilities and talents to their maximum potential. The country's inadequately established industry and research institutes contribute to this difficulty, since they fail to offer the required platforms for people to grow and thrive in their particular disciplines. As a consequence, many brilliant Cameroonians seek chances overseas where they may pursue more meaningful occupations and attain their full potential.

> ***Political Climate:***

The state of politics has a big impact on brain drain. Professionals with talent feel uneasy and underappreciated in nations with political unrest and problems with governance. The persistent possibility of political unrest and unpredictability over the future may induce these people to look for prospects elsewhere. The issue is made worse by public institutions' corruption and lack of openness. Talented people are more inclined to contemplate leaving their native country if they believe that corruption is preventing them from receiving a fair return for their efforts and talents. Furthermore, professionals find it challenging to imagine a day when their expertise would be properly used for the benefit of society due to the lack of confidence in public institutions. In general, competent individuals' decisions to leave their own countries in quest of better prospects and a more stable environment are greatly influenced by the political context.

> ***Mismatch in Education:***

A major contributing element to brain drain in many cases is the presence of an educational mismatch. When the offers of the educational system and the demands of the job market are not aligned, this problem occurs. Armed with their credentials and experience, graduates often encounter a harsh truth: their newly acquired abilities may not be highly valued in their own nation. People who are trying to make a name for themselves in the workplace and get steady jobs often come to the depressing conclusion that their skills don't match the dynamics of the labor market. Even after years of focused study, individuals often find little possibilities to use what they have learned inside the boundaries of their own country. As a result, when confronted with the possibility of underemployment or career stagnation, these very talented people are forced to consider other options. They look for areas or nations where companies actively seek out candidates with their abilities, not just acknowledge them. Their quest for recognition and opportunity drives them to places where their skills may be more fully realized and fairly compensated. The problem of brain drain is primarily driven by the disparity between the skills obtained via education and the needs of the work market. It emphasizes how important it is for decision-makers and academic institutions to foster an atmosphere in which graduates' developed abilities are in line with the changing demands of the local labor market. Only by achieving this kind of alignment will countries be able to fully use their human capital for long-term socioeconomic growth and lessen the negative consequences of brain drain.

> ***Quality of Life:***

The temptation of a better quality of life is one of the main causes of brain drain. People from nations like Cameroon are drawn to developed nations because they provide a number of benefits. For Cameroonians looking for better opportunities, these nations provide an alluring potential with their higher living standards, improved access to healthcare facilities, excellent educational programs, and extensive social services. The whole quality of life includes a number of factors, such as social stability and safety, which have a big impact on people's decisions to migrate. Many people are lured to emigrate in search of a better life for themselves and their family since it offers the possibility of a more stable and affluent future.

**Consequences of Brain Drain**

The emigration of qualified professionals from Cameroon has several adverse effects:

> ***Economic Impact:***

The departure of highly qualified professionals from a nation, known as brain drain, has a significant impact on that nation's economy. The departure of these gifted people strikes a serious damage to a number of industries vital to economic growth. The sectors most severely impacted are technology, healthcare, and education. These industries rely significantly on skilled personnel to drive innovation, productivity, and advancement. These specialists are leaving the country, which has a direct negative impact on production and stifles innovation. The effects of the economy are felt in many areas, impeding development and perhaps lowering the country's competitiveness abroad.

> ***Human Capital Deplition:***

The loss of human capital is one of the most noticeable effects of brain drain, among its many other effects. Skilled people bring important information, experience, and competence with them when they leave a nation. This departure reduces the total skill pool accessible for a variety of efforts in addition to leaving shortages in critical areas. The nation suffers a severe setback in its ability to develop and embrace new technology as a consequence. Without a strong labor force to propel R&D projects, advancement stalls and the country becomes less competitive internationally. Long-term economic development and sustainability are also hampered by the loss of qualified experts, who also interfere with the continuation of important projects and initiatives. Depletion of human capital essentially undermines the nation's chances of success by making current problems worse and making future progression more difficult. In addition to focusing on keeping talent, brain drain prevention strategies should also aim to develop an atmosphere that encourages creativity, keeps talented people in the country, and draws expatriates back. Nations may only fully use their human resource and lessen the negative impacts of brain drain via comprehensive measures.

➤ **Waste in Educational Investment:**
Brain drain has considerably more effects than only emigration. The wasted investments in education are one important consequence. Think about the significant resources invested in teaching and developing people, only to see them leave for possibilities elsewhere. These expenditures, which were meant to develop skill and knowledge inside the nation, ultimately prove to be ineffective. As a consequence, the country underutilizes its human capital, which yields a pitiful return on educational investments. It is similar to planting seeds in rich soil and then letting the field untended, squandering the potential crop.

➤ **Reduce Competitiveness:**
The effects of brain drain in Cameroon are extensive and diverse, affecting not just one industry but also the nation's entire growth trajectory. The decline in competitiveness is one of the most important consequences. Cameroon is suffering from a severe human resource shortage as qualified workers leave the nation in quest of better prospects outside. The nation's capacity to innovate, create new technologies, and boost productivity across sectors is hampered by this lack of experience. The lack of qualified experts makes it harder for Cameroon to compete on the international stage. High-value sectors like technology, healthcare, and engineering significantly depend on having a staff with the necessary knowledge and skills. There is a slowdown in development and innovation when these individuals leave the country because there is not enough skill left to

satisfy the needs of these industries. As a result, local companies could find it difficult to stay up to date with global norms, losing their competitive advantage in both domestic and international markets. In addition, a manpower shortage may discourage foreign investment. Countries with a large pool of skilled laborers who can propel their enterprises ahead tend to draw in investors. Due to the talent exodus, Cameroon may become less of an investment destination as businesses struggle to acquire the necessary level of experience. This might result in a vicious cycle wherein the brain drain is prolonged and prospects for qualified professionals are further reduced due to a lack of investment. Brain drain also affects the education sector. Some of the brightest professors and researchers at universities and research centers leave for better-funded universities elsewhere. This diminishes the ability to teach the next generation of professionals in addition to having an impact on the caliber of research and education. This may exacerbate the brain drain cycle over time by lowering educational standards and decreasing the capacity to create highly qualified graduates. Furthermore, there is a major influence on Cameroon's healthcare industry. There is a scarcity of medical people as a result of physicians, nurses, and other healthcare professionals leaving the country, which has an impact on the quality and accessibility of healthcare services. The population may have worse health outcomes as a consequence, including a greater frequency of untreated illnesses and a generally shorter life expectancy. The remaining healthcare professionals are often overworked, which causes burnout and increased turnover. There are significant economic ramifications. Productivity levels fall when there is a shortage of competent workers, which might hinder economic progress. The nation could find it difficult to diversify its economy and progress up the value chain, continuing to rely on low-wage, low-skilled sectors. An atmosphere that is difficult for socioeconomic growth may be created by this economic stagnation, which can also lead to greater rates of unemployment and poverty.

Additionally, families are often split up when people go abroad in search of better prospects, which has an impact on the social fabric of the country. This may have long-term effects on support networks and community cohesiveness as well as social pressure and changes in family relations. Losing innovators and leaders in the community might reduce social capital, which makes it more difficult to handle issues locally and promote community growth. Brain drain severely lowers Cameroon's competitiveness by reducing the pool of qualified workers needed for innovation, economic expansion, and drawing in outside capital. This problem has an impact on a number of areas, such as healthcare, education, and the general economy. It also creates a vicious loop that impedes the country's ability to grow and encourages further emigration.

> ### *Social Impact:*

Brain drain has long-reaching effects that go well beyond the sudden departure of highly qualified people from a nation. The social fabric of communities is among the most significant effects. Families are often split up when professionals and gifted people leave the country in quest of better prospects. Both the people leaving and their loved ones staying behind may find this separation to be very upsetting, which may cause emotional strain and a feeling of loss in the community. Social cohesiveness may be weakened by the disappearance of important community members who may have played important roles in local cultural, educational, and social activities. As fewer people are left to preserve and transmit common customs and values, the community's sense of identity and togetherness may gradually fade. Aside from these social issues, the quality of vital services may be negatively impacted by the departure of professionals like teachers, engineers, physicians, and nurses. There is already a severe lack of resources for education and healthcare in many developing nations. This problem is made worse by the departure of qualified healthcare workers, which results in longer wait times for medical attention, less access to specialist treatments, and a general deterioration in the quality of healthcare services. This may lead to increased mortality rates, worse health outcomes for the populace, and heightened susceptibility to medical emergencies.

When seasoned instructors go, the education industry is also impacted. Reduced individual attention for pupils, bigger class sizes, and a drop in educational standards might result from the departure of talented instructors. Thus, students get a lesser level of education and are less equipped to make meaningful contributions to their communities and the economy, which further impedes the growth of the next generation. Furthermore, a cycle of underdevelopment and deprivation may result from brain drain. Skilled professionals who leave their home areas deter fresh talent and investment, which feeds the cycle of further emigration due to a lack of opportunities and subpar services. This may result in a cycle of brain drain, where the loss of a generation of experts causes decades-long developmental delays. Because of this, brain drain has a complex social effect that extends beyond the individuals leaving and their immediate families and communities to include larger societal systems that depend on their contributions and skill sets. Long-term effects include frayed ties between neighbors, declining quality of life services, and an ongoing cycle of underdevelopment and emigration that impedes the stability and advancement of the impacted areas.

## Methods for Reducing Brain Drain

In order to counteract the brain drain, Cameroon might use many tactics:

> ➤ *Reforms in the Economy:*

Brain drain mitigation strategies include a range of tactics aimed at addressing the underlying factors that prompt highly qualified individuals to depart from their native nations. Economic changes aiming at fostering an environment that is conducive to talent retention are one of the main methods. It is essential to enhance the economic environment by generating jobs, raising wages, and guaranteeing steady economic growth. People are less inclined to leave their native nation in quest of greater possibilities when they believe that it provides stable work options and stable finances. This strategy is fundamentally based on employment creation. Governments and the private sector must work together to support industries with strong employment potential. This means putting money into industries like manufacturing, healthcare, and technology, which not only have a lot of jobs available, but also want skilled labor. This will make it easier for educated and trained people to find acceptable work back home. Furthermore, as small and medium-sized businesses (SMEs) often employ a sizable number of people, assisting them with grants, loans, and tax breaks may promote the development of jobs. Wage growth is also another important component.

Paying talent well is crucial to keeping them on staff. Skilled professionals are motivated to depart when pay in their native nation are far lower than those provided overseas. Governments have the authority to enact laws that guarantee equitable pay, support workers' rights, and routinely raise salaries to reflect rising costs of living and inflation. Additionally, domestic occupations might become more appealing by providing benefits like healthcare, pensions, and housing, along with performance-based incentives. The foundation of these initiatives is steady economic development. Retaining competent personnel depends on the feeling of security and future opportunities that a strong and expanding economy offers. A stable economy may be attained via prudent budgetary management, infrastructural development, and maintaining an atmosphere that is favorable to business. Through the mitigation of corruption, enhancement of regulatory frameworks, and maintenance of political stability, nations may foster an atmosphere conducive to corporate prosperity and, as a result, increase job prospects. Education and training spending is also essential to economic improvements. Giving workers access to top-notch education and career training gives them the tools they need to fulfill the demands of the contemporary labor market. Collaborations between academic institutions and business may guarantee that graduates are prepared for the workforce and that the curriculum is up to date. Opportunities for ongoing professional development may also aid in the retention of talent by enabling people to progress in their professions without having to relocate overseas. Initiatives for research and development (R&D) may strengthen economic reforms even further. Countries may develop high-tech businesses and knowledge economies that attract and keep qualified workers by encouraging an innovative culture and funding research and development (R&D) initiatives. Governments may encourage R&D by offering tax benefits, subsidies, and the establishment of technology parks and innovation centers. Furthermore, enhancing life quality is crucial to reducing brain drain. Healthcare, safety, infrastructure, and social services are just a few examples of the many factors that influence people's choices to remain or go. A nation with a high quality of life has a better chance of keeping its people. Thus, comprehensive measures that improve urban living conditions, lower crime, and increase public services may significantly lessen brain drain. Reducing brain drain requires a complex strategy built on economic changes. Countries may build an environment that maintains competent individuals and lessens the need for them to look for opportunities overseas by boosting salaries, promoting R&D, investing in education and training, generating employment, and enhancing the quality of life. These tactics help the nation's general social and economic growth in addition to the people who use them.

➤ *Investment in Innovation:*

One of the most important things that can be done to combat the problem of brain drain is to make investments in innovation. Countries have the ability to establish an environment that provides skilled individuals with appealing possibilities by building a healthy ecosystem that encourages research and innovation. This environment may encourage talented professionals to remain in the country rather than looking for more chances elsewhere. The construction of research institutes that are capable of acting as centers for the progress of scientific and technical knowledge is one of the most important approaches. Not only do these institutions make available the infrastructure and resources essential for cutting-edge research, but they also make it easier for researchers, industry specialists, and academic academics to work together. This atmosphere designed for collaboration has the potential to result in ground-breaking discoveries and breakthroughs, which can be the driving force behind economic growth and progress. In addition to research institutes, one of the most important strategies for retaining talent is to provide financial support to innovative new businesses. When they are looking for greater financial assistance and an atmosphere that is more friendly to their initiatives, entrepreneurs and inventors often leave their native nations in quest of better opportunities. These entrepreneurs may be encouraged to develop and expand their firms in the local area by the government via the provision of financial incentives, subsidies, and access to venture capital. Not only does this aid in keeping talent, but it also stimulates the local economy, which results in the creation of more employment possibilities and assists in the development of an innovative culture.

To add insult to injury, the establishment of innovation centers or technology parks may play a significant role in the recruitment and retention of competent workers. These hubs offer a supporting environment that includes state-of-the-art facilities, access to mentoring, and networking opportunities with other entrepreneurs and investors. By building a community of like-minded people, innovation hubs may stimulate cooperation and information exchange, further enriching the innovation environment. Education and continued professional growth are also crucial components of this approach. Investing in high-quality education systems that emphasize STEM (science, technology, engineering, and mathematics) courses may prepare the future workforce with the skills required to prosper in an innovation-driven economy. Additionally, granting scholarships and incentives for advanced study and research inside the nation might assist retain outstanding people. Governments may also establish policies that encourage work-life balance and quality of life improvements, making it more appealing for qualified individuals to live and work in their home country. This involves investing in healthcare, housing, and public transit, as well as encouraging cultural and recreational activities. Overall, a holistic strategy that includes investment in research institutions, support for startups, the formation of innovation clusters, and improvements in education and quality of life may greatly decrease brain drain. By building an atmosphere that encourages and celebrates innovation, nations can retain their finest and brightest brains, promoting sustained economic growth and development.

> ***Enhancing Educational Systems:***

Improving education systems is an important way to counteract brain drain since it guarantees that curricula accurately reflect the demands of the job market. Graduates will have the information and abilities that are in demand in their own nation as a result, which will lessen the motivation to look for chances outside. In order to achieve this alignment, curriculum must be thoroughly reviewed and redesigned to include relevant, real-world skills that satisfy both present and future industry demands. Another crucial component is integrating vocational training into the educational system. With the practical experience and specialized skills that vocational school offers, students may get employed right away after graduation in a variety of crafts and professions. This pragmatic strategy not only improves employability but also cultivates a feeling of relevance and job preparedness in the home labor market. In order to mitigate brain drain, continuous professional development, or CPD, is equally crucial. CPD programs make sure that professionals stay up to date on the latest developments in their professions and maintain their competitiveness. This might include training programs, certificates, seminars, and other educational opportunities that help people stay up to date with developments in the sector and in technology.

Investing in Continuing Professional Development (CPD) allows nations to retain talent by offering clear career development and personal growth routes, which incentivizes qualified people to stay in their native country. Collaboration between businesses and educational institutions may also increase the relevance of education. Creating collaborations between companies and educational institutions may aid in the creation of curricula that adapt to the changing demands of the labor market. Students may get practical experience and industry insights via internships, apprenticeships, and cooperative projects, which will increase their marketability and decrease their propensity to hunt for work overseas. A comprehensive plan to reduce brain drain by improving educational institutions calls for curriculum alignment with industry demands, the incorporation of vocational training, and the encouragement of ongoing professional development. When taken as a whole, these policies improve the domestic job market and increase the attractiveness of

staying in one's native country for qualified workers who want to contribute to its progress.
- ***Political stability and effective governance:***
Mitigating brain drain involves a multidimensional strategy, one of the most critical components of which is maintaining political stability and good administration. This may greatly affect professionals' choices to stay in their native nations rather than exploring chances elsewhere. Firstly, fighting corruption is vital. Corruption reduces faith in public institutions, limits economic prospects, and promotes an atmosphere of uncertainty and inefficiency. By enacting effective anti-corruption measures, governments may strengthen the openness and accountability of public institutions. This entails adopting rigorous rules, guaranteeing their enforcement, and creating a culture of integrity throughout public and private sectors. A transparent and accountable governance system may reassure residents that their nation is devoted to fairness and justice, which in turn can lessen the motivation for qualified professionals to leave. Ensuring political stability is another crucial aspect. Political instability, typified by frequent changes of administration, civil unrest, or violence, provides an uncertain environment that motivates talented people to seek stability elsewhere. Governments may support political stability by maintaining a consistent and fair legislative framework, upholding human rights, and fostering open political procedures that allow for varied representation and

involvement. This stability creates a stable atmosphere where professionals may plan their careers without the worry of unforeseen disruptions.

Good governance goes beyond anti-corruption initiatives and political stability to encompass efficient public service delivery and competent policy-making. Governments must concentrate on developing strong institutions that are capable of executing policies that promote economic growth and social development. This involves investment in infrastructure, education, healthcare, and technology. When professionals perceive that their government is capable of providing great public services and generating possibilities for economic success, they are more inclined to stay in their home nation to contribute to its development. Moreover, building an atmosphere that encourages entrepreneurship and innovation is crucial. Good governance means reducing bureaucratic impediments, simplifying corporate rules, and providing financial incentives for startups and small firms. By promoting a dynamic economic climate, governments may generate multiple possibilities for talented workers, hence lowering the attractiveness of migrating to more developed nations. Finally, engaging the diaspora may also be a useful technique. Governments might develop programs that encourage expatriates to contribute to their home nations via investments, knowledge transfer, and joint ventures. By providing a supportive climate that honors the contributions of both present inhabitants and the diaspora, governments may tap a greater pool of talent and resources for national growth. Political stability and effective governance are basic aspects in the endeavor to minimize brain drain. By tackling corruption, maintaining consistent and inclusive political processes, and providing efficient public services, governments may create a favorable atmosphere that encourages competent professionals to remain and actively contribute to the growth and development of their home nations.

> ***Improvements in Life Quality:***

Investing in healthcare, housing, education, and social services is a multidimensional strategy to minimizing brain drain by boosting the overall quality of life. By prioritizing healthcare, governments may guarantee that residents have access to quality and cheap medical services, which directly adds to their well-being and lessens the attraction of pursuing better healthcare choices overseas. High-quality healthcare systems not only enhance physical health results but also create a feeling of security and stability, encouraging qualified workers to remain within their native nation. Housing is another essential aspect. By building cheap and suitable housing, governments may ease the financial restrictions that typically force qualified professionals to seek opportunities elsewhere. Affordable housing developments may attract young professionals and families by giving them a secure and pleasant living environment, which is vital for long-term planning and stability. Ensuring that housing is accessible and satisfies the requirements of all groups helps build a feeling of community and belonging, making emigration less desirable.

Education has a key role in keeping competent people. By investing in strong educational institutions, governments may create a well-educated citizenry that is capable of contributing to and maintaining economic and social prosperity. High-quality education from basic to tertiary levels guarantees that persons are prepared with the essential skills and knowledge to achieve in their industries. Additionally, investing in continual professional development and lifetime learning opportunities may help retain talent by enabling individuals to progress their careers without having to move. Social services are equally vital in enhancing the quality of life. Comprehensive social services, including child care, elder care, and help for the jobless, may considerably boost the work-life balance and overall happiness of professionals. These services not only offer a safety net during times of need but also indicate a government's commitment to the welfare of its population, generating a feeling of loyalty and belonging. Enhancing the quality of life via smart investments in healthcare, housing, education, and social services may create an atmosphere where talented people feel appreciated, supported, and inspired to remain. By tackling five critical areas, nations may successfully decrease brain drain and retain the talent vital for their growth and development.

> ***Engaging the Diaspora:***

Getting involved with the diaspora is an essential strategy for preventing the loss of intellectual capital, especially for nations like Cameroon that suffer from a substantial loss of talented individuals who leave the country. It is possible to make use of the potential of the diaspora by encouraging people to invest in and contribute to local development initiatives. This is one technique that has shown to be beneficial. One way in which this may be accomplished is by developing specific programs that are designed to assist the transfer of information and skills from individuals who are already residing in another nation back to their home country. There are many different ways to encourage investment from the diaspora, one of which is the creation of diaspora bonds. Diaspora bonds are a sort of sovereign debt that is aimed primarily at the people who have left the nation and are now living outside of it. The issuance of these bonds may provide people of the diaspora a safe and secure means of investing in infrastructure and other important projects, so guaranteeing that their contributions have a direct influence on the development of the target nation. Additionally, the establishment of special economic zones or the provision of tax advantages for enterprises that are managed by diaspora members may be effective in bringing entrepreneurial skill and money back to the United States. It is vital to have programs that promote the transfer of information and skills in order to make use of the expertise of persons who are located overseas. Virtual mentoring programs are one kind of program that may be included in these initiatives. These programs allow professionals from the diaspora to give advice and assistance to their counterparts in the local community online. Furthermore, the organization of frequent conferences, workshops, and seminars that bring together professionals from the local community and specialists from the diaspora may have the effect of fostering cooperation and the sharing of information. Establishing collaborations between local universities and research institutes and those overseas may also encourage academic exchanges and cooperative research activities.

Another strategy is to build platforms and networks that link the diaspora with opportunities in their home country. By way of illustration, internet portals that include a listing of work opportunities, consulting projects, and volunteer jobs have the potential to attract competent persons who are interested in contributing to the growth of their country. Social media groups and professional networks may also serve as essential tools for preserving ties and establishing a sense of community among the diaspora. Engaging the diaspora needs a concerted effort from both government and commercial sectors. Governments may play a crucial role by adopting comprehensive policies and structures that encourage diaspora involvement. This involves creating specific diaspora offices or organizations that supervise and execute outreach efforts. Governments may also focus on easing bureaucratic procedures for diaspora members wishing to invest or return home, such as expediting visa processing and recognizing foreign credentials. Private sector engagement is similarly crucial, as firms may build partnerships and collaborations that tap into the diaspora's knowledge. Companies might organize internship programs that enable young professionals from the diaspora to obtain experience in the local environment, bridging the gap between their foreign education and local industry demands. Additionally, private sector corporations may finance innovation centers and incubators that promote diaspora-led enterprises, building an entrepreneurial environment that benefits from global experiences and ideas. In essence, engaging the diaspora as a method to minimize brain drain comprises promoting investment and enabling knowledge and skill transfer via different programs and projects. By providing an enabling climate and exploiting the potential of the diaspora, nations like Cameroon may convert brain drain into brain gain, encouraging sustained development and progress.

Addressing the core causes and executing comprehensive measures will considerably alleviate the harmful consequences of brain drain in Cameroon and harness the potential of its trained workforce to generate sustainable development and economic progress. Tackling brain drain demands a holistic strategy that goes beyond just generating employment possibilities. It entails improving the entire socio-economic environment, guaranteeing political stability, boosting educational and professional development possibilities, and cultivating a feeling of national pride and dedication. One of the key stages in tackling brain drain is strengthening the socio-economic circumstances inside the nation. This entails creating infrastructure, healthcare, education, and public services to provide a suitable climate for professionals to flourish. By investing in these areas, Cameroon may create a more appealing living and working environment, encouraging competent persons to stay in the nation. Furthermore, giving competitive compensation and perks is vital to keeping talent. This implies harmonizing payment packages with worldwide norms to eliminate the attraction of better-paying possibilities elsewhere.

Enhancing political stability and governance is another essential issue. Political instability and corruption frequently motivate experts to seek opportunities in more stable and transparent contexts. By supporting good governance, guaranteeing the rule of law, and minimizing corruption, Cameroon may develop trust and confidence among its residents, making them more eager to invest their talents and future in the nation. Educational and professional development opportunities must also be highlighted. This requires enhancing the quality of education at all levels, from basic to university, and ensuring that the curriculum is linked with the demands of the contemporary economy. Additionally, offering continual professional development programs and chances for skills enhancement may assist retain talent. Partnerships with overseas universities may give exposure to global best practices and breakthrough technology, further boosting the skills of the local workforce. Fostering a feeling of national pride and dedication is equally vital. This may be done via focused efforts that showcase the successes and contributions of local professionals, as well as by incorporating the diaspora in national development projects. By developing opportunities for the diaspora to contribute to the country's prosperity, either via investment, knowledge transfer, or joint ventures, Cameroon may tap into a large pool of talents and experience.

Moreover, adopting solid regulations to regulate migration properly may assist balance the flow of experts. This involves forging bilateral agreements with other nations to encourage temporary migration and guarantee that skills are transmitted back to Cameroon. Such measures may assist preserve a relationship with the diaspora and promote the return of competent workers after obtaining overseas experience. By addressing the core causes of brain drain and adopting comprehensive policies, Cameroon may establish a supportive environment that keeps its competent workforce. This strategy would not only alleviate the bad consequences of brain drain but also harness the potential of its people capital to generate sustainable development and economic prosperity. Through better socio-economic circumstances, political stability, greater educational possibilities, and a strong sense of national pride, Cameroon may turn brain drain into brain gain, setting itself on a road towards prosperity and resilience.

## C. Addressing Unemployment Crisis
### 1. *Economics Diversification:*
### 1.1 Present-day Economic Situation

Cameroon's economy has both potential and problems as a result of its substantial dependence on extractive sectors, particularly mining, oil, and gas. Despite the fact that these industries greatly boost the GDP of the nation, their dominance comes with a number of dangers and drawbacks. The restricted employment generation that comes with this dependency is one of the main problems. Because extractive sectors often need cutting-edge technology and specialized skills, a sizable section of the population continues to be jobless or underemployed. This problem impedes inclusive progress and widens socioeconomic gaps. Furthermore, the need of diversification is highlighted by Cameroon's economy's susceptibility to changes in the price of commodities globally. Because of its heavy reliance on extractive resources, the country is vulnerable to shocks from the outside world and faces economic instability. In addition to reducing these risks, economic diversification would increase the economy's resistance to shocks from outside. Concerns about the environment also dominate the extractive sectors. The overuse of natural resources often results in environmental deterioration, such as habitat damage, water pollution, and deforestation. In addition to endangering ecosystems and biodiversity, this degradation jeopardizes the long-term viability of these sectors and puts the welfare of nearby populations in jeopardy.

In order to tackle these issues and promote sustainable growth, economic diversification need to be Cameroon's top priority. This can include making investments in industries like manufacturing, tourism, and agriculture, all of which have the ability to boost inclusive development and provide employment. Additionally, the negative effects of the extractive industries on the environment and nearby populations may be lessened by enforcing strict environmental rules and encouraging sustainable practices within these sectors. Additionally, by funding education and career training programs, we can lessen reliance on extractive industries and promote economic resilience by giving workers the skills they need to succeed in a variety of economic sectors.

Although though Cameroon's economy greatly depends on the extractive sectors, their dominance presents a number of difficulties. Cameroon can develop a more robust and inclusive economy that serves all of its residents by investing in human capital, diversifying its economy, and putting sustainable practices into place.

## 1.2 Benefits of Diversification

Diversifying the economy means extending the variety of industries and sectors that contribute to a nation's GDP, minimizing dependence on any one industry. This method may alleviate weaknesses associated with being excessively reliant on a particular sector or export. By spreading economic activity across several sectors, governments may establish a more robust and inclusive labor market, affording opportunities for a larger variety of talents and backgrounds. One of the key advantages of economic diversification is its ability to boost job growth. When a nation invests in numerous businesses, it opens up job prospects across many sectors, lowering unemployment rates and giving citizens with more alternatives for meaningful work. This not only enhances the general level of life but also develops a feeling of economic stability and security within communities. Moreover, economic diversification may play a key role in eliminating poverty. By developing diversified work possibilities, especially in areas like as manufacturing, services, technology, and agriculture, more people have the ability to obtain stable incomes and enhance their quality of life. This, in turn, serves to empower underprivileged groups and alleviate socio-economic inequities. Furthermore, diversity supports sustainable growth by minimizing the environmental effect of economic activity. By investing in green businesses like renewable energy, sustainable agriculture, and eco-tourism, governments may simultaneously develop their economies while lowering their carbon footprint and protecting natural resources for future generations. This coincides with worldwide efforts to mitigate climate change and ensure long-term environmental sustainability. Overall, diversifying the economy is a comprehensive approach that not only promotes economic resilience but also encourages social inclusion, decreases poverty, and contributes to sustainable development objectives. By embracing a varied assortment of companies and sectors, governments may establish resilient economies that are better suited to withstand economic shocks and promote prosperity for all inhabitants. Here are key sectors that may be addressed for diversification:

**a) Agriculture**
- **Innovatio and Modernization:**

Investing in modernization and innovation within the agricultural sector is not just a prudent decision but a transformative one with far-reaching benefits. By incorporating cutting-edge practices, technologies, and infrastructure, nations can catalyze unprecedented growth, sustainability, and resilience in their agricultural systems. Mechanization stands at the vanguard of this revolution. Introducing sophisticated apparatus and equipment streamlines labor-intensive tasks, substantially augmenting efficiency while reducing the burden on manual labor. From cultivating fields to harvesting commodities, mechanization optimizes processes, allowing farmers to maximize their output and minimize their input costs. Moreover, improved irrigation systems represent another cornerstone of modern agricultural practices. By leveraging inventive irrigation techniques such as drip irrigation or precision watering systems, farmers can maximize water usage, mitigate resource wastage, and ensure consistent crop yields even in regions prone to drought or erratic rainfall patterns.

The adoption of high-yield crop varieties is equally pivotal. Through biotechnological advancements and genetic engineering, scientists have developed strains of cereals that exhibit heightened resistance to pests, diseases, and adverse environmental conditions. By cultivating these high-yield varieties, farmers can magnify their harvests while reducing their reliance on chemical pesticides and fertilizers, thereby fostering environmental sustainability and safeguarding public health. Furthermore, investments in infrastructure are indispensable for fostering agricultural modernization. Robust transportation networks, storage facilities, and market linkages facilitate the seamless movement of agricultural produce from farm to fork. By augmenting infrastructure, governments can unleash new market opportunities, enhance agricultural security, and empower rural communities with access to broader economic avenues. Crucially, the convergence of these modernization initiatives not only elevates agricultural productivity but also engenders employment creation across the entire value chain. From manufacturing and servicing agricultural apparatus to research and development in biotechnology, the modern agricultural sector offers a diverse array of employment opportunities, stimulating economic growth and nurturing innovation. In essence, by investing in modern agricultural practices, technology, and infrastructure, nations can set the foundation for a more prosperous, sustainable, and equitable future, where agriculture functions as a beacon of progress and resilience in the face of global challenges.

- **Addition of Value:**

Expanding value addition through the development of agro-processing industries contains immense potential for transforming basic agricultural products into higher-value commodities. This not only enhances economic growth but also generates employment across various sectors such as processing, packaging, and marketing. By leveraging the potential of agro-processing, nations can unleash new avenues for job creation and economic prosperity. One significant benefit of agro-processing is the creation of employment opportunities in rural areas, where agriculture is often the primary source of livelihood. Establishing processing facilities closer to agricultural production sites can stimulate local economies by providing employment to farmers and rural residents. These occupations range from expert positions in food processing and machinery operation to menial labor in packaging and transportation. Moreover, the development of agro-processing industries fosters innovation and technological advancement. Research and development efforts can contribute to the creation of new processing techniques, apparatus, and value-added products, which further enhance competitiveness in domestic and international markets. This innovation-driven approach not only improves product quality and efficiency but also opens up avenues for qualified employment in research and development.

Furthermore, value addition through agro-processing enhances the resilience of agricultural supply chains. By diversifying products and extending their shelf life through processing and packaging, countries can mitigate the risks associated with seasonality and market fluctuations. This stability encourages investment in agriculture and associated industries, leading to sustained job creation and economic growth. Additionally, agro-processing industries play a crucial role in adding value to agricultural exports. Converting basic materials such as cocoa into refined products like chocolate or cassava into flour increases their market value significantly. This not only generates higher returns for farmers and processors but also creates employment opportunities along the entire value chain, from production to distribution. Investments in infrastructure, such as refrigerated storage facilities and transportation networks, are essential for the development of agro-processing industries. Improving logistics and supply chain efficiency enables timely delivery of raw materials to processing units and ensures the distribution of finished products to domestic and international markets. This infrastructure development, in turn, creates employment in construction, maintenance, and logistics management. In summation, developing agro-processing industries to add value to basic agricultural products is a multifaceted approach that contains tremendous potential for employment creation and economic development. By investing in innovation, infrastructure, and human capital, countries can leverage the transformative potential of agro-processing to develop resilient economies and enhance livelihoods for rural communities.

- **Export Promotion:**

Promoting the export of agricultural goods may help countries greatly by expanding their markets and generating more demand for labor. Supply chain logistics must be improved and international standards must be followed in order to fully reap these benefits. Gaining access to foreign markets requires meeting international standards. These standards cover a wide range of topics, including labeling regulations, product quality, and safety. Following them not only guarantees entry into the market but also improves the exporting nation's standing as a dependable provider. Enhancing the logistics of the supply chain is equally important. Effective logistics can guarantee product quality and freshness while cutting costs and lead times. Processes from farm to market, including as distribution, storage, and transportation, must be streamlined. Export promotion may also result in information and technology exchange, which raises the productivity and competitiveness of the agriculture sector even more. Additionally, it may aid in economic diversification, lessening reliance on a small number of commodities and boosting resistance to changes in the market. Encouraging agricultural exports may be a potent instrument for economic growth, but it requires a coordinated effort to satisfy international standards and improve supply chain effectiveness.

## b) Manufacturing:
- **Industrial Zones:**

Industrial zones, which provide specific locations where firms may flourish via specialized economic policies, are essential parts of a nation's economic strategy. Governments may attract international and local investors by offering tax advantages and other benefits via the establishment of industrial parks and special economic zones (SEZs). These areas operate as centers of industrial activity, hosting manufacturing facilities and factories that provide a large number of work possibilities. SEZs provide enhanced infrastructure, reduced regulations, and advantageous tax concessions in an effort to promote economic development. This incentivizes companies to open for business, resulting in more output and employment. Conversely, industrial parks are locations set aside for the purpose of industrial development and provide shared amenities and infrastructure to save expenses for companies. Industrial parks and Special Economic Zones (SEZs) are essential for promoting economic growth and industrialization. They boost local economies, encourage technological transfer, and draw investors. Industrial zones play a major role in job creation and general economic development by offering a favorable business environment.

- **Small and Medium Enterprises (SMEs):**
Small and Medium Enterprises (SMEs) are crucial engines of economic development, stimulating innovation and offering job opportunities. By simplifying access to funding, delivering extensive training programs, and incorporating cutting-edge technology, SMEs may unleash their full potential and contribute considerably to economic growth. Within the industrial sector, SMEs play a significant role in creating a varied variety of items, extending from textiles to equipment. These firms frequently serve as the backbone of local and regional economies, boosting productivity and improving competitiveness in the global market. Access to capital is crucial for SMEs to launch and continue their activities. Whether it's getting loans, accessing venture capital, or using crowdfunding platforms, financial assistance helps SMEs to engage in research and development, modernize their infrastructure, and increase their market reach. Furthermore, training and skill development programs provide SMEs with the information and competence required to handle challenges in the business sector. By increasing management competencies, encouraging technological competence, and promoting entrepreneurship education, these efforts empower SMEs with the means to innovate, adapt, and prosper in an ever-evolving market environment. Integration

of technology is another key part of SME success. Embracing digitalization, automation, and new manufacturing methods may boost productivity, simplify operations, and bolster product quality. Moreover, using technologies such as data analytics, artificial intelligence, and Internet of Things (IoT) helps SMEs to make educated choices, maximize resource use, and remain ahead of the competition. Supporting SMEs via comprehensive policies involving access to financing, training, and technology not only encourages economic growth but also builds a dynamic ecosystem favorable to innovation, entrepreneurship, and sustainable development.

- **Local Content Policies:**

Local content policies are complex tactics adopted by governments to enhance domestic businesses and encourage economic development by promoting the employment of locally obtained materials and resources in manufacturing processes. These programs attempt to foster self-sufficiency, minimize dependency on imports, and solidify the basis of local economies. At their heart, local content regulations are meant to incentivise firms to acquire inputs from domestic sources, so supporting the development of local industries and generating job possibilities within the community. By boosting the usage of locally produced resources, these policies not only increase the competitiveness of domestic producers but also help to the general resilience of the economy against external shocks. Furthermore, the adoption of local content rules generally fits with wider aims of sustainable development and environmental protection. By minimizing the need for long-distance transportation of commodities and encouraging the use of resources that are closer in vicinity, such policies may minimize carbon emissions and relieve strain on natural ecosystems.

Moreover, local content criteria may be incorporated into public procurement procedures, ensuring that government contracts preference local suppliers and contractors. This not only injects cash directly into the local economy but also stimulates the development of local knowledge and technical skills, so boosting the overall competitiveness of domestic businesses. However, although local content regulations provide several advantages, they also bring obstacles and trade-offs. Striking a balance between boosting home sectors and upholding international trade obligations is vital to minimize possible problems with trade agreements and preserve a positive investment environment. Additionally, maintaining the quality and competitiveness of locally supplied materials and products is crucial to minimize market distortions and retain customer trust. Overall, local content regulations constitute a valuable tool for governments to support home sectors, encourage economic diversity, and develop more robust and sustainable economies. Through planned implementation and constant review, these policies may play a crucial role in supporting inclusive development and prosperity at the local, regional, and national levels.

### c) Technology:
- **ICT Development:**

For Cameroon to flourish, infrastructure investments in information and communication technology (ICT) are essential since they have the potential to make the nation a center for digital services. This entails a number of projects including building coding schools to provide young people the fundamental digital skills they need, creating tech incubators to support entrepreneurs and innovation, and extending internet access to more areas. To connect more people to the internet, particularly in rural regions, broadband expansion is essential. It may promote economic development by helping companies to expand into new areas and run more profitably, as well as enhance access to information, healthcare, and educational opportunities. Tech incubators provide money, networking opportunities, and coaching to help firms flourish in a friendly environment. Through innovation and entrepreneurship, these incubators may contribute to the development of a thriving Cameroonian digital ecosystem. Coding schools, which impart coding and other digital skills, are vital to the nation's human capital development. In addition to ensuring that Cameroonians are prepared to engage in the digital economy, this may help close the digital gap. All things considered, funding ICT development may drastically change Cameroon and allow the nation to use technology to further both social and economic advancement.

- **Start-Up Ecosystem:**

Cultivating a vibrant start-up ecosystem entails a comprehensive strategy aimed at promoting innovation and entrepreneurship. This involves easing access to funds, creating mentoring programs, and constructing incubation facilities. By nurturing such an atmosphere, a fertile ground is established for the creation and growth of new initiatives, especially in fields like software development, digital marketing, and e-commerce. The allocation of capital acts as a critical catalyst, helping ambitious entrepreneurs to develop their ideas into sustainable firms. Whether via venture capital, angel investment, or crowdfunding platforms, access to finance may drive the first phases of growth and expansion. Equally crucial is the direction and support offered by experienced mentors who may provide insights, share information, and create significant networking opportunities. Mentorship programs assist entrepreneurs manage the complexity of beginning and expanding a firm, delivering practical guidance and support along the way. Incubation facilities further boost the start-up ecosystem by offering physical areas where entrepreneurs may work, interact, and access vital resources. These places frequently include facilities such as office equipment, networking events, and access to industry experts.

Additionally, incubators may provide customized programs suited to the requirements of start-ups in certain areas, stimulating innovation and driving development. Within this ecosystem, software development, digital marketing, and e-commerce emerge as important sectors suitable for entrepreneurial activity. The fast growth of technology and changing consumer behavior provide numerous chances for creative solutions and disruptive business strategies. Start-ups in software development utilize the power of coding and programming to build software applications, platforms, and services that meet market demands and pain issues. Digital marketing start-ups employ digital platforms and analytics to reach target audiences, engage consumers, and drive conversions. From search engine optimization (SEO) to social media marketing and influencer collaborations, these enterprises utilize a varied variety of techniques to assist companies better their online visibility and build their consumer base. Similarly, e-commerce start-ups capitalize on the expanding trend of online buying, building platforms and marketplaces that allow transactions between consumers and sellers. Whether via specialized market offers, customized shopping experiences, or innovative logistical solutions, these businesses adapt to the increasing wants of today's customers. Supporting a thriving start-up ecosystem via financing, mentoring, and incubation facilities not only encourages economic development but also cultivates a culture of creativity and entrepreneurship. By developing ambitious entrepreneurs and providing them with the appropriate resources and support, society can leverage the transformational potential of start-ups to generate employment, promote technical advances, and accelerate socioeconomic growth.

- **Teck Education:**

Developing the idea of improving STEM education—especially in the context of technology—means taking a multidimensional approach to equipping people with the skills and information they need to navigate the complexity of today's tech-driven world. Fundamentally, the goal of this effort is to develop a skilled labor force that can both meet and exceed the expectations of the ever changing technology industry. The pursuit of STEM education from basic to tertiary levels should be prioritized as a fundamental cornerstone. People who get a solid foundation in science, technology, engineering, and math from an early age are better equipped to acquire the analytical, critical thinking, and problem-solving abilities necessary to succeed in tech-centric contexts. Furthermore, developing a lifelong interest and enthusiasm for these subjects at an early age may have a big impact on career paths by encouraging people to pursue careers in technology-related industries.

In the field of technology education, a wide range of approaches and programs are available with the objective of enhancing the educational process and equipping students with the skills necessary to meet industrial expectations. This includes encouraging interdisciplinary approaches that bridge the gap between STEM disciplines and other fields like the arts, humanities, and social sciences, facilitating hands-on learning opportunities through practical applications and real-world projects, and incorporating state-of-the-art technological tools and resources into educational curricula. Moreover, improving tech education involves more than just conventional classroom settings; it also involves a range of extracurricular activities, corporate collaborations, and mentoring programs. Participating in STEM-related events such as hackathons, robotics contests, and coding clubs not only helps students apply their theoretical knowledge but also develops their teamwork, creativity, and inventiveness. Furthermore, educational institutions may ensure alignment between market needs and their offerings by forming strong ties with industry stakeholders. These collaborations allow the institutions to get insights into new trends, industry best practices, and skill requirements. Essentially, the improvement of tech education is a deliberate attempt to provide people with the abilities, information, and perspective required to prosper in a society that is becoming more and more reliant on technology. Through the promotion of a culture that values continuous learning, flexibility, and creativity, we can develop a workforce capable of meeting the demands and taking advantage of the possibilities posed by the rapidly changing technological world. We can create a future where technology development acts as a catalyst for wealth and progress on a global scale by working together with communities, politicians, industrial partners, and educational institutions.

## d) Services
- **Tourism:**

Developing the tourism sector in Cameroon involves a multifaceted approach that capitalizes on the country's rich cultural heritage, diverse wildlife, and breathtaking natural landscapes. By strategically promoting these attractions, Cameroon can unlock a plethora of opportunities, not only for economic growth but also for job creation across various sectors. One of the primary avenues for job creation lies within the hospitality industry. As tourists flock to explore Cameroon's attractions, there will be an increased demand for accommodation, dining, and entertainment services. This surge in demand can lead to the creation of jobs in hotels, resorts, restaurants, and other hospitality establishments, providing employment opportunities for local residents. Furthermore, the transportation sector stands to benefit significantly from the development of tourism. Improved infrastructure, such as roads, airports, and public transportation systems, will be essential for facilitating the movement of tourists within the country. This, in turn, can generate employment opportunities for individuals involved in construction, maintenance, and operation of transportation networks.

Additionally, the expansion of the tourism sector can spur growth in tour services, including guided tours, travel agencies, and adventure excursions. Local guides, translators, and tour operators will be in demand to provide visitors with enriching experiences and insights into Cameroon's cultural and natural wonders. These roles not only offer employment opportunities but also contribute to the preservation and promotion of Cameroon's heritage. Overall, the development of tourism in Cameroon has the potential to catalyze economic development and create sustainable livelihoods for its citizens. By leveraging its unique cultural assets and natural beauty, Cameroon can position itself as a desirable destination for travelers from around the globe, thereby stimulating growth in key sectors and fostering socio-economic progress.

- *Finantial Services:*

Expanding financial services, comprising banking, insurance, and microfinance, acts as a significant catalyst for supporting company development and producing job possibilities. By improving access to financial products and services, countries may unleash immense potential for growth and development across numerous sectors. Firstly, within the area of banking, increased access to credit facilities helps entrepreneurs and small enterprises to invest in their projects, buy critical resources, and grow their operations. Whether via loans, lines of credit, or novel financing alternatives, such as venture capital or crowdfunding platforms, companies get the financial leverage required to undertake ambitious initiatives and grab emerging possibilities. This injection of cash feeds innovation, boosts productivity, and eventually adds to economic development. Moreover, the growth of insurance services plays a key role in minimizing risks and preserving enterprises from unanticipated adversities. Insurance coverage offers a safety net, insulating firms from possible losses due to natural catastrophes, accidents, or market changes. With proper insurance cover, companies may operate with more confidence, knowing they have a cushion against financial failures that might otherwise damage their operations. Additionally, insurance solutions suited to particular sector demands, such as liability insurance for manufacturers or crop insurance for farmers, respond to different company requirements, supporting resilience and sustainability.

Furthermore, the development of microfinance projects promotes financial inclusion to disadvantaged communities, including low-income people and small-scale enterprises. Microfinance organizations provide accessible loan, savings, and insurance services targeted to the special requirements of underserved groups. By allowing prospective entrepreneurs to create micro-enterprises and providing financial instruments for personal investment and asset accumulation, microfinance encourages grassroots economic growth. Through targeted assistance and capacity-building initiatives, microfinance not only supports wealth creation at the grassroots level but also cultivates a culture of entrepreneurship and self-reliance. In short, the development of financial services exceeds ordinary transactional operations; it acts as a formidable engine for economic empowerment, pushing corporate growth, building resilience, and stimulating job creation. By embracing the transformational power of inclusive finance, societies can unlock the full potential of their entrepreneurial talent, moving them towards sustainable development and shared prosperity.

- *Education and Halth Services:*

Infrastructure investments in the fields of education and healthcare are crucial for the development of society. Governments and communities may promote sustainable development and enhance the well-being of their population by dedicating resources to these areas. Education is the foundation of development. Building schools, colleges, and universities, equipping them with cutting-edge equipment, and guaranteeing that everyone has access to high-quality education are all components of investing in educational infrastructure. This improves the learning environment for children as well as opening new job prospects for educators, administrators, and support personnel. People with higher levels of education are better able to innovate, support the economy, and adjust to the changing needs of the labor market. In a similar vein, creating hospitals, clinics, and other medical facilities as well as modernizing machinery and technology constitute investments in healthcare infrastructure. This increases the population's access to healthcare services while also creating employment for medical professionals including physicians, nurses, and technicians. A strong healthcare system lowers death rates, improves overall quality of life, and produces better health outcomes.

Moreover, there are wider socioeconomic advantages to spending money on healthcare and education. By giving people the information and skills they need to get better employment and have access to better healthcare, they help to reduce poverty. A population that is well-educated and in good health is also better able to sustain long-term economic development and prosperity and is less susceptible to shocks to the economy. Making investments in the infrastructure of healthcare and education not only creates employment but also lays the groundwork for a successful and just society. It is an investment in human capital, and social cohesiveness, increased well-being, and economic productivity are the returns. In order to guarantee the comprehensive development of their communities, authorities need to give priority to these areas.

### 1.3 Strategies for Implementation
**a) Policy Reforms:**

Reforming policies is essential to promoting growth in certain industries. Governments may promote economic activity and innovation by putting in place investment-friendly policies. Various strategies are often used in these changes, such as tax breaks, financial aid, and the simplification of administrative procedures. The growth of sectors that are essential to the economy may be aided by attracting investors and entrepreneurs by lowering administrative costs and removing obstacles to entry. By implementing such programs, governments want to foster an atmosphere that encourages investment and, eventually, advances and prospers the specific industries they are focusing on.

**b) Public-Private Partnerships (PPPs)**

Public-Private Partnerships (PPPs) facilitate cooperation between public and private entities to finance and manage large-scale projects such as industrial parks and infrastructure development. These collaborations take use of the resources and power of the public sector as well as the efficiency and creativity of the commercial sector. PPPs provide companies access to profitable possibilities and government backing, while governments may use the experience, resources, and efficiency of the private sector. Large-scale initiatives that would not be viable for either side to undertake alone due to financial or logistical constraints may now be undertaken thanks to this mutually beneficial partnership.

c) **Capacity building**

Capacity building entails delivering training and skill development programs to workers aimed at preparing them for the needs of developing industries. It focuses on strengthening their talents, knowledge, and ability to successfully traverse and contribute to growing areas. Through capacity development activities, people learn the experience and capacities necessary to adapt to changing market conditions, technology breakthroughs, and organizational demands. It helps people to remain relevant and competitive in the ever-evolving labor market by giving them with the required skills and knowledge to flourish in developing sectors.

d) **Access to Finance**

Encouraging companies, especially Small and Medium Enterprises (SMEs), to get financing is essential to their expansion and prosperity. This entails offering a range of financial tools, including grants, loans, and investment funds, to help companies get the funding they need to launch, run, and grow. A prominent kind of financing used by enterprises is the loan, which they take out from lenders or financial organizations and pay back over time with interest. These loans may be taken out for a number of things, such growing business operations, buying equipment, or paying for overhead. Another kind of funding that is non-repayable is grants. They are often offered by foundations, governments, and non-profits to assist companies operating in certain industries or areas. Grants may be used to innovation, R&D, or other initiatives that support the expansion and development of businesses. Businesses may get funding from investment funds, such venture capital or private equity, in return for a share in the firm. High-growth companies often utilize these funds to finance initiatives related to development or expansion. Encouraging companies, especially SMEs, to have easier access to financing is crucial for promoting innovation, job creation, and economic development. By giving companies the financial resources they need to be successful, we can encourage their expansion and contribute to a booming economy.

To sum this up, Investigating the complex plans of action and tactics needed in several areas is essential to realizing the need of diversifying Cameroon's economy. First of all, Cameroon has enormous unrealized agricultural potential in agriculture. Putting money into post-harvest infrastructure, irrigation systems, and contemporary agricultural methods may greatly increase production, decrease reliance on imports, and open up job possibilities in rural regions. Smallholder farmers may also be empowered to make more productive contributions to the economy by being given access to markets, technology, and funding. The creation of a strong industrial sector must go hand in hand with agricultural growth. Promoting local resource and agricultural processing may foster the development of a trained labor force, increase the value of raw materials, and promote industrial expansion. Furthermore, encouraging both foreign and local investments in manufacturing facilities may result in increased exports, increased competitiveness, and innovation, all of which help to balance trade imbalances and produce income. Beyond that, Cameroon's economic diversification is largely dependent on its ability to fully use technology. Building an innovation environment, increasing internet accessibility, and promoting digital literacy may all help to accelerate the development of IT services and tech startups, establishing Cameroon as a center for digital entrepreneurship and technical innovation in the area. New technologies that have the potential to transform established sectors and open up new job and economic development opportunities include blockchain, artificial intelligence, and renewable energy.

The services industry, especially in sectors like travel, healthcare, education, and finance, has several prospects for diversification at the same time. Through the creation of employment and additional income streams throughout the value chain, investments in hospitality establishments, tourist attractions, and infrastructure development may draw both local and foreign tourists. Enhancing human capital development, productivity, and socioeconomic growth may all be achieved via expanding access to high-quality healthcare and educational services. But a well-thought-out, integrated strategy is needed to carry out these diversification initiatives successfully. To improve the business climate, provide regulatory clarity, and build investor confidence, substantial policy changes are required. Additionally, to promote economic activity and ease commerce, investments in vital infrastructure are necessary, such as energy facilities, transportation networks, and digital infrastructure. Furthermore, in order to provide the workforce with the necessary skills and knowledge for growing sectors, capacity building efforts focusing on entrepreneurial education, vocational training, and skills development are crucial. To maximize funds, exchange knowledge, and advance sustainable development projects, cooperative alliances between the public and commercial sectors, academic institutions, and civil society are essential. Ultimately, expanding Cameroon's economy via economic diversification is not only a wise course of action, but also a critical one in order to promote equitable development, lower the rate of joblessness, and guarantee sustained prosperity. Through directing investments towards agriculture, industry, technology, and services, Cameroon may realize its full economic potential, fortify its economy, and enhance the quality of life for its people. To manage obstacles and seize opportunities in a global economy that is changing quickly, it will be necessary to implement bold reforms, persistent investments, and coordinated efforts in order to realize this goal.

## 2. Investing in Education and Skills Development

### 2.1 Reforming the Education System to Meet Labor Market Needs

Revamping the education system to align with the demands of the job market is crucial for tackling unemployment and promoting economic growth. To ensure that the education system is closely synchronized with the changing requirements of the job market, there are many crucial actions that need to be taken. First and foremost, it is crucial to establish a continuous and active communication between educational institutions and leaders in the business. This partnership facilitates the identification of sought-after skills and competences, which may then be included into the curriculum. By being informed about current industry trends and breakthroughs in technology, educational programs may be tailored to provide students with pertinent and applicable skills. Furthermore, it is essential to integrate a greater amount of practical and experiential training into the educational structure. Internships, apprenticeships, and cooperative education programs provide students the opportunity to get practical experience and develop a more comprehensive understanding of workplace norms and requirements. This strategy not only improves the chances of graduates finding employment but also enables companies to actively participate in the training process, ensuring that the skills being taught are instantly relevant and useful.

Moreover, the curriculum has to be flexible and adaptive. As industries develop, so too must the instructional material. This necessitates the implementation of a dynamic system in which curriculum are constantly evaluated and revised to include the most recent advancements in many disciplines. Implementing modular courses and micro-credentials may assist students gain specialized skills in a shorter time period, allowing for continual learning and adaption to changing employment needs. Investment in teacher training is another key component. Educators need to be well-versed in the newest industry standards and technology technologies to properly educate pupils for the work market. Professional development programs and business collaborations may help instructors keep current and bring practical ideas into the classroom. Additionally, incorporating career advising and job placement services inside educational institutions may bridge the gap between education and work. Career counselors may give students with vital information on labor market trends, job search tactics, and the skills necessary for various career pathways. Effective job placement services may support internships, job fairs, and networking opportunities, helping students move easily from school to employment.

Furthermore, strengthening STEM (Science, Technology, Engineering, and Mathematics) education is crucial in solving the skills gap in many high-demand areas. Encouraging students to seek jobs in these industries may assist fulfill the rising demand for technical competence. This may be done via targeted scholarships, mentoring programs, and generating awareness about the numerous employment prospects accessible in STEM disciplines. Addressing regional and demographic differences in education is also vital to guarantee that all students have equal opportunity to achieve. This requires investing in educational infrastructure in underprivileged communities, giving access to excellent teaching materials, and establishing policies that encourage inclusive education. By leveling the playing field, we can guarantee that talent from all backgrounds is cultivated and exploited efficiently. Connecting the education system with labor market requirements involves a multidimensional strategy combining cooperation between educational institutions, business, and government. By promoting practical skills, assuring curriculum flexibility, investing in teacher training, and offering comprehensive career support services, we can produce a workforce that is well-prepared for the needs of the contemporary economy. This not only solves unemployment but also fosters innovation and economic development.

## a) Curriculum Modernization
- **Industry Collaboration:**

Industry partnership is a vital component in connecting educational curriculum with the ever-evolving needs of the employment market. By working with companies, educational institutions may receive vital insights on the skills and knowledge that are most relevant and in-demand. This partnership helps to guarantee that students are not only well-prepared for current employment needs but also equipped with the abilities required for future developments. One of the key advantages of industry partnership is the opportunity to keep curriculum up-to-date with the newest technical breakthroughs and market trends. Industries are typically at the forefront of innovation, and their contribution may assist educational programs embrace cutting-edge technology and approaches. This guarantees that students are gaining skills that are immediately transferable in the industry, making them more competitive in the job market following graduation. Additionally, industry collaborations may give students with actual, hands-on experience via internships, co-op programs, and real-world projects. These opportunities enable students to apply their academic knowledge in real contexts, obtain significant job experience, and create professional networks. This experience learning is vital in helping students move easily from the classroom to the job. Moreover, cooperation with companies might lead to the

creation of customized training programs suited to certain sectors or employment types. For instance, a cooperation with a tech business may result in the formation of a program focusing on cybersecurity or artificial intelligence, addressing the unique demands of that sector. Such specialized programs may help bridge the skills gap and guarantee that graduates acquire the particular competence sought by companies. Industry engagement also enables the continuing professional growth of educators. By connecting with industry experts, educators may remain current of the newest trends and breakthroughs in their domains, which they can subsequently incorporate into their teaching. This continuing professional development is vital for preserving the relevance and quality of education. Furthermore, agreements with companies may boost the resources accessible to educational institutions. Industries may offer funds, equipment, and other resources that would otherwise be unavailable. This assistance may enrich the learning environment and offer students with access to state-of-the-art tools and technology. In short, working with industry plays a critical role in ensuring that educational curriculum are linked with present and future employment needs. This relationship helps students by delivering relevant information and skills, practical experience, specialized training programs, and better learning tools. It also aids instructors in remaining current with industry advances, eventually leading to a more dynamic and responsive educational system.

- **STEM Emphasis:**

In today's quickly changing labor market, it is imperative to strengthen STEM (science, technology, engineering, and mathematics) education to educate students for areas that are in great demand. STEM education fosters critical thinking, problem-solving, and inventive talents in pupils by providing them with fundamental skills that are highly appreciated in a variety of professions. Students get a solid foundation in scientific principles, technical competency, engineering ideas, and mathematical reasoning via the improvement of STEM education. This extensive body of information guarantees that students can adjust to the changing demands of contemporary work settings in addition to preparing them for specialized vocations. Putting money into STEM education entails giving students access to high-quality materials, current curriculum, and practical learning opportunities. This method makes learning more interesting and efficient by assisting students in applying theoretical information to real-world situations. A solid STEM foundation should also be instilled in children at a young age as this may stimulate their interest and enthusiasm for STEM fields, which can improve their enrollment in advanced STEM programs and jobs. Teachers are essential to this process because they use cutting-edge teaching strategies and keep up with developments in STEM. Opportunities for professional development for educators guarantee that they have the tools necessary to motivate and mentor their pupils. Additionally, collaborations between academic institutions, businesses, and schools may expose students to cutting-edge technology and real-world experiences like mentoring and internship programs. By giving STEM education top priority, we can both train a workforce that will lead future discoveries and meet the expanding need for skilled workers in industries like biotechnology, engineering, and information technology. Maintaining competitiveness in the global economy and tackling difficult issues like climate change, medical improvements, and technology upheavals need a strong focus on STEM. To sum up, enhancing STEM education is a wise investment in the future as it will produce a generation of thinkers and doers equipped to take on the possibilities and problems of the future.

- **Development of Soft Skills:**

Incorporating soft skills development into the coursework is important for training students to thrive in various job settings. Soft skills, which include conversation, teamwork, problem-solving, and critical thinking, are vital for personal and career success. Communication is a basic skill that improves a student's ability to express thoughts easily and effectively. This includes not only speaking and written communication but also non-verbal cues, listening skills, and the ability to change one's communication style to different groups. Integrating speech training into the program can involve activities like group talks, lectures, and joint projects. These tasks encourage students to practice and improve their communication skills in real-world situations, ensuring they can explain their thoughts clearly and coherently. Teamwork is another important soft skill that prepares students for joint work settings. By working in teams, students learn to respect different views, handle disagreements, and leverage each member's skills to achieve shared goals. Team-based projects and tasks help students develop these skills by modeling job situations where teamwork and collaboration are key. Through these situations, students learn the value of dependability, mutual respect, and shared duty, which are necessary for effective teamwork. Problem-solving skills allow students to handle complicated and unforeseen obstacles. Incorporating problem-solving tasks into the program can be done through case studies, models, and project-based learning. These methods urge students to evaluate situations seriously, find possible answers, and apply strategies effectively. By regularly engaged in problem-solving tasks, students develop grit and flexibility, which are essential in dynamic work settings. Critical thinking is the ability to examine material carefully and make reasoned conclusions. Developing critical thinking skills includes pushing students to question beliefs, examine proof, and consider different views.

Integrating critical thought into the classroom can be achieved through discussions, study projects, and critical analysis of books. These activities create an atmosphere where students learn to think freely, make educated choices, and approach problems systematically. By putting conversation, teamwork, problem-solving, and critical thought into the educational system, students are better prepared to face the challenges of modern work settings. These skills not only improve their employment but also arm them with the tools necessary for ongoing personal and professional growth.

### b) Apprenticeships and Vocational Training

- **Technical Education:**

The importance of technical education in preparing students for the employment of the future is becoming more widely acknowledged. Through the inclusion of contemporary trades and technology in vocational training programs, educational institutions are equipping students with the practical skills and real-world experience necessary to succeed in the quickly changing labor market of today. Trades such carpentry, plumbing, and electrical work have traditionally been the emphasis of traditional vocational training. But as companies have developed, there is an increasing need for knowledge in fields like sophisticated manufacturing, renewable energy, information technology, and healthcare technology. By include these subjects in vocational training programs, instructors can make sure that students are not only acquiring in-demand skills but also becoming proficient in cutting-edge technologies that will influence the nature of employment in the future. An essential component of a successful technical education is practical experience. Through the completion of hands-on projects and real-world applications, students may get a better comprehension of the principles being taught. By enabling students to apply their information in real-world contexts, this experiential learning strategy helps close the knowledge gap between theory and practice. Students may work directly with solar panels or wind turbines as part of a curriculum centered on renewable energy, for instance, getting personal knowledge that is incomparable to that which can be obtained just via classroom learning. Furthermore, collaborating with top industry players is often necessary to broaden technical education to include contemporary skills and technology. These partnerships may provide students access to the newest tools and methods, guaranteeing that the instruction they receive complies with current industry requirements. These collaborations may also result in mentoring programs, internships, and job placements, all of which may improve the students' educational experience and employability. A strong technical education system has advantages for the whole economy in addition to specific pupils. The demand for a workforce with current technology skills and the flexibility to take on new challenges is expanding as industries continue to change. Vocational training programs may contribute to closing important labor market gaps and promoting economic development and innovation by providing students with these skills. Moreover, technical education is essential for tackling problems of accessibility and fairness in the classroom. For kids who may not do well in a regular classroom, vocational training programs can provide an alternative to standard academic pathways. People from underprivileged backgrounds may benefit most from these programs as they provide them the qualifications and abilities required to find steady, well-paying professions. Adding contemporary crafts and technology to vocational training programs is an essential investment in the workforce of the future. Through practical experience and instruction that is in line with industry demands, technical education may provide people the tools they need to thrive in a labor market that is changing quickly. In addition to helping the pupils directly, this also advances social justice and more extensive economic development.

- **Apprenticeships:**

Students have the rare and beneficial chance to combine academic learning with real-world, hands-on experience via apprenticeships. Through these programs, people may be paid as they study, giving them financial support while they develop important skills for their chosen industry. Apprenticeships, in contrast to standard educational courses, place a strong emphasis on practical experience, which may greatly improve a student's comprehension and competence in their trade or vocation. Students that participate in apprenticeships work under the supervision and tutelage of seasoned experts. This mentoring is an essential part since it gives apprentices the chance to get direct instruction from people with a wealth of experience and expertise. In addition to offering technical training, mentors also impart knowledge about professional standards, work culture, and best practices within the business. Because of this connection, apprentices are able to learn more deeply in a supportive setting, ask questions, and get prompt feedback. Additionally, apprenticeship programs are designed to accommodate the requirements of the apprentice as well as the employer. The training is guaranteed to be current and immediately related to the work thanks to this tailored approach. Due to the fact that apprenticeships foster a strong feeling of loyalty and engagement in the firm via mentoring and hands-on experience, they often result in greater retention rates. Employers gain from having a staff that is knowledgeable about the unique requirements and procedures of their industry and is qualified and trained. Apprenticeships aid in the development of a variety of soft skills that are essential for job success in addition to the technical abilities learned. Teamwork, problem-solving, time management, and effective communication are among the skills that apprentices acquire. The everyday contacts and responsibilities that come with the apprenticeship help students develop these skills, which will help them lead well-rounded professional lives. Apprenticeships provide a substantial financial benefit. Apprentices may sustain themselves without taking on the debt that is sometimes connected with conventional schooling by earning a salary while undergoing training. Their capacity to concentrate more on their education and career growth is made possible by their financial security. All things considered, apprenticeships provide a hands-on, immersive learning environment that equips students for the demands of the industry by bridging the gap between school and employment. They provide a mutually beneficial partnership in which employers and apprentices get significant advantages, making them a crucial element of contemporary education and professional advancement.

- **Industry Certification:**

Industry certifications are essential for bridging the skills gap between college and work because they provide people the specific knowledge and credentials that are highly sought after in a variety of technologies and occupations. In order to guarantee that the curriculum and examinations are in line with the demands and norms of the workforce today, these certifications are often created in conjunction with companies and experts in the sector. Thus, gaining these qualifications may greatly improve a job seeker's employability and opportunities for advancement. The emphasis placed by industry certificates on real-world, practical experience is one of its main advantages. In contrast to conventional university degrees, which could place more emphasis on theoretical knowledge, industry certifications are intended to provide people the technical know-how and abilities needed to carry out certain work duties efficiently. This realistic strategy guarantees that qualified people are prepared for the workforce and can have a positive impact on their companies' operations right away. Furthermore, these certificates are often seen as a trustworthy sign of a candidate's talents and job preparedness due to the fact that businesses recognize them. The flexibility and accessibility of industry qualifications is another important benefit. Numerous certification programs are accessible to a broad spectrum of people, including those who may already be employed and want to upskill or reskill, via community colleges, vocational institutions, and online platforms. Furthermore, without the long-term commitment and financial strain of a typical degree program, people may swiftly pick up new skills, join the workforce, or progress in their present employment thanks to the comparatively short length of many certification programs. Furthermore, industry certifications are regularly updated to take into account the most recent developments and trends in business practices as well as technology. This gives qualified professionals a competitive advantage by ensuring that they stay up to date with the changing needs of the labor market. Employers might be less concerned about the danger of onboarding new workers when they hire certified people since they know these applicants have the skills and knowledge needed to carry out their jobs well. Industry certifications provide a clear route to employment by offering specific, hands-on training that businesses respect and acknowledge. They provide people with an accessible and adaptable way to acquire the skills required to excel in a variety of trades and technology, improving their employability and prospects for professional advancement.

### c) Education in Entrepreneurship

Teaching people the foundations of launching and managing a company entails giving them a broad range of abilities necessary for navigating the tricky world of entrepreneurship. Financial literacy is essential to this and includes managing cash flow, budgeting, analyzing financial statements, and obtaining finance. A firm understanding of financial concepts empowers prospective entrepreneurs to make well-informed choices, strategize for the future, and guarantee the longevity of their endeavors. Another crucial element is marketing, which calls for an understanding of branding, sales tactics, advertising, and market research. Marketing that works helps companies connect with their target market, stand out from the competition, and develop a devoted clientele. In addition to conventional techniques, it also makes use of digital marketing, which is becoming essential in today's corporate environment. Equally important are management abilities, which include operations, strategic planning, human resources, and leadership. A company with well-managed resources will function smoothly, have motivated and productive workers, and make effective use of its resources. It also requires the ability to solve problems and make decisions, both of which are essential for overcoming obstacles and grasping possibilities. A combination of academic understanding and real-world application is required to teach these foundations. Real-world initiatives, case studies, and simulations may all provide practical experience, and receiving guidance from seasoned businesspeople can provide priceless insights. This all-inclusive method helps people start and expand their enterprises effectively, which promotes innovation and economic expansion.

- **Creativity and Innovation:**

Innovative strategies like project-based learning and the creation of business incubator programs may be used to promote creativity and innovation in educational environments. Project-based learning develops students' creativity, critical thinking, and problem-solving abilities by immersing them in real-world events and problems. Students are free to explore, experiment, and cooperate without the limitations of typical classroom frameworks, which results in creative solutions and original ideas. Programs for business incubators reinforce this philosophy by giving students the chance to start their own businesses and hone their entrepreneurial talents. These courses provide students with the guidance, tools, and encouraging atmosphere they need to develop their concepts, carry out market analysis, and create working prototypes of their goods or services. Through the incorporation of entrepreneurship into the curriculum, educational institutions foster not just student innovation but also an entrepreneurial attitude that equips them for the demands of the contemporary market. By combining project-based learning with business incubator programs, educational institutions may provide an environment that stimulates creativity, encourages innovation, and gives students the tools they need to succeed in a world that is becoming more competitive and complicated. Teachers may empower the next generation of thinkers, problem solvers, and changemakers to create a better future by adopting these cutting-edge teaching strategies.

- **Networking and Mentorship:**
Two of the most important foundations for supporting the success of entrepreneurs are networking and mentoring. Important knowledge and direction are shared by pairing together budding entrepreneurs with seasoned business mentors. These mentors assist mentees navigate the intricacies of entrepreneurship with clarity and confidence by sharing ideas from their own experiences. Additionally, networking opportunities make it easier to create crucial relationships within the ecosystem of entrepreneurs. Engaging with successful business owners broadens one's professional network and provides access to possible partners, collaborators, and investors. Aspiring entrepreneurs may access a multitude of information, resources, and support via networking and mentoring, which gives them more momentum and resilience as they work toward their objectives.

## 2.2 Initiatives for Lifelong Learning and Retraining

In order to keep up with the fast rate of technical progress and economic transformation, it is essential to make a dedicated effort to continuously study and improve the skills of the workers throughout their lives. This phenomenon arises from the profound influence that developing technology and changing economic paradigms have on industries and employment markets. The transformation brought about by automation, artificial intelligence, and digitalization is altering conventional job positions and giving rise to novel ones. This dynamic landscape means that the abilities need now may quickly become outdated in the near future. In order to remain relevant and maintain a competitive advantage, people must actively participate in ongoing education, which entails consistently enhancing their knowledge and abilities. Continuing one's education is essential for adjusting to emerging technology and approaches. As industries progress, the skills needed to succeed in them also advance. For instance, the integration of AI into numerous industries involves not just technical expertise but also the ability to work alongside intelligent systems, evaluate complicated data, and apply findings in novel ways. Moreover, the need for a versatile skill set is also brought about by economic transformations resulting from globalization, market volatility, and changes in consumer behavior. Workers must possess agility, allowing them to quickly adapt and use their skills in various situations. This flexibility is vital not just for personal career advancement but also for organizational resilience. Organizations that allocate resources to the ongoing growth and enhancement of their workforce are more adept at navigating periods of economic uncertainty and seizing emerging opportunities.

Employers have a crucial role in establishing a culture of continual learning. By offering access to training programs, fostering professional growth, and supporting educational efforts, employers may guarantee their staff stays competent and engaged. This investment in human capital is crucial for retaining a competitive advantage and attaining long-term success. Moreover, government policies and educational institutions must match with the expectations of the contemporary labor. This alignment entails providing flexible learning routes, delivering up-to-date curriculum, and ensuring that training programs are accessible to everyone. Public-private partnerships may also boost the success of lifelong learning efforts, pooling resources and expertise to solve skill shortages and prepare workers for future difficulties. In essence, the commitment to lifelong learning and constant upskilling is not only a personal obligation but a social effort. It takes cooperation between people, companies, educators, and governments to establish a vibrant and adaptive workforce. As technology and economies continue to advance, this dedication will be the cornerstone of sustainable growth and innovation, guaranteeing that both people and society can prosper in an ever-changing environment.

## a. Programs for Lifelong Learning

- *Accessible Education:*

In order to provide possibilities for everyone, regardless of their situations in life, accessible education is essential. This objective is greatly aided by the availability of weekend programs, night sessions, and online courses. Students may study from anywhere with the use of online courses, which eliminates geographical obstacles and makes high-quality education accessible to individuals who are isolated or have mobility problems. They provide flexibility, enabling learners to follow their own schedule and at their own speed. This is especially advantageous for those with hectic schedules or erratic lifestyles. Evening programs are designed for working individuals with daytime obligations. With the help of these programs, they may continue their education without having to give up their employment or everyday obligations. This option gives people the chance to attend lessons after completing their daily responsibilities, which helps individuals who may be balancing various duties, such as parents or caretakers. Weekend programs provide an additional degree of freedom, enabling participants to devote their weekends to their academic pursuits. Those who are unable to adhere to a normal weekday routine because of work or other obligations may find this to be very helpful. Weekend programs may be an effective option for working people to further their education since they often provide intense sessions that cover a lot of content in a short amount of time. When combined, these instructional modalities provide a learning environment that is more flexible and inclusive. They acknowledge and cater to the various requirements of adult learners, guaranteeing that postsecondary education is not only reachable but also accommodating to those who are trying to strike a balance between their education and other important facets of their life. Institutions may better assist their students' professional and personal development by introducing these flexible learning choices, which will eventually result in a workforce that is more competent and educated.

- *Modular learning:*

Modular learning focuses on delivering short-term courses and micro-credentials meant to enable people gain new skills without the need for long-term educational commitments. This method to education is very adaptable, enabling people to adjust their learning experiences to their own requirements and schedules. By breaking down education into digestible units, learners may swiftly adjust to the changing needs of the labor market and remain relevant in their jobs. In today's fast-paced world, where technology breakthroughs and industrial needs are always expanding, modular learning offers an effective alternative for continued professional growth. It enables people to refresh their abilities progressively, making it simpler to transfer between various positions or sectors.

These short-term courses and micro-credentials are typically produced in partnership with industry professionals to ensure they fit current market demands and standards. Moreover, modular learning might be more accessible and cheap compared to typical long-term educational programs. It offers up options for a larger audience, including people who would not have the time or financial means to complete a full degree. By concentrating on particular skills and abilities, learners may make concrete professional gains without the lengthy time commitment of conventional education courses. This sort of learning is especially advantageous for working professionals wishing to upskill or reskill without disrupting their professions. It helps them to stay competitive and adapt to new work responsibilities or developing technology. Additionally, organizations gain from a staff that can rapidly learn and deploy new skills, hence boosting overall productivity and creativity inside the firm. In essence, modular learning democratizes education by making it more adaptable to individual and business demands, encouraging a culture of continual learning and flexibility. It enables a more dynamic and resilient workforce capable of flourishing in an ever-changing economic context.

- **Continuing Education Credits:**
Continuing education credits are a valuable tool for professional development, offering employees opportunities to enhance their skills and knowledge. Implementing systems where employees can earn credits for additional training fosters a culture of continuous improvement and career growth. These credits can be accrued through various learning activities such as workshops, seminars, online courses, and on-the-job training sessions. By engaging in these educational pursuits, employees not only gain new competencies but also stay current with industry trends and advancements. This system benefits both the individual and the organization. For employees, it provides a structured pathway for career advancement. They can accumulate credits over time, which can then be used to meet criteria for promotions, salary increases, or even certifications and licenses required in certain fields. This sense of progression and achievement can enhance job satisfaction and motivate employees to take initiative in their personal and professional development. From an organizational perspective, a well-implemented continuing education credit system ensures that the workforce remains skilled and knowledgeable. It helps bridge skill gaps, supports succession planning, and enhances overall productivity. Organizations can tailor the credit system to align with strategic goals, ensuring that the training provided addresses specific business needs and prepares employees for future challenges.

Moreover, this approach demonstrates a commitment to employee growth and development, which can be a significant factor in attracting and retaining top talent. When employees see that their employer invests in their education and career progression, they are more likely to feel valued and engaged. This can lead to higher levels of loyalty and reduced turnover rates. To implement such a system effectively, organizations need to establish clear guidelines on how credits are earned and tracked. This includes defining eligible activities, setting up an accessible platform for logging credits, and communicating the benefits and processes to employees. Regular feedback and assessment can help refine the system and ensure it meets the evolving needs of both the employees and the organization. Continuing education credits play a crucial role in fostering a dynamic and skilled workforce. By providing structured opportunities for learning and growth, organizations can enhance employee satisfaction, support career advancement, and maintain a competitive edge in their industry.

**b. Upskilling and Retraining**

- *Public-private Partnerships:*

Public-private partnerships play a significant role in bridging the gap between the growing needs of the labor market and the skills acquired by the workforce. By engaging with employers to establish retraining programs, these collaborations guarantee that training efforts are not only linked with current industry demands but also enable instant use of skills, hence improving employability and productivity. The dynamic nature of today's businesses, driven by fast technology breakthroughs and fluctuating economic environments, needs a workforce that is always upgrading its skill set. Public-private collaborations exploit the capabilities of both sectors: the public sector's commitment to broad-based educational access and the business sector's expertise into market trends and particular skill shortages. This synergy leads in training programs that are relevant, focused, and effective. Businesses are uniquely positioned to discover the particular talents that are in demand within their industries. By including them in the planning phase of retraining programs, these efforts may be customized to meet particular needs in the job market. This guarantees that participants gain skills that are instantly useful, hence shortening the period between training and employment. For instance, in the computer business, firms might give information on the newest programming languages, software tools, and development processes that are necessary for current projects. This direct channel of contact guarantees that training curriculum are not obsolete and that graduates are job-ready upon completion.

Moreover, these connections typically result in the formation of internship and apprenticeship programs, offering hands-on experience that is crucial for skill growth. These practical components of retraining programs enable participants to apply what they have learned in real-world situations, under the direction of experienced experts. This not only strengthens their new abilities but also boosts their confidence and preparedness to participate successfully from day one. Additionally, public-private cooperation may lead to the creation of novel training models, such as bootcamps and accelerated learning programs, which are geared to satisfy urgent industrial demands. These methods are frequently more flexible and responsive than conventional educational courses, allowing for fast upskilling in high-demand sectors. For example, a combination between a software business and a community college can result in a coding bootcamp that converts persons with no previous programming knowledge into skilled developers in a matter of months. Furthermore, these agreements generally incorporate methods for continuing assessment and modification of the training programs. By regularly monitoring the results and requesting input from both participants and employers, these programs may be fine-tuned to ensure they stay relevant and successful. This iterative method helps to maintain a high grade of training and ensures that the programs change in unison with industry demands. Public-private partnerships also play a crucial role in tackling wider economic and social objectives.

By offering access to retraining for displaced workers and people from marginalized populations, these projects promote diversity and assist to minimize the repercussions of economic upheavals. This not only aids people in getting secure work but also adds to the general resilience and flexibility of the economy. Public-private collaborations are vital in establishing retraining programs that are perfectly suited to the needs of the current job market. By using the expertise and resources of companies, these alliances guarantee that training is relevant, practical, and instantly applicable, so boosting the employability and productivity of the workforce. Through innovative training approaches, hands-on experience, and constant program assessment, these collaborations promote a dynamic and resilient labor market capable of facing the challenges of the future.

- *Government Support:*

Support from the government in the form of financed retraining programs is essential, particularly in areas where technology or globalization are causing economic disruptions. For people whose employment become outdated due to changes in global trade patterns or technological improvements, these efforts provide a lifeline. The government may help people move into developing sectors more smoothly by giving them access to training programs and new skills, which will lower the rates of underemployment and unemployment. Usually designed to meet the demands of the regional economy, these initiatives provide a variety of educational possibilities, from advanced degree programs to vocational training. This guarantees that workers have the necessary skills that businesses in expanding industries want. Furthermore, these initiatives often include collaborations with nearby companies, academic establishments, and neighborhood associations to establish an all-encompassing network of assistance for employees.

The government helps people keep their jobs by funding retraining programs, which also promotes economic adaptation and resilience. By proactively reducing the negative consequences of economic shocks, this strategy fosters societal stability and long-term economic prosperity. Furthermore, by giving underprivileged people the skills they need to compete in the contemporary labor market, government-funded retraining programs may help to reduce economic inequality. All things considered, this kind of government assistance is essential to a strong economic plan as it guarantees that every person has the chance to prosper in a changing economic environment.

- *Technology Bootcamps:*

Technology bootcamps have evolved as a potent and effective way of educating learners with the high-demand skills required in today's quickly expanding employment environment. These rigorous programs are meant to give a fast-track road to competency in essential areas like as coding, data analysis, and digital marketing. Unlike conventional educational methods, bootcamps shorten the learning process into a matter of weeks or months, making them an appealing choice for people seeking speedy entrance or development in digital industries. Coding bootcamps, for instance, concentrate on teaching programming languages and software development skills that are highly sought after by companies. Participants often learn via hands-on projects and real-world applications, enabling them to construct a portfolio of work that may show their talents to future employers. The curriculum generally covers languages and frameworks like JavaScript, Python, Ruby on Rails, and React, among others. By immersing students in a realistic, project-based setting, coding bootcamps guarantee that graduates are job-ready upon graduation. Data analysis bootcamps offer comparable advantages, concentrating on giving students with the capacity to read and manage huge datasets. These programs frequently address subjects such as statistical analysis, data visualization, and machine learning. Tools and tools routinely used in the field, like as SQL, R, Python, and Tableau, are key aspects of the program. As organizations increasingly depend on data-driven decision-making, the need for talented data analysts continues to increase, making these bootcamps a pertinent and relevant training choice. Digital marketing bootcamps address the crucial requirement for proficiency in online marketing methods. Participants learn to negotiate the complicated terrain of digital advertising, search engine optimization (SEO), social media marketing, and content development. The hands-on approach enables students to build and execute marketing initiatives, examine their efficacy, and alter plans based on data insights. This practical expertise is crucial in a profession where trends and technology are continually advancing. The attraction of technology bootcamps resides not just in their ability to swiftly teach technical skills but also in their accessibility and flexibility. Many bootcamps provide both in-person and online choices, appealing to a varied spectrum of learners, including working people wishing to upskill or move into new professions. Additionally, several bootcamps give job placement aid, networking opportunities, and collaborations with IT businesses, increasing the career chances of their alumni. In essence, technology bootcamps provide a dynamic and efficient approach to education in the digital era. By emphasizing on high-demand skills like as coding, data analysis, and digital marketing, these programs educate people for the competitive labor market, typically leading to successful and profitable employment in technology.

## c. Supportive Policies and Infrastructure:

- *Financial Incentives:*

Financial incentives may play a vital role in persuading firms to engage in staff training and devclopment. By giving tax advantages or subsidies, governments may lower the financial burden on companies, making it more possible for them to spend resources towards the continued professional advancement of their workers. This strategy not only helps individual workers by boosting their skills and career opportunities but also adds to the general competitiveness and productivity of the economy. Tax incentives may come in numerous forms, such as tax credits or deductions. For instance, a government may grant a tax credit that enables firms to deduct a particular proportion of their training expenditures from their taxable revenue. This immediate decrease in tax burden may make a major impact in a company's budget, freeing up cash that can be spent in more comprehensive training programs or utilized to expand current ones. Subsidies are another powerful financial strategy. Governments might give direct financial help to pay a part of the training expenses. This might include grants or matching funds where the government matches the amount invested by the employer up to a specified level. These incentives may minimize the initial investment required from the firm, making it more appealing for companies of all kinds, particularly small and medium enterprises that would otherwise struggle to finance such expenditures. The influence of these financial incentives goes beyond the immediate financial comfort for firms. When firms are incentivized to spend in training, they are more likely to have a trained and flexible staff. Employees that get continual training are more suited to manage new technologies and procedures, adjust to industry changes, and contribute to innovation inside the organization. This leads to improved production, better job satisfaction, and reduced turnover rates, providing a more stable and engaged staff. Furthermore, by supporting employee growth, these incentives may assist overcome the skills gap that many businesses suffer. As the need for specialized skills continues to expand, having a staff that is regularly updated with the newest information and abilities is vital. Financial incentives for training may therefore play a vital role in ensuring that the labor market maintains pace with technical improvements and growing industrial needs. Providing tax incentives or subsidies to firms for employee training and development is a strategic investment in the future of the workforce and the economy. It promotes organizations to emphasize employee development, resulting to a more skilled, inventive, and competitive company environment. This not only helps individual firms but also contributes to larger economic stability and prosperity.

- *Career Counseling:*
professional counseling is an essential service aimed to help people in understanding and managing their professional pathways, especially during times of change or while pursuing retraining possibilities. This sort of therapy gives tailored assistance to help individuals determine their abilities, interests, and values, which are vital in making educated choices about their career paths. One of the key goals of career counseling is to assist people explore numerous career possibilities that correspond with their talents and ambitions. This investigation process frequently incorporates extensive examinations, including personality tests, skills inventories, and interest surveys. These technologies allow career counselors to deliver individualized advise, indicating prospective career pathways that clients may not have previously explored. In addition to reviewing career alternatives, career counseling also focuses on helping people understand the current employment market and trends within various sectors. Counselors give insights on which sectors are rising and where there may be a significant need for specific abilities. This information is crucial for persons seeking retraining, since it helps them to pick courses or programs that will boost their employability in the long run. Career transitions may be tough, particularly for people who are changing from one field to another or re-entering the workforce after a long sabbatical. Career counselors play a critical role in these transitions by delivering practical guidance and

emotional support. They assist customers define realistic professional objectives, construct action plans, and build confidence to explore new possibilities. This assistance is especially valuable for people who may feel overwhelmed by the changes or unclear about their future moves.

Moreover, career counseling involves advise on skill development and educational options. Counselors may propose particular training programs, certificates, or degrees that might be good for their clients. They may also give information about financial assistance, scholarships, and other resources to make retraining more accessible. Another key part of career counseling is supporting clients with the job search process. This includes helping individuals construct good resumes, prepare for interviews, and enhance their networking abilities. Career counselors typically conduct mock interviews and give comments on how to present oneself successfully to possible employers. This preparation is vital for people to create a great impression and receive employment offers in their selected professions. Additionally, career counseling services sometimes extend to delivering courses and seminars on different themes linked to professional development. These can include training on leadership skills, time management, or dealing with professional stress. Such programs not only boost an individual's skill set but also prepare them for the varied problems they could experience in their professions. Overall, career counseling is a complete service that assists people at every step of their professional path. Whether someone is trying to change occupations, develop in their present sector, or re-enter the workforce, career counseling offers the essential skills, resources, and direction to help them succeed. By allowing people to make educated career choices and delivering continuous assistance, career counseling plays a critical role in building job satisfaction and long-term professional success.

- *Learning Ecosystem:*

Creating an integrated learning ecosystem requires the cooperation of educational institutions, government agencies, and commercial sector partners to support continuous learning and career growth. This integrated strategy attempts to meet the shifting demands of the workforce and the larger economy by providing learners with seamless access to educational resources, training opportunities, and career assistance throughout their life. Educational institutions play a significant role in this ecosystem by creating and delivering curriculum that are relevant to present and future labor market needs. By cooperating with industry professionals and adding real-world applications, these institutions can guarantee that their programs are relevant and up-to-date. Moreover, schools, colleges, and universities may provide flexible learning choices, such as online courses and modular learning, to fit various student

demands and schedules. Government agencies participate by making policies and giving financing to promote educational programs and workforce development activities. They may encourage cooperation between educational institutions and the commercial sector, ensuring that training programs are linked with national economic objectives and labor market needs. Additionally, governments may create laws that promote lifelong learning, such as tax incentives for continuing education and assistance for vocational training programs. The private sector is also an important component in the learning ecosystem, delivering practical training and job prospects that complement formal education. Companies may cooperate with educational institutions to offer internship programs, apprenticeships, and on-the-job training that provide trainees hands-on experience. Furthermore, employers may contribute insight into developing industry trends and skills needs, helping to influence educational curriculum and training programs. An efficient learning ecosystem encourages continual learning by giving numerous avenues for people to gain new skills and enhance their careers. This includes conventional degree programs, short-term certification courses, professional development seminars, and informal learning alternatives such as online tutorials and community learning groups. By making these materials accessible and integrated, the ecosystem helps learners to simply traverse their educational paths and move seamlessly between various learning stages and career phases. Technology plays a vital role in allowing this integrated learning environment. Digital platforms may simplify the exchange of resources and information among stakeholders, promote the accessibility of educational material, and offer tools for measuring learning progress and results. Additionally, data analytics may be utilized to detect skills shortages, anticipate future job market trends, and adapt educational programs to match the unique requirements of learners and employers. An integrated learning ecosystem that includes educational institutions, government agencies, and commercial sector partners is crucial for enabling continuous learning and career growth. By working together, these stakeholders may create a dynamic and responsive environment that encourages learners to develop the skills they need to flourish in a quickly changing world.

## 2.3 Addressing the Skills Gap

To successfully address the skills gap, a multi-faceted strategy is essential:

**a. Labor Market Analysis**
- *Data-Driven Insights:*

Utilizing labor market data to identify current and projected skill shortages and tailor educational programs accordingly. In today's rapidly evolving job market, it's crucial for educational institutions and policymakers to stay ahead of the curve. By leveraging data-driven insights, we can better understand the changing demands of the workforce and align educational programs to meet these needs. One key aspect of this approach is the use of labor market data. By analyzing trends in job postings, hiring patterns, and economic forecasts, we can identify which skills are in high demand and which are facing shortages. This information allows us to tailor educational programs to focus on developing the skills that are most relevant to employers, ensuring that students are well-prepared for the jobs of the future. For example, if data shows a growing demand for cybersecurity professionals but a shortage of qualified candidates, educational institutions can prioritize the development of cybersecurity programs. Similarly, if there is a decline in demand for certain skills due to automation or other factors, programs can be adjusted to focus on areas where there is greater demand. Overall, by using data-driven insights, we can ensure that educational programs are aligned with the needs of the economy, helping to reduce skill shortages, improve job outcomes for students, and drive economic growth.

- *Employer Surveys:*

Regularly conducting surveys with employers acts as a crucial technique for knowing their developing demands and designing training programs appropriately. By participating in direct interaction with employers, organizations get vital information about the present market environment, new trends, and particular skill sets in need. These surveys provide a proactive approach to matching training activities with market needs, ensuring that participants are equipped with essential abilities to prosper in their particular sectors. Through constant feedback loops, firms may adjust and develop their training programs, building a symbiotic connection between education providers and the workforce. This iterative process not only promotes the employability of individuals but also boosts the overall competitiveness and responsiveness of the workforce to the changing needs of the market.

**b. Promoting STEM and Digital Literacy**
- *Early Exposure:*

The importance of early exposure to STEM (science, technology, engineering, and mathematics) education cannot be overstated when it comes to the development of both curiosity and a level of expertise in these areas. A strong foundation for future learning and development may be established by beginning the introduction of STEM topics from a young age. Learning is made more pleasurable and more successful via the use of this strategy, which capitalizes on the innate curiosity and passion of young children. The cognitive and problem-solving abilities of young people may be considerably improved by exposing them to disciplines that fall within the STEM umbrella. In a way that is both enjoyable and engaging,

children are able to acquire knowledge of difficult ideas via the use of hands-on activities, experiments, and interactive learning. Building simple machines out of materials that are commonly found or understanding fundamental code via apps that are fun to use are two examples of activities that may help demystify these topics, making them more approachable and exciting. Moreover, early education in STEM fields contributes to the development of creative thinking and critical thinking. The ability to approach challenges with an analytical mentality is something that children gain when they are allowed to investigate, question, and experiment their environment. Because of this, kids develop a growth mindset, which allows them to become more at ease with the process of trial and error and to comprehend that failure is an integral part of the learning process. Not only are resiliency and adaptation abilities necessary in STEM industries, but they are also necessary in every other aspect of society. Another key advantage of early STEM exposure is its involvement in closing the gender gap in these disciplines. By portraying STEM disciplines as enjoyable and accessible, educators may overcome prejudices and encourage all students, regardless of gender, to follow their interests. This early intervention is crucial in fostering confidence and competence, ensuring that more girls stay interested with STEM topics as they move through their schooling.

Furthermore, early STEM education is crucial in preparing the future workforce for a quickly developing labor environment. As technology continues to progress, the need for qualified workers in STEM industries is expanding. By teaching children with core STEM abilities, we are preparing them to flourish in a society where technology literacy is increasingly vital. Incorporating STEM education in early life also offers larger social advantages. It supports a culture of creativity and lifelong learning. Children who are exposed to STEM early on are more likely to acquire a love for these disciplines, leading to a higher proportion of adults choosing STEM jobs. This, in turn, may encourage scientific and technical improvements, encouraging economic development and tackling global concerns. In essence, integrating STEM education at an early age is a strategic investment in the future. It not only awakens interest and improves competency in these vital areas but also develops essential life skills, supports diversity, and prepares the next generation for the challenges and possibilities of the future. By creating a solid STEM foundation, we can empower young minds to explore, develop, and thrive.

- *Coding in Schools:*

The rising significance of technology in almost every area of life is reflected in the fact that coding is becoming a required subject in schools. By incorporating digital literacy and

coding into the core curriculum, educators are giving kids the tools they need to succeed in the technology industry in the future. The capacity to comprehend and develop software becomes more useful as society grows more and more dependent on technology. Teaching students to code has several advantages. It encourages creativity, critical thinking, and problem-solving abilities. Pupils get the ability to approach difficult issues systematically and solve them using computational thinking and logical reasoning. This kind of thinking helps them not just with computer science problems, but also with problems in other fields. Additionally, learning to code fosters digital literacy, or the capacity to utilize, comprehend, and communicate with technology in productive ways. Being literate in digital technology is just as important as conventional literacy in a society when digital interfaces are everywhere, from automated systems to cellphones. As a result, students become knowledgeable and competent digital citizens who can confidently and responsibly navigate the digital world. Code is taught in schools as a core subject, preparing pupils for a wide range of jobs. Not only in the IT industry, but in many businesses as well, there is an increasing need for computer-savvy workers. Employers in industries like healthcare, banking, entertainment, and education are looking for more people with coding expertise. Knowing how to code is becoming more useful in the job market, and this trend is probably here to stay. Moreover, early exposure to computer programming might pique a child's curiosity for STEM (science, technology, engineering, and math) disciplines. It may solve the lack of STEM workers in the world by encouraging students to seek postgraduate education and jobs in these fields.

In addition to promoting inclusion and equality, encouraging a wide variety of students to investigate coding may aid in closing socioeconomic and gender inequalities in technology-related sectors. It takes qualified teachers, the right materials, and a well-structured curriculum to implement coding in the classroom. To guarantee that instructors are prepared to teach coding in an efficient manner, schools must make investments in their professional development. Working together with IT firms and academic institutions may improve learning by offering more tools and assistance. All things considered, including digital literacy and coding into the school curriculum is a progressive move that meets the demands of our technologically advanced society. It equips students for a future in which digital competency will be crucial, rather than only for specialized occupations. Schools have a crucial role in creating a workforce that is capable of innovation and success in a rapidly changing technology environment by providing students with these skills.

### c. Fostering Public Awareness

- *Career Awareness Programs:*

Programs that promote career awareness are crucial for closing the knowledge gap between school and the workforce by giving students and job seekers the skills they need to succeed in the dynamic labor market. These courses are essential for exposing students to a wide variety of professions and businesses, which helps them make well-informed decisions and plan their careers for the long run. The main goal of career awareness programs is to increase participants' knowledge of a variety of businesses, particularly those that are new and changing quickly. Through offering insights into industries including advanced manufacturing, healthcare, renewable energy, and technology, these programs assist people in finding possible career paths that suit their skills and interests. This knowledge is essential for pointing students and job seekers in the direction of stable, high-growth regions. Successful career awareness programs often include partnerships between academic institutions, business leaders, and government organizations. Universities and colleges collaborate with companies to provide workshops, seminars, and internships that provide students a hands-on experience in a variety of professional disciplines.

Through these experiences, participants may create professional networks, acquire applicable skills, and get real-world knowledge—all of which are very helpful for future job searches. Programs for career awareness also stress the value of flexibility and soft skills in today's job. The capacity to pick up new skills, collaborate with others, and exercise critical thought is becoming more and more crucial as sectors change constantly. Training in these areas is often included in programs, enabling participants to flourish in fast-paced professional settings. These programs emphasize the value of non-traditional and developing occupations in addition to standard career choices. Through exposure to cutting-edge domains like biotechnology, digital marketing, and artificial intelligence, career awareness programs broaden the scope of opportunities and foster experimentation outside traditional professions. This exposure is especially helpful in assisting people in identifying specialty markets and distinctive career paths. Programs for career awareness also address the changing nature of employment by disseminating knowledge about possibilities in the gig economy and in entrepreneurship. Learners gain knowledge about independent contracting, startup culture, and the abilities required to be successful company owners or independent contractors. With this information, people may take charge of their professional trajectories and pursue both regular work and self-employment. Career awareness programs make sure that participants are able to adjust to future changes as well as be ready for the present work market by emphasizing future trends and real-world applications. This innovative strategy contributes to the development of a flexible and resilient labor force that can handle the demands of a continuously changing global economy. In general, putting career awareness initiatives into place is a calculated investment in the workforce of the future. These programs help people make educated choices, pursue rewarding jobs, and support the expansion and innovation of the economy by educating students and job seekers about developing sectors and career options.

- *Media Campaigns:*

Media campaigns play a pivotal role in emphasizing the importance of skills development and making people aware of the various training programs available. By leveraging various media platforms, these campaigns can reach a wide and diverse audience, ensuring that the message about the value of acquiring new skills is disseminated broadly. To start with, media campaigns can harness the power of social media, which is a highly effective tool due to its extensive reach and ability to engage directly with users. Platforms like Facebook, Twitter, Instagram, and LinkedIn offer opportunities to create targeted advertisements and engaging content that can inform and inspire individuals about the benefits of skills development. Through compelling storytelling, testimonials, and success stories, these platforms can showcase real-life examples of how skills training has transformed lives and careers. Traditional media outlets, such as television, radio, and print media, remain crucial components of an effective media campaign. Television commercials and radio spots can deliver powerful messages that resonate with a broad audience, while newspapers and magazines can provide in-depth articles and features on the subject. By including interviews with experts, case studies, and information on upcoming training opportunities, traditional media can create a comprehensive narrative around the necessity of skill enhancement. Additionally, media campaigns can utilize digital platforms such as websites, blogs, and online forums. Dedicated websites or sections within existing sites can serve as centralized hubs of information, offering details on various training programs, application processes, and potential career paths. Blogs and online articles can provide ongoing updates, tips, and advice, ensuring that the audience remains engaged and informed. Email marketing campaigns are another effective tool. Regular newsletters and email updates can keep subscribers informed about new training opportunities, success stories, and the latest trends in skills development. This direct line of communication ensures that interested individuals receive timely and relevant information, making it easier for them to act on available opportunities.

Public service announcements (PSAs) are also a valuable component of media campaigns. These announcements can be broadcast across multiple channels, ensuring that the message reaches a wide audience. PSAs can be particularly effective in highlighting the societal benefits of skills development, such as increased employment rates and economic growth. Collaborations with influencers and industry leaders can further amplify the reach of media campaigns. Influencers, who often have a substantial and engaged following, can share their personal experiences with skills development and endorse training programs. This approach adds a layer of credibility and relatability, encouraging their followers to explore similar opportunities. Moreover, organizing events such as webinars, workshops, and live Q&A sessions can create interactive platforms for learning and engagement. These events can be promoted through various media channels, attracting participants who are eager to enhance their skills. Recording and sharing these sessions on social media and websites can extend their impact, allowing individuals who could not attend live to benefit from the content. Overall, media campaigns that focus on skills development need to be multifaceted and dynamic, utilizing a mix of traditional and digital media to reach and engage their target audience effectively. By creating compelling content, leveraging various media channels, and fostering interactive engagement, these campaigns can significantly raise awareness about the importance of skills development and the availability of training programs, ultimately leading to a more skilled and empowered workforce.

**d. Initiatives for Inclusive Education:**
- *Equity in Education:*

Equity in education is a fundamental principle aimed at ensuring that all individuals, particularly those from marginalized and underserved communities, have equal access to high-quality educational opportunities. This concept goes beyond mere equality, which implies providing the same resources to everyone; equity focuses on allocating resources and opportunities based on the specific needs and circumstances of different groups to achieve fair outcomes. To address the educational disparities faced by marginalized communities, it is essential to recognize the systemic barriers that hinder their access to quality education. These barriers can include socioeconomic status, geographic location, race, ethnicity, language, and disability, among others. Effective strategies to promote equity in education involve a multifaceted approach that encompasses policy reform, community engagement, and targeted interventions. One critical aspect of promoting equity in education is the provision of adequate funding and resources to schools serving underserved communities. This includes not only financial support but also access to advanced curricula, qualified teachers, modern facilities, and

technological tools. By ensuring that schools in marginalized areas are well-resourced, we can create an environment where all students have the opportunity to succeed academically. Another important element is the development and implementation of inclusive policies that address the unique needs of diverse student populations. For instance, bilingual education programs can support students who are English language learners, while special education services can provide tailored support for students with disabilities. Additionally, culturally responsive teaching practices that recognize and value the cultural backgrounds of students can enhance their engagement and learning experiences. Community involvement is also crucial in advancing educational equity. Engaging parents, caregivers, and community leaders in the education process helps build a supportive network for students and ensures that the specific needs of the community are addressed. Programs that foster family engagement, provide adult education opportunities, and create partnerships between schools and local organizations can strengthen the educational ecosystem. Furthermore, equitable access to higher education and vocational training is vital for breaking the cycle of poverty and enabling social mobility. Initiatives such as scholarships, mentorship programs, and college preparatory courses can help students from marginalized backgrounds pursue higher education and career pathways that were previously inaccessible to them. Vocational training programs tailored to the local job market can also provide practical skills and employment opportunities for individuals in underserved communities. In conclusion, achieving equity in education requires a comprehensive and sustained effort to dismantle the barriers that marginalized communities face and to create an inclusive educational system that serves the diverse needs of all students. By focusing on targeted support, inclusive policies, community engagement, and access to higher education and training, we can work towards a future where every individual has the opportunity to reach their full potential through high-quality education.

- *Gender Inclusion:*

Gender inclusion is vital for encouraging innovation, equality, and societal advancement, especially in professions that have historically been dominated by men, such as science, technology, engineering, and mathematics (STEM) fields. In order to effectively promote gender diversity, it is necessary to implement efforts that are both broad and focused, as well as to establish strong support structures that are tailored to solve the myriad of obstacles that women and other underrepresented genders confront. To begin, during the early intervention process, educational programs are an extremely important component. Educators have the ability to challenge preconceptions and promote interest in STEM disciplines by presenting Science, Technology, Engineering,

and Mathematics (STEM) topics in a manner that is both interesting and accessible of all genders from a young age. It is also possible for mentorship programs to be of great assistance by linking students with role models who are able to provide direction, support, and insight into prospective career options. A picture that is more relevant and aspirational of what a career in these professions may look like can be created by these mentors by demystifying the hurdles that women face in STEM fields and highlighting the accomplishments that women have achieved in these industries. Furthermore, since the pressures of family and profession may have a disproportionately negative effect on women, institutions and organizations need to introduce regulations that encourage a healthy balance between work and personal life. Such policies include, but are not limited to, flexible working hours, parental leave, and on-site childcare services. These approaches not only assist retain talent but also build a more inclusive work environment where workers feel encouraged and respected. Collaborations with other parties are also quite important, in addition to internal policies. It is possible for women to join and prosper in STEM jobs via the formation of partnerships between educational institutions, companies, and non-profit organizations that work together. Scholarship programs, internships, and job placements expressly focused at women may assist bridge the gap from college to work. These programs give practical experience and help create professional networks, which are vital for career success. Moreover, it is vital to address the cultural and organizational prejudices that perpetuate gender imbalance. This may be done by frequent training and seminars on unconscious bias, diversity, and inclusion. Creating a culture of awareness and continual learning helps to remove discriminatory habits and fosters a more inclusive atmosphere. Leadership commitment is vital in this respect; leaders must be loud champions for diversity and actively seek to create and support inclusive policies within their businesses. Visibility and appreciation of women's accomplishments in STEM sectors are also crucial. Celebrating successes via awards, media attention, and public speaking opportunities may influence perspectives and encourage future generations. Highlighting the success stories of women in these fields not only gives role models but also promotes the idea that gender does not affect one's capacity to thrive in STEM. Lastly, feedback systems and frequent review of gender inclusion efforts are important to guarantee their success and sustainability. Organizations should gather and evaluate data on gender diversity, identify gaps, and change their plans appropriately. This continuous improvement strategy helps to build a dynamic and responsive workplace that fosters gender diversity in a meaningful manner.

 In short, fostering gender diversity in STEM and other historically male-dominated areas needs a diversified strategy. Early education, mentoring, supporting policies, external partnerships, cultural transformation, visibility, and continual evaluation are all key components. By adopting these focused efforts and support mechanisms, we can build a more inclusive and inventive future.

In a nutshell, reforming the education system to better match with the requirements of the job market is vital in building a dynamic and flexible workforce. By incorporating more practical and vocational training into the curriculum, we can guarantee that students obtain hands-on experience and technical abilities that are immediately transferable to many sectors. This technique bridges the gap between academic knowledge and practical application, making graduates more instantly employable and more equipped for the needs of their chosen areas.

Emphasizing entrepreneurial education is another key component. By imparting entrepreneurial skills and mentality early on, we can nurture a generation of innovators and problem-solvers who are able to generate their own chances and drive economic growth. Entrepreneurship education emphasizes creativity, resilience, and critical thinking, all of which are vital skills in a continually altering work market. It also offers people with the skills to recognize market requirements, establish business strategies, and manage the complexity of beginning and running a firm. Investing in lifetime learning and retraining programs is crucial for retaining a competitive workforce. As technology evolves and businesses grow, the skills necessary for many occupations are always evolving. Lifelong learning programs allow people to regularly upgrade their skills and adapt to new technology and approaches. Retraining programs are especially crucial for those whose professions are at danger of becoming obsolete owing to automation and other technological improvements. By offering chances for continued education and skill development, we guarantee that people stay relevant and may migrate effortlessly across positions and industries. This comprehensive strategy not only tackles the immediate difficulties of unemployment but also produces a resilient workforce that is prepared for the future. A dynamic workforce, endowed with practical skills, entrepreneurial savvy, and a dedication to lifelong learning, is better positioned to react to the shifting needs of the labor market. This, in turn, encourages economic stability and prosperity, as well as personal and professional satisfaction for people. By implementing these comprehensive actions, we build a sustainable paradigm for workforce development that benefits society as a whole.

## *3. Supporting Micro, Small, and Medium-Sized Businesses (SMEs)*

SMEs are generally acknowledged as crucial to economic development and employment creation. In many countries, they represent the backbone of economic activity, accounting for a major percentage of employment and GDP. Here's an extended look at how aiding SMEs might successfully combat unemployment:

### a. Access to Finance

- *Microfinance and Small Business Loans:*

Limited access to financing is one of the main issues SMEs encounter. It is impossible for these businesses to launch, expand, or continue their activities without sufficient finance. Governments and financial organizations may use a number of tactics to lessen this: Establishing microfinance institutions and small company lending programs has a key role in promoting the growth and development of small and medium-sized companies (SMEs). These financial mechanisms offer the essential money that SMEs typically struggle to access via standard banking channels. By delivering personalized financial solutions, microfinance institutions and small company loan programs may meet the particular requirements of SMEs, allowing them to grow their operations, enhance productivity, and generate additional job opportunities. Microfinance banks often cater to marginalized groups, making modest loans that do not need considerable collateral. This technique is especially advantageous for entrepreneurs and small company owners in developing countries where access to conventional financial services is restricted. By easing access to financing, microfinance helps people to establish new companies or expand existing ones, therefore encouraging economic activity at the grassroots level. The influx of funds helps organizations to invest in new technology, acquire goods, and expand their overall operating capabilities. Similarly, small company loan programs give vital financial help to SMEs, generally with more advantageous conditions than those provided by commercial banks. These programs may feature lower interest rates, longer payback terms, and less rigorous qualifying conditions. Such measures are aimed to alleviate the risks involved with lending to smaller firms, which may lack the financial history or collateral needed by bigger financial institutions. By making money more available, small company loan programs assist SMEs overcome financial constraints that might otherwise restrict their development. The availability of microfinance and small company loans may lead to a large rise in employment. As SMEs acquire the finance required to grow their operations, they may recruit extra people, therefore contributing to job creation and decreasing unemployment rates. This growth not only helps the individual firms but also has a beneficial rippling impact on the larger economy. Increased employment leads to increased disposable incomes, which in turn increases consumer spending and further boosts economic development. Moreover, the help offered by microfinance institutions and small company lending programs may boost the overall sustainability and resilience of SMEs.

With increased access to financing, firms may better manage cash flow, handle economic downturns, and engage in sustainable practices. This stability helps SMEs to contribute more regularly to the economy, producing a stronger and varied economic environment. The formation of microfinance institutions and small company lending programs is a critical approach for fostering the growth and sustainability of SMEs. By providing crucial financial resources, these initiatives help companies to grow their operations, generate employment, and promote economic development. The good influence of such activities goes beyond individual firms, adding to the general health and vitality of the economy.

- *Angel Investors and Venture Capital:*

Promoting angel and venture capital investments has a big influence on how firms grow and evolve, especially startups and early-stage organizations. These kinds of investments provide businesses the much-needed funding they need to create new goods, grow their businesses, and penetrate new markets. Angel investors and venture capital companies provide vital knowledge and mentoring that may be essential for developing enterprises in addition to their financial assistance. Venture capitalists often make investments in businesses that have the potential for rapid development, frequently concentrating on cutting-edge industries like biotechnology, renewable energy, and technology. In return for equity, they provide large investment that enables firms to grow quickly. Venture capitalists' engagement often include operational help, industry contacts, and strategic guidance—all crucial for negotiating the intricate business environment. Their background in creating profitable businesses might assist startups in steering clear of typical traps and making wise choices. Conversely, high-net-worth people who spend their own money in early-stage enterprises are known as angel investors. They often use a hands-on approach, providing guidance and mentoring derived on their own experiences as entrepreneurs. Angel investors may assist firms with improving their business models, creating effective marketing plans, and assembling capable management teams. Angel investors provide individualized attention and flexible investment conditions that may be very helpful for startups that need some extra support to grow to their full potential. An ecosystem of support for startups is created by the mix of finance, knowledge, and mentoring provided by venture capitalists and angel investors. By putting businesses in touch with other investors and building a network of financial resources, these investors often open doors to other investment rounds. This network impact has the potential to draw in partners, top talent, and consumers by increasing market exposure and trust. Additionally, by pressuring businesses to hit benchmarks and grow more quickly than they otherwise could, venture capitalists and angel investors may foster innovation. Both the firms and the investors may profit from these faster returns on investment as a result of the increased expansion. A culture of ambition and constant development is also fostered inside the company by the focus on growth, creating a dynamic and competitive business environment. In general, a key component of the entrepreneurial ecosystem is the promotion of venture capital and angel investments. In addition to giving the firms the money they need to expand, it also gives them access to opportunities, strategic advice, and expertise that are critical for long-term success. The combination of financial assistance and professional mentoring fosters the development of strong companies with the capacity to innovate, grow, and contend on a worldwide scale.

- *Government Public funding and Subsidies:*

The provision of grants and subsidies by the government is an essential component in the process of promoting the expansion and long-term viability of small and medium-sized businesses (SMEs). These initiatives have the potential to dramatically lower the obstacles to entrance and growth that many small and medium-sized enterprises (SMEs) experience by providing financial support. Grants provide monies that are not repaid and may be used for a number of objectives, including investment in research and development, the purchase of technology, and the growth of market opportunities. This kind of assistance may be quite helpful for new enterprises and small businesses that, in the absence of such assistance, could have a difficult time acquiring the cash they want to expand their operations. These subsidies, on the other hand, often take the shape of decreased prices for critical inputs or services, such as energy, raw materials, or labor. These subsidies have the potential to improve the competitiveness of small and medium-sized enterprises (SMEs) by reducing the costs of their operations. Tax incentives further complement these efforts by decreasing the tax burden on SMEs, enabling them to reinvest more of their revenues into their firms. These incentives may take numerous forms, including tax rebates for employing new staff, investing in new technology, or participating in ecologically beneficial activities. By reducing some of the financial constraints, tax incentives make it simpler for SMEs to pursue initiatives that could be too risky or expensive without such assistance. The combined impact of grants, subsidies, and tax incentives produces a more advantageous business climate for SMEs. This supporting structure not only assists in the first phases of company creation but also supports growth and expansion throughout time. With decreased financial limitations, SMEs can concentrate on innovation, efficiency, and growing their operations, which in turn leads to job creation and economic growth. The government's involvement in providing these financial supports is vital since it helps level the playing field for smaller enterprises, allowing them to compete more successfully with bigger, established organizations.

**b. Technical Assistance**

Providing technical help is vital for the development and sustainability of SMEs. This includes:

- *Business Development Services:*

In order to improve the expansion and sustainability of small and medium-sized businesses (SMEs), business development services are essential. By offering thorough training and consulting services, these programs provide organizations the skills and information they need to successfully negotiate the market's intricacies. Business planning is one important area of concentration, where professionals assist SMEs in developing strong plans that complement their long-term objectives. This entails analyzing the market, establishing reasonable goals, and creating workable methods to reach these targets. Another essential element is financial management, which guarantees SMEs can have a healthy cash flow, efficiently control spending, and make wise financial choices. Budgeting, financial forecasting, and comprehending important financial documents are often included in this kind of training. SMEs may make sure their resources are utilized effectively and steer clear of typical financial problems by learning these skills. Customer acquisition and retention depend on marketing, and business development services provide insights into successful marketing tactics. To do this, one must pinpoint target audiences, develop value propositions that are appealing, and use digital marketing technologies to reach a larger audience. SMEs acquire the skills necessary to set themselves apart from rivals and create powerful brand identities. Another key area of emphasis is operational effectiveness, which has a direct bearing on SMEs' capacity to provide goods and services. Process simplification, quality control implementation, and adoption of supply chain management best practices are all part of this field's training. SMEs may save expenses, boost production, and improve customer satisfaction by increasing their operational efficiency. All things considered, company development services provide SMEs a comprehensive growth strategy by addressing important factors that affect their performance. These services help SMEs lay a strong basis for sustained growth by providing continuing assistance and customized guidance, which eventually boosts their productivity and competitiveness in the market.

- *Technology and Innovation Support:*

Facilitating access to new technology and innovations is an important strategy for boosting the productivity of SMEs. By integrating modern technical solutions and promoting creative practices, SMEs may enhance their efficiency, cut costs, and raise their competitiveness in the market. One

successful strategy to achieve this is via collaborations with research institutes and technology centers, which may act as catalysts for innovation and technological improvement. Research organizations, such as universities and specialized research institutes, typically hold cutting-edge information and skills that may be helpful to SMEs. Collaborating with these universities helps SMEs to harness this expertise to produce new products, enhance current processes, and incorporate the newest technology breakthroughs. For instance, SMEs may participate in cooperative research initiatives, access specialized equipment and facilities, and profit from the academic rigor and creativity that these institutions provide. Such cooperation may lead to the production of new intellectual property, affording SMEs a competitive advantage and possible new income sources. Technology hubs and innovation centers also play a vital role in aiding SMEs. These hubs are usually meant to build an ecosystem of innovation, giving SMEs with access to a network of like-minded enterprises, entrepreneurs, and specialists. Within these hubs, SMEs may engage in incubator and accelerator programs, which provide mentoring, tools, and financial possibilities to help bring innovative ideas to market. Additionally, technology centers typically give access to state-of-the-art facilities and infrastructure, which might be too costly for individual SMEs to obtain independently. Moreover, these collaborations may allow knowledge transfer and talent development. By collaborating closely with research institutes and technology centers, SMEs may upskill their staff, ensuring that workers are fluent in the newest technologies and processes. This not only boosts the overall productivity of the SME but also develops a culture of constant development and innovation. Access to new technology and developments also brings up opportunity for SMEs to enter new markets and grow their consumer base. By embracing innovative technology, SMEs may offer distinctive goods and services that satisfy the increasing demands of clients, both locally and worldwide. This flexibility is vital in today's fast-paced market climate, where technical breakthroughs and customer tastes are continuously changing. Allowing access to new technologies and innovations via collaborations with research institutions and technology centers is a significant technique for boosting the productivity of SMEs. These partnerships equip SMEs with the essential tools, expertise, and networks to innovate, expand, and compete successfully in the market. By embracing technology improvements and developing a culture of innovation, SMEs may achieve sustainable growth and long-term success.

- *Capacity Building Programs:*

Capacity development initiatives are crucial for the growth and sustainability of Small and Medium-sized Enterprises (SMEs). These programs are intended to increase the skills and

competencies of both SME owners and their workers, ensuring they are well-prepared to confront the numerous difficulties of company management and growth. One of the key aims of capacity development programs is to give SME owners with the required skills and expertise to make informed strategic choices. This involves training in areas like as financial management, marketing, operational efficiency, and strategic planning. By obtaining a greater knowledge of these important business processes, SME owners may design more successful business models, improve resource allocation, and find new market possibilities. For workers, capacity development programs concentrate on enhancing certain skill sets that are critical for the day-to-day operations of the organization. This might encompass technical training linked to the sector, customer service excellence, sales strategies, and the adoption of new technology. Enhanced staff abilities contribute to enhanced productivity, higher quality of service or product, and more overall efficiency within the firm. Moreover, capacity development programs generally integrate leadership and management training. This feature is especially significant as it assists SME owners and managers to create a leadership style that supports a healthy organizational culture, encourages people, and pushes the firm towards accomplishing its objectives. Effective leadership training may also aid in succession planning, ensuring that there is a pipeline of skilled executives who can carry the firm forward.

In addition to traditional training sessions, capacity development programs may incorporate mentoring and coaching components. These features give SME owners and workers with tailored counsel and assistance from seasoned business experts. Mentoring relationships may give vital insights, practical guidance, and support, allowing participants to overcome particular company issues and establish a better strategic vision. Furthermore, networking possibilities are a big advantage of capacity development programs. By networking with other SME owners, industry experts, and possible partners, participants may exchange ideas, discuss best practices, and cooperate on initiatives. This networking may lead to new business prospects, collaborations, and access to larger markets, leading to the development and expansion of the SME. Incorporating capacity building programs into the business growth plan of SMEs may help strengthen their resilience. Businesses that are better prepared with knowledge and skills are more adaptive to shifting market circumstances and can handle economic risks more successfully. This resilience is vital for long-term sustainability and success in a competitive corporate climate. Overall, adopting capacity development programs is a strategic investment in the future of SMEs. By concentrating on the continual development of skills and knowledge for both owners and staff, these programs guarantee that SMEs are not only capable of managing present company operations effectively but are also well-positioned to pursue growth and expansion prospects. This comprehensive approach to capacity building produces a vibrant and dynamic business environment, where SMEs may flourish and contribute meaningfully to economic growth.

**c. Market Connections**

Creating strong market connections is important for SMEs to reach bigger markets and customer bases. This can be achieved through:

- *Integration into Supply Chains:*

One of the most important tactics for promoting the expansion and sustainability of small and medium-sized businesses (SMEs) is their integration into supply chains. SMEs may profit from major organizations' encouragement to integrate them into their supply chains in a number of ways. This integration gives SMEs a steady and dependable market for their goods and services. For SMEs to maintain stable income streams that can sustain their operations and foster development, there must be a constant demand. Because they are able to anticipate the demands of bigger organizations and modify their operations appropriately, it also helps SMEs plan and scale their production capabilities more effectively. Furthermore, SMEs often have to fulfill certain standards and quality criteria in order to participate in a wider supply chain.

SMEs are compelled by this need to enhance their procedures, use superior technology, and uphold stricter quality standards. This increases SMEs' overall competitiveness and marketability and makes them more appealing to other prospective customers and marketplaces in addition to better serving major businesses. SMEs get important insights and feedback from their ongoing interactions with bigger firms, which they may use to improve their goods and services. From a big business standpoint, adding SMEs to their supply chains may result in more creativity and flexibility. Compared to bigger organizations, SMEs are often more flexible and able to adjust to changes quickly. This flexibility may be especially helpful in sectors of the economy that need rapid reactions to shifts in the market or creative solutions. Large organizations may improve their own operational efficiency and innovative skills by capitalizing on the assets of small and medium-sized enterprises. By encouraging regional companies and creating jobs, the inclusion of SMEs in supply chains benefits the overall state of the economy. SMEs have a major role in creating jobs, and as they expand, so does the economy and employment market. Stronger communities and a more stable economic climate may follow from this. Because SMEs boost the local economy in the areas where they operate, major firms may also benefit from assisting them in terms of their corporate social responsibility profiles. In general, both parties gain from SMEs' incorporation into supply chains. Large firms profit from more flexibility, creativity, and community engagement, while SMEs get the stability and resources required for expansion. Given the competitive corporate environment of today, the economic and social benefits of this kind of integration highlight how crucial it is to cultivate these relationships.

- *Export Promotion Initiatives:*

Export promotion initiatives are vital in assisting small and medium-sized businesses (SMEs) in entering foreign markets, which opens up new income sources and promotes expansion. These programs provide SMEs the tools, direction, and chances they need to grow domestically and internationally. Programs for export promotion help small and medium-sized enterprises (SMEs) in part by providing extensive assistance and training. This comprises courses and seminars covering a range of topics related to global commerce, such comprehending export laws, negotiating cultural differences, and becoming an expert in the logistics of transporting products abroad. These initiatives lower entrance barriers into overseas markets and facilitate small firms' ability to compete globally by providing SMEs with this information. Another important part of export marketing campaigns are trade shows. These occasions provide SMEs a stage on which to present their goods and services to a global clientele. Trade shows provide face-to-face communication between SMEs and possible overseas partners, distributors, and purchasers.

Establishing connections and trust via in-person interaction is crucial for closing international commercial negotiations. Additionally, by attending trade shows, SMEs may learn about regional client preferences, rival tactics, and market trends. This knowledge helps them better customize their products to satisfy demand throughout the world. The development of international alliances via export promotion initiatives is another important factor in the expansion of SMEs. These collaborations might be distributorship agreements, joint ventures, or strategic alliances, among other formats. SMEs may benefit from the local market expertise, distribution channels, and clientele of their overseas partners by working together with well-established companies. This reduces the risks and expenses related to foreign growth while also expediting market access. Moreover, these collaborations often result in innovation and technology transfer, strengthening SMEs' competitive advantage. Export promotion programs often provide SMEs access to financial aid and incentives in addition to these immediate advantages. To encourage exporting, governments and trade associations may provide tax advantages, subsidies, or low-interest loans. By assisting SMEs with the expenses of product adaption, market research, and promotional efforts, these financial supports lessen the financial strain of expanding into new markets. All things considered, export promotion initiatives play a critical role in assisting SMEs in navigating the challenges of global commerce. These initiatives provide SMEs access to new income sources and help them expand sustainably in the global marketplace by delivering financial assistance, education, chances for direct market participation, and strategic relationship development.

- *E-commerce Platforms:*

E-commerce platforms are game-changing technologies that provide small and medium-sized businesses (SMEs) the ability to compete on a global scale by expanding their market reach far beyond local borders. By using these platforms, SMEs may overcome the constraints imposed by physical storefronts and access a huge global pool of prospective clients. Smaller firms may compete on an even playing field with bigger, more established enterprises thanks to e-commerce. SMEs may exhibit their goods and services to a worldwide customer base via the integration of e-commerce, thus boosting their exposure and market potential. These platforms often include a number of features and tools aimed at streamlining corporate processes. For instance, they provide thorough analytics that assist companies in comprehending the preferences and behavior of their customers, allowing for more specialized marketing tactics. Furthermore, the availability of many payment gateways on e-commerce platforms streamlines transactions, facilitating the purchase of products and services by clients from diverse geographic locations. E-commerce platforms can make low-cost marketing options possible. SMEs may use email marketing, search engine optimization (SEO), and social media connections to draw in and keep clients. These marketing tactics are especially helpful for smaller organizations with tighter budgets since they are often less expensive than conventional advertising techniques. E-commerce platforms also improve supply chain management and logistics. Integrated shipping solutions, which make it easier to deliver goods to clients wherever they may be, are available on a lot of platforms. Because it lessens the complexity of international shipping and customs procedures, this is essential for SMEs looking to grow abroad. Better customer service is another important advantage of e-commerce platforms. Live chat, client testimonials, and thorough product descriptions are examples of features that enhance the buying experience and build consumer loyalty. With the help of these technologies, SMEs can interact with clients directly, respond to issues quickly, and establish a solid reputation for their brands. Scalability is also supported by e-commerce platforms. These systems can handle higher traffic and sales volumes as SMEs expand without requiring a substantial extra investment in physical infrastructure. Businesses may successfully manage expansion and maintain a high level of service because to this scalability. To sum up, e-commerce platforms are essential for small and medium-sized businesses (SMEs) that want to grow and compete internationally. They have several benefits, such as increased market awareness, affordable marketing, better logistics, higher-quality customer service, and scalability. SMEs may seize new chances, spur development, and prosper in the cutthroat international economy by using these platforms.

### d. Promoting Entrepreneurship

Promoting entrepreneurship is essential to SMEs' growth. One way to encourage this is by:

- *Entrepreneurship Training and Guidance:*

Entrepreneurial education and mentoring play essential roles in building an entrepreneurial attitude from an early age. Introducing entrepreneurial education in schools and colleges gives students with the required skills and information to discover opportunities, take measured risks, and innovate. This education frequently comprises a curriculum that covers vital subjects such as company planning, financial literacy, marketing, and management. By involving students in real-world projects and problem-solving exercises, they learn to think critically and creatively, crucial attributes for successful entrepreneurs. Mentorship programs enhance formal education by giving students with access to seasoned entrepreneurs and industry experts. Mentors give advice, support, and vital insights that assist budding entrepreneurs negotiate the complexity of beginning and building a firm. These programs may include one-on-one mentoring sessions, seminars, and networking events, providing an atmosphere where new entrepreneurs can benefit from the experiences and failures of their mentors. By incorporating entrepreneurship education and mentoring into the academic system, students get a comprehensive grasp of what it takes to excel in the business world. This combined approach not only develops their business abilities but also promotes their confidence and resilience. Furthermore, it generates a culture of creativity and entrepreneurship that may lead to the formation of new firms and job creation, eventually contributing to economic progress and social improvement.

- *Accelerators and Incubators:*

The creation of business incubators and accelerators may provide nascent enterprises the tools, connections, and guidance they need to expand and thrive. These initiatives provide a variety of crucial services and frameworks for assistance, fostering an atmosphere in which start-ups may prosper. Early-stage entrepreneurs are usually the focus of incubators, which provide reasonably priced office space, administrative assistance, and shared resources like equipment and conference rooms. They often provide support for company growth, including financial planning, marketing strategy, and business plan preparation. With this help, you may drastically lower the risks and operating expenses of launching a new company. Conversely, accelerators often serve more established businesses that have passed the seed stage and are prepared to grow. These

are often time-limited programs, with startup cohorts enrolling concurrently and graduating in a matter of months. Startups may improve their business models, create new products, and become ready for funding with the support of accelerators, which provide rigorous mentoring from seasoned company owners and industry professionals. They often end with a demo day, when entrepreneurs present their ideas to a packed house of prospective investors in hopes of raising the capital required for quick expansion. Accelerators and incubators both provide unmatched networking possibilities. Startups may network with investors, partners, and other like-minded businesspeople by participating in these initiatives. These relationships may open doors to worthwhile joint ventures, client acquisition, and strategic alliances that would be difficult to form otherwise. Furthermore, the legitimacy that comes with belonging to a respectable incubator or accelerator may be a big plus in luring in talent, clients, and more capital. Another essential service that these organizations provide is mentoring. Skilled mentors may provide advice on all facets of managing a company, from daily operations to strategic decision-making. Through improved decision-making, avoiding typical errors, and accelerating their route to success, entrepreneurs may benefit from this mentoring. Having mentors who have successfully navigated the startup environment at one's disposal may be very helpful in helping entrepreneurs remain motivated and focused by offering both emotional support and practical assistance. Startups are also encouraged to create specific targets and milestones in the organized atmosphere of incubators and accelerators, which promotes a results-driven culture. These programs' feedback and accountability procedures make sure that companies stay on course and modify their plans as needed. This organized support network may play a critical role in assisting startups in accomplishing their goals and securing their position in the market. In addition, a lot of incubators and accelerators provide financial possibilities via their network of investors or directly. In return for ownership, startups may acquire seed capital, which gives them the financial runway they need to develop their goods and get into the market. For companies, this first round of investment may be crucial since it frees them up to concentrate on expanding rather than always worrying about obtaining capital. Business accelerators and incubators are essential components of the entrepreneurial ecosystem. They provide a full range of services to businesses, such as accessible capital, mentoring, business development support, inexpensive workspace, and networking possibilities. These initiatives assist new businesses in overcoming the obstacles of early development and laying the groundwork for long-term success by creating an atmosphere that encourages innovation and expansion.

- *Regulatory Reforms:*

Regulatory reforms are a collection of policies designed to reduce the complexity of company registration procedures, remove red tape, and create an atmosphere that encourages entrepreneurship. By removing onerous administrative obstacles that often impede innovation and development, these changes act as a catalyst, making it easier for enterprises to start and thrive. Entrepreneurs may negotiate the regulatory environment more effectively and concentrate their attention and resources on growing their businesses by streamlining registration processes. Furthermore, a supportive regulatory framework inspires confidence in both investors and business owners, cultivating the trust and stability necessary for long-term economic growth. Consequently, regulatory changes are essential for encouraging entrepreneurship, boosting economic expansion, and eventually improving general well-being.

### e. Emphasis on Rural Communities

Encouraging SMEs in rural regions may more successfully combat unemployment by:

- *Developement of Rural Infrastructure:*

Expanding rural infrastructure is crucial for empowering small and medium companies (SMEs) in rural regions. By strengthening infrastructure like roads, telecommunications, and energy supplies, we can nurture a more suitable atmosphere for their growth and development. Improved road networks play a crucial role in linking rural enterprises to markets, suppliers, and customers. They cut transportation costs, permit prompt delivery of products, and provide access to new markets. Additionally, better roads make isolated locations more accessible, promoting investment and economic activity. Enhanced telecommunications infrastructure, particularly broadband internet access, is similarly vital. It helps SMEs to harness digital technology, access online marketplaces, and connect with consumers and suppliers globally. Reliable internet access also offers up prospects for e-commerce, digital payments, and remote jobs, boosting entrepreneurship and innovation in rural regions. Moreover, having a reliable and efficient energy supply is crucial. Reliable energy is a key prerequisite for operating equipment, running companies, and delivering important services. By investing in energy infrastructure, we can alleviate power shortages, cut production costs, and boost the overall competitiveness of rural firms. Developing rural infrastructure is not only about physical development; it is about establishing an environment that encourages entrepreneurship, fosters innovation, and drives economic progress in rural areas. By investing in infrastructure, we can unleash the full potential of SMEs, generate employment, and enhance the quality of life for millions of people in rural regions.

- *Agribusiness Support:*
Encouraging the expansion of agribusinesses and rural companies via tailored programs has the potential to considerably benefit local economies and stimulate job creation. By offering targeted support, such as access to money, specialist training, and market development assistance, these initiatives allow agricultural entrepreneurs to realize their potential and contribute to sustainable economic development in rural regions. This method not only supports entrepreneurship but also increases the agricultural value chain, promotes innovation, and helps the integration of smallholder farmers into bigger markets. As a consequence, communities may enjoy higher economic resilience, better livelihoods, and enhanced food security, eventually increasing overall prosperity and vibrancy in rural areas.

- *Local Market Development:*
Local market development entails supporting the growth and strengthening of markets that operate within a given geographic region. This procedure attempts to promote small and medium-sized firms (SMEs) operating in rural regions by providing them with increased chances to offer their goods and services. By cultivating local marketplaces and value chains, communities may create circumstances where small SMEs can flourish and contribute to the local economy. This may encompass activities such as infrastructure

development, access to financing, talent development, and marketing help customized to the requirements of rural enterprises. Ultimately, boosting local markets may lead to enhanced economic resilience, job creation, and general prosperity within rural areas.

In summary, encouraging small and medium-sized businesses (SMEs) has enormous potential to successfully tackle unemployment. SMEs may become important forces behind long-term economic development and the creation of jobs by focusing on important areas including easing financial access, offering technical support, and creating market connections. Ensuring SMEs have sufficient financial assistance is a key component of this plan. These firms can invest in their operations, grow, and provide job prospects because they have access to financing. Furthermore, providing technical support may improve SMEs' capacities and provide them the ability to successfully manage obstacles and seize opportunities. Furthermore, in order for SMEs to prosper in highly competitive contexts, they must create strong market links. SMEs may expand their operations, find new clients, and diversify their sources of income by linking with larger markets. This promotes the development of jobs. Creating an atmosphere that is favorable to entrepreneurship is also essential. People may be encouraged to start and expand SMEs by laws and policies that encourage innovation, taking calculated risks, and company growth. This will make the economy more robust and dynamic. Ultimately, this all-encompassing strategy creates the groundwork for long-term economic stability in addition to meeting the demands for short-term employment. Through supporting and enabling SMEs to grow, society can create a resilient economic framework that can survive setbacks and guarantee long-term wealth for everybody.

**4. *Enhancing Labor Market Policies***
Enhancing labor market policy is crucial for tackling unemployment efficiently. By enhancing these rules, governments may create an atmosphere that stimulates job development, preserves workers' rights, and builds powerful social safety nets. Here's how these measurements might be built upon:
a. *Job Creation Initiatives:*
   Job development programs are vital for encouraging economic growth and lowering unemployment rates. Governments play a significant part in this process by developing different methods to encourage firms to grow their workforce. One successful technique is via offering incentives such as tax rebates, grants, or subsidies to enterprises that recruit additional personnel. By lessening the financial burden connected with recruiting, firms are more willing to grow their personnel, hence providing additional employment possibilities within the economy. Furthermore, governments may encourage employment creation by supporting entrepreneurship and giving aid to small and medium companies (SMEs). Start-up

enterprises and SMEs are generally substantial contributors to employment creation, since they tend to be more flexible and imaginative in their operations. By granting money, mentoring programs, and access to resources, governments may assist prospective entrepreneurs to develop and expand their enterprises, subsequently producing job possibilities for the workforce. Investing in innovation centers and developing sectors is another efficient approach to encourage employment creation. By supporting settings that encourage innovation and technological growth, governments may attract investment and talent to developing areas. This not only produces employment directly inside these sectors but also has a ripple effect across the economy, as supporting firms and services also enjoy growth. Overall, a complete strategy that includes incentives for firms, encouragement for entrepreneurship, and smart investments in developing sectors is crucial for driving job creation and sustaining sustainable economic growth. By emphasizing these activities, governments may successfully combat unemployment concerns and create a vibrant environment for job seekers and companies alike.

b. *Protecting Worker's Rights*

Expanding on the importance of protecting workers' rights involves delving into various facets of labor laws and regulations. These regulations serve as the backbone for ensuring that workers receive fair treatment and are not subjected to exploitation or unfair practices by their employers. One crucial aspect of

protecting workers' rights is the establishment of minimum wage standards. These standards ensure that workers are compensated fairly for their labor and can afford a decent standard of living. By setting a minimum wage, governments aim to prevent employers from paying unreasonably low wages that would otherwise exploit workers and exacerbate income inequality. Additionally, regulating working hours is essential to prevent overwork and ensure a healthy work-life balance for employees. By setting limits on the number of hours an employee can work in a day or week, labor laws help prevent burnout and safeguard workers' physical and mental well-being. Occupational health and safety standards are another critical component of protecting workers' rights. These standards dictate the conditions under which work should be conducted to minimize the risk of workplace accidents, injuries, and illnesses. By enforcing these standards, governments aim to create safe and healthy work environments where employees can perform their duties without fear of harm. Furthermore, combating workplace discrimination and harassment is paramount to fostering an inclusive and supportive work environment. By implementing measures to address discrimination based on factors such as race, gender, ethnicity, religion, or disability, organizations can ensure that all individuals are treated with dignity and respect. Similarly, tackling harassment in the workplace, whether it be sexual harassment, bullying, or intimidation, is crucial for creating a work culture where employees feel safe and valued. Overall, strengthening labor laws and regulations is essential for protecting workers' rights and promoting fairness, equality, and dignity in the workplace. By addressing issues such as minimum wage standards, working hours, occupational health and safety, discrimination, and harassment, societies can create environments where all individuals can thrive and contribute to their fullest potential.

c. *Social Safety Nets:*

Social safety nets are essential for guaranteeing that people and families have access to the resources they need in financially unstable situations, such job loss or recessions. These nets include a range of services and initiatives aimed at giving those in need access to vital resources and financial support. A crucial element is unemployment benefits, which provide short-term financial assistance to those who have lost their jobs due to no fault of their own. By giving recipients of this aid a source of income while they hunt for new work prospects, it helps stabilize families. Another essential component of social safety nets is healthcare coverage. It is ensured that people and families may get the essential medical treatment without having to put a heavy financial pressure on them by having access to inexpensive healthcare. This is crucial during recessions since losing a job might mean losing employer-sponsored health insurance. This gap

is filled in large part by initiatives like Medicaid and the Affordable Care Act, which provide access to healthcare for those who may not otherwise be able to pay it. Programs for housing aid are also essential to strong social safety nets. These initiatives assist low-income people and families afford secure and long-term housing. There are several different types of assistance available, including emergency shelter programs, public housing, and rental subsidies. Preventing homelessness and advancing general well-being require that individuals have access to safe homes. In order to alleviate food insecurity and guarantee that people and families have access to wholesome meals, food assistance programs are crucial. Programs such as the Supplemental Nutrition Assistance Program (SNAP) give cash support for food purchases, while food banks and community kitchens deliver food directly to those in need. Having access to a sufficient diet is essential for preserving health and allowing people to carry out their everyday activities with efficiency. To make sure that no one, especially the most vulnerable groups, slips through the gaps, it is imperative to strengthen and broaden these social safety nets. Social safety nets assist to lessen the consequences of economic problems and foster social stability by offering a wide variety of support services. In addition to providing families and individuals with crisis help, efficient safety nets also build a more just and resilient community. Funding these initiatives creates an atmosphere where everyone has the chance to develop and contributes to the community's general health and prosperity.

d. *Active Labor Market Programs:*
Programs that actively engage the labor market are crucial for reducing unemployment and promoting workforce development. These programs provide focused assistance to jobless people, particularly those who are confronting major obstacles to finding work, such a lack of education or experience or other socioeconomic difficulties. Job training plans are one of the main elements of these programs. These programs aim to provide employees the specialized skills required in today's labor market. Job seekers are better equipped to fill open jobs when training programs are designed with employers' needs in mind. This improves job seekers' employability and lessens the gap between their skill set and job requirements. Subsidized employment programs, in addition to job training, are essential in motivating firms to recruit people who may not otherwise be able to find work. These subsidies, which partially cover the expenses of recruiting and onboarding new hires, come in a variety of forms, including pay subsidies and tax credits. This not only lowers the financial risk for companies, encouraging them to recruit people from underprivileged backgrounds or with little work experience, but it also helps job seekers get meaningful work experience. An other essential component of ongoing labor market initiatives

is public works initiatives. Through these initiatives, the government invests in community development and infrastructure, giving jobless people options for part-time work. These initiatives might include everything from improving public spaces and services to constructing new roads and bridges. Public works initiatives not only create jobs right away but also help communities in the long run by enhancing infrastructure and boosting local economies. Active labor market initiatives seek to accomplish these goals by working together to lower unemployment, improve worker competencies, and encourage social inclusion and economic prosperity.

e. *Encouraging Lifelong Education:*

Encouraging lifelong learning and ongoing skill improvement is crucial in the quickly changing labor market of today. People are more in need than ever of updating and expanding their skill sets in an age marked by fast technology breakthroughs and changing economic environments. Governments are essential to this process because they make inexpensive education and training programs accessible. These programs may be designed to fulfill the unique demands of the workforce in a variety of ways, such as online courses, apprenticeships, conventional classroom education, and vocational training. Through facilitating greater accessibility and affordability of education and training, governments may enable people to gain new competencies and adjust to changing needs in the job market. Employee employability is improved via empowerment, enabling them to stay competitive and relevant in their industries. It also promotes resilience to economic shocks, like those brought on by advances in technology, intense competition on a worldwide scale, or recessions. People are better prepared to handle professional transitions—whether they are looking to improve in their present positions or make a complete shift to totally different fields—when they have the chance to continually learn and develop. Moreover, encouraging lifelong learning may benefit society as a whole. Increased productivity, economic development, and general quality of life may all be attributed to a highly trained labor force. Additionally, it may lower unemployment rates and aid in bridging skill gaps, which often impede the growth of enterprises. Governments may develop a more flexible and dynamic work force that is equipped to handle future difficulties by funding lifelong learning programs. Encouraging lifelong learning and ongoing skill development is an essential tactic for making sure people are resilient and employable in a labor market that is changing quickly. The provision of easily available and reasonably priced education must be a top priority for governments in order to empower laborers, improve their flexibility, and promote social and economic advancement.

## f. Targeting Vulnerable Groups:

It takes a complex strategy to target vulnerable groups that recognizes and meets the unique requirements and obstacles of every group. Because they lack professional networks and job experience, young people, for example, sometimes have high unemployment rates. Specifically designed programs like mentorships, apprenticeships, and internships may help young people get real-world experience and industry contacts. Their employability may also be increased via educational programs that match skill training with market needs. Women gain from laws that promote work-life balance, especially those who must manage obligations to their families and their jobs. This includes having flexible work schedules, access to dependable and reasonably priced daycare, and parental leave regulations that promote sharing of childcare duties by both parents. Along with assisting women in staying in the workforce, these policies also advance gender equality in labor participation. People with impairments often run up social, economic, and physical obstacles to their job prospects. Anti-discrimination laws must be enforced, assistive technology must be available, and workplace accessibility promoted via inclusive policies. A more inclusive labor market may be created via employer incentives for hiring from this group and job placement services tailored to the talents and skills of people with disabilities. Communities that are marginalized—ethnic minorities, rural populations, or economically disadvantaged groups—often encounter systemic obstacles like prejudice, poor access to high-quality healthcare and education, and geographic isolation. Interventions for these people can include ensuring equitable employment practices, enhancing access to education and vocational training, and promoting local economic growth via microfinance and infrastructure projects. Programs in financial literacy and entrepreneurship may enable members of underprivileged communities to start and run their own companies, therefore promoting economic expansion and independence. Governments may solve the particular difficulties disadvantaged groups have by putting these focused initiatives into practice. Better financial results for individuals are facilitated by this, which also advances more general society objectives of equality and inclusion. Such strategies make sure that economic expansion helps all sections of the population, which lowers inequality and promotes a more cohesive and productive community.

By enacting a comprehensive set of labor market policies, governments may nurture a dynamic and resilient workforce while reducing the harmful consequences of unemployment and underemployment. These initiatives not only assist economic development and social cohesion but also contribute to establishing a more sustainable and fair society.

## 5. Fostering Regional Integration and Trade:

Cameroon's strategic engagement in regional economic communities such as the Economic Community of Central African States (ECCAS) and the African Continental Free Trade Area (AfCFTA) provides tremendous promise for reducing unemployment via many avenues:

a. **Enhanced Trade Opportunities:**

Participation in ECCAS and AfCFTA allows Cameroon to access into bigger markets outside its national limits. By eliminating trade restrictions and providing better access to regional markets, these frameworks help Cameroonian enterprises to increase their consumer base. This expanded market access may lead to more demand for products and services, driving enterprises to scale up production and, therefore, recruit more people. The economic integration under ECCAS (Economic Community of Central African States) and AfCFTA (African Continental Free Trade Area) provides a more competitive environment, boosting innovation and efficiency among Cameroonian enterprises. With fewer obstacles, enterprises may profit from economies of scale, cutting manufacturing costs and making their goods more competitive both locally and globally. Moreover, these trade agreements attract foreign direct investment (FDI) by establishing a more predictable and unified market environment. Investors are more inclined to commit money to an area where they view stable and coordinated trade rules. For Cameroon, this implies an infusion of investment into diverse sectors, such as industry, agriculture, and services, which may lead to technical transfers, skill development, and infrastructural upgrades. The subsequent economic expansion may promote the development of auxiliary businesses and services, producing a more robust economic environment. Cameroon's involvement in ECCAS and AfCFTA also encourages the transfer of knowledge and technology. As firms connect across borders, there is a flow of knowledge and best practices that may increase productivity and creativity inside the nation. For instance, Cameroonian enterprises might borrow innovative farming practices or industrial procedures from their regional competitors, improving their competitive advantage. Additionally, the integration into these bigger markets gives Cameroonian enterprises with significant insights into customer preferences and market trends, which may guide product development and marketing strategies. The increased market access given by ECCAS and AfCFTA may help diversify Cameroon's economy. By expanding out to a range of regional markets, Cameroonian enterprises are less reliant on domestic demand and may offset risks associated with local economic downturns. This diversity is vital for economic stability and progress, enabling firms to explore and exploit new possibilities in other industries and areas. Furthermore, regional economic integration supports infrastructure development. Improved transportation networks, improved logistics, and expanded communication technologies are generally essential to promote commerce across borders. These infrastructure upgrades not only help commerce but also contribute to the general economic growth of the nation, boosting connectivity and cutting the expenses of doing business. Cameroon's involvement with ECCAS and AfCFTA prepares it to exploit a broader, more dynamic market, generating economic development, job creation, and industry diversification. The lowering of trade barriers and better market access provide a suitable climate for corporate growth, innovation, and investment, eventually contributing to the country's socio-economic development.

b. *Attracting Investments:*

Foreign direct investment (FDI) is attracted to Cameroon mostly because of its regional integration. In order to guarantee that their investments have a wider audience and are less vulnerable to the market dangers associated with smaller, isolated economies, investors often search for stable and interconnected markets. Cameroon may present itself as a doorway to a more expansive, integrated market environment by participating in both the African Continental Free Trade Area (AfCFTA) and the Economic Community of Central African States (ECCAS). Cameroon may now provide access to a single market thanks to this integration, which raises the possibility of scale economies and lowers trade obstacles within the area. There are several potential economic advantages for Cameroon from increased FDI. The main benefit is the inflow of money, which is essential for the growth of the economy as a whole as well as for the construction of enterprises and infrastructure. Foreign investments often provide cutting-edge technology and ideas in addition to cash, which is crucial for raising competitiveness and productivity. Technology transfer from more developed nations may assist in modernizing Cameroon's industrial base, resulting in improved production techniques and better-quality products and services.

International business methods and management experience brought by FDI may also improve the abilities of the local labor force. The development of a strong manufacturing sector depends greatly on this knowledge and talent transfer. Local businesses may increase their performance and market reach by using best practices in management, logistics, and operational efficiency. This may thus result in the emergence of many job possibilities in various industries, lowering unemployment and promoting economic growth. A consistent stream of FDI may also diversify Cameroon's economy, lessening its dependence on any one industry and enhancing its ability to withstand shocks to the economy. By using a variety of income sources, a diversified economy is better able to endure changes in international markets and maintain long-term prosperity. As international investors set up shop in Cameroon, they often need products and services from regional vendors, which encourages the growth of small and medium-sized businesses (SMEs). As a result, the economy as a whole is affected, stimulating entrepreneurship and the development of a vibrant private sector. By providing a more expansive, integrated market, regional integration via the ECCAS and AfCFTA greatly increases Cameroon's appeal for foreign direct investment. The resultant flood of foreign investment brings with it finance, technological transfer, and managerial know-how—all critical for industrial development and employment generation. This integration helps to make Cameroon's economy more resilient and diverse while also improving the country's overall economic environment.

c. *Infrastructure Development:*

Significant infrastructural upgrades are required in order to fully benefit from regional integration. Building transportation infrastructure, such as ports, railroads, and roadways, is crucial to enabling the effective movement of people and products. Expanding and modernizing the energy infrastructure guarantees a consistent supply of electricity for home and industrial use. Improving the infrastructure of telecommunications is also essential to the functioning of contemporary businesses, as it facilitates effective communication and information access. The immediate advantage of infrastructure projects is the creation of jobs in the construction and adjacent businesses. Local economies benefit greatly from these occupations, which are spread across a variety of industries and include project management, physical labor, engineering, and design. Beyond only creating jobs directly, supply chain businesses also flourish as a result of the demand for the goods and services required for building. By cutting the expenses associated with logistics and transportation, improved infrastructure lowers the cost of doing business. items may be transported more swiftly and dependably on efficient transportation networks, which minimizes delays and spoiling, especially for perishable items. Enhancements to the energy infrastructure guarantee a steady supply of electricity, reducing interruptions that might stop output and raise operating expenses. Improved communications enable more efficient company processes, from routine correspondence to intricate data transfers, increasing overall efficiency. A region's greater efficiency and lower operating costs draw in more enterprises. Because they know that a strong infrastructure will support their operations and development, businesses seeking to move or expand are more inclined to choose locations in these regions. More jobs may be created as a result of this increased economic activity, not only in the new companies themselves but also in related industries like retail, hotel, and maintenance. Furthermore, a region's overall economic growth is aided by well-developed infrastructure. It encourages increased connection between rural and urban regions, making it easier for farmers and other rural producers to reach markets. This may encourage inclusive development and lessen regional inequities. When it comes to drawing in foreign direct investment (FDI), efficient infrastructure is also essential since investors look for safe, affordable places to base their operations. Infrastructure development is a key component of regional integration, offering both short-term financial gains from the creation of jobs and long-term benefits from raising the competitiveness and efficiency of businesses. It encourages favorable conditions for both local and foreign company activities, lowers costs, and promotes wider economic development, all of which contribute to long-term economic growth and development.

d. Regional Collaboration and Policy Coherence:

Economic integration and development are contingent upon regional collaboration and policy harmonization. Trade and investment flows may be greatly increased by working together with neighboring nations via agreements like the African Continental Free Trade Area (AfCFTA) and the Economic Community of Central African States (ECCAS).

The harmonization of policies and laws is one of the main features of this relationship. One of the main areas of concentration is standardizing customs processes. Countries may expedite and improve the efficiency of the flow of products by lowering border delays and bureaucratic barriers via the establishment of standard customs procedures. Businesses need to embrace this streamlining since it reduces transaction costs and shortens the time it takes to launch goods. Tariff reduction is yet another essential element of harmonizing policies. Excessive tariffs have the potential to hinder commerce by raising the cost and decreasing the competitiveness of imported products. Member nations may cut prices for goods, promote international commerce, and expand the size of the integrated market by reaching an agreement on reduced tariff rates. This has the potential to draw in investment from both domestic and foreign sources hoping to get access to a single market with uniform regulations. It's also critical that quality standards be uniform across nations. Trade may be complicated by the fact that different nations often have different product standards and laws. By harmonizing these standards, it is ensured that goods that satisfy quality criteria in one nation would be immediately compliant in another. This lowers expenses and streamlines the procedure for companies with international operations by eliminating the need for several certificates and tests. This gives customers access to a wider variety of products with assured quality. These policies support the formalization of informal industries while also making cross-border commercial activities simpler for companies. Several tiny enterprises and unofficial vendors have considerable obstacles while navigating complex and erratic regulatory frameworks. Policies that are more streamlined and uniform may encourage these companies to join the official economy. Since formal enterprises are more likely to abide by labor rules, pay benefits, and provide more secure work, this shift may result in improved job security. To summarize, the promotion of a favorable atmosphere for trade and investment is greatly aided by regional collaboration and policy harmonization achieved via the AfCFTA and ECCAS. These programs, which reduce tariffs, standardize customs processes, and unify quality standards, not only increase economic activity but also encourage the formalization of the informal sector, improving benefits and job security for workers across the area.

e. *supporting local businesses and SMEs:*

A key element of regional integration frameworks is support for small and local businesses. These methods are intended to support the growth of small and medium-sized firms (SMEs) by giving them access to opportunities and resources that will enable them to expand their businesses and more successfully compete in wider markets. SMEs are very important to the economy, particularly when it comes to creating jobs. They make a major contribution to the development and stability of local economies by generating employment opportunities. Larger market access is one of the main advantages of regional integration for SMEs. Businesses may expand their consumer base—a crucial component of growth—by operating outside of their local borders. Because of their greater reach, SMEs may take advantage of economies of scale, which lowers costs per unit and boosts profitability. Additionally, these businesses may be exposed to a wider range of customer tastes and increased rivalry as a result of joining a broader market, which might spur innovation and raise the caliber of their output. Regional integration frameworks often include a range of methods to help SMEs. Financial aid and grants play a crucial role in assisting these companies in overcoming their first growth hurdles. A variety of uses for funding exist, including as marketing, increasing manufacturing capacity, and product development. For SMEs who may find it difficult to get loans from conventional banking institutions because they lack collateral or credit history, this kind of financial help is very crucial. Programs for training are still another crucial component of assistance. These courses may provide SME owners and staff the abilities and information required to successfully run and expand their companies. Business management, financial planning, marketing tactics, and the utilization of new technology are a few topics that might be covered in training. These programs guarantee that firms can maintain expansion and handle the complexity of bigger markets by improving the competencies of SME people. Facilitating financing access is another essential component of helping SMEs. Establishing unique credit lines, providing microloans, and creating financial goods designed with small firms' requirements in mind may all help with this. SMEs may grow their operations, add more employees, and invest in new equipment thanks to easier access to financing. Regional integration may also result in the establishment of regional financial institutions, which are better able to provide SMEs the financial services they need since they are aware of the particular difficulties they confront. SMEs are assisted by regional integration frameworks using a variety of strategies, such as subsidies, training courses, and easier access to credit. These kinds of frameworks may greatly increase SMEs' ability to generate employment and support economic development by addressing these areas. The collective influence of these support systems goes beyond specific companies, building a more robust and vibrant local economy.

f. *Promoting Value Addition and Industrialization:*

Through the promotion of the development of regional value chains, integration is the key to realizing the full industrialization potential. Prioritizing value addition within its major sectors—agriculture, mining, and forestry—will benefit Cameroon greatly. Cameroon can make the most of its resources by creating enterprises that turn raw materials into completed goods rather than just exporting raw materials. Then, by being distributed across the area, these completed commodities may promote development and economic progress. By gaining a larger domestic share of the value chain, this strategic move benefits the nation's economy in addition to creating job chances in the manufacturing sector.

*g. Employment in Services Sector:*
There are many potentials that go much beyond the boundaries of physical products when we examine the services sector in the context of regional integration. The interchange of services, including banking, healthcare, education, and tourism, is made easier by the integration of economies within a region. It also promotes the movement of tangible goods. The need for auxiliary services will inevitably increase as international commerce and investment develop. This increase in demand therefore creates a wide range of job possibilities that serve a variety of professional backgrounds. Essentially, the connectivity that results from regional integration serves as a driving force behind the development of the services industry, generating a vibrant environment that offers many opportunities for advancement and employment to those with the necessary skills. For example, in the finance industry, international capital flows need a complex network of financial services, such as investment management, banking, and

insurance. In a similar vein, when educational institutions work to accommodate a more diverse student population, there is an increase in need for curricular development, language training, and academic knowledge. In addition, there is an increase in medical tourism in the healthcare industry as patients go abroad for specialist care and procedures. This increases the need for medical experts and support personnel. At the same time, the travel and tourism sector undergoes a revival thanks to easy travel plans and cultural exchange initiatives that support a flourishing hospitality business and provide jobs in tour guide, hotel management, and event planning. Essentially, there is a dynamic ecosystem where innovation, cooperation, and opportunity meet because of the synergy between regional integration and the services sector, which goes beyond conventional borders. By using integration's transformational power, countries may fully realize the potential of their services sectors, which establishes the foundation for long-term, sustainable economic development and prosperity.

h. *Building Capacity and Developing Skills:*

Through capacity-building programs, regional efforts often play a critical role in improving the skills of a country's workforce. Participating in such projects with regional partners will help Cameroon's inhabitants become far more employable and skilled.

Through this partnership, people may access a range of training and educational opportunities that would not be accessible or would be too expensive if pursued individually. Cameroonian workers may enhance their current skills and learn new ones by taking part in these regional programs, which will increase their competitiveness in the labor market. In an interconnected regional economy where nations compete with one another for investment and economic opportunities, this is especially crucial. Foreign direct investment is generally drawn to areas with a ready supply of trained labor, therefore having a competent workforce is essential. Moreover, maintaining long-term economic growth requires investing in capacity building and skill development. Modern skill proficiency is becoming more important for workers as businesses change and new technologies appear. Regional training programs may provide the instruction and real-world experience required to keep workers flexible and prepared to meet evolving industry standards and demands. These programs increase employability on an individual basis while also promoting economic stability and development on a larger scale. Because skilled people are often more productive, production and efficiency across a range of industries may rise. Consequently, this improves the nation's overall economic performance and creates a more dynamic and competitive market environment. Regional cooperation in capacity development also encourages the exchange of best practices and information transfer.

Information sharing like this may spur innovation and advancements across a range of industries, including manufacturing, services, technology, and agriculture. Cameroon may further propel economic growth by implementing more effective methods and practices by benefiting from the experiences and skills of regional partners. Cameroon stands to gain a great deal from regional efforts aimed at developing its skills and capabilities. They increase the employability of its people, encourage steady economic development, draw in foreign capital, and foster innovation by exchanging information. These initiatives are essential to maintaining the workforce's competitiveness and ability to satisfy the needs of a regionally linked economy.

Cameroon has the potential to dramatically decrease unemployment by actively participating in the Economic Community of Central African States (ECCAS) and the African Continental Free Trade Area (AfCFTA). These initiatives need coordinated policies, major investments in infrastructure, and a focus on increasing the ability of the workforce in order to guarantee long-term economic development and the creation of new jobs.

To summarize, in order to effectively address the issue of unemployment in Cameroon, it is necessary to adopt a comprehensive and coordinated strategy that addresses the fundamental structural difficulties while simultaneously fostering economic growth that is both inclusive and sustainable. The young population of the nation provides a great opportunity; nevertheless, in order to realize this potential, strategic investments and policy changes are not only required but also necessary. The field of education need to be one of the key areas of concentration. To ensure that the workforce is equipped with the information and skills required to prosper in a contemporary economy, it is essential to improve the quality of education as well as the accessibility of training opportunities. This involves not just formal education but also possibilities for occupational training and learning that continues throughout one's life that are in line with the needs of the market. Economic diversification is another essential component that must be addressed. When the economy is too dependent on a small number of industries, it becomes susceptible to shocks from the outside world and restricts the development of new jobs. Cameroon has the potential to develop a more robust and dynamic economic environment that provides a larger range of job possibilities if it is able to encourage development in a number of sectors, including technology, manufacturing, agriculture, and tourism. Supporting entrepreneurship is also vital. Small and medium-sized firms (SMEs) are frequently the backbone of economies, fueling innovation and employment growth. Providing access to capital, simplifying regulatory frameworks, and giving mentoring and business development services may assist ambitious entrepreneurs transform their ideas into viable firms, thereby helping to employment creation. Strengthening labor market policy is equally crucial. This requires ensuring that labor laws safeguard workers' rights while simultaneously stimulating employment development. Effective regulations should combine flexibility with security, allowing firms to adapt and develop while providing workers with stability and equitable treatment. Additionally, improving social protection systems might assist buffer the effect of unemployment and underemployment on vulnerable groups. By tackling five critical areas—education, economic diversification, entrepreneurship, and labor market policies—Cameroon can establish a more equitable and sustainable economic environment. This comprehensive strategy would not only eliminate unemployment but also create long-term economic growth and social development. The outcome will be a better future where all people have the chance to develop and contribute to the nation's success.

*3.4 Healthcare and Education*

Two vital areas that are necessary for every country's socioeconomic growth are healthcare and education. Both sectors in Cameroon confront formidable obstacles that have an impact on the standard of living of the populace as well as the nation's overall growth trajectory.

## A. Healthcare
*i. Access to Healthcare Services:*
One of the primary issues in Cameroon is the restricted availability to healthcare services, especially in rural regions. While larger places like Yaoundé and Douala have comparatively superior healthcare facilities, rural regions suffer from a significant shortage of medical infrastructure and manpower. Many towns are lacking even basic healthcare services, requiring inhabitants to travel vast distances to acquire medical treatment. The discrepancy between urban and rural healthcare access is considerable, with rural residents generally depending on under-resourced clinics that lack vital medical supplies, diagnostic equipment, and skilled healthcare workers. The lack of physicians, nurses, and other healthcare staff is significant, aggravated by the fact that many medical experts choose to work in metropolitan regions where facilities are better and living circumstances are more suitable. In rural locations, the healthcare system confronts various hurdles, including weak transportation networks, which make it difficult for patients to reach hospitals and for medical supplies to be delivered properly. The roads are typically in poor condition, particularly during the rainy season, which may separate populations and limit access to prompt medical treatments. This geographical barrier contributes greatly to the increased death rates and prevalence of avoidable illnesses in these locations. Moreover, the economic limits of the rural people complicate the dilemma. Many persons in these

places cannot afford the expense of healthcare, which involves not just treatment but also transportation to distant medical institutions. This economic barrier leads in a dependence on traditional medicine and home cures, which may not be effective and may occasionally be hazardous. Efforts to enhance healthcare access in rural Cameroon have been impeded by insufficient government financing and logistical constraints. International assistance and non-governmental organizations (NGOs) have sought to replace certain shortages by offering mobile clinics, health education initiatives, and temporary medical missions. However, these projects generally struggle with sustainability and scalability, unable to deliver the long-term answers required for systemic transformation. The absence of healthcare access in rural regions also impacts mother and child health considerably. Pregnant women and small children are especially susceptible owing to the lack of prenatal and postnatal care. The outcome is high rates of maternal and newborn mortality, which might be dramatically decreased with greater access to healthcare services. The restricted access to healthcare services in Cameroon, particularly in rural regions, is a complicated problem driven by poor infrastructure, a dearth of medical professionals, economic restrictions, and logistical difficulties. Addressing these difficulties involves a multidimensional strategy that includes upgrading transportation networks, boosting government investment in healthcare, motivating medical experts to work in rural regions, and ensuring that healthcare is affordable for all populations.

ii. *Quality of Healthcare:*
The quality of healthcare services in Cameroon is typically poor, defined by various systemic challenges that greatly impair the well-being of the people. One important difficulty is the shortage of basic equipment and supplies in many healthcare institutions. This weakness implies that even fundamental medical operations cannot be conducted successfully, leading to a scenario where patients do not get the essential treatment. For instance, many hospitals and clinics suffer from a scarcity of diagnostic equipment, surgical instruments, and pharmaceuticals, which are necessary for treating a range of medical diseases. In addition to the paucity of equipment, there is a serious scarcity of skilled medical workers in Cameroon. This shortage includes physicians, nurses, and other healthcare professionals who are vital for providing excellent treatment. The restricted number of healthcare professionals sometimes results in onerous workloads for the available personnel, leading to burnout and lowering the overall quality of service. This shortage is further worsened by the flight of skilled professionals to other nations in pursuit of better opportunities, creating a vacuum in the healthcare system. The combination of limited resources and a lack of skilled workers leads to inferior treatment and poor health outcomes.

Patients commonly face extended wait periods, misdiagnoses, and poor care, which may aggravate their medical issues. Preventive treatment and health education are also ignored, leading to the rise of avoidable illnesses and disorders. For instance, maternity and child health services are severely impacted, with high rates of maternal and newborn mortality being a disturbing reflection of the healthcare system's deficiencies. Furthermore, the presence of counterfeit pharmaceuticals presents a severe danger to patient safety in Cameroon. These bogus pharmaceuticals, which are frequently useless or hazardous, are common owing to inadequate regulatory frameworks and poor enforcement of pharmaceutical standards. Patients who unintentionally ingest counterfeit pharmaceuticals may suffer from exacerbated health issues or severe responses, weakening faith in the healthcare system. The spread of these substandard drugs hampers treatment efforts and decreases the efficacy of healthcare treatments. Overall, the insufficient quality of healthcare services in Cameroon arises from a combination of equipment and supply limitations, a lack of skilled medical workers, and the persistent problem of counterfeit pharmaceuticals. These factors combined lead to poor health outcomes and emphasize the urgent need for significant changes to strengthen the healthcare system in the nation.

*iii. Health Infrastructure:*
The country's healthcare infrastructure is undeveloped, providing substantial hurdles to the delivery of excellent medical services. Hospitals and clinics, particularly those situated in rural regions, usually function in structures that are in bad condition. These facilities are generally old and not well-maintained, with structural flaws that may impair both the safety and efficacy of healthcare delivery. The old nature of these facilities means they may not satisfy current standards for sanitation, patient comfort, or operational efficiency, which may lead to an unsatisfactory environment for both patients and healthcare personnel. In addition to the physical state of healthcare facilities, there is a noteworthy paucity of sophisticated medical technology. Many hospitals and clinics lack the fundamental equipment needed to conduct a broad variety of diagnostic and therapeutic treatments. This constraint is especially obvious in rural locations, where healthcare practitioners may not have access to basic diagnostic instruments such as X-ray machines or ultrasound scanners, much alone more complex technologies like MRI machines or CT scanners. The lack of these technology makes it impossible to diagnose and treat complicated medical diseases efficiently, necessitating patients to travel considerable distances to metropolitan areas where such treatments are accessible. The scarcity of innovative medical technology also hinders the capacity to deliver complete treatment. Without contemporary technology, healthcare providers

are sometimes unable to deliver the entire gamut of diagnostic tests and treatments. This not only affects the quality of treatment patients get but also delays the identification and management of illnesses, possibly leading to poorer health outcomes. For instance, illnesses that may be recognized early and treated effectively may go unreported until they grow more severe and difficult to cure. Moreover, the absence of modern medical equipment and infrastructure adds to a greater perception of inequity in healthcare access. Urban centers, which often have better-funded and better-equipped hospitals, present a striking contrast to rural areas, exposing the differences between various locations. Patients in rural locations may feel ignored and disadvantaged, knowing that the quality of treatment they get is much lower to that offered in cities. This imbalance may intensify emotions of dissatisfaction and distrust towards the healthcare system, further complicating attempts to improve public health outcomes. Efforts to strengthen the country's healthcare infrastructure must address both the physical status of healthcare facilities and the availability of current medical technology. Investment in the repair and upkeep of hospital facilities is crucial to maintain safe, clean, and efficient conditions for healthcare delivery. Additionally, boosting the availability of innovative diagnostic and treatment technology is vital for strengthening the capability of healthcare practitioners to give complete care. These enhancements will help bridge the gap between rural and urban healthcare facilities, ensuring that all residents have access to the medical care they need regardless of their location. The undeveloped healthcare infrastructure in the nation, defined by crumbling buildings and a lack of new medical equipment, greatly inhibits the capacity to offer high-quality treatment. Addressing these difficulties demands tremendous investment and dedication to updating both the physical facilities and the technical resources accessible to healthcare practitioners. Only via such extensive changes can the healthcare system be reinforced to satisfy the demands of all people efficiently.

iv. *Disease Burden:*
Cameroon suffers a high burden of both infectious and non-communicable illnesses, generating a complicated public health environment that greatly influences the population's well-being and the healthcare system's capability. Communicable illnesses such as malaria, HIV/AIDS, and TB are especially widespread and pose severe public health issues. Malaria is one of the top causes of morbidity and death, particularly among children and pregnant women. Despite attempts to reduce the illness via the distribution of insecticide-treated bed nets and other measures, malaria continues to have a considerable effect on public health. HIV/AIDS is another important health concern in Cameroon. The nation has a high incidence of

HIV, with major efforts being undertaken to limit transmission and offer antiretroviral therapy to individuals infected. However, stigma and limited access to healthcare treatments in particular locations restrict progress in adequately treating the condition. Tuberculosis, typically in combination with HIV, significantly worsens the health condition. The co-infection of HIV and TB exacerbates the challenges in treatment and raises the total illness burden. In addition to the issues provided by communicable illnesses, Cameroon is facing an increasing incidence of non-communicable diseases such as diabetes and hypertension. These chronic illnesses are becoming more widespread owing to changes in lifestyle, urbanization, and food choices. The growth in non-communicable illnesses adds to the already severe burden of communicable diseases, providing a twin problem for the healthcare system. Managing both infectious and chronic illnesses demands large resources, solid healthcare infrastructure, and comprehensive plans to satisfy the complex health requirements of the community. The combined burden of infectious and chronic illnesses exerts great strain on the healthcare system in Cameroon. Healthcare institutions generally contend with insufficient finances, poor infrastructure, and a scarcity of healthcare workers. This pressure is especially visible in rural and underdeveloped communities, where access to effective healthcare is restricted. The healthcare system must balance the immediate, sometimes urgent, needs of addressing communicable illnesses with the long-term, continuous care necessary for non-communicable disorders. Addressing this dual load demands a comprehensive strategy that encompasses prevention, early diagnosis, effective treatment, and ongoing care, with measures to enhance the broader healthcare system to handle these unique problems.

v. *Health Financing:*
Financing healthcare remains a huge concern. Public investment on health is minimal, and out-of-pocket expenditures comprise a substantial component of healthcare financing. This financial stress on families frequently leads to delays in obtaining treatment and contributes to poor health outcomes. The low public investment on health leads in insufficient financing for key health services, restricted access to pharmaceuticals, and understaffed healthcare facilities. Consequently, individuals and families frequently have to face the brunt of medical bills alone, resulting to substantial financial distress. When healthcare expenses are paid out-of-pocket, it may result in catastrophic health expenditures, when people spend a high percentage of their income on healthcare. This circumstance is especially problematic for low-income families, who may skip critical medical procedures owing to the expense, compounding health disparities. Furthermore, the worry of excessive medical costs might dissuade individuals from getting

prompt medical assistance, enabling illnesses to deteriorate and leading to more severe health issues that are costly to address. The dependence on out-of-pocket expenses also underscores the insufficiency of health insurance coverage in many places. Limited access to cheap health insurance implies that many individuals are not protected against the financial risks connected with sickness and injury. In nations where health insurance is available, it frequently does not cover all treatments or may have large co-pays and deductibles, making it difficult for insured persons to finance critical care. Moreover, the low amount of public health spending harms the quality of healthcare services. With minimal money, public health systems struggle to maintain infrastructure, buy sophisticated medical equipment, and provide proper training for healthcare professionals. This may lead to overcrowded facilities, lengthy waiting periods, and subpar treatment, further preventing individuals from getting medical attention when required. Addressing these difficulties demands a diverse strategy. Increasing public investment on health is critical to ensure that basic health services are appropriately financed and available to everyone. Expanding health insurance coverage and decreasing out-of-pocket payments may shield families from financial stress and enhance health outcomes. Additionally, investing in the healthcare staff and infrastructure may increase the quality of treatment and guarantee that health systems are robust and responsive to the requirements of the community. The existing situation of health funding, typified by low public investment and high out-of-pocket expenses, creates enormous hurdles to ensuring fair and effective healthcare. To ameliorate these difficulties, comprehensive policies that boost public health financing, extend insurance coverage, and improve the quality of healthcare services are important.

vi.   *Maternal and Child Health:*
Maternal and child health indices in Cameroon are alarming, showing severe problems within the healthcare system. The nation confronts a high maternal death rate, a serious problem typically attributable to insufficient prenatal care. Many expecting moms may not obtain the essential check-ups and medical care throughout pregnancy, leading to issues that go unnoticed and untreated. This shortage of prenatal care is aggravated by the low number of qualified delivery attendants. In many locations, births are not overseen by skilled healthcare experts, raising the danger of life-threatening problems during delivery. Access to emergency obstetric care is another key challenge. Many women live in places where such services are either unavailable or impossible to get. This restricted access implies that in the case of difficulties, prompt and effective medical care is frequently not feasible, adding to the high maternal death rate. Additionally, healthcare institutions are usually

under-resourced and lack the required equipment and treatments to address crises successfully. The situation for child health is equally bad, with high child death rates widespread throughout the nation. Malnutrition is a key concern, with many youngsters suffering from low food intake and poor dietary variety, which are crucial for their growth and development. This malnutrition lowers children's immune systems, making them more prone to infections and illnesses. Inadequate vaccine coverage further exacerbates the situation. Many children may not get the complete schedule of recommended immunizations, leaving them exposed to preventable illnesses such as measles, polio, and whooping cough. The causes for this low coverage include practical problems, such as vaccine storage and transportation concerns, as well as a lack of knowledge and education among parents about the necessity of vaccines. Access to pediatric treatment is extremely restricted, especially in rural regions. Many children may not get the essential medical treatment when they become sick, and even in metropolitan areas, healthcare facilities are typically overcrowded and under-resourced. This lack of access to appropriate pediatric care implies that many curable illnesses may turn deadly. Overall, the maternal and child health statistics in Cameroon emphasize the urgent need for reforms in the healthcare system.

Addressing these concerns needs a diverse strategy, including boosting access to prenatal and emergency obstetric care, enhancing nutrition and vaccine coverage, and extending access to excellent pediatric treatments. Only through extensive and consistent efforts can these disturbing health indicators be properly handled.

**B. Education**

i. *Access to Education:*
Access to education in Cameroon is distinguished by major discrepancies. While basic education is more accessible, secondary and university education possibilities are restricted, especially in rural regions. This unequal access is formed by different constraints that impair educational success for many youngsters. In rural settings, children frequently face major challenges to getting school. One big problem is the great distance to schools. Many communities lack close educational facilities, requiring youngsters to travel several kilometers everyday to attend lessons. This lengthy drive might be frustrating and taxing, leading to sporadic attendance or full dropout. Additionally, the absence of dependable transportation exacerbates this situation, as many youngsters must walk these great distances, frequently in rough terrain and terrible weather conditions. Socio-cultural issues also have a crucial impact in restricting access to education. In many rural areas, there is a pervasive ethos that values work above education. Children, particularly females, are typically required to participate to domestic

duties, farming, or other sorts of work instead of attending school. This societal expectation throws a great strain on youngsters and may drastically derail their scholastic career. Furthermore, early marriage is another socio-cultural issue that disproportionately impacts girls, restricting their educational chances and increasing gender disparities in schooling. Moreover, the quality of education in rural places is typically affected by poor facilities and resources. Schools in these locations usually suffer from a lack of basic infrastructure such as classrooms, textbooks, and skilled instructors. This resource deficiency not only impacts the learning environment but also decreases the overall quality of education, making it less engaging and effective for pupils. Economic restrictions are another big obstacle to schooling. Many families in rural regions live in poverty and cannot afford the expenditures connected with education, such as uniforms, books, and examination fees. Even while elementary education is technically free, these extra fees might be exorbitant. For secondary and university education, the expenditures are significantly greater, making it essentially unattainable for many rural households. This economic barrier fosters a cycle of poverty and restricted educational achievement. In metropolitan regions, although educational facilities are more accessible, there are still substantial hurdles. Overcrowding in schools is a prevalent problem, resulting to excessive class sizes that may damage the quality of education. Additionally, urban schools typically suffer their own resource restrictions, including insufficient numbers of instructors and inadequate teaching supplies. The government's attempts to enhance access to education have included different programs, including as constructing additional schools, offering scholarships, and establishing regulations aimed at fostering gender equality in education. However, these initiatives have not been adequate to effectively address the deep-rooted difficulties, especially in rural regions. The need for more focused initiatives that address the unique constraints encountered by rural children is crucial to attaining equal access to education in Cameroon. Although basic education is somewhat more accessible in Cameroon, secondary and university education possibilities remain restricted, particularly in rural regions. Long distances to schools, lack of transportation, socio-cultural concerns, poor infrastructure, and economic restraints are important challenges that many students confront. Addressing these difficulties needs extensive and focused initiatives to guarantee that all children in Cameroon have equal access to excellent education.

ii. *The Quality of Education:*
The quality of education in Cameroon is a key problem that impacts the general growth and future possibilities of the country's young. One of the biggest difficulties is the overcrowding of classrooms. Many schools operate with a

student-to-teacher ratio that is substantially too high, which inhibits efficient teaching and learning. Teachers, frequently overwhelmed by the sheer number of students, struggle to offer personalized attention and assistance, which is vital for student comprehension and success. In addition to congestion, the absence of proper instructional resources negatively impairs the quality of education. Many schools do not have adequate textbooks, learning tools, or even basic materials like chalk and paper. This paucity of resources causes instructors to depend on outmoded or improvised materials, which might impair the quality of the instructional information presented to pupils. The lack of contemporary and relevant educational equipment implies that pupils are not exposed to current material and teaching techniques, placing them at a disadvantage compared to their counterparts in better-equipped institutions. Furthermore, the issue of inadequately educated instructors exacerbates the situation. Many educators in Cameroon have not gotten adequate training to manage the different and complicated demands of their pupils. Inadequate teacher training programs fail to provide educators with current pedagogical abilities, leaving them ill-prepared to engage students successfully or to adapt to varied learning styles and demands. This dearth of professional development opportunities for teachers also means that they are frequently ignorant of or unable to use new teaching approaches and technology that might increase learning results. Another important worry is the mismatch of the curriculum with the needs of the employment market. The educational system in Cameroon usually prioritizes rote learning and academic information above practical skills and critical thinking. As a consequence, graduates frequently find themselves ill-prepared for the realities of the job. The skills people learn throughout their schooling do not meet the needs of companies, resulting to a considerable gap between education and career chances. This disparity adds to high levels of unemployment and underemployment among young Cameroonians, who struggle to find jobs that match their abilities. Overall, the quality of education in Cameroon suffers from several structural difficulties that require immediate attention. Addressing these difficulties demands comprehensive changes that include lowering class sizes, providing enough teaching resources, strengthening teacher training programs, and aligning the curriculum with market requirements. By solving these difficulties, Cameroon may develop a more effective and fair educational system that better prepares its students for the future.

iii. *Educational infrastructure:*
Educational infrastructure comprises the physical buildings and resources that enable the delivery of education at institutions such as schools, colleges, and universities. Unfortunately, in many areas of the globe,

educational infrastructure is poor, providing substantial hurdles to the learning process. One noticeable concern is the absence of basic facilities in schools. Clean water, important for hydration and sanitation, is either unavailable or of low quality in many educational facilities. Sanitation facilities, including restrooms and handwashing stations, are often insufficient or non-existent, endangering the health and dignity of children and instructors alike. Additionally, power, vital for current teaching techniques such as multimedia presentations and access to digital resources, is sometimes unstable or absent at schools in underprivileged regions.

The lack of these essential facilities produces a subpar learning environment that hampers student performance and leads to high dropout rates. Without access to clean water and sanitary facilities, pupils may become sick more often, resulting to absenteeism and poor academic success. The absence of energy restricts the use of technology in education, depriving students of opportunity for dynamic and interesting learning experiences. Furthermore, deficient educational infrastructure disproportionately impacts underprivileged populations, compounding existing inequities in access to excellent education. Schools in rural and isolated places are more prone to infrastructure inadequacies owing to limited resources and government prioritizing. Addressing these difficulties needs coordinated efforts from governments, educational institutions, and other stakeholders. Investments in infrastructure renovation initiatives are vital to ensure that all students have access to secure and suitable learning environments. Moreover, measures focused at encouraging sustainable habits, such as water conservation and renewable energy solutions, might help alleviate the effect of infrastructure limits on education. The insufficiency of educational infrastructure, typified by the absence of basic amenities such as clean water, sanitation facilities, and power, impairs the quality of education and perpetuates inequities in learning results. It is vital to prioritize expenditures in infrastructure development to promote inclusive and conducive learning environments for all pupils.

iv. *Teacher Training and Compensation:*

In Cameroon, the field of teacher training and salary provides a multidimensional difficulty. Across the educational landscape, teachers frequently find themselves battling with a confluence of challenges, primary among them being their credentials and salary. A recurring worry centers about the credentials of educators in Cameroon. Many instructors are thought to be underqualified, lacking the requisite training and certifications to successfully transfer information to their pupils. This shortfall in credentials not only impairs the quality of education but also fosters a cycle of insufficiency within the teaching profession. Compounding the problem of credentials is the

evident deficiency of professional development possibilities. Without access to regular training and resources, instructors struggle to remain informed of new teaching approaches and pedagogical breakthroughs. Consequently, the educational experience for pupils suffers, as instructors may depend on obsolete approaches that fail to engage and motivate learning. Beyond professional development, the problem of teacher remuneration looms big. In Cameroon, educators generally battle with inadequate incomes and bad working conditions. This deplorable state of things not only lowers the morale of teachers but also exacerbates the issue of teacher retention. Faced with financial challenges and poor working circumstances, many instructors are obliged to seek employment elsewhere, resulting in disturbingly high turnover rates. Addressing the difficulties surrounding teacher training and remuneration in Cameroon demands a holistic strategy. Efforts must be made to strengthen the credentials of educators via focused training programs and efforts aimed at developing pedagogical abilities. Additionally, emphasizing attractive compensation and improving working conditions may help to motivate outstanding people to continue careers in teaching and alleviate the problem of teacher turnover. Resolving the complexity of teacher training and remuneration in Cameroon is crucial for establishing a conducive learning environment and cultivating the next generation of leaders. By investing in the professional growth and well-being of educators, Cameroon can pave the road for a better future for its education system and the country as a whole.

v. *Gender disparities:*
Gender inequities in education exist as a major topic, with diverse difficulties hampering development. While efforts have been achieved in raising girls' enrollment rates, the path towards gender parity is far from done. A myriad of reasons contributes to this continuing difference, including social conventions and cultural prejudices that promote males' education over girls'. One of the biggest impediments is early marriage, which frequently leads young females to stop their schooling prematurely. Additionally, adolescent pregnancies further increase the dropout rates among females, as they struggle to reconcile the obligations of parenthood with school attendance. These institutional difficulties maintain a cycle of inequity, robbing females of the ability to achieve their academic potential and follow their dreams. Moreover, deep-rooted socio-cultural views continue to devalue female education in many communities. Traditional gender norms and prejudices encourage the perception that females' main task is to accept household chores rather than pursue intellectual achievements. This thinking not only hinders females' educational chances but also promotes greater gender disparities in society. Addressing gender gaps in education needs a comprehensive strategy that targets

both institutional hurdles and social attitudes. Efforts must be taken to eliminate discriminatory practices and create gender-sensitive policies that emphasize girls' education. This involves taking efforts to minimize early marriage and adolescent pregnancies, as well as fighting detrimental assumptions that diminish the importance of girls' learning. Furthermore, empowering females via education not only helps individuals but also has far-reaching ramifications for society as a whole. Educated women are more likely to contribute to economic development, participate in decision-making processes, and fight for gender equality. Therefore, investing in girls' education is not just an issue of social fairness but also a strategic need for sustained growth. Although progress has been achieved in boosting girls' enrollment rates, gender inequities in education continue owing to ingrained societal norms and structural hurdles. Overcoming these problems requires joint efforts from governments, public society, and international organizations to guarantee that all girls have equitable access to excellent education and the chance to achieve their potential.

vi. *Technical and Vocational Education:*

Technical and vocational education (TVET) presents a serious problem in appropriately responding to the needs of today's economy. The skills imparted at vocational training institutes sometimes fail to coincide with the changing needs of the job market, resulting in a considerable gap. This gap between the skills obtained via TVET and those desired by companies exacerbates concerns of unemployment and underemployment. For TVET to successfully meet the urgent requirements of the workforce, a fundamental redesign is essential. This requires not only boosting the quality of education but also guaranteeing its relevance to the growing needs of diverse businesses. A proactive strategy is needed to identify developing skill sets and include them into the curriculum of vocational schools. Additionally, establishing tighter cooperation between educational institutions and companies may give useful insights into the particular skill sets needed by employers. Moreover, investing in state-of-the-art facilities and technology inside vocational training schools is vital to allow hands-on learning experiences. By educating students with practical skills that replicate real-world settings, TVET may better prepare them for smooth transition into the workforce. Furthermore, fostering lifelong learning programs within the TVET framework supports continual skill development, allowing people to adapt to changing market realities throughout their careers. In essence, boosting the relevance and quality of technical and vocational education is crucial for alleviating unemployment and underemployment. By bridging the gap between educational programs and labor market needs, TVET can equip people with the skills essential to flourish in today's competitive job market and contribute significantly to economic growth and development.

vii. *Educational Financing:*

In Cameroon, the sphere of educational funding is marked by a conspicuous insufficiency. The government's provision of cash to education is relatively modest, being a tiny proportion of the entire budget. Consequently, educational institutions regularly find themselves battling with financial restraints, leading them to turn to student fees as a key source of income to support their operations. This excessive dependence on student fees creates a huge obstacle to education for several households throughout the nation. For many, the financial burden caused by these fees proves to be overwhelming, putting access to great education an elusive luxury rather than a basic right. Consequently, a persistent pattern of high dropout rates evolves, as families are compelled to prioritize urgent financial demands above the long-term investment in schooling. The ramifications of this financing shortage ripple across the educational environment, aggravating existing inequities in access and quality. Students from economically disadvantaged homes are disproportionately impacted, thereby expanding the gap in educational performance and perpetuating cycles of poverty and inequality. Addressing the structural shortcomings in school finance is crucial to promote a more equal and inclusive education system in Cameroon. This needs a coordinated effort from both government entities and foreign partners to emphasize education as a critical pillar of development and distribute resources appropriately. Only through ongoing investment and planned interventions can the obstacles to access be addressed, ensuring that every child in Cameroon has the chance to reach their full potential through excellent education.

*C. Interrelation of Healthcare and Education*

The difficulties in healthcare and education are interconnected and have a cascading impact on each other and on the socio-economic development of Cameroon. Poor health may impair educational achievement, since children who are often unwell or hungry are less likely to attend school consistently and do well academically. Similarly, a lack of education may contribute to poor health outcomes, since those with little education are less likely to have the information and means to maintain good health and access healthcare services.

Addressing these difficulties needs a diverse strategy that includes:

- *Improving Infrastructure:* Significant investment in healthcare and educational infrastructure is important to offer a suitable environment for learning and healthcare delivery.
- *Enhancing Quality and Access:* Ensuring that excellent services are available to everybody, regardless of location, is vital.

This involves sending additional healthcare experts and skilled instructors to impoverished communities.
- *Increasing funding:* Adequate financing for both healthcare and education is vital. The government has to prioritize these areas in its budget and seek extra support from foreign donors and private sector collaborations.
- *Promoting Health and Education Synergies:* Integrating health and education activities may have a synergistic impact. For example, school-based health initiatives may enhance kids' health and educational results concurrently.
- *Addressing Gender Disparities:* Special efforts are required to ensure that girls and women have equitable access to healthcare and education. This includes targeted campaigns to minimize early marriages, grant scholarships, and promote gender-sensitive healthcare services.
- *Community Engagement:* Engaging communities in the development and execution of healthcare and education projects may boost their efficacy and sustainability.

In conclusion, healthcare and education are important to the socio-economic growth of Cameroon. Addressing the difficulties in these areas needs extensive and coordinated initiatives to improve infrastructure, enhance quality, raise financing, and promote equality. By investing in the health and education of its population, Cameroon can establish a firm basis for sustainable growth and enhanced quality of life for all its people.

# CHAPTER FOUR

# HUMAN RIGHTS VIOLATIONS

## 4.1 Freedom of Speech and Press

Two essential foundations of democratic society are freedom of speech and the press, which allow people to express their opinions, share information, and hold those in positions of authority responsible. But even though these rights are protected by a number of international treaties and constitutions, they are routinely infringed against all around the world. Human rights breaches pertaining to freedom of expression and the press may take many different forms, from intimidation and censorship to incarceration and harassment.

**a. Censorship in Cameroon:**

In Cameroon, censorship is a widespread problem that reflects larger global patterns in authoritarian governments. Censorship is a common tactic used by governments, like the one in Cameroon, to keep the public under control. This stifling of dissent and suppression of information takes many forms, from overt censorship laws to more covert means of controlling the flow of information. The Cameroonian government often uses the imposition of regulations to limit access to certain websites or publications that are seen to be critical of the system. These regulations attempt to restrict the expression of opposing ideas and keep the public from having access to information that could undermine the legitimacy of the government. Furthermore, media organizations often under pressure from the government to practice self-censorship. If they dare to report on delicate subjects or criticize the government, journalists and reporters are subjected to intimidation methods and threats of retaliation. Because of this, many media outlets choose to stay completely neutral on contentious issues out of concern for what could happen if they speak out against the government. The Cameroonian government uses strategies to maintain control over the digital sector in addition to focusing on conventional media outlets. It's common practice to ban or limit whole web networks and social media platforms to stop the dissemination of information that might contradict the government's narrative. Authorities try to silence opposing opinions and hold onto power by restricting internet speech. All things considered, Cameroonian censorship is the result of a deliberate attempt on the part of the government to control information flow and stifle dissent. The dictatorship seeks to maintain its power and crush any opposition to it by limiting information availability and suppressing freedom of speech. Still, there is a strong network of journalists and activists in Cameroon who are dedicated to reporting the truth and fighting for more freedoms.

**b. Intimidation and Harassment in Cameroon:**

Intimidation and harassment in Cameroon pose major concerns to anyone who attempt to enjoy their basic rights of speech and dissent. Journalists, activists, and regular persons who dare to raise their voices against injustice or oppose the behavior of those in power frequently find themselves targeted by different types of assault. Online trolling and smear campaigns are frequent methods used to denigrate and destroy the credibility of those who speak out. False narratives and malevolent propaganda travel swiftly throughout social media platforms, ruining the names of activists and journalists alike. However, the hazards extend beyond the digital domain. Physical violence and assaults are not prevalent, with people facing the danger of physical damage or even death for daring to defy the existing quo. Assassinations of outspoken voices serve as stark reminders of the consequences connected with speaking truth to power. The persistent climate of dread established by such intimidation measures seeks to quiet criticism and dissuade others from sharing their ideas. The fear of punishment looms large, driving many to self-censor or stop from participating in action entirely. In this environment of fear and constraint, the right to free speech becomes a distant ideal rather than a palpable reality. Upholding the foundations of democracy and defending the rights of people to speak out against injustice is crucial to establishing a society where all voices are heard and appreciated. Efforts to counteract intimidation and harassment must be priority to guarantee the preservation of basic freedoms for all residents of Cameroon.

**c. Legal Restrictions:**

In Cameroon, legal restrictions are purportedly established under the guise of safeguarding national security or maintaining public order. However, these laws frequently serve as tools to stifle dissent and muzzle journalistic freedom. The criminalization of defamation, sedition, and dissemination of "false news" is frequently manipulated to target journalists and activists who uncover corruption or question official narratives. Furthermore, stringent anti-terrorism legislation might be exploited to quash genuine political opposition or marginalize minority perspectives. Such legal frameworks can pose significant challenges to the exercise of fundamental rights and the promotion of transparent governance within the country.

**d. Detention and Legal Proceedings in Cameroon:**

A concerning trend of repression via incarceration and legal action plagues the environment of free speech in Cameroon. Authorities often target journalists, bloggers, and activists, subjecting them to arbitrary detention, arrest, and prosecution on false allegations. These acts are a means of suppressing voices that are critical of the government and of opposition. In particular, the flagrant disrespect for due process is worrisome. Many people who are incarcerated lose their basic rights because they are unable to get legal counsel or fair trials. They face unjust court processes that are sometimes prearranged to produce punitive results, rather than being given the chance to defend themselves. These unfair actions have dire repercussions. If found guilty under these conditions, offenders risk long jail terms or, in extreme situations, the death penalty. Their right to free speech is violated, and others who may consider speaking out against injustices are likewise made afraid by this. These acts have a chilling impact on society as a whole, fostering a climate of fear and self-censorship. People are discouraged from using their own rights to free speech and protest when they see the harsh consequences suffered by those who dare to speak truth to power. To put it simply, the deliberate persecution of bloggers, journalists, and activists in Cameroon not only robs people of their rights but also threatens the basic principles of democracy and human rights. Rather than using coercive methods to stay in power, the government should protect basic liberties and adhere to the ideals of justice.

e. **The prevalence of cyberattacks and digital surveillance in Cameroon:**
Government surveillance and cyberwarfare have become more common in Cameroon as a result of the digital revolution. In order to monitor online communications, track the activities of journalists and activists, and identify potential sources of unrest, authorities have developed complex surveillance systems due to the widespread use of technology. Authorities may identify persons or organizations that are considered threats to the established order by carefully monitoring online activity with the use of this digital surveillance infrastructure. In addition, Cameroonian cyberwarfare is changing quickly. Cyberattacks with malevolent intent are increasingly targeting human rights groups and independent media sources. The goal of these assaults, which are often well-planned and sophisticated, is to undermine these organizations by interfering with their business processes or obtaining private information. These attacks jeopardize these organizations' capacity to protect basic freedoms and operate with efficacy, posing serious challenges to their security and integrity. The repercussions of unrestrained monitoring and cyberattacks are extensive, and the stakes are high in this digital war. They corrode not only the foundations of a democratic society but also personal privacy

and freedom of speech. Strong cybersecurity defenses and alertness against digital intrusions on civil freedoms are progressively necessary as Cameroon negotiates this challenging environment.

**f. Corporate Complicity:**

Corporate complicity in Cameroon refers to the engagement of digital corporations and social media platforms in actions that encourage or facilitate human rights abuses in the nation. These firms possess tremendous power over the diffusion of information and the molding of public opinion. While they have the power to support free expression and democratize access to information, they are also open to criticism for their involvement in censorship, distribution of false information, and amplification of hate speech. In several instances, these platforms have been accused of partnering with authoritarian governments in Cameroon to filter content or supply user data, so contributing in the repression of dissent and increasing human rights violations. This partnership with authoritarian regimes not only contradicts the ideals of free speech and expression but also contributes to the maintenance of injustices against vulnerable people. Tech corporations and social media platforms must realize their position as significant players in global communication and accept responsibility for the repercussions of their activities. By emphasizing ethical standards and following human rights values, these corporations may limit their role in enabling repression and contribute positively to the development of free and open societies in Cameroon and abroad.

In order to address abuses of human rights pertaining to press and speech freedom, governments, civil society groups, the media, and the international community must work together. Protecting journalists and whistleblowers, maintaining the independence of the court, and upholding the rule of law are essential measures in defending these basic rights. Furthermore, establishing media plurality, advancing digital literacy, and holding state and non-state actors responsible for their acts are critical to establishing an atmosphere that supports and nurtures freedom of speech. In the end, defending these rights is not only required by law but also by morality, since it is essential to the growth of democracy, responsibility, and human dignity.

## 4.2 Arbitrary Arrests and Detentions

In Cameroon, arbitrary arrests and detentions have been a continuous problem, adding to the larger range of human rights breaches affecting the nation. The government's security services, including the police and military, have repeatedly deployed arbitrary arrests and detentions as a method to repress dissent, crush political opposition, and retain control over the populace. This practice has notably increased in places impacted by continuing hostilities, such as the Anglophone issue in the Northwest and Southwest regions.

One of the key reasons of arbitrary arrests and detentions in Cameroon is the government's crackdown on persons and organizations viewed as threats to its power or national unity. Dissidents, human rights activists, journalists, and members of opposition parties are routinely targeted without appropriate legal grounds. They are regularly subjected to arbitrary arrest as a method to stifle their voices and dissuade others from speaking out against government policies or abuses. The legal structure regulating arrests and detentions in Cameroon lacks transparency and accountability, allowing security agents to imprison persons arbitrarily with impunity. The Cameroonian Penal Code offers sweeping powers to law enforcement organizations, enabling them to arrest and imprison persons for loosely defined crimes such as "attempted destabilization of institutions" or "threatening national security." This ambiguity gives authorities with significant freedom to interpret and enforce the legislation arbitrarily, ultimately undermining the rule of law and due process rights. Furthermore, arbitrary arrests and detentions are sometimes accompanied by other types of human rights violations, including torture, extrajudicial murders, and enforced disappearances. Detainees are regularly detained incommunicado, denied access to legal counsel, and subjected to protracted periods of pre-trial custody without being officially charged or brought before a court. These methods contradict both local and international legal principles, including the right to a fair trial and the prohibition of torture and cruel, inhuman, or degrading treatment. The problem is aggravated by the absence of adequate supervision measures to hold offenders responsible and offer remedies for victims of arbitrary arrests and detentions. Despite periodic condemnations from international human rights groups and diplomatic pressure from other countries, the Cameroonian authorities have shown little desire to confront these systemic flaws or enact serious changes. In conflict-affected areas like the Anglophone regions, the use of arbitrary arrests and detentions has escalated as part of the government's counterinsurgency operations against separatist organizations. Security forces have been accused of unjustly arresting hundreds of persons suspected of supporting or sympathizing with the separatist movement, including activists, community leaders, and even children. Many of these prisoners are confined in overcrowded and filthy circumstances in improvised detention camps, where they are at danger of torture, sexual assault, and other sorts of abuse. The prevalent culture of impunity surrounding arbitrary arrests and detentions in Cameroon not only weakens the country's democratic institutions and respect for human rights but also perpetuates cycles of violence and instability. Addressing this problem needs broad changes to improve the rule of law, promote judicial independence, and guarantee accountability for security forces' activities. It also demands real communication and participation with impacted communities to address the underlying grievances fuelling conflict and foster reconciliation and social harmony. Until these actions are implemented, arbitrary arrests and detentions will continue to damage the rights and dignity of the Cameroonian people, aggravating the country's human rights situation.

## 4.3 Treatment of Minorities

There are more than 250 different ethnic groups living in Cameroon, a nation in Central Africa with a rich cultural diversity. Each group has its own language and cultural history. Cameroon has had serious problems with regard to the treatment of minorities notwithstanding its great variety. Various sorts of human rights breaches, such as political marginalization and economic and social discrimination, have been seen as a result of these issues. Examining the historical background, contemporary problems, and particular instances of human rights breaches, this section explores how minorities are treated in Cameroon. The colonial history of Cameroon, which included periods of domination by the Germans, the British, and the French, has had a considerable impact on the country's political and ethnic environment. The partition of the nation between areas that speak English

(Anglophone) and French (Francophone) has resulted in a conflict that has persisted for a long time between these two populations. After the country gained its independence, the Francophone-dominated administration consolidated power and resources, which intensified sentiments of marginalization among the Anglophone community as well as other ethnic minorities.

## A. Political Marginalization
### i. Anglophone Crisis:

One of the most obvious instances of problems with minority treatment in Cameroon is the turmoil that has been affecting the Anglophone community. During the year 2016, Anglophone attorneys and educators staged demonstrations against the imposition of French legal and educational systems in their own areas. This was the beginning of the crisis. Historically, Cameroon is split into Francophone and Anglophone areas owing to its colonial history, when the nation was partitioned between French and British colonial administration. Anglophone areas, which account for around twenty percent of the total population, have unique legal and educational systems that are based on the traditions of the United Kingdom. However, throughout the years, there has been a gradual deterioration of these institutions as the central government, controlled by Francophones, has progressively imposed French administrative procedures. These nonviolent rallies were met with severe repression by the government, resulting to widespread instability. The government's

reaction includes arbitrary arrests, torture, and extrajudicial murders, substantially hurting the Anglophone community. Security forces were mobilized to quell the rallies, and allegations surfaced of savage crackdowns, including the use of live fire against unarmed protestors, extensive arrests of activists and bystanders, and the burning of towns suspected of sheltering separatists. This heavy-handed attitude inflamed tensions and created a feeling of unfairness and marginalization within the Anglophone population. The dispute grew into a violent confrontation, with separatist organizations seeking independence for the Anglophone areas, which they name Ambazonia. These organizations say that the only answer to their problems is total independence from Cameroon, given the central government's failure to meet their requests for increased autonomy and respect for their cultural and legal legacy. The battle has resulted in thousands of fatalities and displaced hundreds of thousands, causing a major humanitarian catastrophe. Entire villages have been uprooted, with many fleeing to neighboring Nigeria or becoming internally displaced inside Cameroon. The fighting has also resulted to the destruction of infrastructure, schools, and healthcare institutions, further compounding the misery of the impacted populace. The government's heavy-handed stance and failure to address the problems of the Anglophone minority have been strongly condemned by human rights groups. International agencies like as Amnesty International and Human Rights Watch have recorded several human rights violations perpetrated by both government troops and separatist combatants. These include extrajudicial executions, arbitrary detentions, and torture. Additionally, there have been demands for the Cameroonian government to engage in genuine engagement with the Anglophone leaders to find a peaceful end to the conflict. Despite various attempts at mediation, including moves by the African Union and the United Nations, a durable solution has proved elusive, and the situation continues to worsen, with catastrophic implications for the civilian population caught in the crossfire.

**ii. Political Representation:**

In Cameroon, ethnic minorities have significant obstacles when it comes to political participation. Under the decades-long leadership of President Paul Biya, the Cameroon People's Democratic Movement (CPDM) dominates the country's political scene. Minority groups have been consistently sidelined by this supremacy, giving them little clout or influence in the political system. Frequently criticized for its flaws, the Cameroonian election system is the subject of several accusations of fraud and manipulation. These problems impede the democratic process and impede the different ethnic composition of the nation from being fairly represented. There are several ways that this marginalization

appears. Minority groups often discover that they are shut out of important political roles and procedures. Their unique needs and concerns are not sufficiently addressed at the national level due to their lack of representation. As a result, development initiatives and policies often serve the interests of the prevailing groups, which exacerbates the socioeconomic divide between ethnic communities. There is a noticeable feeling of disenfranchisement among ethnic minorities. Many believe that the political system is biased against them and that their ballots are not valid. This impression is exacerbated by the concentration of power in the hands of a small number of people, mostly members of the governing party, which stifles political plurality and reduces the chances for significant engagement in the political process. Minority groups are thus often forced to depend on unofficial, grassroots networks—which are less effective and more susceptible to governmental repression—to defend their rights and interests. Ethnic conflicts in Cameroon have also been made worse by the absence of political representation. A feeling of unfairness and inequity is cultivated when minority groups are routinely shut out of the political sphere. Because underprivileged people may turn to rallies and other forms of resistance to air their complaints, this may deepen social fragmentation and conflict. This has sometimes led to violent altercations, further destabilizing the area and starting a vicious cycle of discontent and repression. Cameroon's election malpractice-plagued political system, which is controlled by the CPDM, does not adequately represent the ethnic variety of the nation. Ethnic minorities now face serious difficulties as a result, such as marginalization, disenfranchisement, and heightened tensions. To guarantee equitable representation and the participation of all ethnic groups in the political process, addressing these concerns calls for extensive political changes.

**B. Social and Economic Discrimination:**
**i. Economic Inequality:**

Economic differences between different regions and ethnic groups in Cameroon are severe. The northern regions, which are home to the Fulani and other ethnic minorities, are among the poorest in the nation. These areas suffer from underdevelopment, lack of infrastructure, and restricted access to essential services such as healthcare and education. The government's neglect of these communities has created a cycle of poverty and marginalization. In the northern regions, economic activity are predominantly agricultural, with a major dependency on subsistence farming and animal raising. However, these operations are typically impeded by irregular weather patterns, low soil fertility, and restricted access to modern agricultural methods and inputs. This lack of economic diversification renders the northern population exposed to natural shocks and economic downturns, aggravating their financial instability. In contrast, the southern

and central regions of Cameroon, which contain important towns like Yaoundé and Douala, have somewhat better economic circumstances. These locations benefit from more extensive government investment in infrastructure, healthcare, and education. Additionally, they host a bigger percentage of the country's industrial and commercial operations, giving more job possibilities and contributing to a better quality of life. The gap in government resource distribution between the north and south is a crucial component in the economic imbalance. Access to education in the northern areas is extremely restricted. Schools are generally under-resourced, with a scarcity of trained instructors, poor infrastructure, and insufficient teaching resources. This educational deficit adds to poor literacy rates and hinders the youth's ability to develop skills essential for improved work possibilities. In contrast, educational institutions in the southern and central areas are better equipped and provide more extensive educational programs, giving students with greater opportunities for future employment. Healthcare services in the north are equally undeveloped. There are fewer hospitals and clinics, and those that do typically lack vital medical supplies and competent healthcare staff. This deficiency leads to greater incidence of avoidable illnesses and maternal and newborn death. Conversely, the southern and central areas have more established healthcare infrastructures, with more access to medical services and better health outcomes. The absence of infrastructure in the northern areas further limits economic growth. Poor road networks hinder access to marketplaces, making it difficult for farmers to sell their goods or obtain required supplies. Additionally, the lack of consistent power and water supply constrains both everyday living circumstances and the possibility for industrial activity. The economic marginalization of the northern areas is also reflected in political representation and influence. Ethnic minorities in the north have long been underrepresented in the national government, resulting in their demands and challenges getting less attention in national policies and development projects. This political indifference fosters the cycle of poverty, since these places remain deprived of crucial investments and prospects for progress. Efforts to redress these economic imbalances have been intermittent and inadequate. While there have been some government efforts aimed at upgrading infrastructure and social services in the northern areas, they have frequently been poorly handled and lack the requisite size to have a substantial effect. International assistance and development projects have also been adopted, although they too have experienced issues such as corruption, mismanagement, and insufficient local participation. Breaking the cycle of poverty and marginalization in Cameroon's northern regions demands a diversified strategy. It requires major investment in infrastructure, healthcare, and education, with measures to encourage economic diversification and resilience. Enhancing political representation and ensuring that the opinions of the Fulani and other ethnic minorities are heard in national decision-making processes is also vital. Only through persistent and inclusive development policies will the economic imbalances of Cameroon be properly addressed, leading to a more fair and prosperous future for all its regions and people.

**ii. Access to Education and Healthcare:**

Minority populations typically encounter substantial difficulties in obtaining education and healthcare. Schools in minority areas are usually underfunded, with infrastructure that is often subpar and resources that are insufficient to satisfy the requirements of the pupils. These schools may lack fundamental resources such as libraries, labs, and even suitable classrooms, which greatly affects the learning environment. The dearth of trained instructors exacerbates these challenges, since the few educators available are typically overwhelmed by huge class numbers and insufficient instructional resources. This condition produces a circle of educational disadvantage, as kids in minority regions are unable to acquire the quality education required to better their socio-economic standing. The language barrier is another major challenge that minority groups encounter, especially in locations where the prevailing language of teaching is not their native tongue. In Anglophone communities, for example, the imposition of French in schools has been a cause of substantial disagreement. Students who are not proficient in French struggle to grasp the curriculum, resulting to low academic achievement and greater dropout rates. This language difference not only affects students' capacity to study but also impairs their confidence and willingness to continue school. Healthcare facilities in minority neighborhoods are typically substandard, reflecting a greater disregard of these populations. Hospitals and clinics may be under-resourced, missing crucial medical supplies and equipment. There is usually a lack of medical staff, including physicians, nurses, and specialists, which means that inhabitants sometimes have to travel significant distances to receive essential healthcare services. This lack of access may lead to untreated diseases, greater death rates, and a general decrease in the overall health of the population. Preventive treatment and health education, which are vital for preserving public health, are sometimes poor or altogether lacking in these locations. The neglect of education and healthcare in minority populations has serious effects for their well-being and growth. Without access to decent education, people are less likely to acquire well-paying employment, continuing a cycle of poverty. Poor health infrastructure implies that avoidable illnesses may become life-threatening, and chronic problems go uncontrolled, resulting to poor quality of life and lower life expectancy. This systematic neglect not only affects the personal growth of people within these communities but also stifles the economic and social advancement of the places they live. Addressing these disparities requires a multifaceted approach, including increased funding for schools and healthcare facilities in minority areas, targeted recruitment and training of qualified teachers and medical professionals, and policies that respect and incorporate the linguistic and cultural diversity of minority groups. Ensuring fair access to education and healthcare is vital for supporting inclusive growth and increasing the overall quality of life for minority communities.

## C. Cultural Discrimination
### i. Language and Identity:

Language has a key part in the cultural identity of Cameroon's ethnic minorities. In a nation as linguistically varied as Cameroon, where over 250 languages are spoken, language serves not only as a method of communication but also as a symbol of cultural legacy and identity. Each ethnic group in Cameroon values their language as a representation of its distinct customs, history, and worldview. These languages are vital for the transfer of cultural practices, oral histories, and traditional knowledge from one generation to the next. They generate a feeling of belonging and pride among community members, reaffirming their particular identity within the greater national framework. However, the dominance of French in official and public life marginalizes people who do not speak the language well. As a legacy of colonial control, French has been established as the dominant language of government, education, and business in Cameroon. This predominance presents substantial difficulties for persons from ethnic minorities who may not have the same skill in French. The emphasis on French for official issues implies that people who are not proficient experience difficulties in obtaining government services, engaging in political processes, and getting job chances. This language marginalization extends to the public domain, where French predominates in media, signs, and public discourse, further isolating non-French speakers. The imposition of French in schools and governmental contexts in Anglophone areas has been a serious issue, since it weakens the cultural and linguistic legacy of the Anglophone community. In the English-speaking areas of Northwest and Southwest Cameroon, there is a strong history of using English and local languages. However, the central government's policies have frequently prioritized French, resulting local tensions and disputes. The education system, in particular, has been a battlefield where the imposition of French-language curriculum and the recruitment of French-speaking administrators are regarded as attempts to integrate Anglophones into the Francophone majority. This apparent cultural imperialism has fostered discontent and a feeling of unfairness among Anglophones, who believe their identity and language rights are being destroyed. The opposition to French domination in Anglophone areas is not simply about language but also about maintaining cultural autonomy and defending the right to self-determination. Language is strongly connected with identity, and for many Anglophones, the campaign for bilingualism or even a return to a more English-focused educational and governmental system is a chance to recover their cultural heritage. The battle for language rights is therefore part of a wider movement for social and political recognition, attempting to heal past injustices and establish a more inclusive and egalitarian Cameroon. Language is a crucial part of cultural identity for Cameroon's ethnic minorities. The prevalence of French marginalizes non-French speakers, especially in Anglophone areas, where the imposition of French in schools and government contexts is perceived as a threat to their cultural and linguistic legacy. This language marginalization is a source of great grievance and is at the center of wider social and political movements for recognition and equality.

### ii. Indigenous Peoples:

Indigenous peoples of Cameroon, such as the Baka, Bakola, and Mbororo, experience significant discrimination and human rights violations. These groups are routinely forcefully evacuated from their ancestral lands to make room for development projects, logging, and conservation activities. The destruction of their land has catastrophic repercussions on their traditional way of life, food security, and cultural customs. The Baka, Bakola, and Mbororo peoples have lived in peace with their environment for decades, depending on the woods for subsistence, medicine, and spiritual traditions. The rupture of this link owing to evictions and land grabs leads to a loss of biodiversity and environmental degradation, further worsening their marginalization. Moreover, the relocation sometimes drives individuals into new and even unfriendly surroundings where they struggle to adapt and retain their cultural identity. Additionally, indigenous peoples typically lack legal recognition and protection, making it harder for them to assert their rights and receive justice. The legal structure of Cameroon does not fully respect the land rights of indigenous peoples, leaving them susceptible to exploitation and relocation. Without legal recognition, these groups confront substantial difficulties in lobbying for their rights and seeking compensation for their losses. Furthermore, indigenous peoples typically confront systematic discrimination in obtaining education, healthcare, and job opportunities, creating cycles of poverty and social isolation. The marginalization of indigenous populations is reinforced by a lack of political representation, restricting their capacity to influence policies that impact their lives and well-being. Efforts to solve these difficulties are typically impeded by a lack of political will and resources, as well as by established social views that denigrate indigenous traditions and contributions. Despite significant national and international initiatives to promote indigenous rights, the implementation of protective measures remains uneven and inadequate. Advocacy groups and non-governmental organizations play a critical role in increasing awareness and pressing for the implementation of indigenous rights, but their efforts are frequently met with hostility from strong economic and political interests. The predicament of indigenous peoples in Cameroon underlines the need for a more inclusive and equitable approach to development, one that respects and incorporates the rights and knowledge of indigenous populations. Addressing these concerns needs collective work from the government, civil society, and the international community to ensure that the views of indigenous peoples are heard and their rights protected.

## D. Human Rights Violations and International Response

Numerous human rights groups, notably Amnesty International and Human Rights Watch, have recorded extensive violations against minorities in Cameroon. These transgressions involve a variety of grave human rights abuses, including as arbitrary imprisonment, torture, extrajudicial murders, and the damage of property. Arbitrary imprisonment refers to the practice of imprisoning persons without due process or legal grounds, typically targeting those who are viewed as opponents of the government or members of minority groups. Torture includes the deliberate inflicting of extreme pain or suffering, either physical or psychological, and is used to intimidate, punish, or extort information from captives. Extrajudicial murders, when persons are slain by state or non-state entities without legal processes, further show the lawlessness and cruelty endured by minorities. Additionally, the destruction of property, including houses, businesses, and community infrastructures, not only displaces people but also devastates their livelihoods and exacerbates the humanitarian catastrophe. The international world has voiced major concern about the situation in Cameroon, encouraging the Cameroonian government to address the core causes of the disputes and assure the preservation of minority rights. This worry is fueled by reports and personal experiences of the systematic nature of these violations, which imply an intentional campaign to isolate and persecute minority communities. The United Nations and other international entities have constantly urged for dialogue and reconciliation as crucial measures to settle the Anglophone problem and address the larger complaints of minority populations. The Anglophone conflict, in particular, derives from persistent political and cultural difficulties between the mostly Francophone central authority and the Anglophone areas, where citizens have complained of marginalization and discrimination. Despite these appeals for discussion and healing, the Cameroonian government's reaction has been mostly characterized by denial and sustained brutality. This policy involves denying charges of human rights violations, limiting access to impacted regions for impartial observers, and expanding military operations against separatist organizations and civilians. The government's continued denial not only damages trust but also prevents any genuine progress towards resolving the conflict and achieving justice for victims. Continued repression exacerbates the situation, leading to greater human rights abuses and extending the cycle of violence and instability. The international community's efforts for accountability and reform are vital in forcing the Cameroonian administration to alter its direction. However, attaining sustainable peace and justice needs a coordinated effort from both domestic and foreign players to address the underlying challenges, promote inclusive government, and preserve the rights of all individuals.

In summary, The treatment of minorities in Cameroon reveals important human rights concerns that the government confronts. Political marginalization, economic and social discrimination, and cultural restriction have produced a climate of systematic inequity and conflict. The political environment of Cameroon is strongly biased against minority groups, frequently barring them from meaningful involvement in governance and decision-making processes. This exclusion exacerbates sentiments of disenfranchisement and promotes animosity between various ethnic and regional groupings. Economically, minority populations typically encounter difficulties to obtaining resources, education, and work opportunities, resulting to entrenched poverty and social injustice. Social discrimination further complicates these challenges, since minority groups are typically vulnerable to prejudice and uneven treatment in several parts of everyday life.

Cultural oppression is another major part of the issues encountered by minorities in Cameroon. Many minority groups fight to retain their cultural history, languages, and customs in the face of mainstream cultural narratives that strive to homogenize the national identity. This restriction not only erodes cultural variety but also alienates minority populations, widening the gulf between them and the dominant population. The combination of these elements produces a hostile climate where minority rights are regularly infringed, and their voices are ignored. Addressing these difficulties needs a joint effort by the Cameroonian administration, civil society, and the international community. The government must take proactive efforts to foster inclusive governance by ensuring that minority groups are effectively represented in political institutions and have a role in decisions. Legal and institutional changes are important to preserve minority rights and to abolish the structural impediments that perpetuate inequality. Civil society groups serve a critical role in lobbying for minority rights, increasing awareness about their condition, and holding the government responsible for its actions. The international community also has a duty to support these efforts via political pressure, development money, and technical help. International human rights groups may aid by exposing violations, offering venues for minority views, and campaigning for legislative reforms at the global level. Additionally, building a culture of respect and understanding among the many ethnic groups of Cameroon is crucial. This encompasses educational activities that encourage intercultural conversation, tolerance, and mutual respect. Without genuine changes and a commitment to justice, the cycle of violence and marginalization is likely to continue. The endurance of such circumstances threatens Cameroon's stability and development, since unresolved ethnic and regional conflicts may lead to continuous conflict and impair national cohesiveness. Therefore, a comprehensive strategy that tackles the political, economic, social, and cultural components of minority marginalization is vital for ensuring enduring peace and prosperity in Cameroon.

# CHAPTER FIVE

## ENVIRONMENTAL CONCERNS

Cameroon, is blessed with abundant biodiversity and a range of habitats, including forests, savannas, and wetlands. However, the nation has enormous environmental concerns that jeopardize its natural riches and biodiversity. These issues include deforestation, pollution, climate change, and the loss of natural resources.

### 5.1 Deforestation

Deforestation is one of the most important environmental challenges in Cameroon. The nation is home to part of the Congo Basin, which has the second-largest tropical rainforest in the world after the Amazon. This forest is a key carbon sink, biodiversity hotspot, and a crucial resource for local residents. Despite its significance, Cameroon's woods are under significant danger from a mix of logging, agricultural expansion, infrastructural development, and criminal activities.

## A. Causes of Deforerstation in Cameroon:
### i. Logging:
- **Commercial Logging:**

Commercial logging in Cameroon is a difficult topic, typified by the continuous pursuit of profit at the price of environmental protection. The verdant woods of Cameroon, previously brimming with varied flora and animals, are now suffering the unrelenting assault of large-scale logging operations. These operations, driven mostly by worldwide demand for wood, have done catastrophic harm on the country's fragile ecosystems. Legal and illicit logging operations have grown ubiquitous, with both contributing considerably to deforestation. While the government of Cameroon provides logging concessions in an effort to control the business, the enforcement of sustainable standards remains a glaring failure. This inadequate monitoring has empowered many logging businesses to prioritize short-term benefits above the long-term health of the ecosystem. The repercussions of this unfettered exploitation are grave. Vast expanses of virgin forest are being ravaged, leading to habitat loss for innumerable species of plants and animals. Moreover, deforestation exacerbates climate change by releasing carbon held in trees into the atmosphere, adding to global warming. Despite rising concerns from environmentalists and local people, the temptation of profit continues to fuel the unrelenting pursuit of wood exploitation. Urgent action is required to address this critical problem, including tightening legislation, increasing enforcement mechanisms, and encouraging sustainable forestry practices. Only through sustained efforts can Cameroon expect to conserve its outstanding natural legacy for future generations.

- **Illegal Logging:**

Illegal logging presents a huge danger to forests globally, with disastrous environmental, social, and economic effects. In nations like Cameroon, where illicit logging is common, the issue is frequently driven by corruption and a lack of implementation of existing rules. When wood is harvested illegally, it indicates that it is done without the required authority or in violation of restrictions imposed by the government. This may lead to deforestation, habitat damage, and loss of biodiversity. It also deprives local populations of key natural resources and may rise to disputes over land and resources. One of the primary motivations of illicit logging is the need for wood products, both locally and globally. Corruption among authorities responsible for regulating logging operations may lead to the granting of fake licenses or turning a blind eye to unlawful actions. Additionally, insufficient enforcement of rules and regulations makes it simpler for illegal loggers to operate with impunity. Addressing illegal logging involves a multi-faceted strategy that includes strengthening governance, boosting law enforcement, promoting sustainable forest management techniques, and confronting the underlying causes of deforestation, such as demand for wood products. Collaboration between governments, civil society groups, and the commercial sector is important to successfully addressing this problem and safeguarding the world's forests for future generations.

### ii. Agricultural Expansion:
- **Small-scare Farming:**

In Cameroon, small-scale farming is a popular practice among rural communities. Here, subsistence agriculture reigns supreme, with farmers depending on the land to satisfy their fundamental requirements. However, the techniques deployed in this agricultural goal typically come at a considerable cost to the environment. One prominent approach adopted by farmers is slash-and-burn agriculture. This approach includes chopping down trees and bushes before setting fire to the rubble to clear area for farming. While initially beneficial in generating arable land, it comes with terrible implications in the long term. One of the fundamental downsides of slash-and-burn farming is its unsustainability. The ongoing destruction of forests for agricultural reasons depletes the land of its natural resources at an alarming pace. This technique leads to soil deterioration, since the nutrient-rich topsoil is eroded away by wind and rain, leaving behind infertile ground unsuited for agriculture. Furthermore, the loss of forest cover exacerbates environmental challenges such as deforestation and habitat damage. Forests serve a key role in preserving ecological balance, providing homes for various flora and animals, and moderating local temperatures. By recklessly removing enormous areas of wooded land, farmers break this delicate balance, inflicting catastrophic damage to the ecosystem. In addition to environmental difficulties, slash-and-burn agriculture also causes considerable challenges for local populations. As forest cover disappears, so too does the availability of natural resources upon which many rural populations rely for their livelihoods. This may lead to food insecurity, as well as greater rivalry for decreasing resources among nearby groups. In light of these concerns, there is an urgent need for sustainable agriculture techniques in Cameroon. Initiatives focused at fostering agroforestry, soil conservation, and land-use planning may help offset the negative consequences of slash-and-burn agriculture while guaranteeing the long-term sustainability of small-scale farming. By adopting more ecologically friendly practices, farmers may develop the land without jeopardizing the health of the ecosystem upon which they depend.

- **Commercial Agriculture:**

Recent years have seen a sharp increase in Cameroon's commercial agriculture, particularly in the production of cash commodities like oil palm, cocoa, and rubber. Nevertheless, the nation's forests have suffered greatly as a result of this growth. Commercial plantations need a lot of land to be cleared for their creation, which causes deforestation in many different parts of Cameroon. The intensification of agricultural operations has been pushed by the demand for these cash crops on both local and international markets, as businesses want to take advantage of the profitable prospects these commodities bring. Large tracts of formerly wooded land have therefore been transformed into monoculture plantations, where these crops are grown extensively. Large tracts of cleared land are needed for oil palm, cocoa, and rubber plantations in order to cultivate and develop these crops. Important forest ecosystems and biodiversity are lost as a result of this procedure, which entails removing trees and other plants. In addition, deforestation damages local populations' livelihoods that rely on trees for their subsistence and cultural identity, exacerbates environmental degradation, and accelerates climate change. The growing commercial agricultural sector in Cameroon highlights the urgent need for sustainable land management strategies that strike a balance between environmental preservation and economic growth. In order to protect Cameroon's unique biodiversity, maintain important ecosystem services, and guarantee the long-term viability of its agricultural sector, it is imperative that efforts be made to prevent deforestation and encourage responsible land use.

### iii. Infrastructure Development:
- **Road Construction:**

Construction of roads in Cameroon has been a major catalyst for deforestation, playing a crucial part in the country's efforts to expand its infrastructure. Constructing roads and highways often requires the removal of large wooded regions to provide space for new pathways. The act of deforestation directly leads to the disappearance of extensive areas of forest, which play a crucial role in preserving biodiversity and capturing carbon. Furthermore, the consequences of constructing roads go beyond the immediate deforestation. The recently constructed roads and highways provide access to formerly isolated and hard-to-reach regions, enhancing their accessibility for human endeavors. The enhanced accessibility enables loggers to easily access and use forest regions that were previously difficult to reach. Logging, regardless of its legality, contributes to more deforestation when trees are cut down for the extraction of wood and other forest resources. Road development not only facilitates logging but also enables agricultural growth. Agricultural expansion occurs when farmers migrate to more accessible regions, transforming forested areas into cultivated fields. This agricultural encroachment adds to a cycle of deforestation; as additional forest areas are removed to accommodate the rising need for cropland. The implementation of agriculture often results in the formation of villages and infrastructure to facilitate the development of agricultural communities, hence intensifying the depletion of forests. The environmental impacts of road development in Cameroon are diverse. The loss of forest cover disturbs local ecosystems, harming animal habitats and lowering biodiversity. Forests serve a key role in regulating the climate by absorbing carbon dioxide, and their removal adds to increasing greenhouse gas emissions, aggravating climate change. Additionally, deforestation may lead to soil erosion and degradation, reducing the fertility of the land and the health of neighboring water bodies. Efforts to reduce the detrimental consequences of road development on Cameroon's forests need a balanced approach. Sustainable development techniques, such as adopting tight logging rules and fostering reforestation projects, are crucial to protecting the country's natural resources. Additionally, including local populations in conservation efforts and ensuring that infrastructure projects are designed with environmental concerns in mind may help decrease the unfavorable consequences of construction of roads on Cameroon's forests.

- **Urbanization:**

The deforestation problems in Cameroon are mostly a result of the country's urbanization. The clearance of forest land is a direct cause of the fast expansion of cities and the creation of new towns. Numerous socioeconomic considerations, such as population increase, migration from rural to urban regions, and the desire for improved living circumstances and employment possibilities in metropolitan areas, are the main drivers of this development. Large areas of forest land are thus being transformed into commercial, industrial, and residential zones. Urban centers are experiencing population growth, which makes building housing, infrastructure, and public facilities necessary. Due to this need, woods are cleared to create room for new infrastructure, services, and buildings. Furthermore, the absence of sustainable practices and thorough planning in urban areas typically accelerates the destruction of trees. Informal settlements have a major role in deforestation since they usually develop near cities that are expanding quickly. Usually, these towns are built without appropriate regulations, which allows them to expand uncontrolled into wooded areas. Furthermore, the growth of agricultural lands on the edges of Cameroon's towns often coincides with the country's urbanization. The necessity for food production rises with the number of people living in cities. In order to provide room for the growing of crops and the grazing of animals, this agricultural growth often requires the removal of forest area. As a consequence, there is a notable loss of forest cover as a result of the combined effects of urbanization and agricultural growth. Such deforestation has significant negative effects on the ecosystem. In order to sustain biodiversity, maintain the ecological balance, and control temperature, forests are essential. Many plant and animal species in Cameroon are at risk of extinction due to habitat damage brought on by the loss of wooded regions. In addition, it worsens climate change by reducing carbon sequestration, upsetting water cycles, and causing soil erosion. The fast urbanization caused by population expansion and economic progress in Cameroon results in substantial deforestation. Cities are becoming larger and new settlements are being built on top of wooded regions, which is causing serious environmental damage and the loss of the essential ecological services that forests offer.

**iv. Mining:**

- **Mineral Extraction:**

In Cameroon, the exploitation of minerals has a major negative influence on the environment, especially via deforestation. The nation's abundant mineral reserves, including bauxite, diamonds, gold, and other elements, draw significant mining activity. Large tracts of forest must be cleared for these activities in order to make room for extraction sites, access roads, and other infrastructure. Large areas of trees and other vegetation are cut down by mining firms when they enter wooded areas in order to extract the minerals underneath them. This practice disturbs local ecosystems and biodiversity in addition to destroying habitats. Another significant cause of deforestation is the building of access roads. Heavy machinery, equipment, and harvested minerals must be transported along these highways. Many trees must often be chopped down in order to build these routes through deep woods, which splits the forest and makes previously unreachable regions more accessible to exploitation and human activity. This fragmentation may hasten deforestation by encouraging more human intrusion, illicit logging, and agricultural growth. Furthermore, additional area must be cleared in order to build the infrastructure needed for mining activities, such as processing plants, worker housing, and storage facilities.

The aforementioned developments exacerbate the immediate effects of mining by expanding the deforested region and causing soil erosion and sedimentation in adjacent water bodies. The removal of vegetation weakens the soil and increases the likelihood of erosion, particularly after prolonged periods of rain. River and stream sedimentation may have an impact on aquatic life and water quality, posing new environmental problems. Chemicals used in mining operations, such as mercury used in the extraction of gold, may damage water and soil resources. The animal and human populations who depend on these resources for their daily needs and livelihoods are both seriously at danger from this pollution. Long-term environmental deterioration is caused by the combination of mining-related pollution and deforestation, which has an impact on the health and regeneration capacity of forests. Furthermore, it is impossible to overlook the socioeconomic influence on nearby towns. The traditional ways of life of indigenous and local populations—such as hunting, fishing, and gathering—that rely on forest resources are disturbed. These resources become less available as a result of forest cover loss, which causes social dislocation and economic suffering. Even though mining may boost the economy by creating jobs and developing infrastructure, these advantages are often transitory and cannot make up for the long-term costs to the environment and society. The requirement to remove land for mining sites, access roads, and infrastructure has a significant negative influence on deforestation in Cameroon as a result of mineral extraction. Large tracts of forest are destroyed by this practice, which also disturbs ecosystems, contaminates the environment, and has an impact on nearby populations. The combined consequences of these actions highlight the need of sustainable mining methods and regulations that strike a balance between environmental preservation and economic growth.

- **Artisanal mining:**

Artisanal mining, which comprises small-scale and frequently informal mining enterprises, greatly contributes to deforestation. These mining operations are often uncontrolled, resulting to considerable environmental destruction. Miners destroy enormous areas of forest to extract rich minerals and metals, such as gold, diamonds, and tin. The process of harvesting these resources includes destroying trees and plants, which affects local ecosystems and lowers biodiversity. The absence of regulation in artisanal mining implies that there are no imposed requirements for environmental protection. Miners routinely utilize toxic compounds, such as mercury and cyanide, to extract minerals from the ore. These pollutants may pollute soil and water supplies, presenting serious dangers to animal and human populations. Moreover, the disturbance of land produced by mining activities may lead to soil erosion, which further degrades the environment and can result in the loss of productive ground for agriculture. Artisanal mining is typically motivated by economic need. In many developing nations, individuals resort to small-scale mining as a source of income owing to the lack of other work possibilities. This socio-economic factor challenges attempts to regulate and manage artisanal mining activity. Without viable economic alternatives, attempts to restrict these mining activities face considerable obstacles. The effect of artisanal mining goes beyond deforestation and environmental deterioration. It also impacts the health and safety of the miners, who frequently operate in dangerous situations without proper safety equipment or training. The informal nature of these activities implies that miners are at danger of accidents, exposure to poisonous chemicals, and other job risks. Additionally, the existence of informal mining villages may lead to social difficulties, including dispute over land usage, relocation of indigenous groups, and the spread of criminal operations. Efforts to alleviate the negative consequences of artisanal mining include measures to legitimize these businesses, giving miners with legal status and access to safer, more sustainable mining processes. Organizations and governments are striving to develop improved mining processes, minimize the use of toxic chemicals, and restore mined regions. However, the efficacy of these programs relies on the participation of numerous stakeholders, including local communities, governments, and international organizations. Overall, although artisanal mining contributes to economic life, its uncontrolled nature offers substantial environmental and social difficulties. Addressing these concerns demands a comprehensive strategy that combines economic requirements with environmental sustainability and social responsibility.

**v. Fire:**
- **Bushfire:**

Bushfires are a serious hazard to the environment in Cameroon and can cause major damage to the nation's wooded regions. During the dry season, when the dry circumstances allow flames to spread quickly, these fires are very common. A large number of these bushfires are intentionally sparked by people looking to clear land for farming. Slash-and-burn agriculture is a historic technique used to increase soil fertility in preparation for crop production. But the flames have the potential to quickly spiral out of control, consuming more land than planned and penetrating into wooded areas. Unintentional fires are another factor in the issue. Numerous human actions, including the negligent disposal of cigarette butts, neglected campfires, and sparks from moving equipment, might be the source of these. Regardless of where they start, the dry vegetation and strong winds that feed these fires may swiftly spread to include enormous regions. Large swathes of forest, which are essential homes for species and essential to preserving ecological balance, are destroyed as a result of the severe ecological effect. There are several negative repercussions when forests are destroyed by bushfires. As a result of several plant and animal species losing their homes and food sources, biodiversity declines. Local ecosystems may be disrupted and endangered species may be threatened by this habitat degradation. Burning trees also contributes to climate change by releasing large quantities of greenhouse gases, including carbon dioxide, into the environment. The issue is made worse by the loss of vegetation, which also lowers the land's capacity to absorb carbon dioxide. Moreover, the terrain becomes more susceptible to erosion during a blaze. In the absence of plant and tree roots to stabilize the soil, intense rainfall may remove topsoil, resulting in reduced soil fertility and heightened sedimentation in rivers and streams. Further environmental difficulties may arise as a result of this sedimentation's potential to harm aquatic life and water quality. In Cameroon, initiatives to regulate and prevent bushfires include the introduction of more sustainable farming methods, public education campaigns about the risks of uncontrolled flames, and the enforcement of fire usage restrictions. Important elements of a complete fire control plan include reforestation initiatives and the construction of firebreaks, which are vegetation-filled gaps that serve as barriers to impede the spread of flames. Cameroonian bushfires—whether intentional or unintentional—cause serious environmental harm, especially during the dry season. The consequent loss of forest areas underscores the critical need for efficient management and preventive actions since it has far-reaching effects on biodiversity, climate change, and land stability.

## B. Impacts of Deforestation
### i. Biodiversity Loss:

Cameroon's forests are rich in biodiversity, holding a myriad of plant and animal species that are not only unique to the area but also crucial to preserving ecological equilibrium. Among these species, several are endemic, meaning they are found nowhere else in the world, while countless more are classed as endangered. The country's woods serve as vital habitats for these species, providing them with the required resources for life, such as food, shelter, and breeding grounds. Deforestation provides a severe danger to this biodiversity. When forests are cut for logging, agriculture, or infrastructure development, the natural habitats of many species are eliminated or severely fragmented. This habitat loss pulls animals into smaller, isolated pockets of forest, where they may struggle to find adequate food or mates, resulting to a drop in population numbers. The more specialized a species is in its habitat needs, the more exposed it is to the ravages of deforestation. For instance, some tree species that depend on certain soil conditions or animal species with particular food demands may find it hard to adjust to the changing environment. The loss of biodiversity in Cameroon's forests may have far-reaching implications. Each species has a particular role in its environment, contributing to services such as pollination, seed distribution, nutrient cycling, and pest control. The extinction or decline of a single species may disrupt these processes, leading to a cascade of repercussions that endanger the health and stability of the whole ecosystem. For example, the loss of a critical pollinator species might result in diminished reproduction of particular plants, which in turn impacts the animals that rely on those plants for sustenance. Over time, these changes may lead to a less resilient ecosystem that is more prone to diseases, invading species, and the consequences of climate change. Furthermore, the loss of biodiversity also undermines the environmental services that people depend on. Forests serve a key role in supplying clean air and water, controlling climate, and sustaining lives via resources such as wood, medicine, and food. As biodiversity disappears, these services may become less effective, leading to significant issues for local populations that rely on the forest for their daily needs. In essence, the destruction of Cameroon's forests not only threatens the survival of various plant and animal species but also jeopardizes the ecological functions and services that these forests supply. Protecting and conserving biodiversity is vital for ensuring healthy and resilient ecosystems that can support both animal and human populations.

**ii. Climate Change:**

Climate change is substantially affected by the status of the world's forests. Forests operate as major carbon sinks, meaning they absorb carbon dioxide from the atmosphere via the process of photosynthesis. This absorption serves to limit the quantity of this greenhouse gas in the atmosphere, playing a critical part in controlling the Earth's temperature. When forests are healthy and expansive, they can trap significant volumes of carbon dioxide, thereby helping to balance the global carbon cycle. However, deforestation upsets this equilibrium. When trees are taken down, the ability of forests to absorb carbon dioxide is dramatically diminished. This decrease implies that more carbon dioxide stays in the atmosphere, adding to the greenhouse effect and, subsequently, to global warming. Deforestation may occur for several causes, including logging, agriculture, and urban growth. Regardless matter the reason, the loss of wooded regions affects the Earth's capacity to store carbon. Moreover, the situation is aggravated when the removed trees are burnt. The burning process releases the carbon contained in the trees back into the atmosphere as carbon dioxide. This release not only cancels the advantages of the carbon already absorbed but also adds an additional weight of greenhouse emissions. The burning of forests, therefore, promotes the buildup of atmospheric carbon dioxide, worsening the greenhouse effect and speeding up the process of climate change. In essence, trees are crucial in reducing climate change owing to their function as carbon sinks. Deforestation and the consequent burning of trees greatly impair this function, resulting to increased concentrations of greenhouse gases in the atmosphere and an accelerated pace of global warming. The preservation and extension of forests are therefore crucial initiatives in the worldwide fight to mitigate climate change.

### iii. Soil degradation:

Soil degradation is an important environmental problem that severely effects ecosystems, agriculture, and human lives. Trees have a significant role in preserving soil health via numerous ways. They assist reduce soil erosion, which is the process when the top layer of soil is eroded away by wind, water, or other natural forces. This top layer is rich in minerals and organic materials, important for plant development. Trees, with their enormous root systems, anchor the soil, making it more resistant to being washed or blown away. When trees are eliminated via deforestation, this protective function is gone, and soil becomes considerably more prone to erosion. The roots of plants also assist preserve soil structure. Soil structure refers to the arrangement of soil particles into aggregates. Good soil structure increases water infiltration and retention, root penetration, and the flow of air inside the soil, which is crucial for plant health. Tree roots exude organic chemicals that bind soil particles together, promoting soil aggregation. Without trees, the soil structure deteriorates, resulting to compaction, poor water infiltration, and limited aeration. This deterioration may drastically limit the soil's capacity to sustain plant life and reduce agricultural yield. Moreover, trees contribute to nutrient cycling, a process that restores important minerals in the soil. They collect nutrients from deep within the soil and, via the natural process of leaf and branch fall, restore these nutrients to the soil surface. These organic components decay, replenishing the topsoil with minerals like nitrogen, phosphorus, and potassium, which are necessary for plant development. Deforestation breaks this cycle, resulting to a reduction in soil fertility. Without the continual input of organic matter from trees, soils become nutrient-depleted over time, forcing higher usage of artificial fertilizers in agricultural contexts, which may further affect the ecosystem. In addition to soil erosion and lower fertility, deforestation increases the susceptibility of soils to other types of degradation, such as landslides and floods. Trees and their root systems assist stabilize slopes by keeping the soil together and absorbing excess water. When trees are destroyed, the soil loses its stability, making it more prone to landslides, especially in steep or mountainous places. Similarly, without trees to absorb rainwater, the velocity and volume of surface runoff increase, resulting to more frequent and severe floods. This not only washes away the rich topsoil but also may cause major harm to human communities and infrastructure. Overall, the loss of trees via deforestation has severe and harmful consequences on soil health. By preventing erosion, preserving soil structure, and contributing to nutrient cycling, trees play a vital role in ensuring the productivity and resilience of soils. Protecting and restoring wooded areas are key efforts to prevent soil degradation, promote sustainable land use, and maintain ecological and agricultural systems.

**iv. Water Cycle Disruption:**

In Cameroon, the interruption of the water cycle due to deforestation has severe environmental, social, and economic effects. Forests play a key role in managing the water cycle by maintaining a precise balance between precipitation, evaporation, and transpiration. When forests remain intact, they operate as natural sponges, collecting rainwater and gradually releasing it into rivers and streams, which helps to maintain steady water flow and quality. However, deforestation in Cameroon upsets this equilibrium. The removal of trees leads to a reduction in transpiration, the process by which water is absorbed by plant roots and released into the atmosphere via leaves. This decrease in transpiration may lead to reduced atmospheric moisture, which can change local and regional rainfall patterns. Areas that formerly got regular rainfall may endure droughts, while others can suffer from excessive and possibly damaging rainfall, leading to floods. Moreover, without the stabilizing presence of tree roots, the soil becomes more prone to erosion. This erosion may wash away the rich topsoil, further diminishing the land's capacity to sustain plants. The eroded soil typically ends up in rivers and streams, leading to sedimentation, which may impair water quality and alter aquatic ecosystems. This sedimentation also impacts the supply of clean water for human use, agriculture, and industry, generating a ripple effect of issues for populations relying on these water supplies. Additionally, deforestation may contribute to changes in groundwater recharge rates. Forests enhance the entry of water into the soil, replenishing groundwater resources. Without the forest cover, precipitation is more likely to flow off rapidly rather than sinking into the earth, decreasing the natural recharging of aquifers. This may lead to a loss in the supply of groundwater, which many people in Cameroon depend on for drinking water and agriculture. The repercussions on water availability and quality also have substantial ramifications for agriculture, which is a vital sector in Cameroon's economy. Reduced water availability may lead to crop failures and lower agricultural output, impacting food security and livelihoods. Furthermore, changes in rainfall patterns might make conventional agricultural techniques less successful, necessitating adaptation measures that may be expensive and difficult to adopt. The disturbance of the hydrological cycle due to deforestation in Cameroon has far-reaching implications. It modifies rainfall patterns, degrades water quality, impacts groundwater recharge, and has a cascade influence on agriculture and water availability for human and ecological demands. Addressing these concerns needs concentrated efforts in reforestation, sustainable land management, and water conservation measures to restore the balance of the water cycle and reduce the deleterious consequences of deforestation.

**v. Impact on Local Communities:**

The influence on local communities in Cameroon is significant and diverse, reflecting the complex interrelationship between humans and their surroundings. Many communities in this country of Central Africa are strongly dependent on the forest environment for their daily needs, economic security, and sense of self. More than simply a pretty picture, forests are vital to many Cameroonians, giving them access to commodities like fuelwood, food, and medicine. These communities have lived in harmony with nature for centuries, perfecting sustainable traditions. Deforestation, on the other hand, is encroaching and poses a danger to this delicate equilibrium. Deforestation has effects that go well beyond environmental issues. The loss of natural resources threatens economic livelihoods by depriving populations of basic means of survival. Many people are experiencing financial difficulties as a result of the disappearance of conventional sources of nutrition and are finding it difficult to adjust to their fast changing environment. Furthermore, the social fabric of these settlements is deeply entwined with the forest's strands. Particularly indigenous tribes have strong spiritual and cultural ties to their ancestral territories. For them, the forest is a holy area entwined with their identity and history, not just a storehouse of resources. These cultural links are broken when large areas of forest vanish, which causes a deep feeling of loss and displacement. Social disputes often result from deforestation, escalating already-existing tensions among communities. Conflicts over land rights and resource access arise when competition for finite resources heats up. These problems are made worse by the breakdown of social cohesiveness, which leaves communities vulnerable and divided. The precarious state of local communities in Cameroon highlights the critical need for comprehensive conservation initiatives that put the welfare of people and the environment first. A possible way forward is provided by community-led projects and sustainable forest management techniques, which aim to balance local inhabitants' socioeconomic ambitions with conservation objectives. We can create a future where forests flourish alongside the livelihoods and cultural traditions of people who rely on them by giving communities the tools they need to protect their natural heritage.

## C. Efforts to Combat Deforestation
### i. Government Regulations and Policies:

A number of policies and laws have been implemented by the government of Cameroon in order to combat the severe problem of deforestation that is occurring inside the boundaries of the country. The National Forest Policy is an example of such an endeavor. It is a comprehensive framework that was developed to guide the sustainable management of the woods that are located across the nation. These

regulations, which were enacted in conjunction with the Forest Law of 1994, highlight the significance of implementing policies that strike a balance between the protection of the environment and the promotion of economic growth. Promoting sustainable forest management techniques, which put an emphasis on the long-term health and productivity of forest ecosystems, is one of the most important aspects of these strategies. The goal of this strategy is to guarantee that operations such as logging, land conversion, and resource extraction are carried out in a way that minimizes the adverse effects on biodiversity and ecosystem services. This is accomplished by closely monitoring and regulating these activities. In addition, the restrictions that are imposed by the government put a significant focus on conservation activities that are aimed at protecting the abundant biological variety that exists in Cameroon. Through the establishment of protected areas and the implementation of measures to prevent illicit logging and wildlife trafficking, the authorities are working toward the goal of preserving the natural legacy of the nation for successive generations. The engagement of the community is also an essential component of these policies, which acknowledges the significant contribution that local inhabitants play in the responsible management of forests. A feeling of ownership and responsibility for forest resources is something that the government hopes to instill in individuals who are dependent on forest resources for their means of subsistence. This will be accomplished via collaborative management arrangements and projects that are geared at strengthening indigenous and rural communities. Overall, these governmental rules and regulations indicate a commitment to balancing the economic advantages of forest exploitation with the need to safeguard and sustainably manage Cameroon's precious natural resources. The authorities want to address the complex difficulties that are presented by deforestation while simultaneously encouraging environmental resilience and social fairness. They plan to do this by placing a priority on conservation, community participation, and sustainable development.

**ii. Protected Areas:**

Protected areas, such national parks and wildlife reserves, play a key role in maintaining forests and biodiversity. In Cameroon, there are several protected places, such as the famed Dja Faunal Reserve, which has achieved status as a UNESCO World Heritage Site. Despite these efforts, implementing protective measures inside these zones continues to pose considerable hurdles. These protected areas serve as havens for innumerable plant and animal species, providing important habitats and supporting ecological equilibrium. They also help local people by creating chances for sustainable livelihoods via eco-tourism and other activities. However, the viability of these conservation programs rests on vigorous enforcement mechanisms. One of the biggest obstacles encountered in conserving these places is the intrusion of human activity, including illicit logging, poaching, and agriculture. These actions not only harm the biodiversity inside these places but also upset the fragile ecological balance. Additionally, poor money and resources, along with limited ability and training of enforcement authorities, further restrict effective protection.

To solve these difficulties, it is vital to strengthen cooperation between government agencies, local communities, and conservation groups. This involves enhancing monitoring and surveillance activities, boosting public understanding about the need of conservation, and adopting sustainable development strategies that benefit both people and wildlife. Overall, although creating protected areas is a critical step in forest conservation, their long-term viability depends on good enforcement and community participation. By tackling these difficulties, Cameroon may further increase its conservation efforts and assure the preservation of its natural legacy for future generations.

### iii. Community-Based Forest Management:

Community-Based Forest Management (CBFM) offers a vital method in developing sustainable conservation practices within forest ecosystems. At its heart, CBFM underlines the significance of involving local people in the management and maintenance of forests. By handing the duty of forest management to people who inhabit closest to these natural areas, CBFM projects appreciate the rich insights and traditional knowledge offered by indigenous and local communities. CBFM projects focus on the notion of empowerment, giving communities with the tools, resources, and authority required to actively engage in decision-making processes involving forest management. This engagement not only promotes a feeling of ownership and responsibility but also cultivates a greater awareness of the delicate interaction between human activities and forest ecosystems. One of the basic aims of CBFM is to allow local people to receive meaningful advantages from forest resources in a sustainable way. By giving access to these resources for livelihood reasons, such as non-timber forest products, ecotourism, and sustainable wood harvesting, CBFM activities help reduce poverty and promote the socio-economic well-being of local inhabitants. Moreover, community engagement acts as an effective deterrent against illicit logging, poaching, and other ecologically damaging activities. Through active monitoring and enforcement activities, communities may defend against the exploitation and degradation of forest ecosystems, so contributing to the preservation of biodiversity and ecological integrity. CBFM not only improves environmental conservation but also promotes social cohesiveness and cultural resilience among communities. By rejuvenating traditional practices and facilitating intergenerational knowledge transmission, CBFM activities protect cultural identities and enhance community relationships, therefore creating sustainable development that is both environmentally and socially robust. Community-Based Forest Management represents a paradigm shift towards inclusive and participatory approaches to conservation, wherein local communities emerge as indispensable stewards of forest ecosystems, safeguarding these invaluable natural resources for present and future generations.

### iv. Reforestation and Afforestation:

Reforestation and afforestation projects are key components in the quest to restore our ecosystem. Reforestation is the purposeful effort of replacing trees in places that have undergone deforestation, seeking to restore the once-lush greenery that characterized such regions. Conversely, afforestation applies to the purposeful planting of trees in places that were not previously wooded, so boosting the total tree cover and biodiversity of the region. These operations serve diverse goals beyond the simple replenishing of tree populations. One of their key aims is to counteract climate change by sequestering carbon dioxide from the atmosphere via the process of photosynthesis. As trees grow, they absorb carbon dioxide during photosynthesis, so limiting the greenhouse effect and helping to control world temperatures. Furthermore, regeneration and afforestation activities play a crucial role in restoring ecosystem functions that have been degraded owing to deforestation and land degradation. Forests are not merely aggregations of trees; they are complicated ecosystems that sustain a multitude of flora and fauna, manage water cycles, prevent soil erosion, and offer homes for many species. By re-establishing wooded regions, these efforts strive to resume these critical ecological services, therefore supporting ecological balance and sustainability. In addition to their environmental advantages, reforestation and afforestation operations also carry socio-economic value. They provide job prospects, especially in rural regions where livelihoods are frequently based on natural resources. Moreover, by boosting ecosystem services such as water control and soil fertility, these initiatives may contribute to better agricultural production and food security. Regeneration and afforestation activities are crucial instruments in the battle against environmental degradation and climate change. By restoring forests and growing tree cover, we not only minimize the ill consequences of deforestation but also pave the path for a more sustainable and resilient future for both people and ecosystems alike.

**v. International Cooperation and Funding:**

In order to combat deforestation, Cameroon works in conjunction with international organizations, non-governmental

organizations (NGOs), and donor nations. The purpose of this partnership is to address the complicated problems that are associated with the preservation of forests and the management of land in a sustainable manner in the nation. This initiative is mostly comprised of programs such as the Central African Forest Initiative (CAFI) and the REDD+ (Reducing Emissions from Deforestation and Forest Degradation) mechanism. These programs provide both financial and technical assistance to conservation efforts, and thus are an important component of this effort. As a result of the provision of resources and knowledge that would otherwise be unavailable to the nation, these initiatives are of critical importance in the process of establishing a framework for the sustainable management of forests. Through these activities, Cameroon is able to execute programs that concentrate on lowering the pace of deforestation and encouraging sustainable farming practices, which are crucial for maintaining biodiversity and mitigating climate change. Along with this, the relationship serves to enhance the capacity of local people and institutions, which in turn enables them to manage forest resources more efficiently and ensures that conservation initiatives are both inclusive and useful to the local inhabitants. Initiatives that seek to repair degraded lands, maintain existing forests, and enhance the lives of people who are dependent on forest resources may get financial assistance from CAFI and REDD+. This support assists in financing initiatives that have these goals. The supply of cutting-edge instruments for monitoring forest cover, determining carbon stocks, and putting into practice the most effective methods for sustainable forest management are all examples of the technical help that these efforts provide. Additionally, these initiatives promote the sharing of information and activities that create capacity, therefore assisting local players in adopting new techniques and technology in the field of forest conservation. In addition, the participation of international organizations and donor nations lends a degree of responsibility and openness to the efforts that are being made to battle deforestation. Regular monitoring, reporting, and verification methods guarantee that the funds are spent properly and that the initiatives achieve their intended goals. This joint strategy not only tackles the immediate challenges to Cameroon's forests but also helps to the worldwide battle against climate change by lowering greenhouse gas emissions from deforestation and forest degradation. In summary, Cameroon's engagement with international organizations, NGOs, and donor nations via initiatives like CAFI and REDD+ plays a significant role in reducing deforestation. These relationships offer important financial and technical assistance, develop sustainable land management practices, and help create local capabilities, all of which are crucial for the long-term protection of Cameroon's forests and the well-being of its inhabitants.

**vi. Sustainable Agricultural Practices:**

Promoting sustainable agriculture methods in Cameroon may greatly lessen the impact on forests. One viable strategy is agroforestry, which includes incorporating trees into agricultural areas. This strategy not only produces a varied variety of goods including fruits, nuts, and lumber but also gives significant ecological advantages. Trees in agroforestry systems aid in preserving soil fertility by fixing nitrogen, minimizing erosion, and boosting water retention. Additionally, they offer a habitat for animals and help to biodiversity protection. Conservation agriculture is another key approach. It stresses little soil disturbance, preserving a permanent soil cover, and varied plant species. These measures enhance soil structure and health, boost organic matter content, and minimize the demand for chemical inputs. By enhancing soil health, conservation agriculture boosts crop yields and resistance to climate change, which in turn lessens the need to remove new forest area for agriculture. Both agroforestry and conservation agriculture contribute to sustainable land use and aid in reducing climate change by sequestering carbon in plants and soil. They also boost food security by enhancing agricultural output sustainably. Implementing these methods involves knowledge and assistance for farmers, including access to suitable technology and financial incentives. Building the capacity of local communities via training and extension services may encourage the implementation of these sustainable practices. Moreover, policies that encourage sustainable agriculture and conserve forests are vital for providing an enabling environment for these activities to flourish.

**vii. Education and Awareness:**

Cameroon is home to rich and diversified forest ecosystems that are crucial not only to the country's environmental health but also to its social and economic well-being. These woods offer home for a vast diversity of plants and wildlife, many of which are indigenous or endangered. They have a key role in controlling the climate, sustaining water cycles, and avoiding soil erosion. Additionally, they sustain the lives of local populations via resources including wood, non-timber forest products, and chances for ecotourism. Raising awareness about the significance of forests and the repercussions of deforestation is vital in Cameroon. This process starts with instructional campaigns that target diverse populations, from kids to policymakers. By incorporating forest conservation into school curriculum, pupils may learn from an early age about the critical roles that forests offer and the implications of deforestation. These teaching programs may be supported with workshops and seminars for adults, especially in rural regions where people are directly reliant on

forest resources. Public awareness initiatives may also play a vital role in enlightening the general audience. These campaigns may employ media such as radio, television, and social media to reach a large audience. Highlighting tales of successful forest conservation initiatives and the benefits received from them might persuade communities to embrace sustainable practices. These anecdotes may highlight how protecting trees contributes to long-term economic stability, boosts biodiversity, and helps prevent climate change. Stakeholders, including government officials, commercial sector entities, and non-governmental groups, must be involved in these awareness campaigns. Policymakers need to appreciate the value of forests to pass and enforce effective conservation legislation. The business sector, especially enterprises engaged in logging and agricultural, should be encouraged to adopt sustainable practices. NGOs may help these efforts by campaigning, fundraising, and conducting conservation programs. Sustainable approaches that need to be supported include selective logging, agroforestry, and community-based forest management. Selective logging entails cutting just particular trees and conserving the overall structure and health of the forest. Agroforestry incorporates trees and shrubs into agricultural landscapes, offering environmental advantages while supporting agriculture. Community-based forest management helps local communities to manage and profit from forest resources sustainably. The long-term advantages of forest protection are varied. Healthy forests assure the continuous availability of resources for future generations. They sustain biodiversity, which is vital for ecological resilience and human well-being. Forests also operate as carbon sinks, collecting carbon dioxide from the atmosphere and helping to reduce climate change. By reducing soil erosion, trees preserve water supplies and maintain soil fertility, which is necessary for agriculture. Boosting awareness about forest conservation in Cameroon is crucial for protecting these critical ecosystems. Through extensive educational initiatives, public awareness campaigns, and stakeholder involvement, communities may be taught about sustainable practices and the long-term advantages of forest protection. This united effort will help guarantee that Cameroon's forests continue to grow, maintaining biodiversity, regulating the climate, and offering economic and environmental benefits for years to come.

In conclusion, Deforestation in Cameroon presents a severe danger to the country's ecology, biodiversity, and the well-being of its people. The substantial loss of forest cover disturbs ecosystems, resulting to the fall of animal populations and the destruction of important habitats. This environmental harm extends to the local inhabitants that depend on trees for their livelihoods, including agriculture, hunting, and gathering. The consequent loss of

resources exacerbates poverty and food insecurity, further destabilizing these communities. Addressing deforestation in Cameroon needs a holistic strategy that covers numerous essential initiatives. Robust policy implementation is required, combining the enforcement of current environmental laws and the formulation of new rules to safeguard wooded areas. Government authorities must work carefully to monitor illicit logging operations and sanction individuals who break forestry regulations. Community engagement is equally crucial, since local communities are both the stewards and beneficiaries of forest conservation activities. Educating communities about sustainable land-use practices and including them in decision-making processes helps develop a feeling of ownership and responsibility toward forest preservation. Sustainable land-use practices are another crucial component in fighting deforestation. Promoting agroforestry, where trees are incorporated into agricultural systems, may help sustain biodiversity while delivering economic advantages to farmers. Encouraging the use of non-timber forest products, such as fruits, nuts, and medicinal plants, may alleviate the demand on forests for wood extraction. International collaboration is also vital, since deforestation is a worldwide problem that demands collaborative response. Partnerships with international organizations, foreign governments, and NGOs may offer the essential resources, experience, and funds to assist conservation activities in Cameroon. By safeguarding its woods, Cameroon can assure the preservation of its rich natural legacy, which includes rare species and habitats found nowhere else on Earth. Furthermore, forest protection helps to worldwide efforts to counteract climate change and biodiversity loss. Forests operate as carbon sinks, absorbing carbon dioxide from the atmosphere and lessening the consequences of climate change. Additionally, sustaining biodiversity is crucial for ecosystem stability, resilience, and the general health of the planet. Therefore, Cameroon's efforts to control deforestation not only help the local environment and inhabitants but also have far-reaching benefits on a worldwide scale. Through a mix of strong legislation, community participation, sustainable practices, and international cooperation, Cameroon can effectively address the problems presented by deforestation and assure a sustainable future for its forests and people.

## 5.2 Wildlife Conservation

Wildlife conservation in Cameroon is a major concern owing to the country's high biodiversity, which includes several indigenous and endangered species. However, the nation's wildlife faces grave challenges from poaching, habitat loss, and weak enforcement of conservation regulations. Below is a thorough overview of the animal conservation difficulties and initiatives in Cameroon.

## A. Biodiversity and Endangered Species

Cameroon is home to a varied diversity of wildlife, including major populations of big animals such as elephants, gorillas, chimpanzees, and a range of antelope species. The country's rainforests, especially those in the Congo Basin, are among the most ecologically rich locations on the globe. Key wildlife sites include the Korup National Park, the Dja Faunal Reserve, and the Campo Ma'an National Park, all of which contain several rare species.

Endangered species in Cameroon include:

**i. Western lowland gorillas:**

Western Lowland Gorillas are a critically endangered species largely found in the deep rainforests of southeastern Cameroon, as well as in other regions of Central Africa including the Republic of the Congo, Gabon, Equatorial Guinea, and the Central African Republic. They inhabit lowland tropical forests and swamp forests, where they serve a key role in maintaining the ecological balance. As herbivores, they mostly devour fruit, leaves, stems, and other plant components, which makes them significant seed dispersers, contributing to forest regeneration and biodiversity. These gorillas are noted by their lower size compared to other gorilla subspecies, with males averaging between 300 to 450 pounds and females generally weighing about 150 to 250 pounds. They have a unique chestnut-brown coat and a more noticeable forehead crest. Western Lowland Gorillas are noted for their social structure, living in groups lead by a dominant silverback male, who is responsible for the safety and coordination of the group. These groupings, or armies, generally consist of many females and their progeny. The population of Western Lowland Gorillas has been significantly damaged by human activities. Habitat loss is one of the biggest dangers they face, as substantial logging, agricultural expansion, and infrastructural development continue to encroach upon their natural habitats. This fragmentation of forests not only decreases the available living area for the gorillas but also separates groups, making it harder for them to find mates and retain genetic variety. Poaching is another serious issue. Despite being protected by law in many countries, gorillas are nevertheless targeted for bushmeat, and babies are occasionally taken for the illicit pet trade. The bushmeat trade is fueled by both local subsistence needs and international markets, creating a difficult challenge for conservation efforts. Additionally, illnesses such as the Ebola virus have had catastrophic impacts on gorilla populations, causing high mortality and further threatening their existence. Conservation initiatives are underway to conserve these lovely animals. Organizations are focusing on developing and preserving protected areas, enforcing anti-poaching legislation, and supporting community-based conservation projects. These projects attempt to prevent human-wildlife conflict and offer alternative livelihoods for local populations, so decreasing their dependence on hunting and habitat degradation. Research and monitoring are also key components of conservation measures, helping to track gorilla populations and understand their behavior, health, and ecological requirements. The situation of the Western Lowland Gorilla illustrates the wider concerns of biodiversity loss and the need of maintaining natural environments. Protecting these gorillas needs a holistic strategy that tackles both the acute dangers to their existence and the underlying socioeconomic issues causing these challenges. By conserving the Western Lowland Gorilla, we also conserve the complicated web of life that relies on healthy, functioning ecosystems in Central Africa.

ii. **African Elephants:**

African elephants in Cameroon comprise both forest and savanna elephants, both confronting serious risks that endanger their existence. These gorgeous creatures are susceptible to intensive ivory poaching, motivated by the huge demand for ivory in many regions of the globe. Poachers target elephants for their tusks, which are subsequently sold on the black market, frequently subsidizing other illicit operations. The constant poaching has led to a dramatic drop in elephant numbers, driving them closer to the verge of extinction. In addition to poaching, habitat fragmentation is a serious danger to elephants in Cameroon. As human populations rise and expand, natural habitats are progressively encroached upon for agricultural growth, urbanization, and infrastructural developments. This fragmentation of their habitat hinders the elephants' ability to wander freely and obtain adequate food and water, crucial for their survival. It also leads to increasing human-elephant conflicts, as elephants occasionally travel into human settlements in search of resources, resulting to property destruction and presenting threats to both people and elephants. Efforts to safeguard African elephants in Cameroon include anti-poaching patrols, greater enforcement of wildlife protection legislation, and work to build and maintain wildlife corridors that link fragmented habitats. Conservation groups are also striving to increase awareness about the situation of elephants and the need of protecting their natural habitats. Despite these efforts, the problems remain great, needing continual and coordinated activities at both local and international levels to secure the survival of these iconic species.

iii. **Cross River Gorillas:**
Cross River Gorillas, the world's rarest great ape, are severely endangered with a population of fewer than 300 individuals. These gorillas inhabit the deep mountain woods near the border areas of Cameroon and Nigeria. They are a subspecies of the Western Gorilla, technically known as *Gorilla gorilla diehli*. Their survival is constrained to a fragmented range of around 12,000 square kilometers, principally inside the

Cross River State of Nigeria and the Takamanda National Park in Cameroon. The existence of Cross River Gorillas is gravely endangered by habitat degradation and human activity. Deforestation for agricultural expansion, logging, and infrastructural development has substantially diminished their habitat. Moreover, poaching, while illegal, nevertheless happens and presents a major harm to these already constrained populations. Local populations sometimes rely on the woods for their livelihoods, which may lead to conflict and further harm the gorillas. Conservation initiatives are important for the survival of Cross River Gorillas. Various groups and governments are attempting to safeguard their habitat and decrease human-gorilla conflict. These efforts include creating protected areas, supporting sustainable land use practices, and incorporating local populations in conservation programs. Research and monitoring initiatives are also necessary to better understand the gorillas' behavior, environment, and health, contributing in the creation of successful conservation policies. Despite these hurdles, there have been some advances in the conservation of Cross River Gorillas. Initiatives like the development of the Kagwene Gorilla Sanctuary in Cameroon and community-based conservation programs in Nigeria have showed potential. Additionally, international assistance and cooperation have played a significant role in these initiatives, contributing financing, knowledge, and advocacy for the conservation of this unique ape. The situation of the Cross River Gorillas underlines the greater challenges of biodiversity loss and the urgent need for comprehensive conservation initiatives. Protecting these gorillas not only helps conserve a unique species but also defends the greater environment, which benefits several other animals and local human communities. Continued efforts and improved awareness are important to guarantee that future generations may experience the presence of these wonderful animals.

## iv. Drills:

Drills, a monkey species closely related to baboons, are experiencing major risks from poaching and habitat degradation in Cameroon. These attractive creatures are noted for their striking look, with bright faces and muscular bodies. Despite their stunning characteristics, drills are at danger of extinction because to the effects of human activity. Hunting provides a direct danger to drills, since they are regularly targeted for bushmeat. Additionally, habitat loss is a big worry, as deforestation and agricultural growth continue to encroach onto their natural habitats. As a consequence, drills are increasingly restricted to fragmented and diminishing sections of forest, further worsening their vulnerability. Conservation activities are vital for the survival of drills. Conservation groups and local people are working together to safeguard their remaining habitats, create protected areas, and raise awareness about the necessity of keeping these unique primates. By addressing the risks confronting drills, we may help guarantee that they continue to flourish in the wild for decades to come.

## B. Major Threats to Wildlife
- **Poaching and Illegal Wildlife Trade:**

Poaching, a widespread activity across the globe, is the unlawful hunting, capture, or killing of wild animals. One of the key motivations for poaching is the extraction of bushmeat, which is the meat of wild animals caught for food. In areas where other food sources are sparse, bushmeat is an important protein source for local people. However, unrestricted bushmeat hunting may cause significant ecological imbalances by decreasing animal populations and interrupting food systems.

Another concerning facet of the illicit wildlife trade is the trafficking of particular animal parts, such as ivory and pangolin scales. Elephants are cruelly pursued for their tusks, which are highly valued for their decorative and therapeutic benefits. Similarly, pangolins, the world's most trafficked animals, are hunted for their scales, which are mistakenly thought to have therapeutic virtues in certain cultures. The voracious demand for these animal items, particularly in Asian markets, pushes poachers to mercilessly exploit fragile species, bringing several to the verge of extinction. Despite worldwide attempts to fight the illicit wildlife trade via laws, law enforcement, and conservation programs, poaching persists. The appeal of large revenues, combined with a lack of efficient enforcement procedures in many places, fuels the continued existence of this illegal activity. Furthermore, corruption, insufficient resources, and poor governance enhance the difficulties in combating poaching operations. The effects of poaching and illicit wildlife trading go well beyond the immediate impact on animal populations. The extinction of essential species harms ecosystems, causing cascading impacts on biodiversity and ecological stability. Furthermore, animal exploitation often happens in protected areas, undermining conservation efforts and jeopardizing the lives of local populations who rely on tourists. Addressing the complicated problem of poaching and illicit wildlife trading requires coordination among governments, law enforcement agencies, conservation groups, and local populations. Efforts should be directed at lowering demand for wildlife goods via education and awareness campaigns, improving law enforcement and judicial systems to discourage poachers, and encouraging sustainable livelihood options in impacted communities. Only by joint effort and collective responsibility can we expect to reduce the destructive effect of poaching and protect the world's valuable biodiversity for future generations.

- **Habitat Destruction:**

The loss of habitat is a serious problem that is made worse by several human activities, especially in Cameroon. The main cause of the destruction of natural ecosystems is deforestation, which is mostly linked to the growth of agriculture, logging, and infrastructural development. The region's forest cover has significantly decreased as a consequence of the pervasive use of slash-and-burn agriculture and the construction of large plantations focused on commodities like cocoa and palm oil. The complex ecosystems and biodiversity found in these woods are under danger, and the livelihoods of indigenous populations who depend on these natural resources for both subsistence and cultural traditions are also at risk due to this trend.

- **Human-Wildlife Conflict:**

As human societies continue to develop and spread into previously unspoiled natural regions, confrontations between people and animals have grown increasingly common. One prominent consequence of this growth is the development of confrontations between people and animals. In instance, creatures like elephants and monkeys regularly go into agricultural regions, destroying crops and inflicting severe damage. This conduct causes a circle of retribution, as farmers, suffering economic losses and risks to their livelihoods, turn to murdering these animals in efforts to defend their crops and guarantee their food. This phenomena, known as human-wildlife conflict, offers major problems for conservation efforts and biodiversity protection. Not only does it jeopardize the existence of some species, but it also exacerbates conflicts between local populations and wildlife officials. Finding sustainable methods to alleviate these conflicts is vital for the long-term coexistence of people and animals. This can entail adopting measures such as creating physical barriers to preserve crops, applying non-lethal deterrents to dissuade animals, encouraging alternative livelihoods for impacted populations, and cultivating better understanding and tolerance between humans and wildlife. Ultimately, resolving human-wildlife conflict involves a multidisciplinary approach that includes the needs and viewpoints of both human and animal populations, looking for solutions that are fair, effective, and ecologically sustainable.

- **Climate Change:**

Climate change presents a severe danger to Cameroon's ecosystems, with potentially far-reaching repercussions. One of the most apparent repercussions is observed in the modification of rainfall patterns, which may disrupt agricultural cycles and water availability, harming both human populations and animals. Moreover, the increasing frequency of severe weather occurrences, such as droughts, floods, and storms, further exacerbates these issues. These catastrophes may inflict significant damage to infrastructure, crops, and livelihoods, making it difficult for people to recover and adapt. Additionally, climate change may contribute to habitat degradation, as increasing temperatures and shifting precipitation patterns affect the composition and structure of ecosystems. This degradation may result in the loss of biodiversity, as animals struggle to adapt to rapidly changing circumstances or are pushed to relocate to more appropriate environments. Overall, the repercussions of climate change on Cameroon's ecosystems are complex and interwoven, having the potential to have wide-ranging effects on both the environment and human communities. Addressing these difficulties will need concerted actions at the local, national, and international levels to minimize greenhouse gas emissions, adapt to changing circumstances, and safeguard sensitive ecosystems and populations.

### C. Conservation Efforts and Initiatives

Cameroon has attempted many initiatives to address animal conservation, combining both government action and the activities of non-governmental organizations (NGOs).

- **Protected Areas and National Parks:**

Cameroon features a network of protected areas committed to conserving its unique wildlife and natural environments. Among these sanctuaries, many highlight as bastions of conservation efforts, exemplifying the nation's dedication to protecting its biological legacy. Korup National Park rises tall as a symbol of Cameroon's devotion to animal protection. Nestled inside its verdant expanse, a plethora of rare and endangered species find sanctuary, protected from the hazards of habitat degradation and poaching. The park's beautiful landscapes teem with life, giving a look into the rich network of wildlife that flourishes inside its confines. The Dja Faunal Reserve maintains a position of distinction among Cameroon's protected regions, obtaining classification as a UNESCO World Heritage site. This distinction highlights its importance as a worldwide asset, worthy of greatest care and regard. Within its broad bounds, a patchwork of ecosystems intertwines, giving a habitat for innumerable species, some found nowhere else on Earth. Campo Ma'an National Park, another diamond in Cameroon's conservation crown, demonstrates the nation's persistent determination to preserve its natural marvels. Here, in the untamed nature, uncommon wildlife walk freely, their existence secured by the park's attentive caretakers. Within its bounds, a delicate equilibrium is maintained, sustaining both the plants and wildlife that call it home. These protected areas represent more than just parcels of land; they are witness to Cameroon's continuous dedication to biodiversity protection. Through their preservation, future generations will inherit not simply a heritage of natural beauty, but a legacy of care and responsibility towards the planet's precious resources.

- **Anti-Poaching Measures:**

The battle against poaching is a multidimensional operation, with governments and international groups working hand in hand to conserve species. Anti-poaching patrols, strengthened by cooperation from worldwide organizations, act as frontline guards of endangered species. Through rigorous training and the supply of vital equipment, rangers are equipped to preserve sensitive ecosystems from the clutches of poachers. Moreover, monitoring measures have been enhanced, deploying cutting-edge technology to monitor and stop unlawful activity. This proactive strategy not only deters prospective criminals but also promotes the fast capture of those who dare to abuse animals for profit. Furthermore, legal frameworks have been tightened to guarantee that punishment is speedy and harsh for individuals found guilty of poaching. Stricter punishments serve as a deterrence, reflecting the unyielding attitude against the terrible act of wildlife crime. In essence, the coordinated efforts of countries and international organizations underline a determined commitment to conserving biodiversity and defending the fundamental worth of all living species. Through unshakable commitment and concerted effort, we seek to assure a future where wildlife lives undisturbed by the danger of poaching.

- **Community-Based Conservation:**

Engaging local people in conservation activities is crucial for the ultimate preservation of wildlife. Such projects strive to empower and engage community people directly in conserving their surrounding ecosystems and the animals living them. By developing a feeling of ownership and responsibility among residents, community-based conservation projects attempt to alleviate concerns such as poaching and habitat loss. These attempts aim on supplying viable alternatives to detrimental behaviors, so lowering the dependency on activities like poaching and unsustainable land usage. One of the key techniques is the development of eco-tourism, which not only produces cash for communities but also supports the preservation of natural environments. Through eco-tourism initiatives, communities may display the beauty of their environment while also benefitting economically, strengthening the desire to maintain it. Additionally, community-based conservation programs typically include sustainable agricultural techniques. By supporting approaches that are both ecologically beneficial and economically feasible, such as organic farming or agroforestry, these initiatives enable communities feed themselves without intruding on animal areas. Moreover, such measures help to the protection of soil fertility and water resources, maintaining the long-term health of the ecosystem. Education also plays a significant part in community-based conservation initiatives. By promoting awareness about the necessity of animal conservation and the implications of habitat damage, these efforts build a culture of conservation among local communities. Educational programs may include workshops, seminars, and outreach activities meant to involve community people of all ages and backgrounds. Community-based conservation incorporates a comprehensive approach to wildlife preservation, acknowledging the link between people well-being and the health of the ecosystem. By actively incorporating local people in conservation efforts and offering them with sustainable options, these projects provide a possible avenue towards live together with nature.

- **International Cooperation and Funding:**

Cameroon has profited from support offered by renowned worldwide conservation institutions such as the World Wildlife Fund (WWF), the Wildlife Conservation Society (WCS), and the African Wildlife Foundation (AWF). These organizations have played a vital role in furthering conservation activities inside the nation by contributing financial resources, specialist technical expertise, and operational help for a multitude of conservation programs.

- **Research and monitoring initiatives in Cameroon:**

Research and monitoring efforts in Cameroon play a crucial role in knowing the dynamics of animal populations and measuring the efficiency of conservation policies. One such organization, the Great Apes Survival Partnership (GRASP), dedicates its energies to performing detailed surveys, methodically documenting the movements of animals, and digging into the complex intricacies of human activities' ramifications on the local wildlife. These activities are crucial in creating a greater knowledge of Cameroon's biodiversity and establishing educated conservation strategies aimed at protecting its rich natural legacy for generations to come.

### D. Challenges and Future Directions

Despite these efforts, major obstacles remain in properly protecting Cameroon's biodiversity. These include:

- **Insuficient Funding:**

Insufficient funding is a big barrier to conservation efforts globally. Without the appropriate financial means, programs focused at maintaining and safeguarding natural habitats, endangered species, and ecosystems fail to fulfill their goals efficiently. The repercussions of lack finance are substantial and far-reaching. Conservation groups and agencies are regularly obliged to cut down their activities, lowering the quantity and scope of initiatives they may undertake. This constraint affects their capacity to handle important environmental challenges completely. Moreover, limited financing harms the viability of conservation activities over the long run. Without continuous financial backing, projects may be unable to maintain vital infrastructure, execute important research and monitoring programs, or involve local communities successfully. Furthermore, the effect of limited financing goes beyond conservation groups to include governmental institutions and lawmakers. Budget limitations may lead to lower appropriations for environmental protection initiatives, undermining enforcement mechanisms and regulatory frameworks meant to conserve natural resources. Ultimately, the absence of proper financing for conservation jeopardizes the health and resilience of ecosystems, threatens biodiversity, and weakens attempts to solve global environmental concerns such as climate change. To overcome this challenge, it is vital for governments, private donors, and international organizations to prioritize and enhance investment in conservation activities, assuring their efficacy and sustainability for the benefit of current and future generations.

- **Weak Governance and Corruption:**

Corruption, a ubiquitous evil in many cultures, presents a severe danger to wildlife conservation efforts when paired with poor governance and insufficient implementation of conservation laws. In such situations, persons tasked with conserving natural resources may resort to bribery, extortion, or other types of illegitimate enrichment, jeopardizing the integrity of conservation projects. Without powerful enforcement measures and severe monitoring, illicit activities like as poaching, deforestation, and habitat degradation may flourish, exacting a high toll on endangered species and fragile ecosystems. This weakens not just the inherent worth of biodiversity but also jeopardizes the ecological services required for human well-being, such as clean air, water, and climate control. Moreover, corruption erodes public trust and confidence in conservation agencies, impeding collaboration and cooperation among stakeholders. It generates a culture of impunity where violators go unpunished, continuing a cycle of environmental degradation and social injustice. Addressing corruption and building governance structures are so important for successful wildlife protection. This requires developing open and responsible policies, boosting law enforcement capabilities, and creating increased interaction and participation from local communities. By eliminating corruption and fostering good administration, we can better conserve our natural legacy for future generations.

- **Population Pressure:**

Population increase and poverty are key factors contributing to the problems faced by animals. As the world population continues to rise fast, especially in emerging nations, there is greater demand on natural resources and ecosystems. This population pressure frequently leads to habitat damage, fragmentation, and degradation, which are key causes of species decline and extinction. Moreover, poverty exacerbates these concerns since people living in poverty may depend significantly on natural resources for their subsistence, leading to unsustainable activities such as overexploitation of forests, poaching, and illicit wildlife trading. These behaviors not only affect species directly but also destabilize ecosystems, leading to cascade consequences on biodiversity. Balancing human needs with environmental aims is vital for sustainable development. It entails tackling the core causes of population increase and poverty via education, access to family planning services, poverty alleviation methods, and sustainable resource management. Additionally, adopting conservation-friendly practices and laws, such as protected areas and wildlife corridors, may help offset the consequences of population pressure on animals and their ecosystems.

To boost wildlife conservation in Cameroon, there is a need for more investment in conservation initiatives, tighter enforcement of regulations, and greater engagement of local populations in sustainable practices. Additionally, international cooperation and the integration of conservation aims into larger development plans are vital to guarantee the long-term preservation of Cameroon's unique biodiversity.

## 5.3 Climate Change Impact

Cameroon is facing significant challenges as a result of climate change, which are having a negative impact on the country's economies, diverse ecosystems, and the overall health of its people. The country of Cameroon, which is located in Central Africa, is endowed with an abundance of biodiversity, which includes mountainous areas, coastal regions, savannas, and rainforests. On the other hand, these ecosystems are more susceptible to the effects of climate change, which makes the environmental problems that are already present much more severe and introduces new threats to the sustainable development of the whole nation. One of the most notable repercussions of climate change in Cameroon is the alteration of weather patterns, which has led to an increase in the frequency and severity of extreme weather events. Agricultural activity has been disrupted and food security has been put at risk as a result of the growing frequency of erratic weather patterns, prolonged droughts, and abrupt floods. Due to the fact that their livelihoods are heavily dependent on rain-fed agriculture, small-scale farmers, who make up a considerable portion of the population, are particularly vulnerable to these fluctuations.

An further effect that climate change is having on Cameroon is a rise in the country's average temperature. The melting of glaciers on Mount Cameroon and other high elevations is caused by higher temperatures, which in turn changes the water supply farther downstream and poses the risk of water shortages. This has repercussions for hydropower generation, a vital source of energy in the country. Moreover, rising temperatures provide perfect settings for the development of diseases such as malaria and dengue fever, imposing extra pressure on the healthcare system and public health infrastructure. Cameroon's coastal regions are also susceptible to the effects of climate change, which include the increase in sea level and the erosion of coastal areas. In addition to putting coastal residents and infrastructure at risk, rising sea levels also pose a threat to essential ecosystems like coral reefs and mangrove forests. These ecosystems provide vital services such as coastal protection, fish habitat, and carbon sequestration, making their loss an issue of great worry for both the environment and the economy.

Furthermore, climate change exacerbates present environmental challenges in Cameroon, such as deforestation and biodiversity loss. Forests perform a critical role in regulating the climate by absorbing carbon dioxide, but deforestation for agriculture, logging, and infrastructure development affects this function. Loss of forest cover not only increases to greenhouse gas emissions but also decreases the resilience of ecosystems to climate change impacts, jeopardizing the country's natural heritage and the services it delivers to society. Addressing climate change demands joint actions at the national, regional, and international levels. In Cameroon, efforts aimed at building climate resilience and cutting greenhouse gas emissions are underway. The government has prepared a National Climate Change Policy and Action Plan, which comprises measures for adaptation and mitigation across various sectors, including agriculture, energy, and forestry. Additionally, Cameroon is a participant to international agreements such as the Paris Agreement, pledging to take actions to limit global temperature rise and adapt to its implications. However, major impediments continue in transforming policy intentions into concrete actions on the ground. Limited financial resources, inadequate infrastructure, and institutional capacity restrictions impede the implementation of climate change adaptation and mitigation initiatives. Moreover, fighting climate change demands collaboration across sectors and stakeholders, including government agencies, civil society organizations, academia, and the business sector.

International cooperation and aid are also important for Cameroon to appropriately combat climate change. Developed countries have an obligation to aid impoverished nations like Cameroon in adapting to climate change and shifting to low-carbon development routes. This comprises giving financial resources, technical transfer, and capacity-building aid to enhance resilience and lower emissions. In conclusion, climate change provides serious issues to Cameroon's ecosystem, economy, and society. Addressing these concerns involves comprehensive strategies that combine climate adaptation and mitigation initiatives across sectors and stakeholders. By investing in climate resilience and sustainable development, Cameroon can retain its natural resources, safeguard vulnerable populations, and construct a more resilient and prosperous future for all its citizens.

# CHAPTER SIX

## REGIONAL CONFLICTS

### 6.1 ANGLOPHONE CRISIS

The ongoing political and social tensions in Cameroon between the government, which is predominately Francophone, and the English-speaking regions of the country, specifically the Northwest and Southwest, are referred to as the Anglophone Crisis, also known as the Anglophone Problem or the Cameroon Anglophone Crisis. Historical, cultural, and linguistic divides that stem from the colonial past are the cause of this dilemma.

### A. Historical Context

The Anglophone Crisis refers to the continuing socio-political unrest in Cameroon, resulting from past colonial divides and modern frustrations. The origins of this dilemma trace back to the late 19th and early 20th centuries when European countries, mainly France and Britain, conquered Cameroon. Following World War I, the area was partitioned between these colonial powers, with France holding the main portion and Britain governing smaller portions in the northwest and southwest sections. This colonial divide established the seeds of linguistic and cultural inequalities that continue to shape Cameroon's socio-political environment. The territories under British administration, notably the northwest and southwest, embraced English as the official language and preserved many British administrative structures and judicial systems. Meanwhile, the districts under French rule generally employed French as the official language and conformed to French administrative methods.

Over time, these language and cultural contrasts, worsened by uneven growth and resource allocation, generated frustrations among English-speaking Cameroonians, who felt sidelined and discriminated against by the Francophone-dominated central government. The Anglophone Crisis erupted in late 2016 when lawyers and teachers in the Anglophone areas protested against the imposition of French-language practices in English-speaking institutions. The government's heavy-handed reaction to these rallies, including arrests and crackdowns, further exacerbated tensions and fueled bigger demonstrations seeking more autonomy or independence for the Anglophone areas. The war has subsequently resulted to extensive bloodshed, human rights violations, displacement of residents, and economic disruption, with both government security forces and armed separatist organizations engaged in crimes. Efforts to settle the problem by means of negotiation have been mostly ineffective, and the situation continues turbulent, with no clear conclusion in sight.

**B. Cultural and Linguistic Division**

Cultural and Linguistic Division: The linguistic and cultural division between the English- and French-speaking parts of Cameroon lies at the heart of the Anglophone Crisis. This division originated during the colonial era, when Cameroon was split between French and British colonial authorities. The nation's task upon independence was to bring these two disparate areas—each with its own language and customs—together. English is the main language used in administration, law, and education in Cameroon's English-speaking areas, which include the Northwest and Southwest. These areas have created a unique cultural identity that highlights aspects of their Anglophone past, such as the administrative procedures, educational system, and common law of Great Britain. The Anglophone community has protected and valued this identity, seeing it as an essential part of their social and cultural fabric. On the other hand, the majority of Cameroon is Francophone, with French being the most often spoken language. French is the dominant language in courts, government offices, and schools in the Francophone areas, which adhere to the civil law system that was carried over from the

French colonial era. The two regions' operations and interactions with the federal government have significantly diverged over time as a result of this linguistic and administrative duality.

The predominance of French language and culture in national affairs has long made Anglophones feel neglected. They contend that the Francophone majority-led central government often ignores their demands and enacts laws at odds with their language and cultural heritage. Numerous reasons, such as uneven resource distribution, sparse political representation, and the placement of administrators who speak French in Anglophone areas, have made this feeling of marginalization worse. Decades of unrest among Anglophones have culminated in demonstrations, strikes, and calls for more autonomy or even independence. When attorneys and educators in the Anglophone areas staged demonstrations in 2016 against what they saw as the Francophone legal and educational systems' imposition, tensions sharply increased. Anglophone discontent was further stoked by the government's strong reaction to the demonstrations, which included violence and arrests. Since then, the problem has grown into a larger struggle as armed separatist organizations have formed to defend the Anglophone areas' independence. Significant bloodshed, mass population displacement, and a humanitarian disaster have resulted from this war. Thousands of people have been forced to from their homes, schools have been closed, and communities have been devastated. The military reaction of the government has come under fire for violating civilian rights and using disproportionate force, which has made the situation worse for the populace. The deep effects of language and cultural divides in post-colonial nations are brought to light by the Anglophone Crisis. It emphasizes how crucial it is to resolve minority complaints and make sure that all areas have equal access to resources and representation. Finding a peaceful and long-term solution to the war is still a major problem for Cameroon, one that calls for communication, rapprochement, and sincere attempts to heal the rift between its Francophone and Anglophone people.

**C. Political Grievances**

The Anglophone majority in Cameroon has long voiced deep-seated frustrations over discrimination and marginalization by the Francophone-dominated administration. This resentment derives from a historical environment where English-speaking areas feel constantly ignored in national decision-making processes and development aspirations. The notion is that the government favors Francophone areas, awarding them more money and development initiatives, which exacerbates the feeling of injustice among Anglophones. The discrepancies are notably visible in different governmental areas, including as infrastructure, healthcare, and education, where Anglophone regions claim to get substandard investment compared to their Francophone counterparts. This apparent neglect has produced a feeling of disenfranchisement and alienation among the Anglophone population, who believe that their concerns and interests are not effectively represented or handled by the central government. Additionally, Anglophone attorneys and teachers have been in the forefront of demonstrations against the imposition of French legal and educational systems in their territories. The legal system of Francophone Cameroon follows the French civil law heritage, whilst the Anglophone areas have generally adhered to common law ideas. This collision of legal systems has led to major tension, with Anglophone attorneys contending that the imposition of French legal norms compromises their judicial independence and erodes the legal traditions that have long been a part of their regional identity.

Similarly, in the educational sector, the preponderance of the French language and the Francophone curriculum is regarded as an effort to integrate Anglophone pupils into a system that does not represent their linguistic and cultural history. Anglophone instructors have challenged these efforts, arguing that such policies disrespect the particular educational requirements of English-speaking kids and undermine the quality of education in their areas. These complaints have spurred a larger movement for greater autonomy or even independence from Cameroon, since many Anglophones think that their ambitions for fair treatment and self-determination can only be satisfied via considerable political restructuring. The perception of exclusion and the government's apparent unwillingness to address these concerns have further reinforced the demands for change, making the Anglophone conflict a key subject in Cameroon's national debate.

## D. Emergence of Secessionist Movements

The year 2016 saw a notable intensification of the Anglophone Crisis in Cameroon, coinciding with the rise of separatist groups throughout the nation. The conflict started when educators and attorneys in Cameroon's Anglophone regions—the Northwest and Southwest—started protesting against the government's decision to assign French-speaking judges and educators to their courts and educational institutions. The common law and English language foundations of the Anglophone legal and educational systems, which contrast with the civil law and French language systems that are more widespread across the nation, were seen as being directly threatened by this imposition. As soon as more Anglophones became aware of the first demonstrations by teachers and attorneys, a bigger movement advocating for more autonomy and acknowledgment of their cultural and linguistic identity was born. Many of the movement's supporters demanded total independence from Cameroon and the creation of an independent English-speaking state as the movement evolved and its demands got more extreme.

Several separatist organizations arose in reaction to these increasing demands, the most well-known of which were the Ambazonia Defense Forces and the Ambazonia Governing Council. Leading the separatist movement, these organizations are actively attempting to establish a new state they call "Ambazonia." The English-speaking parts of Cameroon, which the separatists contend have traditionally been neglected and underrepresented in the government mostly composed of Francophones, would be included in this proposed state. The Anglophone Crisis has been greatly exacerbated by the rise of these separatist groups, which has resulted in extensive bloodshed and instability in the impacted areas. In response, the Cameroonian government has often used harsh measures, like as military operations and crackdowns on alleged separatist activities. This has increased Anglophone discontent and resistance. This cycle of protest and repression has given rise to a prolonged war that has serious humanitarian ramifications, such as extensive disruption of everyday life, fatalities, and displacement. Deep-rooted problems of linguistic and cultural division within Cameroon are highlighted by the Anglophone Crisis and the emergence of secessionist movements like those calling for Ambazonian independence. This emphasizes the necessity of an inclusive and thorough dialogue to address the core causes of the conflict and open the door to a peaceful resolution.

**E. Violence and Government Crackdown**

Human rights organizations have harshly criticized the Cameroonian government's handling of the protests and separatist movements. The use of disproportionate force by security personnel against nonviolent demonstrators has been charged, including the dispatch of police and military troops to put an end to protests. These interventions often turn into violent altercations that leave unarmed individuals injured or dead. Human rights organizations have reported on random arrests, in which people are held without cause or established charges. Arrestees often endure severe circumstances while in detention, such as torture and other cruel treatment. There have also been several reports of security personnel murdering people without a trial who are thought to have supported separatist groups, raising serious concerns about extrajudicial murders. In the Anglophone areas, where there is already a strong feeling of marginalization and oppression, these acts have exacerbated animosity and distrust among the populace.

Separatist organizations have responded by attacking infrastructure and government troops, further escalating the region's instability. These organizations have attacked police stations, military checkpoints, and other symbols of state power in their quest for independence or more autonomy for the Anglophone areas. Separatist rebels have been carrying out ambushes, bombings, and killings among other acts of violence, which have created an atmosphere of dread and instability. For the civilian population, this never-ending cycle of conflict has had disastrous results. There have been several deaths and serious injuries as a result of people being caught in the crossfire. Numerous individuals have been displaced due to the fighting, with thousands of people leaving their homes in order to avoid the carnage. The circumstances faced by displaced persons are terrible, and they often lack access to needs like food, clean water, and healthcare. The precarious security situation limits the involvement of foreign assistance agencies, exacerbating the humanitarian catastrophe.

The lengthy violence has severely damaged social and economic infrastructure, impairing livelihoods, healthcare, and education. Children's access to education has been violated and their possibilities for the future are compromised as a result of the closure or destruction of schools in the impacted communities. Additionally, attacks on or obstructions to health institutions have complicated the provision of basic medical services. Farm productivity has collapsed and firms have closed, causing economic activity to come to a standstill. The ensuing economic crisis makes the problems that the general public faces worse, making them more vulnerable and impoverished. The absence of a sincere conversation between separatist leaders and the administration has impeded efforts to end the issue. Though significant progress is still difficult, the international world has advocated for a peaceful conclusion and respect for human rights. The intricate interactions between armed opposition and government persecution are exemplified by the situation in Cameroon, underscoring the pressing need for all-encompassing and inclusive strategies to address the underlying issues and promote enduring peace.

**F. International Response**

The Anglophone Crisis has garnered a great amount of attention from the international world, which has been very loud in its appeals for negotiation and a peaceful settlement to the dispute. The violence has been denounced by a number of countries, international organizations, and human rights organizations, and they have encouraged both the government of Cameroon and the separatist parties to participate in constructive discussions. Although these efforts have been made, the majority of attempts at mediation have been unsuccessful. This is mostly due to the stubbornness of both sides, who continue to be staunch in their fundamental demands. The government of Cameroon is adamant about preserving the country's territorial integrity and central authority, and it is unwilling to make any substantial concessions that may result in the country's secession or transition to federalize its administration. On the other side, the separatist forces are inspired by long-standing complaints over the political marginalization and cultural oppression of the Anglophone areas. They desire significant autonomy or outright independence for the Anglophone regions. Despite several interventions from the international community, the peace negotiations have been unable to make any forward due to this impasse.

Regional institutions such as the African Union (AU) and the Economic Community of Central African States (ECCAS) have been especially active in attempting to mediate the situation. The African Union (AU) has made many calls for a halt to the violence and has promoted inclusive discourse. It has also emphasized the need of tackling the fundamental problems of governance and representation. The European Court of Arbitration for Sport (ECCAS) has also volunteered its services as a mediator in the disagreement; however, its efforts have been received with scant success. There are a number of obstacles that both groups must overcome, such as having little influence on the parties involved and the complicated political dynamics that exist inside Cameroon.

Additionally, Western governments and the United governments have voiced alarm about the humanitarian consequences of the fighting. The UN has emphasized the displacement of hundreds of thousands of people and the awful circumstances faced by those caught in the crossfire. International NGOs and human rights groups have recorded several violations by both government troops and separatist combatants, significantly complicating attempts to broker peace. Although the international reaction to the Anglophone Crisis underlines a genuine desire for a peaceful settlement, the route to accomplishing this remains laden with impediments. The refusal of both parties to compromise on their core beliefs has stalled mediation attempts, and the regional and international entities concerned continue to struggle to bring about a durable settlement.

**G. Impact on Humanity**

Devastating humanitarian effects have resulted from the ongoing fighting, with thousands of people seeking safety in neighboring Nigeria and hundreds of thousands of people internally displaced. Many families have been forced to from their homes due to the continued violence, and they are now seeking shelter in host communities that are sometimes ill-equipped to care for them or in improvised camps. These internally displaced people (IDPs) deal with a number of serious issues, such as low food supply, restricted access to clean water, and inadequate housing. These communities are more vulnerable as a result of not having access to basic requirements, which has exacerbated malnutrition and health problems.

Due to government limitations and instability, humanitarian agencies have found it difficult to reach impacted people, which has made the suffering of civilians in the Anglophone areas worse. It has become dangerous for aid workers to provide necessary services because of the unstable security situation, which is characterized by regular battles between armed groups and government troops. The provision of humanitarian aid is further hampered by barricades, threats of violence, and outright assaults on relief convoys. Humanitarian organizations are also facing further challenges as a result of government limitations on the flow of persons and supplies.

The issue has become worse since help is not getting to those who need it, and many impacted people are still unable to get vital assistance. Health care services are severely burdened; owing to security concerns, hospitals and clinics sometimes operate at reduced capacity or close entirely. Due to this, people are unable to get medical attention for common health problems as well as injuries sustained during conflicts, further taxing the already vulnerable healthcare system.

The violence has had a significant effect on education as well, with numerous schools being damaged or shuttered. Significant educational interruptions affect children and young people in the impacted areas, which not only negatively impacts their learning in the short term but also negatively impacts their opportunities for the future. The psychological effects on kids and their families are severe because the trauma of being uprooted and exposed to violence has a negative effect on mental health and general wellbeing. The conflict's overall economic effects have made the humanitarian issue worse. Because of the damage to property, the disruption of markets, and the loss of revenue streams, many individuals have lost their means of subsistence. The impacted populations' poverty and resilience have worsened as a result of this economic volatility, making it much harder for them to recover from the crisis. There are many and serious humanitarian effects from the prolonged fighting in the Anglophone areas. There is a great deal of need and suffering as a result of the mass emigration of people and the difficulties humanitarian groups have in delivering relief. The interrelated consequences for economic stability, education, and health highlight how urgently a comprehensive and long-term approach to solve the issue and assist the impacted communities is needed.

**H. Prospects for Resolution**

Despite repeated efforts at mediation and peace discussions, the Anglophone Crisis remains unsolved, with intermittent violence continuing to afflict the area. Efforts by international organizations and neighboring nations to mediate have so far not resulted to a durable peace. The complexity of the issue, entrenched in historical, cultural, and political inequalities, have made settlement impossible.

A durable solution to the conflict will likely entail meaningful engagement between the Cameroonian government and Anglophone leaders, resolving complaints relating to governance, resource distribution, and language policy. The government's centralization plans and the marginalization of the Anglophone minority have been key to the conflict. Many Anglophones feel marginalized and desire more autonomy or perhaps independence. Addressing these complaints demands a comprehensive strategy that goes beyond simple surface improvements. It entails reworking the political system to allow for increased regional autonomy, fair resource distribution, and the preservation of the Anglophone identity within a largely Francophone nation.

Language policy is another crucial part of the situation. The imposition of French in schools and other institutions has been a significant cause of dispute. A resolution would seek measures that acknowledge and encourage bilingualism, ensuring that English-speaking Cameroonians have equal opportunities and representation. This might require modifying the educational curriculum, ensuring that both English and French are utilized in public administration, and conserving the cultural history of the Anglophone districts.

However, forging a consensus among firmly entrenched opinions and a history of distrust offers a tough task. The Anglophone community's calls for federalism or independence are met with hostility from the administration, which concerns that such concessions might lead to greater fracturing of the nation. Moreover, the existence of violent separatist organizations complicates the issue, since these groups are typically not affiliated with moderate Anglophone leaders and have distinct aspirations for the region's future. Trust-building techniques are crucial for any genuine discourse to take place. Confidence-building actions might include the release of political prisoners, a suspension of hostilities, and assurances of safety for people working in the peace process. International players might play a vital role by offering mediation assistance and ensuring that both parties stick to agreements.

The African Union, United Nations, and other international entities should foster discourse and propose frameworks for conflict settlement that have been effective in other situations.

Economic incentives might also be part of the answer. Development programs focused at boosting infrastructure, education, and healthcare in the Anglophone areas might alleviate some of the underlying socio-economic gaps. Creating employment opportunities and supporting economic development might help ease some of the issues that drive the violence. Additionally, honest and equitable resource distribution would be vital in creating confidence and proving the government's commitment to resolving Anglophone issues. Although the chances for settlement of the Anglophone Crisis remain dubious, a multidimensional strategy that involves real conversation, political and economic changes, and international backing provides a route towards peace. Overcoming the deeply rooted distrust and diverse objectives of the parties concerned will be tough, but with continued work and kindness, a durable settlement is feasible.

## 6.2 BORDER DISPUTES

Throughout its history, Cameroon, a country in Central Africa, has had several boundary conflicts. Geopolitical tensions, ethnic differences, and colonial legacies have all contributed to these confrontations. It is necessary to examine the historical background, the particular areas at issue, and the current ramifications in order to fully comprehend the intricacy of these debates. Many of Cameroon's border issues have their origins in the country's colonial past. Cameroon was first colonized by Germany in the late 19th century; after Germany's loss in World War I, the country was split between French and British domains. These areas, which eventually became United Nations trust territories, were allocated to Britain and France by the League of Nations. The limits of Cameroon were established by this partition, but it also planted the seeds for many disputes.

In 1960, Cameroon separated from France, and in 1961, it did the same from Britain. After the reunification of the French and British territories, the newly formed country was left with the arbitrary boundaries set by the colonial powers, which did not accurately represent the ethnic and cultural reality of the region. Many border conflicts with neighboring nations have resulted from this.

## A. Key Border Disputes
### i. The Bakassi Peninsula Dispute

The Bakassi Peninsula Dispute: The Bakassi Peninsula, rich in oil and fisheries, has been a key subject of conflict between Cameroon and Nigeria. The controversy over Bakassi comes from colonial treaties, specifically the 1913 Anglo-German Treaty, which set borders between German Cameroon and British Nigeria. These colonial-era treaties failed to account for the various ethnic and cultural landscapes of the area, resulting to ambiguities and contestations over territorial control. Post-independence, both Nigeria and Cameroon claimed claim to the peninsula, with Nigeria alleging historical and ethnic links, while Cameroon based its claim on colonial limits. Tensions intensified throughout the 1990s, culminating in military clashes and loss of life. The issue reached a critical point in 1994 when Cameroon filed the dispute to the International Court of Justice (ICJ), seeking a judicial settlement. The ICJ's 2002 verdict backed Cameroon, citing the 1913 treaty and subsequent accords as the foundation for its conclusion. Despite Nigeria's initial reluctance to cooperate, international pressure and diplomatic talks led to the signing of the Green Tree Agreement in 2006, easing the gradual transfer of sovereignty to Cameroon. The transfer process was plagued with problems, including opposition from local communities who identified as Nigerian and were apprehensive about their future under Cameroonian control. Nigeria and Cameroon, with backing from the international community, tried to resolve these issues via different measures, including citizenship possibilities and protection of rights for impacted populations. The Bakassi issue shows the difficulties of colonial legacies in Africa, where past treaties frequently meet with present realities, needing sophisticated and diversified methods to conflict settlement.

- **Conflict and Resolution:**

The Bakassi Peninsula, situated on the boundary between Nigeria and Cameroon, has long been a problematic territory owing to its significant oil riches and important maritime position. Historically, the border demarcation between the two nations was imprecise, leading to rival claims over the land. The conflict drew worldwide prominence when tensions between Nigeria and Cameroon intensified in the early 1990s, resulting in both states sending military troops to exert authority over the area. This military standoff underlined the enormous stakes involved, given the peninsula's economic and geopolitical importance. In 1994, Cameroon attempted a peaceful settlement by referring the case to the International Court of Justice (ICJ). The ICJ, entrusted with adjudicating international conflicts, performed a detailed assessment of the historical data, including colonial-era treaties and maps. After long consideration, the ICJ rendered its verdict in 2002, deciding in favor of Cameroon. The court's verdict was based on historical records that backed Cameroon's claim to sovereignty over Bakassi. The ICJ finding needed a practical and diplomatic response to execute the court's decision. This led to the Greentree Agreement in 2006, a major pact signed by both nations under the auspices of the United Nations. The agreement provided a precise procedure for Nigeria to remove its military presence and transfer administrative sovereignty of the Bakassi Peninsula to Cameroon. Despite this official agreement, the transfer was riddled with obstacles. Local residents, many of whom identified as Nigerian, rejected the shift in sovereignty, fearing economic relocation and cultural marginalization. The resistance sometimes materialized in skirmishes between local groups and Cameroonian authorities, but these episodes were infrequent compared to the large-scale military engagements of the past. The Nigerian government, although ostensibly supportive of the transfer, had to handle internal political pressures and the concerns of the Bakassi population. Over time, attempts were made to resolve these issues via negotiated settlements and developmental assistance aimed at incorporating the peninsula into Cameroon's administrative structure. Despite the hurdles, the conclusion of the Bakassi Peninsula issue serves as a major example of international judicial arbitration and diplomatic diplomacy. The ICJ verdict and the accompanying Greentree Agreement demonstrated the ability for international law to settle complicated territory disputes and for diplomacy to assist peaceful transitions. Today, although certain problems remain unsolved at the local level, the major military battles over Bakassi have faded, clearing the way for a more stable and cooperative relationship between Nigeria and Cameroon.

## ii. Dispute with Equatorial Guinea
- **Maritime Borders:**

Cameroon and Equatorial Guinea are immersed in a severe dispute over their maritime borders in the resource-rich Gulf of Guinea. This argument principally centered over the rights to extract valuable offshore oil sources. Unlike typical land boundary conflicts, this debate is centered on the economic zone and continental shelf under the sea, which are vital for obtaining significant natural resources. The Gulf of Guinea is a hotspot for oil exploration, and both Cameroon and Equatorial Guinea have significant interests in increasing their claims to these offshore deposits. The region's oil potential makes the marine borders a very sensitive and strategic issue for both nations, directly effecting their economic interests and national development goals. The disagreement over marine borders is not only a bilateral problem but it has larger ramifications for regional stability and cooperation. The determination of maritime borders affects each nation's rights to explore and utilize natural resources, and differences may lead to tensions or even violence if not handled wisely. Both Cameroon and Equatorial Guinea have engaged in different diplomatic and legal attempts to press their rights and negotiate a settlement. However, the complicated nature of maritime law and the huge economic stakes involved make this a tough matter to settle. The argument over these limits underlines the significance of unambiguous and mutually agreed-upon marine demarcations. It also underlines the importance of international authorities and legal frameworks, such as the United Nations Convention on the Law of the Sea (UNCLOS), in providing principles and processes for resolving such conflicts. The current discussions and any ultimate conclusion will establish key precedents for similar issues in the area and beyond. In essence, the disagreement between Cameroon and Equatorial Guinea over maritime limits in the Gulf of Guinea is a major issue fueled by the desire to control and profit from offshore oil riches. This issue, focusing on economic zones and continental shelves, emphasizes the larger consequences for regional stability, legal frameworks, and international diplomacy in managing and resolving maritime conflicts.

- **Resolution Efforts:**

Both nations have engaged in bilateral discussions and sought arbitration to settle their maritime borders. These discussions have been critical in resolving the difficult problems regarding the delimitation of maritime boundaries, which are significant owing to the region's substantial oil and gas deposits. The need to properly define these limits has been motivated by the need to promote oil exploration and prevent problems that may come from overlapping claims. The conversations have been held in a spirit of collaboration, with both governments declaring a desire to peaceful conclusion. In recent years, great work has been made in amicably delineating the maritime boundary. Both nations have demonstrated a willingness to compromise and work together to find mutually beneficial solutions. This collaboration is not only significant for the local stakeholders but also establishes a favorable example for the settlement of similar problems in the area. The attempts to identify the border have required considerable technical and legal debates, depending on international marine law and precedents established by earlier boundary conflicts. The African Union and United Nations have played significant roles in resolving these debates. Their presence has offered a neutral venue for discourse and helped guarantee that the process is performed fairly and honestly. The African Union, in particular, has been crucial in strengthening regional stability and collaboration. By fostering discussion between the two nations, the African Union has worked to de-escalate tensions and develop a culture of partnership. The United Nations has also participated to the resolution attempts by giving knowledge and assistance via its specialized organizations. The UN's engagement shows the need of international collaboration in resolving conflicts and highlights the worldwide relevance of sustaining peace and security in the area. Through different efforts, the UN has pushed both nations to adhere to international legal principles and to seek a settlement that respects the rights and interests of all parties concerned. Overall, the settlement efforts between the two nations reflect a commitment to peaceful dispute resolution and regional collaboration. These measures have not only aided oil exploration but also boosted bilateral ties and helped to the greater objective of regional stability. By continuing to engage in constructive communication and seeking the cooperation of international organizations, both nations are striving towards a durable and mutually beneficial settlement to their maritime border issue.

### iii. Dispute with Chad
- **Lake Chad Basin**

The Lake Chad Basin is a complicated and disputed area where the nations of Cameroon, Chad, Nigeria, and Niger intersect. This region has long been a hotbed for conflicts, partly owing to the imprecise and changeable nature of its limits, which are greatly impacted by the fluctuating waters of Lake Chad. Over the decades, Lake Chad has seen tremendous shrinkage, with its surface area falling considerably owing to both natural and manmade reasons. This drastic drop in size has escalated rivalry over the increasingly restricted land and water resources, leading to recurrent disputes among the countries that share the basin. The declining waters of Lake Chad have not only affected the natural terrain but also intensified socio-economic stresses. Communities who formerly depended on the lake for fishing, agriculture, and cattle now find their livelihoods endangered. As water levels decrease, the fertile land that gets exposed sometimes becomes the subject of territorial claims. These claims are exacerbated by the historical uncertainties and the absence of clear demarcation lines, resulting in overlapping and disputed ownership. Moreover, the shrinking lake has had serious ecological repercussions, affecting local ecosystems and the wildlife that formerly flourished in the area. The environmental deterioration has had a ripple effect, deepening poverty and pushing migration, which further strains ties among the basin nations. The rivalry for depleting resources has led to militarism and regular confrontations, as each country strives to exert control over critical regions. Efforts to manage and resolve these issues are complicated by the participation of various parties, including local communities, national governments, and international organizations. Attempts at collaboration, such as the Lake Chad Basin Commission, have been undertaken to solve these concerns together. However, political instability, economic constraints, and differing national interests frequently limit the efficacy of such programs. In essence, the Lake Chad Basin issue highlights a multidimensional dilemma where environmental, economic, and political components overlap. The shifting nature of Lake Chad's waters has left a legacy of loosely defined borders, leading to continuous battles over land and water resources among Cameroon, Chad, Nigeria, and Niger. The region's future rests on the capacity of these countries to work and create sustainable ways to manage their common resources and reduce the repercussions of environmental change.

- **Boko Haram Insurgency:**

The existence of Boko Haram in the area has had a big impact on the conflict with Chad. The political and territorial conflicts between the surrounding nations have become more complicated as a result of the insurgency led by Boko Haram, one of the deadliest and most persistent terrorist groups in West Africa. Due to the group's assaults, kidnappings, and raids, a significant portion of the Lake Chad Basin has

become unstable, making it very difficult for Nigeria, Chad, Niger, and Cameroon to successfully control their borders. These nations now need to work together more in the area as a result of the chaos brought forth by Boko Haram. Joint military actions have been triggered by the insurgency since different countries are finding it difficult to control the bloodshed within their borders. Multinational task forces and regional coalitions have been formed as a result of the frequent need for intense coordination and cooperation in these operations. Despite being crucial for preserving security and thwarting the terrorist threat, these initiatives have often eclipsed the underlying territorial issues. Resolving the territorial disputes has also taken resources and attention away from managing the danger posed by Boko Haram. The pressing need to tackle security issues has often superseded the pursuit of protracted diplomatic discussions or litigious settlements of boundary conflicts. Tensions have increased as a result of the insurgency since the regions under dispute are strategically important to counterterrorism activities, making them even more disputed. In addition, Boko Haram's presence has had an impact on the civilian populations in the contested areas, resulting in humanitarian problems and forced migration. The flow of internally displaced people and refugees has created an additional degree of complexity to the problems associated with border control. Cross-border collaboration is often necessary for humanitarian assistance and relief operations, but it may be hampered by lingering conflicts and a lack of trust between the participating nations. The Boko Haram insurgency has had a major impact on the conflict with Chad by causing instability in the area, requiring combined military operations, casting doubt on territorial disputes, taking resources away from diplomatic initiatives, and making humanitarian efforts more difficult. This complex effect draws attention to how security and territorial integrity are intertwined in the area and emphasizes the difficulties in resolving deeply ingrained and complex disputes.

### iv. Northern Borders with Nigeria
- **Cross River State:**

Over the years, there have been a number of small skirmishes centered around the northern borders with Nigeria, mostly in Cross River State. Local grievances and conflicting claims over land and natural resources are usually the root cause of these conflicts. The populations who reside on both sides of the border and depend significantly on the land for agriculture and other sources of income are often at the center of the underlying problems. Because the border area has a wealth of natural resources, there may sometimes be disputes about who is entitled to use and possess them. In the past, this region's boundaries have been unclear, which has exacerbated conflict amongst the populations. Traditional land claims often overlap due to the absence of distinct, internationally recognized borders, which causes conflicts. The economic activities that are common in the area and are essential to the local economies—such as farming, fishing, and logging—also intensify these disagreements. Conflicts may readily emerge when resources, such as fishing waterways or arable land, are sought by groups in Cameroon and Nigeria. These conflicts are also significantly influenced by the socioeconomic dynamics in the Cross River State region. Many communities have family and historical links on both sides of the border, demonstrating the strength of ethnic and cultural relationships that exist across it. These connections may sometimes promote collaboration and harmonious cohabitation, but they can also cause conflict when one party believes that relatives living on the other side of the border are invading their resources or territory. Authorities from Cameroon and Nigeria have intervened locally in discussions to try to settle these conflicts. These fixes, meanwhile, often only last a short while and don't deal with the underlying reasons of the disputes. These problems may be lessened by the establishment of precise and widely accepted boundary demarcations, but these procedures are difficult to carry out and need for the participation of both local and national administrations. There are modest but ongoing land and resource conflicts along Nigeria's northern borders, especially in Cross River

State. Local grudges, economic ties, and imprecise boundary definitions all contribute to these confrontations. To find long-lasting and peaceful solutions, resolving these problems calls for a holistic strategy including both local and national players.

- **Settlement Efforts:**

Settlement attempts along the northern borders with Nigeria have been a complicated and continuous process, partly motivated by the need to settle conflicts and disputes stemming from ambiguous demarcations. Local border commissioners have been essential in these efforts, frequently interacting closely with traditional leaders who hold substantial power in their communities. These leaders provide a wealth of local expertise and a profound awareness of the cultural and historical background, which is crucial for successful mediation. The fundamental purpose of these settlement attempts has been to obtain a better delineation of the boundaries, which traditionally have been poorly defined. This lack of clarity has frequently led to misunderstandings and disagreements between populations on either side of the boundary. By creating well-defined boundaries, the commissions strive to limit the possibility for violence and build a feeling of stability in the area. Promoting cross-border collaboration has also been a prominent emphasis of the settlement efforts. This collaboration is considered as a method to establish confidence and enhance relations between the neighboring communities. Various efforts have been attempted to foster combined economic activity, cultural exchanges, and coordinated security measures. These activities are meant to provide a framework where both parties may gain mutually, thereby diminishing the incentives for conflict. The success of these attempts has been uneven. In certain regions, the delineation and cooperation activities have contributed to major improvements in relations and stability. In some places, obstacles continue owing to deep-seated distrust, the presence of armed organizations, and economic inequities. Nevertheless, the continued efforts of local border commissioners and traditional leaders continue to play a key role in aiming for a peaceful and cooperative border zone.

## B. Contemporary Implications
### i. Economic Repercussions:

Cameroon's economy is significantly impacted by border conflicts, which affect a number of industries as well as the country's general economic stability. Because of the wealth of natural resources, notably oil and fisheries, in locations like Bakassi and the Gulf of Guinea, control over these territories is highly important. For example, the Bakassi Peninsula has huge oil deposits, which are a significant source of income for the nation. Uncertainties and disagreements over who owns and controls such resource-rich areas may discourage investment and spark disputes that impede extraction and production. As a result, the potential revenue from oil exports, which are essential to the nation's economic stability, is reduced, which has an impact on the whole economy. Furthermore, the Gulf of Guinea is a vital fishing zone, and disagreements over maritime borders may have an effect on this sector, which supports large local economies and provides jobs for a large number of people. In order to guarantee that fishing operations may be conducted without fear of violence or legal challenges, stable and recognized boundaries are necessary. Uncertainty near borders may also encourage illicit fishing, which damages fish populations and undermines the resource's sustainability. Furthermore, one of the main elements luring in foreign investment is border stability. Investors want to know that the political and legal landscape is stable and that their investments will be safe. Due to the unpredictability created by border disputes, investors are hesitant to commit capital to projects that may be threatened by political or territorial conflicts. On the other side, a stable border situation offers a more predictable investment climate, luring both international and local investors to fund initiatives that have the potential to strengthen the economy. Furthermore, there are often high diplomatic and legal expenses associated with resolving border disputes. To safeguard its interests, Cameroon has to participate in international legal proceedings, talks, and sometimes even military spending. These expenses take funds away from other important sectors that are necessary for long-term economic growth and development, such infrastructure development, healthcare, and education. Dealing with border conflicts may have a significant opportunity cost since maintaining and guarding borders takes up resources that might have been utilized to boost the nation's economic prospects Maintaining secure and internationally recognized borders is essential to Cameroon's economic strategy as well as to the country's overall security. Cameroon may more effectively use its natural resources, draw in international investment, and direct resources toward development objectives by settling border disputes and maintaining stable boundaries. The nation's long-term economic development and prosperity depend heavily on this stability.

**ii. Security Concerns:**

Security problems in places with unresolved border conflicts are extensive and diverse. These disagreements typically lead to heightened regional instability since they create a vacuum when government is weak or disputed. Such volatility offers ideal ground for several security issues, including the rise of insurgent organizations. For instance, in locations where the boundaries are not well defined or enforced, organizations like Boko Haram might abuse the situation, utilizing these territories as safe havens to conduct operations and grow their influence. These rebel organizations thrive in the uncertainty and lack of authority that unsettled boundaries provide, hindering attempts by national governments to administer and defend their territory. The existence of these organizations in border regions not only harms local communities but also weakens regional security. Insurgent operations might flow over into neighboring nations, increasing bloodshed and instability. This cross-border character of the danger needs coordination amongst nations sharing these vulnerable borders. Effective handling of these security challenges needs comprehensive cross-border collaboration, including coordinated military activities, information sharing, and concerted endeavors to upgrade border security infrastructure. Such collaboration may be tough to develop owing to differing national interests, political will, and resource restrictions. Nonetheless, it is vital for building a more stable and safe workplace. Without joint efforts, insurgent organizations would continue to exploit the holes in security, resulting to continuous bloodshed and instability. The consequences of these unsolved issues and the existence of rebel organizations extend beyond immediate security concerns, hurting economic growth, humanitarian situations, and overall regional stability. To address these concerns thoroughly, it is important for concerned states to participate in diplomatic efforts to settle border disputes and create clear and mutually accepted borders. Additionally, there must be a coordinated effort to enhance governance and development in border areas, giving local populations with the support and resources they need to resist insurgent forces. By integrating diplomatic, military, and developmental policies, governments may better handle security concerns and strive towards long-term stability in areas afflicted by unresolved border conflicts.

### iii. Border Disputes:

Border disputes have a considerable influence on Cameroon's diplomatic ties with its neighboring nations. The stability of these partnerships is vital for the general peace and security of the area. Peaceful settlement of these disagreements is vital not only for preserving friendly connections but also for encouraging regional integration and collaboration. When border disputes emerge, they may lead to tensions and strained ties between nations. This may result in economic disruptions, hamper commerce, and impact the movement of people across borders. Diplomatic attempts to address these disagreements are so crucial. Cameroon, like many other nations, typically depends on regional and international organizations to mediate and expedite discussions. The African Union (AU) is one of the primary organizations engaged in settling such crises. The AU provides a venue for discourse and offers procedures for peaceful conflict settlement. It works towards developing collaboration and understanding among member nations, striving to establish a stable and integrated African continent. The AU's engagement is vital in ensuring that any agreements made are respected and executed by the parties concerned. International mediation organizations also play a significant role in these processes. These groups contribute objectivity and knowledge, helping to manage the difficulties of border conflicts. They provide legal and diplomatic instruments to address the core causes of disputes and to suggest lasting solutions. Their participation is frequently important to break deadlocks and to assist solutions that could be difficult to accomplish via bilateral discussions alone. Effective mediation and dispute resolution help to the enhancement of diplomatic ties between Cameroon and its neighbors. Successful settlement of border conflicts not only eliminates sources of stress but also creates confidence and fosters collaboration in other areas such as commerce, security, and cultural exchange. This, in turn, promotes greater aims of regional integration, which are necessary for economic growth and stability in Africa. Thus, the peaceful settlement of border conflicts is not only a question of current conflict management but also a strategic approach to long-term regional stability and development. Diplomatic relations benefit enormously from these efforts, building a basis for sustainable peace and joint development.

**iv. Humanitarian Issues:**
Border conflicts sometimes have substantial humanitarian ramifications, hurting the lives and well-being of local inhabitants in numerous ways. One of the most direct and noticeable repercussions is the relocation of

communities. When boundaries become problematic, communities that formerly lived in relative tranquility might find themselves in the heart of violence, leading to mass displacement. Families are compelled to leave their homes, frequently with little warning, resulting in a loss of shelter, security, and stability. Displacement affects everyday life and erodes social structures, since individuals are transferred to regions where they may not have access to basic requirements or familiar support networks. This may lead to overcrowded and under-resourced refugee camps, where living conditions are harsh and resources are few. Another important effect of border conflicts is the loss of livelihoods. Many border areas are home to agricultural populations who depend on the land for their subsistence. When these regions become disputed, farmers and workers might lose access to their fields and workplaces. This disturbance not only affects food security for those directly concerned but also hurts the larger community that relies on the product and economic activity provided by these lands. In addition to agriculture, local economies may suffer as trade routes are interrupted and markets become unavailable, thus compounding poverty and economic instability. Human rights violations are also a regular and terrible effect of border conflicts. In zones of war, the rule of law typically breaks down, and military and paramilitary groups may operate with impunity. This may lead to a variety of violations, including arbitrary incarceration, torture, and extrajudicial murders. Women and children are especially vulnerable, with heightened risks of assault, exploitation, and abuse. The volatility and anarchy of contested border regions create a climate where human rights are regularly abused without accountability. The situation in places like Bakassi demonstrates the delicate interaction between national interests and local hardship. The Bakassi Peninsula, for instance, has experienced extended conflict between Cameroon and Nigeria, resulting to substantial suffering for the local population. These communities frequently find themselves caught in the crossfire, enduring ongoing instability and peril to their lives. The peninsula's population have endured relocation, loss of their traditional fishing livelihoods, and a significant shortage of essential services and infrastructure owing to the continuous war. Such protracted suffering adds to a cycle of poverty and despair, making it difficult for impacted communities to recover even when peace initiatives are launched. The humanitarian challenges emerging from border conflicts demand broad and persistent international attention. Addressing these difficulties entails not only settling the political and territorial disputes but also delivering urgent humanitarian help and long-term development support to impacted communities. Ensuring that displaced individuals get proper help, reconstructing damaged economies, and preserving human rights are essential elements in reducing the detrimental impacts of border conflicts and establishing sustainable stability and peace.

## Conclusion:

Border conflicts in Cameroon are strongly entrenched in its colonial past and have been affected by economic, security, and humanitarian considerations. The history of colonization has left behind arbitrarily defined boundaries that do not fit with the cultural and ethnic landscapes, producing friction and conflict. These conflicts are further compounded by the existence of significant natural resources in disputed regions, which heighten economic tensions and rivalry. Additionally, the instability that results from these disagreements disrupts communities, displaces people, and produces humanitarian crises that drain local and national resources.

Despite these hurdles, there has been substantial progress in settling certain border disputes. A classic example is the conclusion of the Bakassi Peninsula war with Nigeria, accomplished by the involvement of the International Court of Justice (ICJ) and subsequent bilateral accords. This result highlights the ability of international mediation and respect to legal frameworks in obtaining peaceful ends. However, other issues remain unsolved, providing continuous obstacles to regional security and prosperity. The peaceful settlement of these issues is crucial for sustaining long-term stability and stimulating growth in Cameroon and its surrounding nations. This demands a multidimensional strategy incorporating international mediation, bilateral discussions, and regional collaboration. Such initiatives not only attempt to alleviate urgent conflicts but also to develop foundations for enduring peace and collaboration. Effective settlement procedures may assist lessen security concerns, increase economic partnership, and create mutual understanding among the relevant parties. The future trajectory of these border conflicts will greatly effect Cameroon's national security, economic development, and regional diplomatic ties. A stable and secure border environment is crucial for economic progress, since it facilitates commerce, investment, and development activities. Conversely, unresolved conflicts may lead to lengthy conflict, economic stagnation, and strained diplomatic connections. Therefore, it is necessary for Cameroon and its neighbors to emphasize diplomatic engagement, legal arbitration, and cooperative initiatives to address and resolve border problems completely. In summary, although the historical backdrop and intricacies of border conflicts in Cameroon provide substantial problems, there are avenues to settlement that may pave the way for a more peaceful and prosperous future. Through continuing dedication to peaceful discussion and international collaboration, Cameroon and its neighbors may address these conflicts, strengthening security and encouraging regional prosperity.

## 6.3 REFUGEE CRISIS

Cameroon, a nation in Central Africa, has been enduring major regional wars that have led to a severe refugee problem. The Far North Region's Boko Haram insurgency, the Northwest and Southwest regions' Anglophone issue, and other internal conflicts are some of the root causes of this catastrophe. The inflow of refugees from surrounding countries and the internal and external displacement of Cameroonians are the two main features of the country's refugee issue. An extensive analysis of the causes, effects, and reactions from many stakeholders of the refugee situation in Cameroon will be provided in this section.

### A. Causes of the Refugee Crisis
- **Boko Haram Insurgency:**

The Far North Region of Cameroon has been greatly impacted by the Boko Haram insurgency, which started in northeastern Nigeria. Many Cameroonians have been forced to from their homes as a result of the group's violent actions, which include assaults on communities, bombings, and kidnappings. Nigerian refugees have also fled to Cameroon as a result of the war in an attempt to escape the bloodshed.

- **The Anglophone Crisis:**

When teacher and lawyer demonstrations in Cameroon's Anglophone regions turned into a larger conflict in late 2016, the Anglophone crisis began. Separatist organizations promoting Ambazonian independence emerged as a result of the government's severe suppression of these demonstrations. A large number of people have been compelled to seek safety in Nigeria, a neighbor, as a result of the ongoing fighting between government troops and separatist militias.

- **Internal Displacement:**

Cameroon has seen internal displacement as a result of community violence, land disputes, and other minor conflicts in addition to these two main crises. Inadequate infrastructure and restricted access to basic services in many regions of the nation exacerbate the problem of internal displacement.

## B. Scale and Scope of the Crisis

- **Internally Displaced Persons (IDPs):**

Hundreds of thousands of people are internally displaced in Cameroon, according to recent reports. These IDPs are mostly found in the Far North, Southwest, and Northwest areas. These areas are known for their high levels of instability, which make it difficult to provide aid and impede humanitarian access.

- **Cameroonian Refugees:**

The Central African Republic (CAR) and Nigeria are the two main surrounding nations from which Cameroon receives a large number of refugees. In addition to thousands of refugees entering Cameroon as a result of the unrest in the CAR, Boko Haram's actions are primarily to blame for the inflow from Nigeria. The lack of infrastructure and resources in the nation makes it difficult to accept these migrants.

- **Foreign Refugees from Cameroon:**

A significant number of refugees from Cameroon have fled to Nigeria as a result of the Anglophone issue. Numerous difficulties that these refugees encounter include poor housing, restricted access to schooling, and inadequate medical care. International groups and the Nigerian government have been attempting to help, but the scope of the problem often exceeds the resources that can be allocated.

### C. Effect on Humanitarian Issues

- **The standard of living in Refugee camps:**

The living circumstances in host nations like Nigeria and the refugee camps in Cameroon are often appalling. Common problems include overcrowding, insufficient healthcare facilities, poor sanitation, and restricted access to clean water. Particularly in youngsters, these circumstances exacerbate the high rates of malnutrition and the spread of illnesses.

- **Upheaval in Education:**

For many youngsters, the fighting and relocation have caused serious disruptions to their schooling. Schools have been demolished, taken over by armed organizations, or shuttered because of unrest. Additional obstacles to schooling for refugee children include linguistic challenges, a dearth of educational resources, and psychological trauma resulting from their experiences.

- **Psychological Trauma:**
Because of the violence and dislocation, they have endured, both IDPs and refugees suffer from severe psychological trauma. Many have either been the victims or witnesses of atrocities such as sexual assault, kidnappings, and murders. The trauma's long-term effects are made worse by the dearth of mental health treatments.

## D. Assistance and Response

- **Government Reaction:**
Frequently chastised for its management of the wars, the Cameroonian government has found it difficult to provide sufficient support to internally displaced people and refugees. The continued security difficulties, insufficient funding, and ineffective bureaucracy are impeding efforts to solve the refugee situation.

- **International Aid:**
International organizations are essential to the relief effort. These include the International Organization for Migration (IOM), the United Nations High Commissioner for Refugees (UNHCR), and other non-governmental organizations (NGOs). Numerous services, including as emergency housing, food assistance, medical treatment, and educational help, are provided by these groups. Nevertheless, their activities' reach and efficacy are often constrained by a lack of finance and practical difficulties.

- **Regional Community Assistance:**

  By accepting and assisting refugees, local people in Cameroon and its surrounding nations have shown incredible solidarity. But this kindness may cause host communities and refugees to become tense and adds to the already burdened local resources.

## E. Prospects and Difficulties

- **Safety Issues:**

  One of the biggest obstacles to solving the refugee problem is the persistent instability in areas impacted by conflicts. Delivering assistance is made more difficult by the fact that armed groups often threaten humanitarian workers and that entry to certain places is still restricted.

- **Finance and Resources:**

  The amount of refugees in Cameroon is significantly more than what can be handled. International financing is often inadequate, which causes gaps in vital services like safety, education, and healthcare.

- **Enduring Remedies:**

  For the refugee issue to be resolved in the long run, it is imperative that the underlying causes of the conflicts be addressed. In order to tackle Boko Haram, this involves fostering communication between the government and separatist parties in the Anglophone areas, strengthening regional security cooperation, and tackling more general challenges of governance and development in Cameroon.

**Summary:**

A complex and interconnected set of conflicts has resulted in a complicated humanitarian disaster in Cameroon: the refugee crisis. The government of Cameroon, foreign relief agencies, and host communities face major issues as a result of the extent of internal and cross-border displacement. In order to effectively address this issue, extensive and well-coordinated activities are needed that aim to promote long-term peace and development in the area in addition to offering urgent aid. To lessen the suffering of those impacted and to encourage a secure and successful future for Cameroon, the international community's ongoing commitment and assistance are crucial.

# CHAPTER SEVEN

## INTERNATIONAL RELATIONS

### 7.1 RELATIONS WITH NEIGHBORING COUNTRIES

Cameroon, situated in Central Africa, has an intricate network of global connections that are shaped by its colonial past, advantageous geographical position, and varied ethnic makeup. The country's foreign policy is influenced by the need for regional stability, pursuit of economic advancement, and establishment of diplomatic relations with significant world powers. The country has a well-established practice of non-alignment and diplomacy, aiming to preserve peaceful ties with its neighboring countries and the wider international community. Cameroon is bordered by Nigeria to the west, Chad to the northeast, the Central African Republic (CAR) to the east, and Equatorial Guinea, Gabon, and the Republic of the Congo to the south. Each of these connections is unique and shaped by historical, political, economic, and security factors.

## A. Nigeria:

The relationship between Nigeria and Cameroon is complex and diverse, influenced by both cooperation and past conflicts. One of the most notable conflicts has been the Bakassi Peninsula dispute, which involves a peninsula that has large quantities of oil and gas. In 2002, the International Court of Justice (ICJ) made a significant decision by granting title of this peninsula to Cameroon, resolving the dispute. Although Nigeria originally protested the verdict, the government finally obliged and withdrew its soldiers in 2008, marking an important step toward settling the territorial issue and building a climate of better diplomatic ties between the two countries. Economic connections between Nigeria and Cameroon are strong, marked by major commercial exchanges and coordinated infrastructural endeavors. Both countries get advantages from their participation in regional institutions like the Economic Community of West African States (ECOWAS) and the African Union (AU), which strive to promote regional integration and collaboration. These associations not only promote economic cooperation but also foster political and security alliances that are essential for maintaining regional stability. Despite these favorable economic and diplomatic gains, Nigeria and Cameroon confront enduring problems, notably in the sphere of security. The Boko Haram insurgency presents a huge danger to the northern parts of both nations, producing severe instability and humanitarian issues. To confront this common problem, Nigeria and Cameroon have engaged in cooperative military operations and substantial information sharing. These joint measures are vital in reducing the effect of Boko Haram and sustaining regional security. The relationship between Nigeria and Cameroon is one of both conflict and collaboration, primarily impacted by historical disputes like the Bakassi Peninsula problem and current security issues like as the Boko Haram insurgency. Nonetheless, their economic links and membership in regional organizations underline a commitment to maintaining peace and development in West Africa.

**B. Chad**

Cameroon and Chad share a border and have traditionally maintained amicable ties, underpinned by shared security interests and economic collaboration. This cooperation is backed by their involvement in regional organizations like as the Economic Community of Central African States (ECCAS) and the Lake Chad Basin Commission, both of which concentrate on regional stability and development. These organizations enable collaboration on a variety of subjects, from economic growth to environmental management, and offer a forum for the two nations to coordinate their policies and activities for mutual benefit. The war against

Boko Haram has further reinforced their alliance, as both countries confront severe security difficulties from the terrorist organization. Boko Haram's actions in the Lake Chad Basin have destabilized the area, resulting to loss of life, displacement of people, and interruption of economic activity. In response, Cameroon and Chad have expanded their coordination on military operations and border security to battle this mutual adversary. Joint military activities, information sharing, and coordinated patrols are critical components of their plan to lessen the danger presented by Boko Haram. These security measures are necessary not just for national stability but also for the safety of citizens and the safeguarding of economic activity in impacted regions. Economically, the completion of the Chad-Cameroon pipeline is a monument to mutual reliance. This pipeline, which delivers oil from landlocked Chad to Cameroon's Atlantic coast, is crucial for Chad's economy, providing a major export route for its oil. For Cameroon, the pipeline brings in transit fees and develops commercial connections with its neighbor. This infrastructural project highlights the necessity of their economic collaboration, illustrating how natural resources may act as a bridge for regional integration. Additionally, this initiative has stimulated the development of auxiliary businesses and services, contributing to economic growth in both nations. The relationship between Cameroon and Chad demonstrates how adjacent nations may exploit their physical closeness and common issues to develop healthy bilateral connections. Their collaboration in security and economic activities displays a holistic strategy to tackling regional concerns, fostering stability, and boosting growth possibilities for their people.

### C. Central African Republic (CAR)

The relationship between Cameroon and the Central African Republic (CAR) is profoundly linked with the continuous turmoil in the CAR. Cameroon has taken on a crucial role in tackling the humanitarian situation created by the violence in the CAR. This commitment involves offering asylum to thousands of CAR refugees who have left their homes owing to conflict and upheaval. By extending asylum and help to these displaced persons, Cameroon exhibits a strong commitment to regional peace and humanitarian aid. The refugee crisis has needed tremendous resources and coordination from Cameroon, highlighting the complicated and hard nature of this humanitarian operation. In addition to humanitarian help, security cooperation represents a crucial part of the bilateral ties between the two nations. Cameroon has actively engaged in regional peacekeeping operations and supported several international measures aimed at stabilizing the CAR. This includes contributions to multinational troops and engagements with international organizations focused on peace and security. Such measures reflect Cameroon's proactive position in encouraging peace and stability in the area, realizing that the security of one country substantially effects its neighbors. Trade between Cameroon and the CAR, albeit minimal, bears great significance. Cameroon operates as a major transit route for supplies entering and departing the CAR, providing a lifeline for the landlocked nation. The transportation and commerce infrastructure in Cameroon promotes the transit of necessary goods, consequently boosting the CAR's economy despite its internal issues. This economic relationship underlines the reliance of the two countries and the strategic imperative of maintaining stable and effective trading channels. Overall, the relationship between Cameroon and the Central African Republic is distinguished by considerable humanitarian and security components, as well as important economic linkages. Cameroon's position in offering asylum to CAR refugees, contributing in peacekeeping activities, and enabling commercial routes demonstrates its commitment to regional security and collaboration.

## D. Equatorial Guinea

Equatorial Guinea and Cameroon maintain a complicated relationship that oscillates between economic cooperation and diplomatic disputes. The two nations have a history defined by intermittent border conflicts, notably over coastal borders and oil-rich areas. These conflicts generally originate from the large oil and gas riches available in the area, which both governments are hungry to exploit.

Despite these thorny problems, the nations have largely resolved their disputes via diplomatic channels and regional institutions, avoiding significant wars. Economic links between Equatorial Guinea and Cameroon are especially strong, driven mostly by the lucrative oil and gas industry. Both nations gain large earnings from their natural resources, and this economic connection encourages a cooperative dynamic. Equatorial Guinea's participation in the Central African Economic and Monetary Community (CEMAC), which includes Cameroon, further increases economic integration. CEMAC offers a framework for these nations to interact on monetary policy, economic planning, and trade, fostering a stable economic climate in the area. The link goes beyond economy into regional security and stability measures. Both Equatorial Guinea and Cameroon engage in projects aimed at tackling security concerns in Central Africa. This involves collaboration in combatting piracy in the Gulf of Guinea, managing cross-border crime, and handling insurgencies that threaten regional security. By working together on these security problems, the two nations hope to establish a safer and more stable environment favorable to economic growth and development. Although Equatorial Guinea and Cameroon periodically suffer political problems owing to border disputes and rivalry for natural resources, their relationship is generally defined by strong economic cooperation. Through regional organizations like CEMAC, they participate in economic integration and cooperate on security efforts, cementing their dependency and commitment to regional stability.

### E. Gabon

Gabon and Cameroon share a border and have always maintained amicable ties. Both nations are key members of the Central African Economic and Monetary Community (CEMAC) and the Economic Community of Central African States (ECCAS), which encourage regional economic and political cooperation. This common membership supports several joint measures aimed at boosting trade, investment, and general economic integration within the area. The economic link between Gabon and Cameroon is especially solid in the forestry and oil industries, areas where both nations have major resources and interests. The trade of products and services in these sectors not only increases their economies but also deepens their interdependence, establishing a stable and mutually beneficial cooperation. Diplomatically, Gabon and Cameroon have maintained solid ties, frequently working together on critical regional concerns. Environmental protection and sustainable development in the Congo Basin, a vital region for both nations, are essential to their collaboration efforts. By tackling these concerns jointly, they intend to conserve one of the world's most significant natural areas while supporting sustainable economic activities. Furthermore, the two countries participate in cooperation efforts focused at infrastructure development. These initiatives generally entail cross-border collaboration, boosting connectivity and promoting easier commerce and mobility between the nations. Such measures not only strengthen the physical infrastructure but also pave the path for greater economic integration and stronger bilateral connections. Overall, the relationship between Gabon and Cameroon is defined by a combination of economic partnership, diplomatic stability, and shared regional aspirations. This comprehensive alliance shows the need of cooperation in solving both economic and environmental concerns, eventually contributing to the prosperity and stability of the Central African area.

### F. Republic of the Congo

Relations between Cameroon and the Republic of the Congo are strongly established in common economic interests and a shared commitment to regional cooperation. Both nations are members of the Central African Economic and Monetary Community (CEMAC) and the Economic Community of Central African States (ECCAS), organizations that strive to develop economic integration and political cooperation within the area. These connections promote many cooperation initiatives, including the harmonization of policies, the promotion of regional commerce, and the construction of infrastructure projects that benefit both countries. Economic links between Cameroon and the Republic of the Congo are especially solid in the oil and wood industries, which are essential to the economies of both nations. The Republic of the Congo, rich in oil deposits, depends largely on the export of petroleum products, whereas Cameroon, with its enormous forest resources, is a prominent participant in the wood business. The trading of these goods not only bolsters the economies of both countries but also produces countless business possibilities and employment, promoting a symbiotic economic connection. Beyond economic partnership, bilateral cooperation between Cameroon and the Republic of the Congo extends to security problems. The two nations are committed to working together to solve mutual security concerns such as cross-border crime, illicit logging, and regional instability. Joint security efforts and information-sharing systems have been formed to fight these concerns, strengthening the safety and stability of the area. This collaboration is vital in combating dangers that transcend national boundaries, providing a coordinated and effective response. Diplomatic relations between Cameroon and the Republic of the Congo are marked by strong ties and regular high-level exchanges. Leaders from both countries frequently participate in communication to discuss subjects of common interest and to establish cooperation projects aimed at fostering peace, security, and prosperity in Central Africa. These exchanges assist to build the links between the two nations, promoting a sense of cooperation and mutual respect. The relationship between Cameroon and the Republic of the Congo highlights the relevance of regional alliances in solving both economic and security concerns. Through organizations like CEMAC and ECCAS, and through their own bilateral initiatives, these nations work together to construct a more connected and stable Central African area. Their relationship acts as an example for other countries in the region, illustrating how cooperation can lead to shared wealth and peace.

## Conclusion

Cameroon's foreign relations with its surrounding nations are complicated and motivated by a mix of historical connections, economic interests, and security concerns. The nation's strategic approach to diplomacy and regional cooperation has helped it to maintain stable and fruitful ties with its neighbors, despite periodic conflicts and obstacles. Historically, Cameroon has deep-rooted relationships with its surrounding nations, resulting from colonial legacies and common cultural and ethnic bonds. These historical linkages frequently impact the character of its diplomatic relations, promoting a feeling of unity and mutual understanding. Economically, Cameroon is a prominent participant in regional trade, exploiting its geographical location to enable commerce and economic integration within Central Africa. The nation's economy, being one of the most varied in the area, enables it to participate in favorable trade agreements, which in turn encourage regional economic stability and prosperity. Security issues are an important component of Cameroon's international relations, especially given the problems provided by terrorism, armed conflicts, and cross-border crimes. Cameroon cooperate extensively with its neighbors to solve these security concerns, engaging in cooperative military operations and information sharing. This collaboration is vital for sustaining regional stability and defending national security. Cameroon's membership in regional organizations, such as the Economic Community of Central African States (ECCAS) and the African Union, indicates its dedication to regional cooperation. These forums offer Cameroon with options to influence regional policy and contribute to collaborative efforts in tackling shared concerns. Through these organizations, Cameroon actively supports projects aimed at building peace, stability, and prosperity throughout Central Africa. Overall, Cameroon's approach to its foreign relations is defined by a balanced combination of diplomacy, economic engagement, and security cooperation. This policy has helped the nation to manage the complexity of regional dynamics efficiently, ensuring that it remains a crucial role in the search for a peaceful and prosperous Central Africa.

## 7.2 FOREIGN AID AND INVESTMENT

In order to shape Cameroon's international relations, propel its economic growth, and handle a variety of socioeconomic issues, foreign assistance and investment are essential. For Cameroon, the relationship between foreign investment and assistance is crucial since the country aims to use these outside resources to support social services, build infrastructure, and boost economic development. The details of foreign investment and assistance in Cameroon are examined here, along with their origins, effects, and difficulties.

### A. Foreign Aid Sources

Numerous bilateral and multilateral entities, such as international organizations, foreign governments, and non-governmental organizations (NGOs), provide help to Cameroon.

- **Bilateral Aid:**

Bilateral aid refers to the help offered by one nation directly to another, often via government channels, without middlemen or multilateral agencies engaged. In the case of Cameroon, bilateral assistance agreements are particularly formed with various Western countries, with France, Germany, and the United States being important partners in this respect. France, maintaining historical colonial links with Cameroon, continues to play a vital role in delivering bilateral assistance to the nation. This help is generally allocated toward key areas like as education, healthcare, and infrastructure development. Given the common historical and cultural linkages, France's support holds a special relevance in defining Cameroon's growth trajectory. Germany, another significant bilateral assistance partner for Cameroon, concentrates its support on environmental conservation efforts and vocational training projects. This coincides with Germany's focus on sustainable development and capacity building, seeking to empower Cameroonian communities to overcome environmental concerns and boost skills for economic growth and prosperity. The United States also stands as a major contributor to Cameroon's growth via its bilateral assistance programs. Notably, the President's Emergency Plan for AIDS Relief (PEPFAR) constitutes a flagship effort through which the U.S. delivers major help in battling HIV/AIDS and strengthening healthcare systems in Cameroon. This partnership highlights the common commitment to solving major health concerns and fostering well-being in the area. Overall, Cameroon's bilateral assistance partnerships with Western countries demonstrate a broad approach to development cooperation, including multiple sectors and priorities customized to fit the country's particular needs and difficulties. Through these relationships, efforts are made to create sustainable development, enhance livelihoods, and build mutual bonds across states.

- **Multilateral Aid:**
Multilateral aid refers to the financial help and technical support offered to Cameroon by

different international institutions, notably the World Bank, the International Monetary Fund (IMF), the African Development Bank (AfDB), and the European Union (EU). These institutions play a significant role in assisting Cameroon's development aspirations across many sectors. Through international assistance, Cameroon gets funds for different programs, encompassing infrastructure development, healthcare, education, and governance changes. This help is crucial in resolving critical issues and ensuring sustained growth within the nation. Specifically, the World Bank and the IMF have been essential in executing structural adjustment programs meant to stabilize Cameroon's economy and allow long-term development. These initiatives frequently comprise policy changes intended at strengthening budgetary discipline, fostering private sector growth, and improving governance processes. Overall, multilateral assistance constitutes a joint effort between Cameroon and foreign partners to encourage economic growth, enhance social welfare, and boost the nation's chances for a successful future.

- **NGOs and International Foundations:**

NGOs and foreign foundations play a major role in Cameroon, serving diverse social needs ranging from healthcare and education to human rights and rural development. These organizations work with a purpose to create a concrete influence on the lives of Cameroonians, seeking to reduce poverty, increase access to critical services, and promote social justice. Among the key participants in Cameroon's NGO sector is Médecins Sans Frontières (Doctors Without Borders), recognized for providing emergency medical help in crisis circumstances. CARE International is another significant organization, noted for its holistic approach to poverty eradication and community development. Additionally, the Bill & Melinda Gates Foundation, with its emphasis on global health and development, has been essential in funding projects to tackle illnesses like malaria and enhance healthcare facilities in Cameroon. Through their programs and activities, these NGOs and foundations contribute substantially to Cameroon's development efforts, working in conjunction with local communities, government agencies, and other stakeholders. Their participation emphasizes the necessity of international collaboration and joint effort in solving the difficult issues confronting the country.

**B. Impact of Foreign Aid**

Foreign aid has had a mixed effect on Cameroon. While it has permitted substantial breakthroughs in some fields, it has also drawn criticism for encouraging reliance and inefficiency.

**i. Positive Impacts:**
- **Health:** Aid has been vital in battling illnesses like HIV/AIDS, malaria, and TB. Programs financed by PEPFAR and the

Global Fund have supplied pharmaceuticals, preventative measures, and healthcare infrastructure.
- **Education:** Educational initiatives sponsored by bilateral and multilateral assistance have enhanced access to elementary and secondary education, especially in rural regions. Scholarships and training programs have also improved higher education prospects.
- **Infrastructure Development:** Aid has sponsored key infrastructure projects, including roads, bridges, and energy projects. For instance, the Lom Pangar dam, supported by the World Bank and other donors, intends to enhance energy supply and water management.
- **Governance and Institutional Strengthening:** Aid programs have supported governance reforms, judicial enhancements, and anti-corruption initiatives. These efforts are meant to increase openness and accountability in public administration.

ii. **Negative Impacts:**
- **Dependence:** A significant critique of foreign assistance is that it might generate a dependence syndrome, where the receiving nation depends unduly on help rather than building its own sustainable economic policies.

- **Inefficiency and Corruption:** There have been cases when assistance monies were squandered or siphoned off owing to corruption. This has led to inefficiencies and the failure of some assistance initiatives to achieve their desired effects.
- **Conditionalities:** Aid from foreign financial institutions sometimes comes with rigorous requirements that might lead to socio-economic disturbances. Structural adjustment efforts by the IMF, for instance, have occasionally resulted in public sector downsizing and subsidy reduction, impacting the vulnerable communities.

### C. Foreign Investment

Foreign direct investment (FDI) is another essential component of Cameroon's international economic connections. The government of Cameroon has made attempts to attract FDI by strengthening the business environment and giving incentives to international firms.

### i. Investment Climate and Incentives

- **Regulatory changes:** Cameroon has attempted many regulatory changes to attract international companies. These include streamlining corporate registration procedures, increasing property rights, and upgrading legal frameworks to safeguard investors.
- **Incentives:** The government gives numerous incentives such as tax rebates,

customs exemptions, and access to land. Special economic zones have been formed to give extra incentives to investors.

ii. Key Investment Sectors:
- **Oil and Gas:** The hydrocarbon industry remains a key draw for international investment. Companies from China, the United States, and Europe are active in exploration and production operations.
- **Agriculture:** Agriculture is an important industry for foreign investment, given Cameroon's abundant agricultural resources. Investments are geared towards large-scale growing, processing, and export of products including cocoa, coffee, and rubber.
- **Infrastructure:** Foreign investment in infrastructure projects, including transportation, telecommunications, and energy, is crucial. Projects like the Kribi Deep Sea Port and the Lom Pangar Dam have major international participation.
- **Mining:** The mining industry, notably for minerals like bauxite, iron ore, and cobalt, draws international investment. Exploration and extraction efforts are sponsored by firms from Australia, China, and other nations.

iii. **Challenges and Risks:**
- **Political and Security Risks:** Political instability and security

difficulties, particularly in the Anglophone areas, represent major risks to international investment. Investors are apprehensive about possible disruptions caused by hostilities and political instability.
- **Bureaucratic Hurdles:** Despite improvements, bureaucratic red tape and inefficiencies continue to hinder the investment process. Investors frequently suffer difficulties in getting permissions and licenses.
- **Corruption:** Corruption is a prevalent problem, impacting both local and international investors. Bribery and embezzlement may damage investor confidence and lead to excessive expenditures.
- **Infrastructure Deficits:** While there are continuous improvements, insufficient infrastructure, notably in transportation and electricity, remains an issue. Poor infrastructure may raise operating costs and lower the attractiveness of investment possibilities.

In conclusion, the influence of foreign assistance and investment in Cameroon's international relations cannot be emphasized. These variables play a key role in establishing the country's socio-economic environment, impacting many areas from health and education to infrastructure development. Foreign assistance has been crucial in generating good changes, allowing progress in critical sectors. However, it also introduces difficulties like as reliance and corruption, which need to be managed efficiently. On the other side, foreign investment presents enormous potential for economic development, particularly in industries like oil and gas, agriculture, and infrastructure. The infusion of foreign money may drive job creation, innovation, and general economic growth. Nonetheless, for Cameroon to fully exploit the advantages of international assistance and investment, it must tackle internal hurdles such as political instability, corruption, and bureaucratic inefficiency. By confronting these concerns head-on, Cameroon may create a more favorable climate for sustainable growth and promote stronger international connections. This requires developing transparent governance processes, improving regulatory frameworks, and fostering accountability at all levels of government. Ultimately, by using foreign assistance and investment successfully, Cameroon may speed its road towards prosperity and boost its status on the world arena.

## 7.3 DIPLOMATIC EFFORTS

Cameroon has a complex tapestry of diplomatic contacts formed by its historical, geographical, and economic factors. The country's diplomatic activities have been varied, covering regional, continental, and global venues, showing its commitment to supporting peace, stability, and development both locally and globally. Here, we look into the diplomatic attempts of Cameroon on several fronts:

## A. Regional Diplomacy:
- **Central African Region:**

In the realm of regional diplomacy, the Central African area stands as a nexus of interrelated states, each with its particular difficulties and possibilities. Among these states, Cameroon emerges as a vital participant, exerting substantial influence within important regional institutions like the Economic Community of Central African States (ECCAS) and the Central African Economic and Monetary Community (CEMAC). Within these forums, Cameroon plays an active and involved role, contributing to diplomatic talks that aim to encourage economic integration, nurture peace, and boost security throughout the Central African breadth. Through its engagement, Cameroon not only reflects its own interests but also functions as a light for cooperation and collaboration among surrounding governments. With a dedication to communication and consensus-building, Cameroon seeks to solve the many concerns affecting the region, from economic imbalances to geopolitical conflicts. By harnessing its diplomatic skills and regional connections, Cameroon attempts to pave the way for a more stable, wealthy, and linked Central African environment.

- **Conflict Resolution in Cameroon:**

Cameroon, as a proactive member of the international community, has made substantial efforts in resolving disputes among its surrounding nations, notably in the Central African Republic (CAR). Through its diplomatic channels and active participation, Cameroon has played a significant role in supporting peace and security in the area. One prominent facet of Cameroon's engagement is its participation in peacekeeping operations sanctioned by both the United Nations and the African Union. By deploying soldiers and resources, Cameroon has proved its commitment to settling disputes and restoring order in regions impacted by violence and instability. In addition to its military efforts, Cameroon has also employed diplomatic discourse and negotiation to address the core causes of conflicts and foster reconciliation among warring groups. Through diplomatic channels, Cameroon has encouraged communication between warring parties, providing a favorable climate for peaceful settlement and sustained peacebuilding initiatives. Furthermore, Cameroon's role in conflict resolution goes beyond its local boundaries, indicating its commitment to regional peace and security. By actively engaging in peacekeeping operations and resolving disputes, Cameroon has emerged as a vital role in fostering peace and security within the Central African region. Overall, Cameroon's efforts in conflict resolution demonstrate its determination to fostering peace, stability, and prosperity both inside its borders and throughout the larger African continent. Through its diverse strategy combining military intervention, diplomatic negotiation, and regional collaboration, Cameroon continues to contribute substantially to the settlement of conflicts and the progress of peacebuilding efforts in the area.

## B. Africa's Sub-Saharan Region
- **Diplomatic Relations:**

Located in the center of Sub-Saharan Africa, Cameroon actively cultivates bilateral ties with a number of African countries. These diplomatic initiatives are essential to improving collaboration in a number of areas, such as commerce, healthcare, and education. Cameroon hopes to further socioeconomic development and boost regional cohesion via these diplomatic connections. This is especially crucial in an area where poverty, illness, and political unrest are just a few of the many problems. Cameroon's commitment to advance the interests of the continent as a whole is shown by its efforts to forge solid bilateral connections with other African nations. Cameroon aims to provide all Africans a more affluent and peaceful future by cooperating with its African partners.

- **Regional Integration:**

Cameroon's involvement in regional groups such as the Economic Community of West African States (ECOWAS) underlines its commitment to promote economic cooperation

and integration across the West African area. By cooperating with ECOWAS, Cameroon engages with neighboring nations to confront common issues and capitalize on mutual possibilities. Through this collaboration, Cameroon not only benefits from the combined power of the region but also plays a crucial role in creating its economic and political environment. One of the major aims of ECOWAS is to foster economic growth and stability via regional integration. Cameroon's membership in ECOWAS projects helps ease the free movement of products, services, and people across borders, which is vital for promoting commerce and investment in the area. Additionally, Cameroon's involvement in ECOWAS decision-making processes enables it to contribute to the creation of policies that encourage regional economic growth and development. Furthermore, Cameroon's involvement with ECOWAS offers a venue for encouraging political conversation and collaboration with other member nations. By working together under the framework of ECOWAS, Cameroon and its neighbors can handle mutual security issues, promote good governance, and maintain democratic ideals. This partnership not only supports regional stability but also increases Cameroon's reputation on the world scene. Cameroon's involvement in regional entities like ECOWAS indicates its commitment to promote economic cooperation and integration in West Africa. By actively engaging in ECOWAS activities, Cameroon contributes to the region's economic progress, political stability, and general prosperity.

## C. International Diplomacy
- **United Nations:**

Cameroon plays an active role in international diplomacy, notably within the United Nations (UN) framework. The nation is a member of the UN General Assembly and other UN organizations, where it participates in debates and decision-making on a broad variety of global topics. One significant area of attention for Cameroon is campaigning for climate change mitigation measures. As a nation that is susceptible to the repercussions of climate change, such as desertification and severe weather events, Cameroon acknowledges the need of taking action to solve this global problem. Additionally, Cameroon is dedicated to helping UN peacekeeping missions across the globe. The country has provided soldiers and resources to UN peacekeeping operations, indicating its commitment to upholding international peace and security. Furthermore, Cameroon is a fervent champion of human rights on the world scene. The government regularly participates in talks on human rights problems within the UN and other venues, pushing for the preservation and advancement of human rights globally. Overall, Cameroon's strong engagement in the United Nations and other international entities indicates its dedication to tackling global concerns and contributing to international peace, security, and development.

- **Bilateral Partnerships:**

Bilateral relationships serve as key conduits for Cameroon's involvement with states globally, exemplifying its dedication to diplomacy and collaboration on the international scene. Through diplomatic channels, Cameroon creates and maintains connections with a vast range of nations, spanning continents and cultures. These partnerships transcend beyond conventional diplomatic formality, including cooperation activities in diverse sectors. Trade serves as a cornerstone of Cameroon's bilateral ties, promoting the interchange of products and services with partner states. Through mutually advantageous trade agreements, Cameroon exploits its resources and commodities, supporting economic progress and stability. Investment flows reciprocally between Cameroon and its partners, boosting growth across numerous industries and promoting innovation and entrepreneurship. Moreover, bilateral ties act as conduits for technology transfer, allowing Cameroon to access and utilize developments from partner states. This interchange strengthens Cameroon's technical environment, boosting its companies and enhancing its capacities in sectors such as infrastructure, healthcare, and education. Cultural interaction represents another vital component of bilateral ties, developing mutual understanding and respect between Cameroon and its peers. Through cultural exchanges, Cameroon shows its rich past and customs while accepting the variety of its partner countries. This cultural discussion fosters people-to-people relationships, transcending geographical limits and building lifelong partnerships. Collectively, these bilateral agreements correspond with Cameroon's socio-economic development goal, enhancing its resilience and competitiveness in the global arena. By using the talents and resources of partner countries, Cameroon achieves its strategic goals and strengthens its global status. Through persistent cooperation and mutual respect, bilateral ties continue to move Cameroon towards greater wealth and importance on the international stage.

- **Multilateral Engagements:**

Multilateral engagements represent a cornerstone of Cameroon's foreign policy agenda. The nation actively engages in a varied variety of multilateral forums, including important ones like as the Non-Aligned Movement, the Commonwealth, and the Organization of Islamic Cooperation (OIC). These forums serve as crucial spaces for Cameroon to communicate and work with a broad range of countries, transcending geographical borders and ideological divides. Within these venues, Cameroon employs its diplomatic presence to advocate for its interests, contribute to global discussions, and establish alliances with likeminded governments.

Whether it's addressing urgent concerns like climate change, economic growth, or peacekeeping activities, Cameroon understands the inherent benefit of multilateral collaboration in confronting common difficulties that transcend state boundaries. Furthermore, involvement in these multilateral groups offers Cameroon with opportunity to connect with a varied variety of ideas and experiences, increasing its own grasp of global issues and shaping its own policy. By actively participating in multilateral forums, Cameroon underlines its commitment to collective action, international solidarity, and the pursuit of shared objectives for the development of its inhabitants and the global society as a whole.

## D. Economic Diplomacy

- **Trade and Investment Promotion:**

Economic diplomacy is a strategic technique through which nations like Cameroon employ their diplomatic networks to boost trade and investment prospects. This entails leveraging links with other countries to attract foreign investments and strengthen economic relations. Cameroon's efforts in economic diplomacy are reflected in its active participation in different international trade fairs, business conferences, and investment summits. Through these venues, Cameroon demonstrates its economic potential and appeal as an investment destination to major partners globally. By participating in economic diplomacy, Cameroon aspires to not only attract international investments but also to foster sustainable economic growth and development. Through collaborative efforts with other countries, Cameroon aspires to develop mutually beneficial alliances that boost economic success and strengthen its global competitiveness.

- **Development Cooperation:**
Development cooperation in Cameroon is characterized by strong diplomatic efforts aimed at getting development aid and technical help from a number of bilateral and multilateral partners. These programs are vital for tackling the nation's socio-economic concerns, including poverty reduction, healthcare improvement, educational upgrading, and infrastructure development. Cameroon's government collaborates with a broad variety of foreign donors and development groups to generate the required money for these programs. By building links with nations and international organizations, Cameroon wants to create partnerships that may give both financial help and technical knowledge. This collaborative approach is vital for the execution of sustainable development initiatives. Poverty reduction remains a prominent emphasis of these activities. Through collaborations, Cameroon wants to execute initiatives that promote economic possibilities, improve living circumstances, and boost social services for its people. These programs generally involve microfinance efforts, vocational training, and assistance for small and medium-sized firms,

which are crucial for job creation and economic development. In the healthcare sector, Cameroon engages with international health organizations and donor nations to enhance medical facilities, provide access to vital medications, and battle illnesses such as malaria, HIV/AIDS, and TB. These agreements also promote the training of healthcare workers and the implementation of health education initiatives, which are crucial for improving public health outcomes. Education is another significant area where development cooperation plays a critical role. By collaborating with educational foundations, international development organizations, and foreign governments, Cameroon aims to expand its educational infrastructure, offer teacher training, and promote access to excellent education at all levels. These activities seek to lower illiteracy rates and guarantee that more children, particularly females, have the chance to attend school and finish their education. Infrastructure development is also an important component of Cameroon's development cooperation agenda. The government wants funding for developing and renovating roads, bridges, ports, and energy infrastructure, which are crucial for economic growth and increasing the quality of life for its population. These infrastructure developments not only ease commerce and investment but also give job opportunities and help to general economic stability. Overall, Cameroon's participation in development cooperation is a diversified strategy that harnesses foreign help to meet its socio-economic difficulties. By obtaining development aid and technical support, Cameroon wants to establish a more wealthy, healthier, and educated society, providing the framework for long-term sustainable development.

### E. Peace and Security
- **Regional Stability:**

Peace and security are vital foundations for the stability and prosperity of any country, and Cameroon plays a key role in fostering these values both inside its boundaries and in the greater Central African area. Through its active involvement in different regional security frameworks and peacekeeping operations, Cameroon tries to provide a stable and secure environment that encourages economic progress and social development. One of the key ways Cameroon contributes to regional peace and security is via its involvement in cooperative security activities with neighboring nations. These joint initiatives are vital in confronting transnational dangers that do not respect national boundaries. For example, Cameroon works closely with Nigeria, Chad, and Niger in the Multinational Joint Task Force (MNJTF) to battle the Boko Haram insurgency. This partnership has been vital in minimizing the danger presented by this terrorist organization, which has generated substantial instability and humanitarian problems in the Lake Chad Basin.

In addition to counter-terrorism operations, Cameroon also works on countering piracy, notably in the Gulf of Guinea, which is one of the world's most pirate-prone locations. The country's naval forces are participating in regional maritime security efforts, conducting patrols and cooperating with other states to guarantee safe and secure maritime routes. This not only safeguards the marine sector and coastal towns but also helps to the overall economic stability of the area. Organized crime, including people trafficking, drug smuggling, and weapons trafficking, is another important danger to regional security. Cameroon interacts with international organizations, such as Interpol and the United Nations Office on Drugs and Crime (UNODC), to increase its law enforcement capacities and improve cross-border collaboration. By strengthening its capabilities to identify and intercept criminal networks, Cameroon helps to impede the activities of organized crime organizations that endanger security and development. Moreover, Cameroon's commitment to peacekeeping is evidenced by its contributions to United Nations (UN) and African Union (AU) peacekeeping operations. Cameroonian military and police officials have been sent to war zones in Africa, giving critical help in keeping calm and safeguarding people. These missions not only help to the stability of conflict-affected regions but also boost Cameroon's image as a responsible member of the international community devoted to global peace and security. Internally, Cameroon has adopted numerous steps to guarantee internal peace and security. The government has spent in upgrading its military and police forces, enhancing their capabilities to react to internal security concerns. This involves combatting internal insurgencies, managing refugee flows from adjacent war zones, and resolving socio-political problems inside the nation. By maintaining a robust and responsive security infrastructure, Cameroon aspires to establish a secure environment favorable to economic growth and social harmony. Cameroon's diversified approach to peace and security involves active regional collaboration, engagement in international peacekeeping, and solid domestic security measures. Through these measures, Cameroon not only strengthens its internal stability but also helps to the wider security and prosperity of the Central African area.

- **Conflict Prevention:**

Conflict prevention in Cameroon is a complex strategy aimed at sustaining peace and stability inside the nation and the greater area. The Cameroonian government aggressively seeks diplomatic routes to avert disputes by encouraging communication and reconciliation among its varied ethnic, religious, and linguistic populations. This entails regular involvement with community leaders, religious figures, and local stakeholders to resolve issues and create mutual understanding. By fostering open

communication and teamwork, the government seeks to minimize potential tensions and settle issues before they develop into violence. In addition to domestic initiatives, Cameroon invests in preventative diplomacy to address possible causes of instability in the area. This means engaging in regional organizations and efforts that promote peace and security, such as the African Union and the Economic Community of Central African States (ECCAS). Through these venues, Cameroon engages with neighboring nations to combat cross-border concerns, like as terrorism, organized crime, and refugee flows. By working cooperatively, the area can devise comprehensive plans to avert disputes and guarantee stability. Moreover, Cameroon's preventative efforts include economic and social programs aimed at eliminating poverty and inequality, which are typically underlying causes of conflict. The government invests in education, healthcare, and infrastructure to enhance the quality of life for its residents, hence minimizing the chance of social unrest. Efforts to foster inclusive governance and political engagement also play a vital role in conflict prevention. By ensuring that all sectors of society have a role in decision-making processes, Cameroon creates a feeling of ownership and responsibility among its inhabitants. International collaborations and assistance are also crucial to Cameroon's conflict prevention strategy. The country engages with foreign organizations, such as the United Nations and numerous non-governmental organizations, to receive technical support, finance, and experience in peacebuilding initiatives. These collaborations increase Cameroon's ability to manage difficult problems and execute effective conflict prevention measures. Cameroon's strategy to conflict prevention is broad and proactive, involving diplomatic engagement, regional cooperation, socioeconomic growth, inclusive governance, and international collaborations. Through these measures, Cameroon aspires to provide a secure and peaceful environment for its varied people and contribute to regional stability.

To sum up, Cameroon's diplomatic endeavors are distinguished by a dedication to cultivating regional integration, advocating for peace and security, propelling economic progress, and augmenting its worldwide involvement. In order to further its national interests, the ambitions of its people as a whole, and the goals of the international community, Cameroon uses bilateral and multilateral diplomacy to forge alliances, settle disputes, and confront shared difficulties.

# CHAPTER EIGHT

## VOICES OF CHANGE

### 8.1 CIVIL SOCIETY MOVEMENTS

It is impossible to overstate the importance of civil society groups in Cameroon when it comes to pushing for social justice, political change, and human rights. A wide variety of organizations are included in these movements. These organizations include non-governmental organizations (NGOs), grassroots movements, religious groups, and professional associations. Civil society in Cameroon has been tenacious and inventive in its efforts to fight for change, despite the fact that it operates in a hostile environment that is defined by persecution and oppression from the government. This section examines the historical backdrop of civil society movements in Cameroon, as well as essential organizations, significant accomplishments, obstacles, and the hopes for the future of these groups. Civil society movements in Cameroon may be traced back to the colonial period, when organizations emerged to protest colonial control and push for independence. These groups were founded in order to help Cameroon achieve its independence. A short era of political plurality occurred in Cameroon when the country gained its independence in 1960. However, the country quickly returned to a one-party state under the leadership of President Ahmadou Ahidjo, and then again under the leadership of President Paul Biya. Both the rise of civil society and the suppression of dissent were hampered by the political context, which was oppressive. The political liberalization that took place in Cameroon at the beginning of the 1990s was a watershed moment for the country's civil society. The dictatorship of Biya, which was under to criticism from both inside the country and from the international community, implemented multiparty politics and allowed for more freedom of association. During this time period, there was a proliferation of groups that were part of civil society. Many of these organizations played important roles in campaigning for democratic changes, human rights, and good governance.

**A. Key Organizations and Movements**
**i. Cameroon Association of Non-Governmental Organizations (CANGO):**
The Cameroon Association of Non-Governmental Organizations (CANGO) was created in the early 1990s with the main purpose of integrating numerous non-governmental

organizations (NGOs) functioning inside Cameroon. Its establishment was an important step towards strengthening the efficacy and impact of civil society efforts in the nation. CANGO works as an umbrella organization, meaning it serves as a central body that brings together a varied variety of NGOs under one collective structure. This structure provides for improved coordination and cooperation among member groups, allowing them to work more effectively towards shared objectives. One of the major tasks of CANGO is to enhance cooperation among its member NGOs. This requires arranging frequent meetings, conferences, and forums where members may exchange information, debate difficulties, and deliberate on collective actions. Through these coordinated efforts, CANGO helps to guarantee that the operations of various NGOs do not overlap needlessly and that resources are utilized properly. This coordination is vital in a scenario where multiple NGOs may be working on comparable problems but from different viewpoints or in various parts of the country. In addition to coordinating, CANGO is extensively engaged in capacity development for its member organizations. This component of its activity is targeted at increasing the capacities of NGOs to successfully carry out their objectives. Capacity development may take several forms, including training seminars, technical help, and giving access to important resources and information. By strengthening the skills and expertise of NGO personnel and volunteers, CANGO assists these organizations to better their project execution, management practices, and overall organizational growth. Advocacy is another key component of CANGO's efforts. The group functions as a voice for its members, supporting their concerns at national and international levels.

CANGO participates in advocacy on a broad variety of problems, including health, education, governance, and human rights. By lobbying government agencies, interacting with politicians, and participating in public discussions, CANGO tries to influence policy and decision-making processes in favor of its members' interests. This advocacy effort is vital for building an enabling climate in which NGOs may function more efficiently and have a bigger influence on the communities they serve. CANGO's emphasis areas reflect the broad and urgent demands of Cameroonian society. In the health sector, member NGOs could concentrate on topics such as maternity and child health, HIV/AIDS prevention and treatment, and enhancing access to healthcare services in disadvantaged communities. In education, CANGO members could be active in programs aiming at boosting school enrollment rates, enhancing the quality of education, and encouraging adult literacy. Governance-related activities might include initiatives to improve openness, accountability, and public involvement in political processes. Overall, the Cameroon Association of Non-Governmental

Organizations plays a significant role in the country's civil society environment. By bringing together NGOs from all sectors, giving them with the assistance they need, and lobbying on their behalf, CANGO works to magnify their influence and contribute to the social, economic, and political growth of Cameroon.

## ii. Transparency International Cameroon

Transparency International Cameroon, as a division of the worldwide anti-corruption group Transparency International, plays a significant role in the fight against corruption inside Cameroon. It has established itself as a dominant force campaigning for openness, accountability, and integrity in both governmental and commercial activities. The group participates in numerous actions aiming at exposing corrupt practices, educating the public, and promoting governmental changes to build a more open and accountable environment. One of the major operations of Transparency International Cameroon is performing detailed research and analysis to uncover and expose corruption. This entails collecting data, conducting surveys, and generating reports that identify locations where corruption is most widespread. These reports are vital tools for increasing awareness among the public and policymakers about the degree and effect of corruption in the nation. In addition to research, Transparency

International Cameroon is actively engaged in advocacy and lobbying operations. The group strives to influence legislation and policy choices to increase openness and accountability. This involves interacting with government officials, lawmakers, and other stakeholders to advocate anti-corruption legislation and policies. Through these activities, Transparency International Cameroon works to build a legislative and institutional environment that deters corrupt behaviors and holds perpetrators responsible.

Education and public awareness efforts are also vital to the organization's aim. openness International Cameroon offers workshops, seminars, and public forums to educate individuals about their rights and the necessity of openness and accountability. By equipping people with information, the group aspires to build a culture of honesty and civic duty. These instructional programs are especially crucial in a nation where public understanding of corruption concerns may be low. Furthermore, Transparency International Cameroon offers assistance and protection for whistleblowers. Recognizing the hazards encountered by persons who reveal corrupt practices, the group gives legal advice and aid to whistleblowers to safeguard their safety and security. This assistance is crucial in encouraging more individuals to come forward with knowledge on corruption, hence boosting the efficacy of anti-corruption activities. The organization also interacts with other civil society groups, the commercial sector, and international organizations to improve the joint fight against corruption. By developing relationships and networks, Transparency International Cameroon increases its effect and leverages extra resources and experience. These alliances are vital for building a united and coordinated strategy to addressing corruption at both national and international levels. Transparency International Cameroon's activities have resulted to considerable gains, including improved public knowledge of corruption concerns, the adoption of anti-corruption measures, and more scrutiny of government and corporate practices. However, the organization continues to encounter problems, such as political pushback, limited resources, and the endemic nature of corruption in numerous sectors. Despite these hurdles, Transparency International Cameroon is devoted to its goal and continues to play a critical role in promoting transparency, accountability, and good governance in Cameroon.

### iii. Network of Human Rights Defenders in Central Africa (REDHAC)

The Network of Human Rights Defenders in Central Africa (REDHAC) is a vital organization committed to defending and enhancing the rights of human rights defenders throughout Cameroon and the greater Central African area. This organization plays a key role in assisting people and organizations that campaign for human rights, ensuring they may continue their work despite the various hurdles they confront. REDHAC offers crucial legal aid to human rights defenders, helping them negotiate the sometimes complicated and hostile legal environments they confront. This legal help is crucial for activists who are routinely targeted by authoritarian governments and endure legal harassment, arbitrary arrests, and detentions. By granting legal assistance, REDHAC guarantees that these defenders have the necessary means and counsel to protect themselves and their rights. In addition to legal help, REDHAC gives logistical aid to human rights advocates. This might involve providing safe locations for activists who are under danger, promoting communication and coordination among different human rights organizations, and supplying financial assistance for various activities and situations. This logistical assistance is crucial for preserving the operating capacity of human rights groups and ensuring that activists may continue their work without interruption.

Moreover, REDHAC is heavily concerned in recording human rights violations in the area. By meticulously documenting instances of violations, REDHAC helps raise worldwide attention to the suffering of human rights advocates and the larger society. This documentation is vital for advocacy activities, since it offers solid proof that can be used to compel governments and international authorities to take action against perpetrators of human rights violations. Through its comprehensive support structure, REDHAC increases the resilience and effectiveness of human rights activists in Central Africa. The group not only helps safeguard individual activists but also promotes a more vibrant and integrated human rights network. By doing so, REDHAC helps greatly to the promotion and preservation of human rights in an area that regularly experiences severe political and social turbulence. Overall, the Network of Human Rights Defenders in Central Africa (REDHAC) is a cornerstone in the battle for human rights in Cameroon and the Central African area. Its multidimensional approach to helping human rights defenders—through legal, logistical, and documentation efforts—ensures that these critical players may continue their work in campaigning for justice, freedom, and equality.

### iv. Ecumenical Service for Peace (SEP)

Ecumenical Service for Peace (SEP) is a faith-based organization devoted to promoting peace, justice, and human rights inside Cameroon. The group works in a number of activities aimed at encouraging peaceful cooperation and resolving social injustices. Through advocacy, SEP attempts to increase awareness about crucial problems impacting communities and encourage legislative changes that favor peace and human rights. The group also lays a significant focus on education, giving training and tools to equip people and communities with the information and skills required to advocate for their rights and participate in constructive conversation. SEP's mediation efforts are especially crucial in the light of the continuing violence in the Anglophone areas of Cameroon.

The Anglophone crisis, which started as a political argument about the marginalization of English-speaking Cameroonians, has evolved into a violent confrontation between separatist organizations and government troops. In this hazardous context, SEP has played a significant role in encouraging conversation between contending groups and resolving conflicts to avoid further escalation of violence. In addition to its dispute resolution activities, SEP works on different programs aimed at improving social cohesion and aiding disadvantaged groups. These programs frequently involve community-building activities, assistance for displaced individuals, and attempts to address underlying causes of conflict such as poverty and inequality. By addressing both current needs and long-term structural challenges, SEP helps to developing a more equal and peaceful society. Overall, the Ecumenical Service for Peace stands out as an important institution in Cameroon's civil society scene. Its comprehensive approach to peacebuilding—encompassing advocacy, education, and mediation—demonstrates a genuine commitment to establishing sustainable peace and safeguarding human rights in the face of difficult and ongoing problems.

**v. Cameroon People's Party (CPP)**

The Cameroon People's Party (CPP) stands out as a prominent force in Cameroon's political scene, not only for its function as a political party, but for its vast efforts in organizing civil society around critical causes. The CPP has been in the forefront of advocating for political change, striving to establish a more democratic and fair society in Cameroon. Its efforts are focused at tackling fundamental difficulties within the country's political structure, encouraging a more transparent and responsible administration. One of the primary areas of the CPP's advocacy is the battle against corruption. Corruption is a prevalent problem in Cameroon, impacting numerous industries and damaging public faith in political institutions. The CPP has vigorously advocated for anti-corruption legislation, attempting to uncover corrupt practices and hold public officials responsible. This involves fighting for stronger legal frameworks, more implementation of current anti-corruption legislation, and enhanced openness in government operations. Electoral openness is another major focus of the CPP's activities. The party has been vociferous on the need for free and fair elections, which are crucial to a functioning democracy. This entails pushing for improvements in the electoral process to guarantee that elections are conducted in a transparent way, free from manipulation and fraud.

The CPP has advocated for the formation of independent electoral bodies, the adoption of trustworthy and tamper-proof voting technology, and the safeguarding of voters' rights to participate in the election process without intimidation or force. Through its advocacy, the CPP has played a critical role in organizing civil society, urging ordinary individuals to join in the political process and demand improved government. The party's actions generally involve organizing public rallies, educational campaigns, and community forums to increase awareness about political and social concerns. By doing so, the CPP serves to empower people, providing them the skills and information they need to fight for their rights and hold their leaders responsible. In summation, the Cameroon People's Party is more than simply a political body; it is a catalyst for change inside Cameroonian society. Its continuous pursuit of political reform, anti-corruption legislation, and election openness has made it a vital participant in the struggle for a more democratic and egalitarian Cameroon. Through its initiatives, the CPP continues to inspire and organize civil society, establishing a culture of active civic involvement and responsibility.

**vi. North West and South West Women's Task Force (SNWOT)**

The North West and South West Women's Task Force (SNWOT) is a famous organization devoted to fighting for women's rights and promoting peace in the conflict-affected Anglophone parts of Cameroon. This group has emerged as a key force amid the present crisis, which has profoundly impacted the lives of many, particularly women and children. SNWOT operates with a broad approach to tackle the numerous issues encountered by women in these regions. One of its key missions is to support women who have been directly harmed by the conflict, providing them with crucial resources and assistance. This aid spans from psychological treatment to economic empowerment efforts, seeking to help women rebuild their lives and recover their independence in the wake of the upheaval. In addition to direct support services, SNWOT plays a crucial role in peacebuilding operations. The organization actively engages in conversations and negotiations, attempting to provide a platform where women's voices may be heard in the peace process. They organize and participate in various conferences, bringing together stakeholders from different sectors to discuss and devise strategies for a permanent peace. By pushing for the involvement of women in peace discussions, SNWOT assures that the perspectives and needs of women are not overlooked in the hunt for a solution to the conflict. SNWOT's operations extend to raise awareness about the suffering of women in the crisis zones.

Through campaigns and collaboration with other civil society organizations, they try to highlight the special obstacles encountered by women, such as gender-based violence, displacement, and lack of access to healthcare and education. By focusing emphasis on these difficulties, SNWOT wants to gain both national and international support for their cause. Education and capacity-building are also crucial to SNWOT's mission. They conduct training sessions and seminars aiming at teaching women with the skills and knowledge essential to advocate for their rights effectively. These programs cover a wide array of themes, including leadership, conflict resolution, and human rights. By providing women with these abilities, SNWOT not only enhances their ability to engage to the peace process but also builds a sense of agency and resilience throughout the community. Moreover, SNWOT engages with other organizations, both within and outside Cameroon, to strengthen their effect. Through these ties, they are able to share resources, expertise, and ideas, enhancing their overall effectiveness in addressing the needs of women in the combat zones. These alliances also assist to develop a bigger coalition of activists working towards a common purpose of peace and gender equality. The North West and South West Women's Task Force stands as a testament to the power of grassroots movement in effecting social change. Their work underscores the significance of involving women in all phases of peacebuilding and post-conflict rehabilitation. By protecting women's rights and working for their inclusion in peace processes, SNWOT not only meets acute humanitarian needs but also aids to the long-term stability and development of the Anglophone territories of Cameroon.

## B. Major Achievement
### i. Advocacy for Electoral Reforms:

Civil society groups in Cameroon have played a major role in campaigning for electoral changes, notably contributing to the move towards more transparent and fair election procedures. Their relentless efforts have raised attention to the need for integrity in elections and have impacted numerous critical improvements within the electoral structure. One of the noteworthy results emerging from this lobbying is the formation of Elections Cameroon (ELECAM), an independent election administration authority. Prior to ELECAM's inception, the election process in Cameroon was frequently criticized for being strongly controlled by the government, leading to questions about impartiality and fairness. Civil society groups urged for the development of an independent body that could supervise elections with more impartiality and openness. The founding of ELECAM constituted a major step forward in resolving these issues, since it attempted to limit government intervention and increase the confidence of the election process. Moreover, these groups have not only concentrated on the development of ELECAM but have also been actively engaged in monitoring its actions to ensure it achieves its goal properly. They have participated in voter education efforts, teaching residents about their voting rights and the necessity of participation in elections. By educating voters with information, civil society has helped improve voter participation and develop a more engaged and educated electorate.

In addition to instructional activities, civil society organizations have also performed a watchdog role, watching elections to discover and report anomalies. Their presence has helped to enhance accountability and openness during elections, since they give independent evaluations of the electoral process. This monitoring has been vital in identifying instances of fraud, voter intimidation, and other malpractices, therefore exerting pressure on authorities to solve these concerns. Furthermore, civil society groups have participated in conversation with government officials and political players to argue for comprehensive election changes. Through workshops, conferences, and policy papers, they have given evidence-based proposals targeted at strengthening the voting system. These attempts have led to debates on different facets of electoral reform, such as voter registration procedures, the transparency of vote counting, and the impartiality of election officials. The lobbying of civil society groups for election changes in Cameroon has resulted in substantial successes. The formation of ELECAM as an autonomous entity is a monument to their influence and tenacity. Their continual efforts in voter education, election monitoring, and policy advocacy have cumulatively led to steps towards more free, fair, and transparent elections in Cameroon.

## ii. Human Rights Awareness and Protection:

Cameroon has made substantial improvements in human rights awareness and protection, mostly spurred by the continuous efforts of civil society groups. These organizations have played a crucial role in recording and exposing human rights violations, which include the maltreatment of disadvantaged populations, the incarceration of political prisoners, and acts of governmental brutality. By methodically compiling evidence and delivering thorough reports on these crimes, they have effectively increased awareness both inside Cameroon and on international forums. This heightened awareness has been helpful in gaining support from worldwide human rights groups and putting pressure on the Cameroonian government to take meaningful efforts towards resolving these concerns. The documentary efforts have not only brought to light the hardships of underprivileged populations but also revealed the systemic nature of the crimes, spurring demands for greater changes. The civil society's publications typically contain statements from victims and witnesses, adding a human face to the data and making the predicament of these persons more accessible and serious. International media coverage and the cooperation of global human rights watchdogs have magnified these voices, establishing a network of accountability that the administration cannot simply ignore. Moreover, the greater knowledge has led to a more educated and engaged citizenry in Cameroon. People are now more aware of their rights and are abler to demand justice and responsibility. Civil society groups have also been essential in providing legal help and advocacy for victims, ensuring that their claims are heard and that they get the necessary support to seek restitution. The pressure on the government has resulted in some good improvements, but the process is frequently gradual and riddled with problems. There have been times when the government, in response to both internal and foreign criticism, has made vows to investigate abuses, free political prisoners, and engage in conversation with opposition organizations. While these efforts are important, they are frequently considered as first movements that need ongoing lobbying and monitoring to guarantee long-term effect and true progress in human rights circumstances. In summary, the greatest successes in Cameroon regarding human rights awareness and protection may be credited to the continuous efforts of civil society groups. Their effort in recording and exposing violations has increased awareness, rallied worldwide support, and placed pressure on the government to address these essential challenges. These groups have established a forum for victims' voices to be heard, supported legal proceedings, and developed a more aware and proactive citizenry. Although obstacles continue, the progress accomplished underlines the essential role of civil society in furthering human rights and keeping the government responsible. The continuing efforts continue to shed a light on injustices, pressing for persistent progress in the preservation and promotion of human rights in Cameroon.

### iii. Anti-Corruption Efforts:

In the sphere of anti-corruption initiatives, Transparency International Cameroon and many other anti-corruption organizations have pushed major investigations into corruption issues inside the country. Through their meticulous effort, they have effectively brought to light several cases of corruption that would have otherwise stayed secret. These findings have spurred heightened public awareness and scrutiny surrounding unethical activities common among political institutions and other areas of society. The disclosure of these corruption scandals has not only helped to throw light on the severity of the problem but has also stimulated a need for accountability and transparency among the Cameroonian people. Citizens are more outspoken in their rejection of corrupt practices and are actively pressing for tough measures to eliminate corruption at all levels of administration. Furthermore, the continuous efforts of these anti-corruption organizations have prompted the government to take some type of action against implicated officials and companies participating in corrupt operations. While the nature of these measures may vary, ranging from administrative punishments to judicial procedures, they still constitute a step towards tackling the prevalent problem of corruption inside the nation. Overall, the continuous devotion of Transparency International Cameroon and its peers in the anti-corruption movement has substantially helped to establishing a culture of accountability, integrity, and transparency inside Cameroon. Their unrelenting dedication to eliminating corruption serves as a light of hope for a future where ethical government triumphs, and the interests of the population are valued above all else.

### iv. Peacebuilding and Conflict Resolution:

Considerable progress has been achieved in Cameroon toward peacekeeping and conflict resolution, especially in light of the ongoing unrest in the Anglophone areas. Organizations from the civil community have become essential in promoting harmony and stability. They have led conversation attempts to bridge gaps between opposing groupings via their coordinated efforts. These conversations are essential forums for promoting understanding, communication, and eventually the settlement of disputes. Furthermore, civil society organizations have played a crucial role in delivering vital humanitarian relief to areas devastated by the fighting. Their services include food distribution, medical supply distribution, and emotional help for victims of violence. In conflict-stricken communities, these groups help to restore some semblance of resilience and normality by attending to the urgent needs of the impacted populace. Civil society plays a more significant part in Cameroon's peacebuilding initiatives than only acting as a mediator and source of aid. Additionally, these organizations take part in lobbying and advocacy campaigns, raising the voices of underrepresented groups and promoting inclusive laws that remedy underlying concerns. They work to create an atmosphere that is favorable to long-term peace and development via their advocacy work. The proactive participation of civil society groups is largely responsible for Cameroon's significant accomplishments in peacebuilding and conflict resolution. Navigating the complexity of the continuing conflict and guiding the country towards a road of reconciliation and permanent peace has been made possible by their unwavering devotion, fortitude, and commitment to resolving humanitarian needs and promoting discussion.

**v. Women's rights and gender equality:**

Gender equality and women's rights have made great progress in Cameroon, thanks in large part to the committed work of groups such as SNWOT. Because of their steadfast dedication, they have raised the conversation about women's rights and created a more activist and conscious national environment. These measures have had a noticeable effect, as seen by real legislative changes that show how important gender parity is becoming more and more. In addition to increasing awareness, SNWOT's activism has sparked significant improvements that attempt to remove obstacles standing in the way of women's advancement and empowerment. Through advocating for women's rights, SNWOT has played a role in creating a more just and inclusive community where women have the chance to prosper and have a significant impact on Cameroon's growth. They have ignited a movement that keeps pushing toward a day when gender equality is not only an ideal but a basic reality via their coordinated efforts.

## C. Chanllenges
### i. Government Repression:

Civil society groups in Cameroon, despite their noteworthy successes, meet enormous barriers, particularly in the form of government persecution. The authorities routinely turn to measures of intimidation, harassment, and arbitrary arrests as reactions to civic activity. Moreover, legal measures constraining the freedom of assembly and speech are used as instruments to crush any kind of criticism. This pervasive repression undermines the basic rights of individuals and obstructs the development towards a more inclusive and democratic society.

### ii. Limited Resources:

Challenges are plentiful, particularly in the setting of restricted resources inside Cameroon. Civil society groups, essential in campaigning for many causes and pushing social change, find themselves coping with a severe constraint—limited financial and logistical resources. This shortage provides a tremendous challenge, restricting their potential to implement programs with efficiency and to spread their impact beyond communities. Operating with restricted resources constrains the breadth and depth of their influence. Without appropriate financing, these organizations confront difficulty in executing their programs, conducting research, and delivering crucial services to their target groups. Additionally, logistical restrictions impair their capacity to mobilize effectively, impeding their outreach efforts and restricting their involvement with stakeholders. This shortage isn't only an annoyance but a barrier that stifles the possibility for genuine advancement. It limits the breadth of interventions, curtails innovation, and weakens sustainability initiatives. Moreover, it exacerbates existing inequities, as underprivileged populations suffer the burden of the shortage in services and advocacy. Addressing these resource restrictions needs new techniques and coordinated initiatives.

Whether by creating collaborations with donors, utilizing technology for cost-effective solutions, or campaigning for governmental changes to better financing systems, there exists a range of options to offset these issues. Ultimately, overcoming these restrictions is vital for building an atmosphere where civil society groups may survive and successfully promote the issues that are instrumental for social development and fairness in Cameroon. Through strategic planning, resource mobilization, and collaborative action, the capacity to surpass these hurdles and create significant change is within grasp.

**iii. Internal Divisions:**

The issues within Cameroon's civil society are varied, mainly defined by internal differences that impair its collective efficacy. These divides emerge in different ways, including fragmentation and a conspicuous dearth of coordination among the profusion of civil society organizations functioning inside the country. Such disagreement dilutes their influence, making their efforts less forceful than they may be. One key aspect contributing to this fragmentation is the variety of ideas, methods, and interests among various groupings. Each company frequently clings strongly to its own set of views, procedures, and goals, which may not necessarily line with those of others. This imbalance creates rivalry rather than collaboration, resulting to a lack of synergy in their attempts. Moreover, diverse strategic approaches further worsen the lack of coherence within Cameroon's civil society scene. Some organizations may emphasis campaigning and lobbying, while others tend towards direct action or community mobilization. Such variations in approach can inhibit successful cooperation, since varied techniques may result in opposing objectives and plans. Additionally, the lack of a unifying framework or platform for conversation and collaboration exacerbates these internal differences. Without mechanisms for constructive participation and consensus-building, civil society organizations struggle to establish common ground and create coalitions to solve shared problems. Overall, the internal divides within Cameroon's civil society offer considerable hurdles to its combined efficacy. Overcoming these challenges demands a determined effort to build more unity, collaboration, and coordination across varied organizations, therefore boosting their power to advocate for real change and solve important social concerns.

**iv. Security Concernss:**

Security concerns in Cameroon, particularly in the Anglophone regions, represent a formidable challenge. The persistent conflict in these areas not only jeopardizes the safety of civilians but also presents grave risks to civil society activists. Operating in perilous environments, these individuals courageously navigate through a landscape fraught with danger. Their dedication to promoting societal change and advocating for human rights often places them squarely in the crosshairs of threats emanating from various quarters, including state apparatuses and non-state actors. In the face of such adversity, they persist in their endeavors, undeterred by the ever-present specter of violence and intimidation.

**v. Public Perception:**

In Cameroon, civil society organizations face a myriad of challenges, chief among them being the issue of public perception. This intricate landscape is marked by a struggle to secure trust and garner support from the populace, particularly in areas where government propaganda paints them as external entities or sources of instability. The foundation of a vibrant civil society lies in its ability to engage and mobilize citizens towards common goals, advocating for their rights and interests. However, in Cameroon, this fundamental relationship is often strained due to the pervasive influence of government narratives that depict these organizations as foreign proxies or agents of chaos. This narrative, perpetuated through various channels of communication, ranging from state-controlled media to official statements, creates an environment of suspicion and skepticism towards civil society initiatives. As a result, efforts to address pressing issues such as human rights abuses, social injustice, or environmental degradation are met with resistance and skepticism from segments of the population. Moreover, in regions where the government holds significant sway over public opinion, civil society organizations find themselves marginalized and ostracized, further impeding their ability to effect meaningful change. This marginalization not only undermines the credibility and legitimacy of these organizations but also hampers their capacity to mobilize resources and advocate effectively on behalf of marginalized communities. To overcome these challenges, civil society organizations in Cameroon must engage in concerted efforts to bridge the gap between perception and reality. This necessitates transparent communication strategies that debunk misconceptions and highlight the positive impact of their work on society. Additionally, forging alliances with like-minded entities and fostering grassroots support can help counter the influence of government propaganda and build a stronger foundation of trust within the communities they serve. Ultimately, the struggle for public perception in Cameroon underscores the broader battle for democracy and social justice in the country. By confronting and overcoming these challenges, civil society organizations can play a pivotal role in advancing the collective interests of the Cameroonian people and fostering a more inclusive and equitable society.

### D. Future Prospects

The future of civil society movements in Cameroon bears both promise and worry. The perseverance and resolve of activists continue to drive progress, but sustainable influence will require overcoming the aforementioned issues. Key areas of attention for the future include:

**i. Strengthening Networks and Coalitions:**

Expanding on the future possibilities of Cameroon, one key path for growth lay in the establishment of networks and alliances among civil society organizations. By creating deeper relationships and alliances within this sector, there exists a significant potential to increase their combined power and influence. Such coordinated undertakings open the door for more powerful lobbying campaigns and the pooling of resources. Through these networks and alliances, civil society organizations may raise their views on vital topics, ranging from human rights and social justice to environmental protection and economic growth. By joining under shared aims and objectives, these organizations may harness their combined skills, knowledge, and resources to create real change within Cameroonian society. Moreover, developing stronger networks and coalitions allows information sharing and capacity growth among participating organizations. This helps them to learn from one other's experiences, adopt best practices, and create new solutions to solve common difficulties more effectively. Additionally, these coordinated activities may boost the visibility and credibility of civil society groups, both locally and abroad. A cohesive front makes a better case for lobbying activities and promotes higher credibility among politicians, funders, and other stakeholders.

Overall, the future prospects of Cameroon rest greatly on the capacity of civil society organizations to establish powerful networks and alliances. By working together towards similar aims, people may fulfill their full potential and promote constructive change for the good of Cameroonian society as a whole.

**ii. Engaging Youth:**

The young population in Cameroon constitutes a strong force for change. Engaging young people in civil society activities may infuse fresh energy and ideas into the movement. Young Cameroonians, who make up a considerable section of the population, provide new viewpoints and a readiness to question the current quo. This group is more digitally adept, frequently more aware of global trends, and usually more flexible to change. Empowering the young requires giving forums for their voices to be heard and for their ideas to be acted upon. This may be done via several approaches, including educational initiatives, leadership training, and increasing involvement in local government. Schools and colleges may serve as breeding grounds for future leaders by integrating civic education into their curriculum and fostering student-led activities that address community concerns.

Furthermore, social media and other digital platforms provide significant methods to organize and connect young people. By exploiting these channels, kids may organize campaigns, exchange information, and work on initiatives that promote social change. These digital natives may utilize their abilities to drive movements, create awareness, and mobilize support for diverse causes, making the internet a key venue for activism and involvement. Youth participation also includes establishing environments where young people feel appreciated and their contributions acknowledged. This means not just incorporating people in decision-making processes but also ensuring they have the resources and support required to execute their ideas. Mentorship programs, where experienced leaders assist new activists, may help bridge the gap between generations and build a collaborative atmosphere. Moreover, tackling the socio-economic difficulties encountered by the young, such as unemployment and restricted access to excellent education, is vital. Providing chances for skill development, entrepreneurship, and vocational training may help young people become more self-reliant and capable of driving economic and social change. When young people are economically empowered, they are more likely to engage actively in civic society. To continue young participation, it is necessary to acknowledge and celebrate their successes. Acknowledging their work via prizes, public acknowledgment, and media attention might drive additional young people to become engaged. Additionally, having youth councils or advisory boards inside organizations helps institutionalize their involvement and guarantee their opinions are constantly heard in policy-making. Involving young in Cameroon's civil society is crucial for developing a dynamic, inclusive, and progressive movement. By tapping into the creativity, enthusiasm, and inventive spirit of young people, Cameroon can establish a stronger, more resilient civil society capable of solving current and future issues.

### iii. Leveraging Technology:

Cameroon, a nation rich in cultural variety and natural riches, has a complicated socio-political situation. Despite the problems created by official prohibitions and budget limits, the future prospects for civil society in Cameroon are optimistic, especially with the opportunity to harness technology. Digital platforms provide a potent medium for advocacy, mobilization, and information distribution, offering new channels for civil society to raise their voices and reach bigger audiences. In the field of advocacy, technology may be a game-changer. Digital channels such as social media, websites, and blogs enable civil society organizations (CSOs) to disseminate their thoughts with a greater audience, both locally and worldwide. These forums give a venue for increasing awareness about vital topics such as human rights, governance, and social justice. By leveraging online campaigns, petitions, and virtual events, CSOs may engage supporters, raise attention to their problems, and put pressure on legislators and international authorities to take action. Mobilization initiatives can benefit tremendously from the use of technology. In a nation where actual meetings might be banned or difficult to plan owing to logistical and budgetary restrictions, internet platforms provide an alternative method to bring people together. Social media and messaging applications allow the coordination of virtual meetings, webinars, and online conversations, boosting the sharing of ideas and cooperation among activists, community leaders, and the general public. This may lead to a more cohesive and successful civil society movement, capable of pushing change even in adverse settings. Information distribution is another vital area where technology may have a major influence. Access to credible and timely information is crucial for an educated and engaged citizenry. Digital platforms enable CSOs to circumvent conventional media routes, which may be susceptible to government control or censorship, and directly communicate news, reports, and research results with the public. This provides individuals with the information they need to hold their government responsible and engage more actively in civic life. Additionally, technology may assist the gathering and analysis of data, allowing CSOs to better understand the challenges they are addressing and to build evidence-based plans and solutions.

Moreover, the use of technology may allow civil society in Cameroon to create networks and relationships, both locally and globally. Online platforms enable opportunity for CSOs to interact with like-minded groups, exchange information, and cooperate on initiatives. This may expand their ability, widen their reach, and raise their influence. International relationships, in example, may bring in extra resources, experience, and support, allowing Cameroonian CSOs to overcome some of the restrictions they confront at the local level. Although the obstacles confronting civil society in Cameroon are enormous, the strategic use of technology provides a method to overcome some of these hurdles. By embracing the potential of digital platforms for advocacy, mobilization, and information distribution, CSOs may expand their effectiveness, reach, and impact. This, in turn, may lead to a more robust and resilient civil society, capable of driving good change and advancing democracy, human rights, and social justice in Cameroon.

**iv. International Support and Solidarity:**

The future possibilities for civil society activists in Cameroon are closely tied to international support and solidarity. The involvement of international organizations and foreign governments is vital in providing critical resources and protection for these activists, who frequently face tremendous dangers and hurdles in their work. By offering financial aid, technical support, and training programs, foreign entities may help improve the capacity of local civil society groups, allowing them to function more efficiently and sustainably. Moreover, solidarity from the global community plays a key role in amplifying the voices of Cameroonian activists. When foreign entities, like the United Nations, European Union, and other non-governmental groups, express concern and call for action, it garners worldwide attention and puts pressure on the Cameroonian government to conform to human rights norms. Statements, resolutions, and campaigns from these bodies may expose abuses and argue for the protection of activists, therefore creating a climate where their activities are more likely to be noticed and preserved.

Furthermore, diplomatic participation from other countries may also act as a strong deterrent against repression. By creating conversations and implementing sanctions or other diplomatic actions in reaction to human rights breaches, international countries may influence the conduct of Cameroonian authorities. This sort of international pressure may lead to the execution of changes and the development of a safer environment for civil society to function. In addition to direct assistance and campaigning, international solidarity generates a feeling of global connection among activists. By linking Cameroonian activists with their counterparts in other countries, worldwide networks and coalitions may exchange methods, give moral support, and jointly press for change. This connection strengthens the resilience of civil society in Cameroon, as activists may take confidence from knowing they are part of a wider movement devoted to protecting human rights and democratic values. Ultimately, the prospects for civil society in Cameroon will mainly rely on the continuous commitment of the international community to assist and stand in solidarity with local activists. By continuing to donate resources, advocate for human rights, and engage diplomatically, foreign players may assist establish an atmosphere where civil society can grow and contribute to the progress of democracy and justice in Cameroon.

### v. Legal and Institutional Reforms:

Legal and institutional changes in Cameroon are necessary for the nation's development toward a more open and democratic society. Advocacy for these changes remains an important priority, since they address basic features of government that may support stability, justice, and progress. One of the major issues needing emphasis is the independence of the court. An independent judiciary is the cornerstone of a fair legal system, ensuring that laws are administered uniformly and impartially. In Cameroon, attempts to promote judicial independence would comprise steps to safeguard judges from political pressure, better their professional training, and secure enough financing for the court. This would aid in strengthening public faith in the judicial system and ensure that justice is delivered without partiality or corruption. Reforming election rules is another essential part of the wider legal and institutional changes required in Cameroon. Transparent and fair election procedures are important to democracy. Reforms might include the creation of more strong measures to combat election fraud, ensuring equitable access to media for all political parties, and guarantee the integrity of voter registration processes. Additionally, forming independent electoral organizations that supervise elections without state influence will strengthen the credibility of election outcomes and the legitimacy of elected leaders. Strengthening procedures for accountability is also crucial. This may be done by expanding the authority and resources of anti-corruption authorities, adopting strong checks and balances within governmental institutions, and encouraging openness in public administration. Whistleblower protection laws and public access to government information may empower individuals to hold their leaders responsible. Moreover, building a culture of accountability needs strong civil society involvement. Non-governmental organizations, the media, and community groups play a significant role in monitoring government actions and lobbying for changes. Supporting these institutions via legal safeguards and financial help may increase their effect on governance. Overall, the future prospects for Cameroon rest on the effective execution of these legislative and institutional changes. Such reforms not only pave the path for a more democratic society but also help to economic progress and social stability. By tackling these important areas, Cameroon may develop a more robust and fair society where the rule of law prevails, and people' rights are respected.

In conclusion, civil society movements in Cameroon play a key role in the nation's drive for democracy, human rights, and social justice. Despite confronting enormous hurdles, these movements have accomplished important milestones and continue to be a light of hope for change. The continuous activities of civil society will be essential in defining the future of Cameroon, encouraging a more inclusive and democratic society.

## 8.2 YOUTH ACTIVISM

Activism among young people in Cameroon has emerged as a crucial force for bringing about social, political, and economic transformation. By virtue of the fact that more than sixty percent of the population is under the age of twenty-five, the vitality, inventiveness, and ambitions of young Cameroonians play an essential part in determining the future of the nation. This part of the article examines the dynamics of youth activism in Cameroon, including its problems and the influence it has on a variety of different communities. In the context of history. Throughout the course of Cameroon's history, young people have been actively engaged in political and social activities;

yet, their position has changed throughout the course of time. Throughout the time of colonial rule, a significant number of young people were actively involved in the fight for independence, taking part in demonstrations and political groups. After the country gained its independence, youth groups continued to play an important role in the political scene, especially during times of political instability and economic difficulties.

## A. Contemporary Youth Activism

In modern Cameroon, youth activism emerges in numerous ways, from grassroots movements to internet activism. The emergence of social media has given young activists with tremendous tools to organize, create awareness, and campaign for change. Key places where youth activism is especially prevalent include:

### i. Political Activism

- **Electoral Participation:**

Political activism among young Cameroonians is a dynamic and increasing phenomenon, notably in the field of electoral participation. This participation emerges in numerous ways, expressing a strong desire to affect the political scene and push for change. Young people in Cameroon are more participating in electoral processes, exhibiting a dedication to molding their country's future. They participate as voters, exercising their right to vote and making educated choices regarding politicians and policies. This engagement is vital, considering that the young demographic constitutes a major section of the population. Moreover, young Cameroonians are not simply

passive participants but are increasingly standing forward as candidates in elections. They offer fresh views and new ideas to the political arena, questioning the current quo and pushing for causes that connect with their generation. This tendency is a good indicator of a more inclusive and representative democratic process. However, the route to expanding young participation in elections is laden with hurdles. One important hurdle is the limited political chances open to young people. The political scene of Cameroon is frequently controlled by an older political class, who have long maintained power and are reluctant to change. This dominance may limit the political aspirations of younger persons and make it harder for them to obtain a footing in the political realm. Additionally, there are structural barriers that restrict youth engagement. These include a lack of resources, such as finance for campaigns, and restricted access to political networks that are vital for electoral success. Despite these difficulties, young Cameroonians are finding methods to navigate the political system and make their opinions known. The steady growth in young involvement in elections is a tribute to their perseverance and drive. It also demonstrates the possibility for a livelier and dynamic political climate in Cameroon. As young people continue to participate in political processes, they bring with them the promise of innovation and change, challenging conventional power structures and pushing for a more inclusive and equitable society. This trend of rising political involvement among young Cameroonians is vital for the country's democratic growth. It guarantees that a varied variety of opinions and viewpoints are reflected in the political process, resulting to more thorough and effective government. As this momentum increases, it is necessary for both the government and society at large to promote and encourage the political involvement of young people, recognizing their critical role in molding the future of Cameroon.

- **Movements and Protests:**

Youth-led protests and movements have gained prominence as a means of voicing political complaints and promoting change. Driven by a yearning for fairness and an improved future, youth have spearheaded several noteworthy demonstrations across. These demonstrations are often sparked by a variety of problems, including election fraud, corruption in the administration, and violations of human rights. Young activists' tenacity and organization have drawn attention to their problems on a global scale, highlighting the strength and significance of movements headed by young people. An important instance of a protest spearheaded by young people is the Anglophone Crisis that started in Cameroon in 2016. Long-standing hostilities between the nation's Anglophone and Francophone areas gave rise to the conflict. The government, which was mostly Francophone, made Anglophones feel alienated and discriminated against, thus

they began to seek more autonomy and respect for their cultural and linguistic rights. In these events, youth were crucial in planning demonstrations, spreading awareness via social media, and engaging with law enforcement. Their participation was crucial in drawing attention to the larger problems of governance and human rights in Cameroon as well as the suffering of the Anglophone regions on a global scale. Protests spearheaded by young people have often successfully combated election fraud. Young activists have organized to call for free and fair elections because they are often demoralized by unethical behavior that compromises democratic processes. They have exerted pressure on authorities to eliminate election malpractices and assure transparency via nonviolent rallies, sit-ins, and internet initiatives. On occasion, their efforts have resulted in the installation of safeguards for future elections, the resignation of dishonest officials, and important political changes. Another problem that has sparked youth-led uprisings worldwide is government corruption. Young people are demanding justice and transparency in the streets because they are angry over the misappropriation of public monies and the leaders' lack of responsibility. In order to raise awareness of the concerns, these demonstrations often include artistic and nonviolent forms of resistance such street art, music, and performance. Young activists create a feeling of community and solidarity among themselves and their supporters by participating in these activities, in addition to expressing their disagreement. Protests staged by young people have sometimes been sparked by violations of human rights. Young people have rebelled against injustice, including gender-based violence and police brutality, in several nations. Their activism has been distinguished by a readiness to defy authority and take serious risks, such as being physically attacked or arrested. Social media's worldwide reach has given them a greater voice, enabling them to enlist the aid of supporters abroad and increase pressure on their governments to protect human rights. Young protestors' tenacity and inventiveness have often resulted in significant change. Their campaigns have brought about changes to laws, the removal of dishonest officials, and an increase in public understanding of social justice concerns. Furthermore, these demonstrations have shown how important it is for youth to shape the future of their communities. They continue to motivate and inspire new generations of activists with their dedication to justice, equality, and democracy.

- **Civil Society Organizations:**

Civil society organizations (CSOs) in Cameroon play a key role in influencing the social and political environment of the nation. These groups, spearheaded by youthful activists, are devoted to supporting democracy, human rights, and good governance. They operate as crucial intermediaries between the

government and the population, fighting for openness, accountability, and inclusive governance. Young activists within these CSOs are typically at the forefront of initiatives to build a more participatory political climate. They add new ideas and enthusiasm to the cause, which is vital for pushing change in a culture where conventional power structures may be firmly entrenched. By concentrating on democracy, these groups aim to guarantee that elections are free, fair, and transparent, campaigning for measures that prevent electoral fraud and support the integrity of the democratic process. They also engage in voter education initiatives, urging residents, particularly the young, to use their right to vote and participate actively in the political process. In addition to democracy, human rights are another major emphasis area for these CSOs. They monitor and report on human rights violations, giving help and advocacy for victims. This entails tackling concerns such as freedom of speech, assembly, and the press, as well as combatting prejudice and violence against disadvantaged groups. By raising awareness and offering a venue for discourse, these groups attempt to build a culture of respect for human rights across Cameroon. Good governance is a further significant issue, with CSOs aiming to promote government accountability and transparency. They do research, produce publications, and host conferences to address governance concerns, trying to influence policy and decision-making processes. By offering training and resources, these groups equip young people with the skills and information required to engage in civic activities, participate in public discussions, and hold their leaders responsible. Through numerous programs and projects, civil society groups provide young activists with the skills essential for successful advocacy and leadership. They provide training on issues such as civic education, leadership skills, and the use of digital resources for action. These efforts assist young people understand their rights and obligations as citizens, encouraging them to become active participants in their communities and the greater political arena. Moreover, CSOs typically function as a support network for young activists, giving mentoring and possibilities for cooperation. This feeling of community may be crucial in maintaining the momentum of social and political movements, as it enables activists to exchange experiences, learn from each other, and develop solidarity. Overall, civil society groups in Cameroon are vital in advancing democratic principles, preserving human rights, and guaranteeing effective governance. By enabling young activists, they contribute to develop a more engaged, knowledgeable, and active citizenry capable of achieving genuine change in the nation.

**ii. Social Activism:**
- **Gender Equality:**
Social activity in Cameroon has experienced a tremendous spike, particularly among the

young who are enthusiastic about pushing change and tackling numerous social concerns. One of the primary areas of attention for these young campaigners is gender equality. They are ardently campaigning for women's rights and working relentlessly to eliminate gender-based violence. Their efforts are broad and cover a variety of initiatives aimed at increasing the participation of women in leadership positions throughout many sectors of society. Youth activists in Cameroon are utilizing numerous platforms and technologies to disseminate their message and connect with the community. Social media, in particular, has become a strong channel for raising awareness and rallying support. Through campaigns, online conversations, and educational articles, they are able to reach a large audience and generate a discourse around the essential topics of gender inequality and women's empowerment. In addition to internet activism, these young campaigners are also organizing and engaging in on-the-ground efforts. Workshops, seminars, and community forums are often organized to educate people about gender equality and the significance of women's rights. These meetings generally contain conversations on how to detect and combat gender-based violence, giving practical methods and assistance to those impacted. By building safe places for discourse and learning, activists are attempting to break the shame and silence that frequently accompany problems of gender violence. Moreover, the struggle for gender equality in Cameroon entails campaigning for policy reforms at many levels of government. Youth activists are interacting with lawmakers, pressing for policies that will offer greater protection and opportunity for women. This includes requests for tighter legislation against gender-based violence, policies that encourage women's involvement in politics and business, and efforts that help women's education and economic development. Educational institutions are another crucial battleground for these campaigners. By partnering with schools and institutions, they attempt to incorporate gender studies into the curriculum and develop a culture of respect and equality from an early age. Programs and groups devoted to gender equality are being formed, giving students with the information and resources to become champions for change within their local communities. Additionally, connections with foreign organizations and NGOs are helping to enhance the effect of local initiatives. These alliances typically give resources, training, and a bigger platform for Cameroonian activists to discuss their experiences and methods. The assistance from global organizations not only confirms their work but also gives new options for development and impact. Overall, the devotion and resourcefulness of young activists in Cameroon are driving substantial progress in the struggle for gender equality. Their entire strategy, which includes awareness-raising, education, lobbying, and policy change, is building a more inclusive and equitable society. Through their continuous efforts, they are challenging the current quo and paving the way for a future where gender equality is not only a dream but a reality.

- **Education and Employment in Cameroon:**

Young activists committed to building a better future for their generation in Cameroon have turned their attention to the intertwined concerns of education and employment. Since both the high rates of young unemployment and the quality of education are vital to the nation's socioeconomic growth, these activists are tackling these urgent problems. One major problem is the quality of education in Cameroon. Even with government attempts to enhance the educational system, many schools continue to struggle with a shortage of basic supplies, trained instructors, and functional facilities. As a consequence, learning environments are often unfavorable to gaining the skills required for future work. The new curriculum that cater to the needs of the labor market, enhanced teacher preparation programs, and more financing for schools are among the many educational changes that young activists are fighting for with great fervor. Because they think that a strong educational system is the cornerstone of a thriving society, they are advocating for laws that will guarantee that every kid has access to a top-notch education. These campaigners are addressing the problem of excessive young unemployment at the same time. The abilities that young people have and what businesses are looking for don't match in Cameroon's labor market. Many recent graduates experience widespread discontent and unstable economic conditions as a result of their inability to find employment that aligns with their abilities. In response, youthful activists are pushing for more employment prospects and the creation of vocational training programs that provide youth with employable, real-world skills. They contend that vocational education is essential for closing the achievement gap between school and the workforce and giving young people the skills they need to be successful in a variety of fields. In addition, these advocates are trying to establish collaborations between academic institutions and industry to guarantee that training curricula correspond with industry standards. They want to develop a more responsive and dynamic educational system that can change to meet the changing demands of the job market by encouraging these kinds of partnerships. This strategy not only lowers unemployment but also boosts economic expansion by developing a workforce that is more knowledgeable and talented. Young activists use a variety of channels in their endeavors to garner support and increase awareness. To reach a larger audience, they host neighborhood seminars, interact with legislators, and use social media. Their objective is to build a wave of support for the reforms required to drastically alter Cameroon's work and educational environments. These youthful leaders are paving the way for a day when all young Cameroonians will have access to meaningful career opportunities and high-quality education via their tenacious lobbying and creative problem-solving. The development of Cameroon depends on the initiatives of its young activists to raise standards of education and lower the rate of youth unemployment. They are tackling two of the most important problems of their age by supporting the reform of education and the creation of more work possibilities. Their efforts are crucial to building a wealthier and just society where youth may reach their full potential and make valuable contributions to the advancement of the country.

- **Health and well-being:**

Health and well-being are important areas of concentration in Cameroon and include a wide range of topics, such as mental health, HIV/AIDS awareness, and sexual and reproductive health. In order to effectively address these issues, a multimodal strategy is needed, often lead by youth-led projects that are essential to enhancing community health outcomes. In Cameroon, where access to comprehensive sexual education and reproductive health care is restricted, sexual and reproductive health is a major problem. Due to a lack of appropriate knowledge regarding sexual health, a large number of young people are becoming pregnant at an early age and contracting STIs. Initiatives organized by young people have become more important in closing this gap. Peer education programs, which teach young people to inform their peers about safe sexual behaviors, contraception, and the value of routine health check-ups, are often a part of these projects. These initiatives seek to empower young people to make knowledgeable choices about their bodies and lessen the stigma associated with sexual health concerns by encouraging candid conversations and supplying trustworthy information. HIV/AIDS is still a major public health concern. HIV/AIDS incidence remains a serious danger, especially among young people, despite advancements in treatment and awareness. Youth-led programs play a critical role in raising public awareness about and preventing HIV/AIDS. Young leaders try to bust myths and misunderstandings about the illness via community outreach, educational initiatives, and the provision of instructional materials. Among these initiatives include the planning of workshops and seminars that educate attendees on HIV prevention techniques such condom usage, the means of transmission, and the significance of routine testing. These campaigns also often support improved access to antiretroviral medication (ART) for those living with HIV, with the goal of enhancing their quality of life and lowering the virus's transmission rates. Mental health is another crucial area of concern. Because of cultural stigma and a lack of resources, mental health disorders are often underrecognized and badly managed. A reduced quality of life and untreated disorders result from many people's restricted access to mental health treatments, particularly in rural regions. Through raising awareness and offering assistance, youth-led projects are starting to shift the narrative around mental health. Creating safe venues where youth may talk about mental health difficulties without worrying about being judged is a common goal of these efforts. Among the tactics used include peer counseling programs, mental health classes, and raising awareness via social media. These programs seek to lessen stigma and increase access to treatment by promoting improved mental health services and normalizing discussions about mental health. Cameroonian health and well-being are complex concerns requiring all-encompassing and creative solutions. In order to address issues of mental health, HIV/AIDS awareness, and sexual and reproductive health, youth-led programs are essential. By means of peer education, community outreach, and advocacy, youthful leaders are catalyzing constructive transformation and striving for a more educated and healthy society.

### iii. Environmental Activism
- **Climate Change:**

Environmental movement in Cameroon is gaining speed, driven primarily by a rising awareness of climate change and its implications. Young Cameroonians are in the vanguard of this movement, recognizing the urgent need to address environmental deterioration and push for sustainable practices. This increased awareness has inspired the establishment of several youth-led environmental groups and movements committed to promoting conservation, sustainability, and climate justice. These teenage activists are working in a range of projects to counteract the ill consequences of climate change. They conduct awareness programs to educate the public on the necessity of environmental conservation and the repercussions of disregarding it. These campaigns generally involve workshops, seminars, and community outreach initiatives that stress the important role of sustainability in ensuring a livable future. Through these initiatives, young Cameroonians are building a culture of environmental responsibility and pushing their classmates to adopt eco-friendly practices. In addition to instructional initiatives, these youth-led groups are actively engaged in hands-on conservation projects. They engage in tree planting efforts, which assist to repair damaged areas and prevent deforestation. These forestry efforts not only improve biodiversity but also function as carbon sinks, minimizing the effects of greenhouse gas emissions. Moreover, young environmentalists in Cameroon are striving to conserve the country's unique natural legacy by lobbying for the preservation of national parks and wildlife reserves. Climate justice is another essential

part of their work. Young Cameroonians recognize that the repercussions of climate change are not uniformly spread, with underprivileged people typically suffering the brunt of environmental deterioration. To combat this, they are promoting policies and programs that encourage fair access to resources and opportunities for all residents. They advocate for legislative reforms that guarantee environmental protection laws are followed and that communities most impacted by climate change get the help they need to adapt and prosper. Furthermore, these youth-led initiatives are embracing social media and digital platforms to magnify their message and reach a broader audience. By employing these technologies, they may organize support, communicate information, and interact with worldwide environmental groups. This worldwide link strengthens their work and helps them to learn from and contribute to the greater environmental movement. The passion of young Cameroonians to environmental advocacy is a tribute to their commitment to safeguarding a sustainable future. Their efforts are not only raising awareness about the critical need for climate action but are also generating concrete change in their communities. Through education, conservation initiatives, campaigning for climate justice, and the use of digital platforms, they are making important steps towards a more sustainable and equitable society. Their involvement acts as an inspiration and a call to action for others to join the battle against climate change and environmental destruction.

- **Community initiatives in Cameroon:**

Community initiatives in Cameroon are crucial in developing environmental stewardship and strengthening sustainable practices. One such program is tree planting, which has garnered great popularity across several locations. Young activists spearhead these activities, organizing tree planting events to oppose deforestation, increase biodiversity, and minimize the consequences of climate change. These activities generally include local schools, companies, and community organizations, establishing a collaborative attitude and a shared responsibility towards the environment. By integrating broad parts of the public, these programs not only increase the quantity of trees but also educate participants about the role of trees in preserving ecological balance and delivering ecosystem services. Another major area of concern is waste management. With increased urbanization, garbage disposal has become a major problem in many Cameroonian cities. Young activists have taken the lead in tackling this issue by organizing clean-up initiatives and campaigning for improved trash management procedures. These efforts entail cleaning public places, educating locals on the significance of appropriate garbage disposal, and encouraging recycling. By actively engaging in these clean-up initiatives, community members become more aware of the repercussions of littering and the advantages of having a clean environment. Moreover, these projects generally partner with local authorities to enhance garbage collection services and promote legislation that encourage sustainable waste management. Clean-up initiatives are also an important part of community projects in Cameroon.

These projects are aimed to organize volunteers to clean up communities, streets, rivers, and beaches. Such actions not only increase the visual attractiveness of these locations but also decrease pollutants and promote public health. The effectiveness of clean-up initiatives rests on the passion and dedication of young activists who utilize social media and other platforms to promote awareness and encourage involvement. These actions typically gain media attention, further amplifying the message and driving other communities to pursue similar projects. Overall, community initiatives in Cameroon, especially those headed by young activists, play a key role in fostering environmental care. Through tree planting, garbage management, and clean-up efforts, these projects involve communities in meaningful acts that contribute to a healthier and more sustainable environment. By developing a feeling of communal responsibility, these programs help create resilient communities that are better suited to manage environmental concerns. The engagement of young people in these activities also guarantees that future generations are aware of and dedicated to conserving their natural environment.

## B. Challenges Facing Youth Activists

Despite their zeal and efforts, young activists in Cameroon encounter various challenges:

### i. Political Repression in Cameroon:

Political repression in Cameroon is defined by the government's strong reaction to dissent and activity, which has been a major problem in the country's recent history. The administration adopts a variety of techniques to quell dissent and preserve power, frequently resorting to arrests, detentions, and intimidation of activists. These acts are aimed to create an atmosphere of fear that inhibits people from participating in political activities or voicing dissident viewpoints. Arrests and detentions are regular measures employed by the Cameroonian government to stifle dissidents. Activists, opposition leaders, and even regular residents who express their disagreement with the administration might be subjected to arbitrary arrest. These people are routinely jailed without charge for lengthy periods, and their family may be kept in the dark about their location or legal status. The absence of transparency and due process in these instances highlights the authoritarian character of the administration and its readiness to disregard legal standards to stifle dissent. Intimidation techniques further aggravate the climate of dread. Activists regularly claim being followed, getting threatening phone calls, or being subjected to physical attacks. These approaches are not just intended at the persons directly participating in activism but also serve as a warning to those who may contemplate speaking out. The widespread feeling of monitoring and probable retaliation produces a chilling effect, prohibiting individuals from engaging in political activities or supporting opposing groups. The effect of this repression goes beyond the immediate victims. The larger society is impacted as well, with many individuals growing weary of partaking in any type of political conversation. This suppression of free speech and assembly undermines the democratic process and diminishes civic society. It also inhibits attempts to solve social and economic challenges, since fear of punishment discourages free discussion and cooperation on solutions.

In addition to these direct efforts, the government also takes legal and administrative procedures to limit the activity of opposition parties and non-governmental organizations (NGOs). Laws controlling public meetings, media, and non-profit activities are regularly used to curb the operations of organizations seen to be critical of the government. This legislative structure, combined with the arbitrary execution of laws, further constrains political space and perpetuates the oppressive climate. The international community has voiced alarm about the political repression in Cameroon, encouraging the government to respect human rights and democratic ideals. However, the reaction from the Cameroonian authorities has frequently been dismissive, with the government presenting such accusations as foreign intervention in local matters. This approach hinders attempts to redress the human rights violations and encourages a feeling of impunity among those responsible for the repression. Overall, the strong reaction to dissent and activity in Cameroon has generated an environment of fear that stifles political involvement and weakens the foundations of democracy. The persistent use of arrests, detentions, and intimidation, together with restrictive legal measures, guarantees that opposition voices are muted and that the government's grip remains unquestioned. This repression not only effects the immediate targets but also has far-reaching implications for the political and social fabric of the nation.

**ii. Limited Resources in Cameroon:**

Several youth-led groups and movements in Cameroon are greatly impacted by the problem of inadequate resources. These organizations, which are led by enthusiastic young people hoping to make a difference, are often limited by a lack of funding. They find it difficult to attract a wider audience and maintain their projects over the long run in the absence of sufficient funding. These groups continue to push for significant social change and address urgent concerns in spite of the lack of funding support. To make the most of the resources at their disposal, they use their imagination, ingenuity, and willpower. Still, the fact remains that the limitations imposed by little finance impede their potential influence. This financial crisis has far-reaching effects. It not only makes it more difficult for youth-led groups to carry out their initiatives successfully, but it also makes it more difficult for them to interact with a larger audience and rally support for their causes. As a consequence, significant voices and efforts would not be heard, and crucial problems might not be resolved in Cameroonian society. To realize the full potential of youth-led projects in Cameroon, the problem of few resources must be resolved. This calls for coordinated efforts from a range of stakeholders, including governmental agencies, businesses, and international organizations, to provide these groups financial assistance, chances for capacity-building, and networking platforms. Through supporting young people's efforts and investing in them, Cameroon can create a more active civil society and promote good change across the country.

### iii. Lack of Political Will:

Young activists' complaints and concerns have not been met with a real political desire to act. Despite declarations of change and discussions, these pledges are often not followed through on, leaving people feeling very disappointed and disenchanted. This absence of political will takes many different forms. First of all, the government often responds to young demands with flimsy solutions, including committee formation or the introduction of unconstitutional projects with no real commitment or follow-through. When this happens, young activists who had hoped for significant change often feel betrayed. Politicians may also speak in a way that seems to promote topics that young people are passionate about, but their actions may be in direct opposition to these claims. For instance, they can pledge to combat youth unemployment but fall short of putting in place measures that provide meaningful work possibilities. Moreover, there is a clear lack of political will shown by the unwillingness to have an honest and open discussion with young activists. The government often sees them as challengers to the status quo rather than as partners in development, which prevents genuine interaction and cooperation. All things considered, Cameroon's lack of true political will thwarts attempts to address the grievances of young activists and impedes the development of a more just and inclusive society. The cycle of dissatisfaction and disappointment is likely to continue in the absence of a genuine commitment to reform, further undermining public confidence in the administration and fostering social unrest.

**iv. Fragmentation:**

The young activist community in Cameroon is often found to be fractured, with many organizations pursuing their goals mostly independently rather than cooperatively. This disarray is a serious problem as it may dilute the efforts of the activists and lessen their potential influence as a whole. The wide variety of problems that these organizations concentrate on, which might include social justice, political change, environmental preservation, and more, is one of the primary causes of this fragmentation. Every group has a tendency to put its own cause first, which often results in a lack of cooperation and coordination with other organizations. This problem is further made worse by the activist community's lack of leadership and efficient communication. These groups struggle to identify common ground and work toward shared objectives in the absence of clear lines of communication and strong leadership to guide them. The fragmentation of Cameroonian young activist organizations must be addressed by promoting more cooperation and collaboration. This might include developing forums for communication and information exchange in addition to deciding on shared objectives and tactics that all parties can support. Together, these organizations can have a greater effect and raise their voices, which can eventually help bring about constructive change in Cameroon.

## C. Impact of Youth Activism
### i. Policy Changes:

The power structures of Cameroon have been shaken by youth activism, which has led to important policy reforms in a number of industries. The effects have been especially noticeable in the areas of employment and education. Young activists have successfully pushed for measures meant to address the urgent problem of youth unemployment via persistent campaigning and mobilization. The programs and initiatives created specially to provide young Cameroonians the chance to find fulfilling jobs and advance their country have been sparked by their unwavering efforts. A rising understanding of the critical role that children play in determining the destiny of our nation is reflected in these policy reforms. Youth activists have not only gained observable advancements in employment and education by raising their voices and advocating for their issues, but they have also shown the effectiveness of grassroots movements in bringing about constructive change. Youth activism is expected to continue to be a major factor in policy change and advancement as Cameroon navigates its ongoing socioeconomic problems. Young activists are changing the country through cooperation, ingenuity, and unyielding resolve, opening the door for a more promising and inclusive future for all Cameroonians.

**ii. Increasd Awareness:**
The activism of young people in Cameroon has become a strong force, focusing attention on important problems ranging from abuses of human rights to the urgent need for gender equality and the preservation of the environment. Young activists have been successful in magnifying these concerns and

attracting attention to the importance they have within Cameroonian society as a result of their fervent lobbying and relentless efforts. Individuals from many walks of life have been encouraged to actively engage with these concerns and provide their support to the causes championed by these teenage activists as a result of this increased knowledge, which has sparked a larger social conversation. As a consequence of this, a discernible momentum has been established, which has enabled the movements for human rights, gender equality, and environmental preservation to advance with a renewed strength and resolve.

### iii. Empowerment:

Through activism, young people in Cameroon have developed skills, knowledge, and confidence. This empowerment not only enhances their personal growth but also fortifies the whole of civic society. Participating in activism empowers young people by giving them a forum to express their concerns and advocate for change, therefore cultivating a feeling of agency and responsibility. While engaging in different causes, these youthful activists develop crucial abilities such as leadership, coordination, public speaking, and strategic planning. These talents may be applied to other aspects of their life, improving their opportunities for education and job advancement. Furthermore, activism provides young people to a broad spectrum of information, from comprehending social and political challenges to learning about human rights, environmental sustainability, and economic justice. This information expands their horizons and enables them to become better-informed and actively involved citizens. It also helps students to critically assess the difficulties encountered by their communities and propose unique ways to overcome them. The confidence earned via advocacy is another key part of empowerment. As young people experience the visible consequence of their actions, they feel more confidence in their capacity to create change. This confidence is vital for personal growth and for the development of future leaders who are devoted to constructive societal reform. Collectively, the empowering of young activists helps to the building of civil society. A dynamic civil society is defined by active and engaged individuals who work together to solve shared concerns and promote the common good. By engaging in activism, young people in Cameroon are helping to develop a stronger and resilient civil society. Their engagement stimulates increased civic participation, establishes a culture of responsibility and openness, and promotes social cohesiveness. Ultimately, the empowering of young activists leads to a more democratic and inclusive society, where varied views are heard, and collective action drives development.

**iv. Social Innovation:**
Social innovation refers to the creation and implementation of innovative ideas,

methods, and practices aimed at tackling social concerns and increasing the quality of life for communities. In Cameroon, young activists play a vital role in this process, harnessing their ingenuity and excitement to achieve genuine change. Their new ideas can lead to the finding of unique solutions that may be ignored by more standard techniques. These young innovators are not restricted by the standard ways that have previously been utilized to solve societal concerns. Instead, they rely on their experiences, understanding of local circumstances, and frequently a profound feeling of urgency to build significant projects. Their contributions may cover numerous fields such as education, healthcare, environmental sustainability, and economic empowerment. For instance, in the area of education, young Cameroonian activists can design novel teaching techniques or educational programs that make learning more accessible and enjoyable for children in impoverished neighborhoods. These initiatives may combine technology, such as mobile applications or online platforms, to reach students in distant places. By doing so, they assist bridge the educational gap and educate young people with the skills they need for the future. In healthcare, creative solutions could include community health programs that target unique local health concerns. Young activists might launch mobile clinics or health education initiatives that encourage preventive care and healthy lives. These measures not only enhance acute health outcomes but also provide a basis for long-term community resilience.

Environmental sustainability is another crucial issue where young Cameroonian activists are making an impact. They could pioneer programs that encourage sustainable agriculture, trash reduction, or renewable energy. By creating a culture of environmental responsibility, they assist communities adapt to and minimize the consequences of climate change. Economic empowerment is also a big emphasis for many young social innovators. They may build microfinance programs, offer vocational training possibilities, or assist local business. These activities may increase economic growth, eliminate poverty, and enhance the general well-being of the community. The effect of these young activists goes beyond the immediate advantages of their endeavors. By exhibiting the potential of creative thinking and community participation, they encourage others to become engaged and contribute to social change. Their work generates a feeling of optimism and possibilities, illustrating that even the most entrenched issues can be handled through creativity and teamwork. Young Cameroonian activists are at the vanguard of social innovation, employing their unique views and techniques to solve urgent societal concerns. Their efforts not only give emergency answers but also create the capacity for long-term community resilience and well-being. Through their work, they are crafting a more inclusive, sustainable, and prosperous future for everybody.

## D. Case Studies of Youth Activism
### i. The Anglophone Crisis:

In considering the role of youth activism in the Anglophone Crisis, it becomes obvious that young activists have played a key and dynamic role in pushing for the rights and interests of the Anglophone community. The Anglophone Crisis, rooted in historical grievances and linguistic divides between the Anglophone and Francophone regions of Cameroon, has seen significant contributions from young people who have tirelessly worked towards seeking peaceful resolutions and ensuring that the voices of their communities are heard on both national and international stages. One of the key strategies through which young activists have contributed to the movement is via the planning of demonstrations. These rallies, frequently defined by their nonviolent nature and inventive techniques, have acted as significant venues for voicing opposition and demanding for justice. The youth-led protests have highlighted concerns like as prejudice, marginalization, and the demand for more autonomy for the Anglophone areas. These demonstrations have not only increased awareness locally but have also caught the attention of international media and human rights groups, ultimately magnifying the cause. In addition to organizing demonstrations, young activists have been actively participating in conversation with authorities. Recognizing the significance of discussion and communication in conflict resolution, these young leaders have attempted to bridge the gap between the government and the Anglophone populace. Through their efforts, they have endeavored to promote talks that may lead to real solutions and have frequently functioned as middlemen to relay the concerns and desires of their communities. This participation has not been without hurdles, since it includes negotiating a complicated political terrain and frequently confronting pushback from those in power. However, the perseverance and endurance of these young activists have been important in keeping the discourse alive.

Another key feature of youth action in the Anglophone Crisis is the focus on establishing worldwide awareness. Young activists have exploited numerous venues, including social media, international forums, and collaborations with global organizations, to cast a focus on the situation. By sharing tales, reports, and personal descriptions of the situation on the ground, they have been able to gain assistance from the worldwide community. This support has materialized in different ways, including words of sympathy, humanitarian help, and pressure on the Cameroonian government to address the problems of the Anglophone people. The influence of young activism in the Anglophone Crisis is varied. It has not only pushed the misery of the Anglophone community to the forefront but has also enabled a generation of young people to take an active part in defining their future. The boldness and tenacity of these young activists serve as a monument to the potential of youth in pushing social and political change. Their actions have proved that even in the midst of tragedy, young people can be a force for good development, campaigning for peace, justice, and the acknowledgment of their rights.

**ii. Social Media Campaigns:**

Social media campaigns have developed as a formidable tool for digital activism, allowing individuals and organizations to mobilize support and amplify their voices on urgent problems. A significant example is the #BringBackOurInternet movement, which protested against internet shutdowns in the Anglophone areas of Cameroon. This campaign graphically highlights how social media may be exploited to attract worldwide attention to local concerns and apply pressure on governments. In 2017, the Cameroonian government implemented an internet blackout in the English-speaking portions of the nation, a move that was generally considered as an effort to quash dissent and conceal the voices of those demonstrating against perceived marginalization by the Francophone-dominated administration. In response, young Cameroonians went to social media channels to create the #BringBackOurInternet movement. Utilizing Twitter, Facebook, and other social media platforms, activists shared their tales, spread information about the effect of the closure, and asked for worldwide support. The movement immediately gathered traction, with hashtags like #BringBackOurInternet trending internationally. This extensive digital activism not only increased awareness about the situation in Cameroon but also placed enormous pressure on the government to restore internet connection. The worldwide reach of social media enabled the campaign to interact with international organizations, human rights groups, and powerful personalities who amplified the message further.

The efficacy of the #BringBackOurInternet movement shows many crucial features of successful social media campaigning. Firstly, it highlights the capacity of social media to transcend geographic borders, allowing local concerns to attract worldwide attention. Secondly, it emphasizes the power of collective action, as the campaign recruited a wide coalition of supporters who shared, retweeted, and lobbied for the cause. Lastly, the campaign shows how digital platforms may be utilized to hold governments responsible, particularly in circumstances where conventional media could be banned or limited. Overall, the #BringBackOurInternet movement is a powerful illustration of how social media can be a catalyst for change, allowing people to question injustices and speak for their rights on a worldwide platform.

### iii. Environmental Initiatives:

Environmental initiatives are vital in tackling the mounting issues faced by climate change, deforestation, and pollution. Organizations like Green Cameroon are at the vanguard of these initiatives, propelled by the passion and devotion of young activists determined to having a concrete influence on the environment. One of the primary efforts conducted by Green Cameroon is reforestation. This entails planting trees in deforested or degraded places to restore ecosystems, mitigate climate change, and conserve biodiversity. Trees perform a key function in absorbing carbon dioxide, stabilizing soil, and providing homes for innumerable species. By involving local communities in tree planting activities, Green Cameroon not only rejuvenates the natural environment but also promotes a feeling of ownership and duty among the participants. Environmental education is another cornerstone of Green Cameroon's programs. By incorporating environmental subjects into school curriculum, they want to produce a generation of ecologically concerned citizens. This education includes a broad variety of themes, including the significance of conservation, the repercussions of pollution, and sustainable behaviors. Through participatory workshops, field excursions, and classroom teachings, students get a greater knowledge of their responsibility in safeguarding the environment. This information helps students to make educated choices and advocate for sustainable practices in their own lives and communities. Community clean-up activities are also a significant element of Green Cameroon's activity. These efforts target the immediate issue of pollution, especially plastic trash, which is a big problem in many locations. Volunteers gather together to remove rubbish from streets, waterways, and public areas, increasing the cleanliness and health of their surroundings. These efforts not only beautify the neighborhood but also prevent hazardous pollutants from entering rivers and ecosystems, where they may cause considerable damage. Additionally, clean-up programs frequently contain educational components that increase awareness about the significance of good garbage management and recycling.

The actions conducted by groups like Green Cameroon illustrate the potential of grassroots activism in pushing environmental change. By integrating hands-on activities with education and community participation, they offer a multidimensional strategy that treats both the symptoms and core causes of environmental challenges. Through reforestation, they restore and safeguard essential ecosystems. By teaching the next generation, they assure long-term commitment to environmental care. And via clean-up programs, they attack pollution head-on, building a cleaner, healthier neighborhood.

These activities show the significance of local involvement in the global battle against environmental deterioration. While large-scale policy and international agreements are necessary, the work done by local groups and individuals is as critical. They not only execute actual solutions on the ground but also encourage others to join the cause, producing a ripple effect of good change. Green Cameroon's programs illustrate how devoted people and communities can join together to make a huge effect, illustrating that collective action, no matter how little it may appear, can lead to large and enduring environmental changes.

In conclusion the activism of young people in Cameroon is a force for change that is both energetic and dynamic. Young activists continue to work for a brighter future, tackling crucial concerns in the political, social, and environmental realms, despite the fact that they are confronted with tremendous challenges. Their efforts not only contribute to advances that are occurring right now, but they also build the framework for social transformations that will occur in the long run. The voices of Cameroon's young people will continue to be vital in determining the direction that the nation will take in the future as they continue to organize and agitate.

## 8.3 ROLE OF THE DIASPORA

As a strong force for social, political, and economic change inside Cameroon, the Cameroonian diaspora has developed as a prominent force from the country. The term "diaspora" refers to the population of Cameroonians who have relocated to other areas of the globe, such as Europe, North America, and other regions, even if they continue to have strong links to their country. Expats like these make use of their resources, abilities, and networks in order to exert influence on change in a variety of different ways. A number of important aspects may be used to get an understanding of the function that the diaspora plays:

### A. Economic Contributions
### i. Remittances:
- The Cameroonian diaspora considerably contributes to the economy via the remittances they send back home. These cash transfers are a significant source of assistance for families and communities, playing a vital role in supporting family incomes. By giving contributions, diaspora members assist pays important expenditures such as healthcare, education, and everyday living costs. The influence of these remittances goes beyond immediate financial comfort, as they allow families to invest in their children's education, which may lead to long-term economic benefits and social mobility. Moreover, remittances typically act as seed funding for small company endeavors, supporting

entrepreneurship and local economic growth. These investments may lead to the production of new employment and services, further encouraging economic activity within the neighborhood. By sponsoring diverse entrepreneurial initiatives, the diaspora not only helps individual families but also contributes to larger economic development and creativity. In many circumstances, remittances are vital in reducing poverty and increasing economic stability. They offer a financial safety net that may safeguard families from economic shocks and downturns. For instance, during moments of economic crisis or when natural catastrophes hit, remittances may be a lifeline, helping affected communities recover and rebuild more efficiently. The collective impact of these remittances is tremendous, since they constitute a major infusion of foreign cash into the national economy. This inflow may enhance the country's balance of payments and raise foreign currency reserves, which are crucial for preserving economic stability and enabling international commerce. Overall, the remittances provided by the Cameroonian diaspora play a diverse role in sustaining individual families, stimulating entrepreneurial activity, and contributing to the national economy's stability and development. These financial contributions

illustrate the vital relationship between the diaspora and their home nation, illustrating how migration may positively effect economic growth.
- Remittances also contribute to the national economy. The infusion of foreign cash may enhance the country's balance of payments and boost the financial sector. For example, the World Bank claimed that remittances to Cameroon amounted to several hundred million dollars yearly, delivering a considerable boost to the economy. The infusion of foreign cash via remittances helps to stabilize the national currency and may minimize the country's dependence on international borrowing. This consistent influx of income from overseas typically goes straight to families, improving their spending power and encouraging local consumption. Additionally, remittances might enhance the national savings rate, since recipient households may deposit a part of the cash in local institutions. This enlarged savings base may then be leveraged by financial institutions to offer loans and other financial goods, ultimately promoting investment and economic development. Moreover, remittances may play a major role in poverty reduction. For many families, these monies are an essential source of income, typically used to meet basic requirements like as food, healthcare, and education. By reducing financial limitations, remittances provide improved access to services that increase quality of life and

human capital development. In turn, this may lead to increased productivity and economic production in the long term. Remittances can contribute to community development, since pooled monies are often utilized for local infrastructure projects or small company endeavors, boosting entrepreneurship and job creation. In the larger economic environment, remittances may offer a cushion against economic shocks. During moments of economic depression or natural catastrophes, the constant stream of remittances might provide a type of economic resilience, helping to maintain consumption and avert further economic crises. The regular nature of remittance payments gives them a steady source of foreign money, which is especially useful for nations with unpredictable export income or those highly dependent on a small range of export items. Furthermore, remittances may impact macroeconomic policy. The beneficial effect on the balance of payments and foreign currency reserves may offer policymakers with additional flexibility in controlling monetary policy and exchange rates. This financial infusion may also decrease the pressure on central banks to maintain high interest rates to attract foreign investment, allowing for a more balanced approach to economic growth and development. Overall, remittances constitute a major and diverse contribution to the national economy, impacting many levels from family income to national financial stability and economic policy. The considerable input of cash from outside underlines the interconnection of global and local economies, underscoring the significance of migrant workers' contributions to their home nations' economic well-being.

ii. **Investment in Development Projects:**
- The advancement and prosperity of Cameroon is greatly dependent on the diaspora's contributions to development projects. A large number of diaspora residents direct their resources into various fields, greatly influencing the nation's social and economic fabric. Real estate is one well-known investment category. Diaspora investors contribute to the local economy by building residential and commercial properties, therefore alleviating the housing crisis. Building new structures boosts associated businesses like building supplies and services in addition to creating instant job opportunities. Another important industry gaining from diaspora investments is healthcare. Access to medical services is facilitated by the construction of healthcare facilities, such as hospitals and clinics, by Cameroonians living overseas. In places with little or nonexistent healthcare infrastructure, these interventions are crucial. Improved healthcare facilities result in lower death rates, improved health

outcomes, and an all-around higher standard of living. Furthermore, these initiatives often provide cutting-edge medical procedures and technology, improving the quality of treatment that the community may get. Since education is essential to growth, a large number of diaspora investors finance the establishment and upkeep of schools as a priority. These educational establishments, which span from elementary schools to universities, provide much-needed chances for knowledge acquisition and skill advancement. More young people have access to high-quality education, which gives them the information and abilities they need to make significant economic contributions to the nation. Furthermore, educational institutions founded by diaspora investment often provide financial help and scholarships, opening up access to education for a larger range of people. The diaspora's funding of infrastructure projects is essential to Cameroon's progress. Roads, bridges, and other critical infrastructure projects improve connectivity, ease commerce, and stimulate the economy. Improved infrastructure lowers transportation costs, connects rural and urban regions, and facilitates easier access to services and markets. These advancements are essential for promoting regional integration and guaranteeing equitable economic growth across the nation. The country is affected in a variety of ways by the Cameroonian diaspora's involvement in development initiatives. They improve living conditions, provide employment, and support long-term economic growth. Through focusing on important areas like infrastructure, real estate, healthcare, and education, these investments contribute to the development of a stronger, more resilient Cameroon. The diaspora's engagement enhances the development process by contributing not just financial resources but also a variety of viewpoints and skills.

- Diverse diaspora networks and groups have made a substantial contribution to development efforts. These organizations have been essential in helping to combine resources so that bigger, more significant initiatives may be undertaken. Initiatives that may otherwise be beyond the scope of individual efforts have been supported by diaspora groups thanks to their combined organizational skills and financial power. Typically, these diaspora groups work closely with Cameroonian local bodies to make sure their contributions are meaningful and sustainable. They may match their programs to the real needs and objectives of the communities they want to serve by collaborating with regional partners. In order to include local knowledge and skills and ensure that initiatives are not only well-received but also successfully handle the targeted difficulties, this partnership often entails extensive preparation and coordination. Furthermore, the participation of diaspora networks in development initiatives creates a feeling of connection and ownership between the populations living abroad and their own nation. The durability of development initiatives depends on long-term involvement and continuous support, both of which might come from this relationship. The constant exchange of resources, expertise, and information between the diaspora and the local populations in Cameroon thereby increases the effect of these investments. All things considered, the involvement of diaspora groups in development initiatives emphasizes how critical it is to use international networks to spur local development. They play a critical role in closing gaps, allocating funds, and promoting sustainable development, guaranteeing that the returns on their investments last long into the future.

## B. Social and Cultural Impacts
### i. Promotion of Education and Health:
- The diaspora has been actively engaged in promoting education and health in Cameroon, which has had a tremendous influence on both of these areas. Through the provision of scholarships, they guarantee

that a large number of young Cameroonians who may not have been able to afford to continue their study may have the opportunity to get a great education. These scholarships are often awarded to students at a variety of educational levels, ranging from elementary school to tertiary school, and they pay the costs of tuition, books, and other vital educational materials. This financial assistance not only assists students on an individual basis, but it also fosters an environment that values education and places an emphasis on academic achievement among communities. Additionally, the diaspora makes a contribution to education by donating instructional resources to educational institutions. These gifts consist of various learning aids, such as textbooks, laptops, laboratory equipment, and other materials that are often in short supply in many schools around Cameroon. By giving these resources, the diaspora helps bridge the gap between resource-rich and resource-poor educational institutions, enabling a fairer learning environment. In addition to this, they have played a significant role in the establishment of schools in disadvantaged regions, which has resulted in an increase in the number of possibilities available to students who may otherwise have restricted access to education. The contributions made by the diaspora are considered to be of comparable importance in the field of medicine. Communities that do not have sufficient healthcare facilities are often provided with vital medical services by these organizations, who frequently finance and operate health clinics. These clinics not only provide immediate health benefits but also act as training grounds for local healthcare workers, therefore boosting local capacity. The engagement of the diaspora extends to the contribution of medical supplies and equipment, both of which are essential in enhancing the quality of healthcare services. Items like as surgical equipment, diagnostic devices, and medications may make a major impact in the treatment offered to patients. Moreover, the diaspora routinely organizes medical missions, when healthcare experts come to Cameroon to give free medical treatments, perform operations, and provide training to local medical personnel. These missions assist address critical health needs and transfer sophisticated medical techniques and technology to the local healthcare system. Additionally, via public health initiatives and educational programs, the diaspora promotes awareness about major health concerns, supporting preventive measures and better lives. Overall, the diaspora's efforts in promoting education and health have a major social and cultural influence on Cameroon. They not only increase the quality of life for many people but also build a feeling of solidarity

and connectivity amongst Cameroonians at home and abroad. This assistance helps generate a better educated and healthier population, which is crucial for the country's long-term growth and prosperity.
- Diaspora professionals, especially those in the medical and academic areas, regularly return to Cameroon for short-term missions, playing a significant role in boosting the country's progress. These experts bring with them a plethora of specialized skills and information that may have a big influence on local communities and organizations. In the medical area, physicians, nurses, and other healthcare professionals provide services that may not be easily accessible in Cameroon. They undertake difficult treatments, give expert advice, and occasionally introduce novel medical methods and technology. This immediate involvement not only improves patient care but also offers local medical workers with crucial hands-on training. In the academic world, diaspora scholars contribute by participating in teaching, research partnerships, and curriculum creation. They bring fresh instructional approaches and cutting-edge research procedures, promoting an atmosphere of creativity and critical thinking. Their commitment typically goes beyond the classroom, as they mentor students and younger professors, helping to develop a healthy academic community. These exchanges lead to knowledge transfer that may enhance the

quality of education and research in Cameroonian institutions. The advantages of these missions are manifold. They assist bridge the gap between local capabilities and international standards, generating a ripple effect that goes beyond the immediate length of the visit. Local professionals learn new ideas and abilities, which they may subsequently distribute within their own networks. Additionally, the presence of diaspora experts may inspire and drive local talent, highlighting the potential that can result from international cooperation and continual professional growth. Moreover, these trips typically lead to the formation of long-term relationships and networks that may permit continued assistance and resource sharing. Such relationships are crucial for sustainable growth, since they offer a framework for continual interchange of knowledge and resources. This continual engagement helps guarantee that the advantages of the diaspora's participation are not short-lived but lead to sustainable advances in local capacity. Overall, the services of diaspora professionals during their short-term missions to Cameroon are significant. They serve a crucial role in boosting local capacity via the provision of specialized services, training, and information transfer, hence supporting growth and advancement in the medical and academic domains.

ii. **Cultural exchange and preservation:**
- Cultural exchange and preservation play a crucial role in sustaining and promoting the rich cultural legacy of Cameroon, notably via the efforts of the Cameroonian diaspora. Acting as a critical connection between their hometown and the broader world, the diaspora acts as a conduit for spreading and enjoying Cameroonian culture globally. The Cameroonian diaspora organizes and participates in a range of events and festivals that exhibit the country's unique cultural traditions. These events generally feature traditional music and dance performances, food showcases including Cameroonian cuisine, and art displays emphasizing the country's cultural legacy. By bringing these cultural components to a worldwide platform, the diaspora not only celebrates its ancestry but also educates and engages audiences from all backgrounds, promoting a wider awareness and knowledge of Cameroonian culture. Cultural groups formed and maintained by Cameroonians abroad play a key role in these endeavors. These organizations generally concentrate on encouraging cultural events and giving opportunities for Cameroonian artists, singers, and performers to display their abilities. They may also provide language lessons, workshops, and seminars to educate people about Cameroon's history, traditions, and customs. Such programs assist to

maintain the cultural knowledge and traditions that could otherwise be at danger of dying away, particularly among younger generations who may be more detached from their origins. In addition to actual events and organizations, the internet era has created new pathways for cultural exchange. Social media platforms, online forums, and virtual events enable Cameroonians throughout the globe to engage with each other and with worldwide audiences. Through various digital channels, people share tales, music, art, and cultural insights, creating a dynamic and accessible archive of Cameroonian culture that transcends geographical bounds. The significance of these initiatives goes beyond simple preservation; they also contribute to the dynamic growth of Cameroonian culture. Exposure to diverse cultures and ideas frequently leads to a fusion of traditions, resulting in new, hybrid cultural manifestations. This continual interaction and adaptation guarantee that Cameroonian culture stays lively and current, changing in response to modern influences while keeping its essential character. Moreover, the existence of a vibrant and active Cameroonian cultural scene overseas helps strengthens the country's image and visibility on the world arena. It generates a feeling of pride and identity among

Cameroonians, both at home and in the diaspora, and promotes a good narrative about Cameroon to the broader world. This cultural diplomacy may also create doors for other types of international cooperation and exchange, including economic and educational prospects. The Cameroonian diaspora plays a key role in cultural interchange and preservation. Through events, organizations, internet platforms, and daily encounters, they convey Cameroonian culture to a worldwide audience, assuring its continuous life and relevance. This not only helps conserve the rich cultural history of Cameroon but also enhances the worldwide cultural landscape, encouraging mutual understanding and respect among many cultures.

- Cultural interchange and preservation in Cameroon also play a significant part in conserving the nation's rich legacy and identity. One of the key ways this is done is via the efforts of the Cameroonian diaspora, who actively try to conserve cultural customs and languages even while living overseas. This devotion guarantees that newer generations, who may have been born and nurtured outside of Cameroon, stay linked to their heritage. By participating in cultural events, festivals, and educational programs, these communities create an atmosphere where traditions are not only remembered but actively lived and experienced. This develops a strong feeling of identification and community among the younger

generations, helping them understand and respect their ancestry. The preservation of languages is a fundamental part of this cultural continuity. In a nation with over 250 languages, the diaspora plays a vital role in preserving these languages alive. Parents and community leaders typically promote the use of local languages at home and at community meetings. This not only helps youngsters learn and practice their ancestral languages but also reinforces the cultural values and tales buried in the language. Through storytelling, music, dance, and religious traditions, the diaspora passes the essence of Cameroonian culture to the next generation. Cultural festivals and activities conducted by the diaspora are also essential in this interchange and preservation process. These gatherings generally involve traditional music, dancing, cuisine, and costume, giving a forum for cultural expression and education. They serve as a bridge between the ancient and the contemporary, enabling younger Cameroonians to experience the richness of their culture firsthand. These celebrations typically draw not just members of the diaspora but also individuals from other groups, encouraging intercultural understanding and respect. Educational endeavors are another key approach by which the Cameroonian diaspora assures cultural preservation. Language schools, cultural seminars, and internet platforms provide options for learning about Cameroonian history, languages, and customs. These educational initiatives are vital in a worldwide society where cultural integration may often lead to the extinction of individual cultural identities. By offering organized learning opportunities, the diaspora helps younger generations create a firm foundation in their cultural heritage. Moreover, technology has become a vital instrument in the preservation of Cameroonian culture. Social media platforms, websites, and digital archives enable for the exchange of cultural information across boundaries. This internet presence not only preserves the culture available to individuals living abroad but also provides a worldwide network of Cameroonians who can share and enjoy their history together. Online communities and forums offer areas for debate, support, and the sharing of cultural information, ensuring that traditions continue to adapt while keeping faithful to their origins. Through these numerous channels, the Cameroonian diaspora plays a key role in cultural exchange and preservation. Their efforts guarantee that cultural traditions and languages remain lively and relevant, promoting a strong feeling of identity and community among newer generations. This constant connection to their origins helps individuals negotiate their identities in a global world, retaining a balanced appreciation of both their ancestry and their present surroundings.

## C. Political Influence and Advocacy
### i. Advocacy for Democratic changes:
- The Cameroonian diaspora plays a key role in pushing for political influence and democratic changes inside Cameroon. Leveraging their positions in diverse host nations, members of this diaspora utilize their relative freedoms and resources to shine attention on the serious challenges impacting their country. Their advocacy activities are varied and include raising awareness of human rights violations, corruption, and the absence of democratic government in Cameroon. One key part of their lobbying is the usage of media outlets. Diaspora groups regularly organize and engage in campaigns using social media, blogs, and other online forums to share information about the political situation in Cameroon. By doing so, they hope to organize worldwide assistance and attract global attention to the difficulties faced by their country. This digital activity is crucial in evading the restrictions and control typically placed by the Cameroonian government on local media outlets. In addition to internet lobbying, members of the Cameroonian diaspora participate in more conventional kinds of political activity.

They organize protests, marches, and public demonstrations in places throughout the globe, particularly in countries with major Cameroonian communities including the United States, Canada, and different European nations. These activities are aimed to gain media attention and compel foreign governments and international organizations to take a stance on problems relating to Cameroon's political environment. Another crucial channel of advocacy is lobbying. Diaspora leaders and groups regularly engage with policymakers and lawmakers in their home countries to address the situation in Cameroon. They give evidence of human rights breaches and lobby for foreign policy initiatives that might assist support democratic changes in Cameroon. This can include appealing for penalties against Cameroonian authorities engaged in corruption or abuses, campaigning for more humanitarian relief, or calling for election observation by foreign agencies. Moreover, the diaspora actively supports grassroots movements and opposition organizations inside Cameroon. This assistance might take the shape of financial help, strategic counsel, and the development of forums for these organizations to communicate their issues worldwide. By strengthening local activists, the diaspora helps maintain the momentum for democratic change from inside the nation. Educational programs are another significant facet of the diaspora's advocacy efforts. Many in the diaspora try to educate both the foreign community and Cameroonians about the significance of democratic ideals and human rights. They conduct conferences, seminars, and workshops that bring together academics, activists, and politicians to debate and propose methods for political transformation in Cameroon. Lastly, the Cameroonian diaspora regularly engages with international non-governmental organizations (NGOs) and human rights groups. These collaborations boost the credibility and reach of their lobbying activities. By partnering with existing groups, the diaspora may more successfully lobby for international action and assistance. The Cameroonian diaspora's campaign for democratic changes is a multidimensional and dynamic activity. Through media campaigns, public rallies, lobbying efforts, support for local activists, educational projects, and alliances with foreign groups, they try to bring about major political change and maintain democratic ideals in Cameroon.

- Diaspora groups regularly organize rallies, campaigns, and lobbying activities targeting international organizations, foreign governments, and human rights authorities to place pressure on the Cameroonian government for changes. These initiatives are vital in raising worldwide attention to concerns inside Cameroon, which may otherwise be neglected or disregarded. The demonstrations often take place in large cities throughout the globe where there is a substantial Cameroonian diaspora presence. By doing so, they want to create awareness among the worldwide public and media, emphasizing the human rights violations and political persecution happening in Cameroon. Campaigns by diaspora organizations sometimes use social media activity, which is a potent tool for conveying their message swiftly and broadly. These campaigns might involve petitions, coordinated social media postings, and virtual events that engage a bigger audience. The idea is to generate a prolonged and amplified voice that cannot be readily rejected. By employing hashtags, films, and personal testimony, these campaigns may personalize and humanize the challenges experienced by folks in Cameroon, making it more relevant and urgent for worldwide observers. Lobbying activities are another essential component of the diaspora's agenda. Members of the diaspora regularly meet with politicians, diplomats, and officials of international organizations to promote their cause. These meetings are intended at influencing foreign policy choices and promoting the introduction of sanctions or other measures against the Cameroonian administration. Lobbying may also entail presenting thorough reports and evidence of human rights breaches, giving a factual foundation for international agencies to take action. The engagement of expatriate organizations in such initiatives reflects a profound dedication to affecting change in their home country. Despite living distant from Cameroon, they have a deep connection to their hometown and feel a duty to speak for others who are unable to do so from inside the nation. Their attempts are frequently greeted with pushback from the Cameroonian government, which may consider their actions as a challenge to national sovereignty. However, the diaspora's constant efforts help keep the focus on Cameroon and sustain pressure on its government to adopt changes. Through these combined efforts of rallies, campaigning, and lobbying, diaspora organizations play a key role in the worldwide struggle for justice and democratic reform in Cameroon.

### ii. Support for Opposition groups:
- The diaspora offers enormous support to opposition groups and political parties in Cameroon via numerous sources. One key kind of support is financial aid, which enables opposition organizations fund their activities, arrange events, and maintain their operations. This financial assistance is vital for opposition parties, since it helps them to fight more effectively against the frequently

better-funded incumbent administration. The diaspora's donations may finance campaigns, pay logistical expenditures, and help the families of political activists, ensuring that opposition views continue to be heard despite financial restraints. In addition to financial assistance, the diaspora gives strategic counsel that may be important for the success of opposition groups. Many persons in the diaspora have received significant knowledge and views by living in diverse political and socio-economic situations. They bring this information to bear on the tactics adopted by opposition groups in Cameroon. This could include advise on political campaigns, public relations, and grassroots mobilization. The diaspora's feedback may assist opposition leaders polish their messaging, enhance their organizational structures, and devise more effective strategies to communicate with the voters. Furthermore, the diaspora participates in worldwide networking, which serves to increase awareness of the political situation in Cameroon on a global platform. By engaging with international organizations, foreign governments, and global media, the diaspora may expose human rights violations, election anomalies, and other challenges affecting the opposition in Cameroon. This worldwide attention may put pressure on the Cameroonian administration to change and can also gather support for opposition groups from the global community. The diaspora's capacity to organize worldwide networks guarantees that the concerns and goals of Cameroonian opposition organizations are recognized beyond national boundaries, which may lead to greater diplomatic and humanitarian help. By amplifying the opinions of local opposition organizations, the diaspora plays a key role in influencing political discourse inside Cameroon. The diaspora may utilize many forums, including social media, international conferences, and advocacy campaigns, to attract attention to the opinions and demands of opposition parties. This amplification serves to undermine the government's narrative and gives a venue for other opinions. It supports a more diversified and dynamic political discourse, promoting a climate where alternative views and policies may be examined by the public. Overall, the assistance from the diaspora considerably strengthens the ability of opposition forces in Cameroon. Their financial contributions, strategic counsel, and international connections are important in advancing democratic principles and ensuring that opposition voices remain an integral part of the political scene. Through these initiatives, the diaspora not only supports the opposition but also helps to the greater movement for political change and democratic government in Cameroon.

- Social media and internet platforms have become crucial instruments for the Cameroon diaspora to participate in political activity. These platforms allow real-time communication, coordination of actions, and distribution of information, thereby improving the effect of their efforts. In recent years, the worldwide scope and accessibility of social media have presented the Cameroon diaspora with unparalleled chances to engage in political conversation and activity. Through networks like Facebook, Twitter, Instagram, and WhatsApp, users can communicate news, ideas, and updates quickly, providing a dynamic and participatory atmosphere for political involvement. The capacity to interact in real-time is vital for the Cameroon diaspora, particularly when addressing critical political concerns or organizing demonstrations and rallies. Social media helps activists to swiftly recruit supporters, manage logistics, and react to developing situations. For instance, during moments of political turmoil or election cycles, diaspora members may utilize these platforms to communicate crucial information, call for action, and offer live updates, ensuring that their voices are heard despite geographical boundaries. Moreover, digital platforms improve the coordination of operations across multiple areas and time zones. Activists may organize and execute coordinated activities, such as worldwide demonstrations or online campaigns, by

using the connection afforded by these technologies. This degree of cooperation boosts the visibility and effect of their work, attracting attention to their problems and generating worldwide support. The capacity to plan events and activities jointly, regardless of physical location, helps the Cameroon diaspora to maintain a coherent and united face in their activity. The transmission of information is another significant part of how social media and digital platforms aid the Cameroon diaspora in their political involvement. These sites serve as crucial conduits for exchanging news, exposing human rights violations, and increasing awareness about political events in Cameroon. By circumventing conventional media gatekeepers, diaspora members may highlight topics that may be underreported or neglected by major media channels. This democratization of information allows a broader spectrum of voices and opinions to be heard, leading to a more educated and active global society. Furthermore, social media helps the Cameroon diaspora to form networks and alliances with other activist groups, NGOs, and international organizations. These ties may give extra resources, enhance their messages, and create forums for cooperation. The capacity to reach a worldwide audience also implies that the diaspora may interact with and influence international public opinion, perhaps leading to increasing diplomatic pressure on the Cameroonian government to address their concerns. In essence, social media and digital platforms have transformed the way the Cameroon diaspora participates in political action. These technologies give the means for real-time communication, efficient coordination of actions, and extensive distribution of information, all of which boost the effectiveness of their efforts. By harnessing these tools, the Cameroon diaspora may overcome geographical boundaries, organize more effectively, and guarantee that their voices contribute to the global debate on political and social concerns impacting their nation.

## D. Challenges and Opportunities
### i. Challenges:
- The Cameroon diaspora makes considerable contributions to their home country, but faces constraints that might limit its efficacy and influence. Bureaucratic difficulties are one of the most significant impediments. These may take many forms, including costly and onerous administrative procedures that make it impossible for diaspora members to do business, invest, or participate in development initiatives. For example, obtaining appropriate permissions, licenses, or approvals often requires negotiating a labyrinth of paperwork and extended wait periods, which may be frustrating and cause

delays in project execution. Political opposition is another key difficulty for the Cameroonian diaspora. In certain circumstances, the political atmosphere in Cameroon may be hostile to outsider participation, particularly from expatriate populations seen to be critical of the administration or advocating for changes. This opposition might originate from a fear of losing authority or influence, as well as doubts about the motivations of diaspora programs. Such political impediments might limit diaspora groups' activity, restrict access to government officials, or even openly oppose their goals. A lack of coordinated strategy within the diaspora itself might be a difficulty. The Cameroonian diaspora is varied, consisting of people and organizations with various origins, interests, and techniques. This variety might result in fragmented efforts and a lack of cooperation. Without a cohesive approach, diaspora programs risk duplicating efforts, competing for the same resources, or failing to capitalize on the community's combined strength. This dispersion may dilute the overall influence of diaspora contributions, making it more difficult to achieve long-term, sustainable results. Tensions between diaspora projects and local authorities or communities in Cameroon might exacerbate the situation. These conflicts are often caused by divergent ideas, goals, or development methodologies. Local governments and communities may see diaspora programs as oppressive or divorced from real-world circumstances. There may be worries regarding the motivations driving diaspora activity, particularly if it is seen as meddling or attempting to control local agendas. Furthermore, cultural misconceptions or communication gaps might escalate tensions, resulting in resistance or lack of collaboration from local groups. Despite these limitations, the Cameroonian diaspora has various possibilities that may be used to strengthen its effect in the home country. The expanding trend of digital connection, along with developments in communication technology, has made it simpler for diaspora members to remain in touch with Cameroon, exchange expertise, and cooperate on projects remotely. This technology bridge has the potential to assist overcome some of the logistical and geographical constraints that have historically hampered diaspora involvement. Furthermore, the diaspora's exposure to other cultures, educational systems, and professional contexts provides individuals with distinct skills, information, and views that may be beneficial to Cameroon's progress. By bringing these talents and experiences back home, diaspora members may provide new solutions, best practices, and global standards that promote advancement in a variety of areas, including

education, healthcare, business, and technology. The Cameroonian diaspora has the ability to mobilize substantial financial resources via remittances, investments, and charitable donations. These money flows may help fund local development initiatives, provide financing for new firms, and contribute to social welfare programs. By wisely diverting these resources, the diaspora may help Cameroon's economy thrive and improve living conditions. Furthermore, the diaspora may serve as an effective advocacy organization, raising awareness and generating support for Cameroon on a global scale. Through lobbying, networking, and collaboration with global organizations, the diaspora may influence policy, attract foreign assistance, and generate possibilities for Cameroon in the global arena. This activism may assist solve some of the country's underlying difficulties, including governance challenges, human rights concerns, and socioeconomic disparities. To summarize, although the Cameroon diaspora has considerable problems, such as bureaucratic impediments, political opposition, and internal division, there are several possibilities that may be used to effect good change in the home country. The diaspora may overcome these challenges and contribute significantly to Cameroon's growth by utilizing technology breakthroughs, transferring skills and expertise, mobilizing financial resources, and participating in global activism.

- Another challenge is the sustainability of diaspora-led initiatives. Ensuring long-term effect requires regular involvement, competent management, and connection with Cameroon local needs and circumstances. Diaspora-led projects frequently begin with strong energy and excitement but sustaining this momentum may be challenging over time. Regular contact and constant cooperation from the diaspora community are vital to keep these programs alive and growing. This takes a commitment that may be hard to keep, particularly when people balance their personal and professional lives in their host nations. Proper management is another key component. Effective project management requires not just initial planning but also continual monitoring, adapting to changing conditions, and handling unanticipated obstacles. This may be especially challenging in a distinct cultural and logistical setting like Cameroon, where local dynamics, legislative frameworks, and socio-economic situations may vary greatly from those in the diaspora's home nation. Building local relationships and integrating community stakeholders from the onset may help reduce some of these problems, ensuring that projects are handled in a manner that is both efficient and culturally respectful. Alignment

with local needs and circumstances is vital for the success and longevity of any initiative. Diaspora activities must be built on a detailed awareness of the local terrain, including economic circumstances, social conventions, and existing infrastructure. Projects that fail to address these elements risk becoming irrelevant or even detrimental. Engaging local communities in the planning and implementation phases may give significant ideas and build a feeling of ownership and teamwork. This local engagement helps to guarantee that the initiatives are not only approved but also supported and maintained by people who benefit from them. Furthermore, finance might be a considerable impediment. While early donations could come from diaspora members, long-term viability frequently needs various financing sources. This might involve local government backing, foreign help, business sector investment, or community-based fundraising activities. Developing a thorough financing plan that integrates these numerous sources will assist guarantee that projects have the financial stability required to continue beyond the first stages. Monitoring and assessment are also key components of sustainable programs. Regularly monitoring the impact and success of initiatives enables for modifications and improvements to be made, ensuring that the programs stay relevant and valuable throughout time. This process involves precise metrics and a methodical approach to data gathering and analysis, which may be resource-intensive but is crucial for showing success and gaining continuous financing. The longevity of diaspora-led programs in Cameroon rests on continued participation from the diaspora community, effective management methods that are responsive to local settings, and the capacity to access various financing sources. Additionally, regular monitoring and assessment are important to modify and develop these initiatives, ensuring they suit the changing demands of the local community.

## ii. Opportunities

- The increasing impact of the Cameroonian diaspora offers a wealth of opportunities for the country's development and progress. Through enhanced collaboration between the diaspora and local entities, Cameroon can harness this potential to tackle its pressing issues more effectively. This collaboration can facilitate knowledge and skills transfer, technology exchange, and investment influx into key sectors. Additionally, it can promote cultural exchange and understanding, fostering a sense of unity and shared purpose among Cameroonians both at home and abroad. By leveraging the strengths and resources of the diaspora, Cameroon can accelerate its development and create a more prosperous future for all its citizens.

- Making use of the skills and expertise of the diaspora, especially in domains like technology, entrepreneurship, and governance, has enormous potential to promote innovation and advancement. Proactive measures that promote knowledge sharing and capacity building may have a substantial positive impact on Cameroonian institutions as well as local communities. Through using the vast knowledge and expertise of people outside, Cameroon may take advantage of fresh perspectives, methods, and connections to further its growth. By means of strategic collaboration and allocation of resources towards initiatives that promote knowledge transfer and skill development, the country can unlock growth opportunities, encourage entrepreneurship, and fortify governance structures. These actions will ultimately contribute to the nation's population's prosperity and sustainable development.

In summary, the Cameroonian diaspora is a significant component in the drive for change in Cameroon. Their economic contributions, social effect, cultural preservation initiatives, and political lobbying substantially affect the country's growth trajectory. While limitations persist, the potential for good change via expanded diaspora participation remains enormous. By utilizing the full potential of the diaspora, Cameroon may achieve more equitable and sustainable development, eventually benefitting from the worldwide connections and different viewpoints that its expatriate population provides.

# CHAPTER NINE

## PROSPECTS FOR THE FUTURE

### 9.1 CHALLENGES AND OPPORTUNITIES

Because of its variety in geography and culture, Cameroon is often referred to as "Africa in miniature" and is now at a turning point in its growth. Although the nation has many obstacles to overcome, it also has a lot of chances that might help it achieve sustained growth and development. This in-depth research looks at Cameroon's obstacles as well as possible paths forward.

### A. Challenges in Cameroon

**i. Issues with Political Instability and Governance:**

In Cameroon, political instability is still a major problem. The nation has gone through moments of turmoil, especially in the Anglophone parts where violent confrontations have resulted from aspirations for further autonomy. Corruption and a lack of transparency are examples of governance problems that impede efficient public administration and reduce public confidence in institutions.

**Impact:**
- Because of perceived volatility, there is less foreign investment.
- Development in areas impacted by war has stalled.
- Slow policy implementation and inefficient utilization of resources.

## ii. Development and Economic Diversification:

The two main drivers of Cameroon's economy are agriculture and oil. Because of this reliance, it is susceptible to changes in the price of commodities globally. Furthermore, the majority is in the informal sector, which restricts tax collections and makes comprehensive economic planning difficult.

**Impact:**
- Economic susceptibility to shocks from outside.
- Limited growth in employment and disparities in wealth.
- Sluggish modernization and industrialization advancement.
- 

## iii. Deficits in Infrastructure:

The nation has serious infrastructural problems, including as insufficient energy supplies, inadequate transportation networks, and restricted access to sanitary facilities and clean water. These shortfalls lower the standard of living for residents and obstruct economic activity.

**Impact:**
- Higher operating expenses and decreased market share.
- Limited population access to necessary services.
- Obstructed commerce and regional integration.

## iv. Education and Health:
The health and education sectors of Cameroon are underfunded and confront several difficulties. Three main issues are the prevalence of infectious illnesses, the state of healthcare facilities, and the lack of qualified medical workers. Problems in education include crowded classrooms, a lack of resources for instruction, and poor teacher morale.

**Result:**
- Reduced life expectancy and poor health outcomes.
- A mismatch in skills between the work market and low educational attainment.
- Social disparity and poverty over generations.

## v. Damage to the Environment:
The natural resources of Cameroon are being threatened by environmental problems such pollution, soil erosion, and deforestation. Natural catastrophes and unpredictable weather patterns are brought on by climate change, which intensifies these issues.

**Result:**
- A decline in food security and agricultural output.
- A loss of ecological equilibrium and biodiversity.
- Communities' heightened susceptibility to climate-related catastrophes.

## B. Opportunities in Cameroon
### i. Reforms in Politics and Institutions:
An atmosphere that is more stable and transparent may be achieved by addressing concerns of governance and political instability via reforms. Peace and stability may be fostered by bolstering democratic institutions, advancing inclusive governance, and strengthening the rule of law.

**Potential:**
- Increasing economic growth and drawing in foreign investment.
- Better public service performance and citizen contentment.
- Improved status abroad and collaboration within the area.

### ii. Innovation and Economic Diversification
One way to lessen the economy's susceptibility to external shocks is to diversify it beyond the oil and agricultural sectors by making investments in industries like manufacturing, technology, and services. Promoting innovation and entrepreneurship, particularly among young people, may be the engine of economic change.

**Prospect:**

- Reduction of unemployment and creation of long-term jobs.
- Greater self-sufficiency and economic resiliency.
- Increased ability to compete in local and international markets.

### iii. Development of Infrastructure

Developing infrastructure, especially those related to energy, transportation, and information and communications technology, may greatly increase economic activity and raise living standards. The required resources may be mobilized via international collaboration and public-private partnerships.

**Prospect:**
- Improved connection and lower operating expenses.
- Greater population access to necessary services.
- Promoted economic cooperation and commerce within the Central African continent.

### iv. Enhancements in Education and Health

Better health and greater educational achievement may result from strengthening the health and education systems via improved financing, capacity development, and policy changes. Certain demands may be met by placing an emphasis on basic healthcare and vocational training.

**Prospect:**
- A population that is healthier and more productive.
- A workforce with the skills to propel economic expansion.
- A decrease in socioeconomic disparities and an improvement in social unity.

## v. Environmental Management That Is Sustainable

Cameroon's natural resources may be safeguarded and long-term ecological balance can be ensured by tackling climate change and implementing sustainable environmental management techniques. Encouragement of conservation and renewable energy projects may be quite important.

**A possibility:**
- Enhanced food security and agricultural production. The conservation of natural environments and biodiversity.
- Risk mitigation associated with climate change and green growth promotion.

## C. Strategic Directions for Progress

In order to use these prospects and tackle the obstacles, Cameroon has the option to pursue many strategic approaches:

### i. Inclusive Political Dialogue:
Encouraging inclusive communication between various social and political groups in order to resolve disputes and promote patriotism.

### ii. Reforms to Economic Policy:

Putting into practice measures that encourage economic diversity, assist small and medium-sized businesses (SMEs), and draw foreign direct investment.

**iii. Infrastructure Investment:**
Giving priority to funding important infrastructure initiatives, using global alliances, and guaranteeing open fund management.

**iv. Healthcare and Education Reform:**
Increasing funding for the education and health sectors, boosting community-based health and education initiatives, and strengthening professional development and retention programs.

**v. Environmental Sustainability:**
creating and upholding legislation to save the environment, encouraging the use of renewable energy sources, and participating in global climate efforts.

**vi. Digital Transformation:**
Using digital technology to enhance business, government, healthcare, and educational systems in order to promote efficiency and creativity.

In conclusion, the capacity of Cameroon to successfully negotiate the intricate interplay of possibilities and challenges will determine its future prospects. Cameroon may put itself on a road to sustainable development by tackling challenges with governance, diversifying the economy, making infrastructure investments, enhancing health and education, and encouraging environmental sustainability. In order to accomplish these objectives and guarantee a successful future for all Cameroonians, the government, business community, civil society, and foreign partners must work together in harmony.

## D. Recommendations for Change

Cameroon, a Central African nation, has a plethora of socio-political, economic, and environmental difficulties that demand extensive changes for sustained growth and stability. Recommendations for change in Cameroon may be grouped into five important areas: governance, economic growth, social services, infrastructure, environmental conservation, and human rights. Each of these sectors is crucial for the country's prosperity and the well-being of its citizens.

### 1. Governance and Political Reform
#### a. Enhancing Political Stability:

Political stability is important to every country's growth. Cameroon has suffered political turmoil, notably with the current Anglophone issue. To address this:

- **Dialogue and Reconciliation:** Initiate inclusive discussions including all stakeholders, including opposition parties, civil society, and representatives from the Anglophone areas, to resolve issues and establish common ground.
- Decentralization: Strengthen the process of decentralization to ensure local governments have the authority and

resources to solve local concerns effectively. This may help decrease tensions and build a feeling of responsibility among local communities.

### b. Combating Corruption

Corruption is a key hindrance to growth in Cameroon. Measures to counter corruption include:

- **Strengthening Anti-Corruption Agencies:** Empower organizations like the National Anti-Corruption Commission (CONAC) with greater authority and resources to investigate and prosecute corruption cases.
- **Transparency and Accountability:** Implement comprehensive procedures for transparency in public budgets and procurement processes. Encourage the use of digital channels to eliminate human touch and diminish corruption chances.

### 2. Economic Development
### a. Diversification of the Economy

Cameroon's economy is mainly based on oil and agriculture. Diversifying the economy is vital for resilience against market swings.

- Promoting Industrialization: Invest in industrial areas such as manufacturing and processing businesses. This may generate employment and provide value to raw resources.
- Supporting SMEs: Provide financial and technical assistance to small and medium-

sized firms (SMEs) to foster innovation and entrepreneurship.

**b. Enhancing Agricultural Productivity**
Agriculture is a key industry that frequently underperforms owing to poor assistance.
- **Modernizing Agriculture:** Promote the adoption of modern agricultural methods and technology. Provide access to high-quality seeds, fertilizers, and irrigation systems.
- **Training and Education:** Offer training sessions for farmers on sustainable agriculture methods and market trends.
- 

### 3. Social Services
**a. Education** Education is the cornerstone of sustainable development.
- **Access to excellent Education:** Ensure that all children, particularly in rural and conflict-affected regions, have access to excellent education. This involves establishing additional schools, providing learning materials, and educating instructors.
- **Curriculum Reform:** Update the curriculum to incorporate technical and vocational training that matches with market demands. Emphasize STEM (Science, Technology, Engineering, and Mathematics) education to prepare pupils for future employment markets.

**b. Healthcare**
Improving healthcare services is crucial for a healthy population.

- **Universal Healthcare Coverage:** Work towards attaining universal healthcare coverage, ensuring that all people have access to critical health services without financial difficulty.
- **Healthcare Infrastructure:** Invest in healthcare infrastructure, especially in rural regions. Ensure that hospitals and clinics are fully equipped and staffed.

## 4. Infrastructure Development

Transportation Efficient transportation networks are vital for economic growth.

- **Road and Rail Networks:** Develop and maintain road and rail networks to promote connectivity inside the nation and with neighboring countries. Prioritize initiatives that boost access to markets and minimize transportation costs.
- **Public Transportation:** Improve public transportation systems in metropolitan areas to alleviate traffic congestion and pollution.

### b. Energy

Reliable energy supply is crucial for growth.

- **Renewable Energy:** Invest in renewable energy sources such as solar, wind, and hydropower to diversify the energy mix and minimize dependency on fossil fuels.
- Rural Electrification: Expand the electrical system to rural regions to boost local development and enhance living conditions.

## 5. Environmental Conservation
### a. Forest Management
Cameroon's woods are crucial for biodiversity and climate control.
- **Sustainable Logging Practices:** Enforce rules and regulations to ensure that logging is performed responsibly. Encourage reforestation and afforestation efforts.
- **Protected Areas:** Expand and successfully administer protected areas to maintain biodiversity and safeguard endangered species.

### b. Climate Change Adaptation
Climate change presents enormous hazards to Cameroon's ecology and economy.
- **Adaptation Strategies:** Develop and execute climate change adaptation strategies that address vulnerabilities in agriculture, water resources, and coastal zones.
- **Community Involvement:** Engage local people in conservation initiatives and climate adaption programs to promote sustainability and resilience.

## 6. Human Rights and Social Justice
### a. Protecting Civil Liberties
Ensuring the preservation of civil rights is vital for a fair society.
- **Freedom of Expression:** Safeguard freedom of speech and press. Protect journalists and activists against harassment and persecution.
- **Legal Reforms:** Reform the judicial system to guarantee independence and

impartiality. Provide training for law enforcement on human rights problems.

**b. Gender Equality**

Promoting gender equality is crucial for socioeconomic growth.

- **Empowering Women:** Implement policies that enhance women's education, employment, and involvement in decision-making processes.
- **Combating Gender-Based Violence:** Strengthen legislation and enforcement against gender-based violence. Provide support services for survivors, including legal aid and healthcare.

In summary, implementing these ideas needs a collective effort from the government, civic society, foreign partners, and the commercial sector. Each suggestion targets a unique facet of Cameroon's complex socio-economic and political situation, trying to build a more stable, affluent, and egalitarian country. Sustainable development in Cameroon rests on the country's capacity to accept change and execute changes that address both current and long-term issues.

# CHAPTER TEN
# CONCLUSION

"The Cry of Cameroonians" is a profound literary masterpiece that goes deep into the heart and soul of Cameroon, chronicling the numerous problems and successes of its people. The end of this book draws together the different strands that have been weaved across its chapters, bringing a contemplative and optimistic finish to the tales given.

**Thematic Recapitulation**
In the end, the author revisits the fundamental issues that have been covered throughout the book. These themes include the war for independence, the continuing fight for political and social justice, the rich cultural history of Cameroon, and the tenacity of its people. The conclusion underlines how these themes are interrelated and how they define the identity and destiny of the country.

**Reflection on Historical and Contemporary Issues**
The author gives a thoughtful appraisal of both historical and current concerns affecting Cameroon. This encompasses the colonial heritage, the effect of globalization, and the internal political strife. The conclusion

highlights the need of knowing these concerns in a historical perspective to realize the present state of things in Cameroon adequately.

**Voices of the People**

A key component of "The Cry of Cameroonians" is the voices of the regular people. The conclusion underscores the value of these voices, underlining that the fundamental power of Cameroon rests in its people. Their experiences of struggle, resilience, and optimism are what give the country its distinctive character. The author reiterates the importance to listen to these perspectives to solve the country's concerns effectively.

**Call for Unity and Action**

One of the primary themes in the conclusion is a call for unity and collaborative action. The author contends that for Cameroon to progress ahead, it must embrace unity across its different ethnic and cultural groupings. This unity is vital for resolving the socio-economic and political difficulties that the nation confronts. The conclusion urges on leaders and people alike to work together towards a shared objective of advancement and development.

**Hope for the Future**

Despite the multiple problems outlined in the book, the end delivers a message of optimism. The author believes in the ability of Cameroon to overcome its obstacles and reach greatness. This optimism is anchored in the perseverance and resourcefulness of its people, as well as the rich natural and cultural resources that the nation boasts.

## Lessons and Recommendations

The conclusion also includes practical lessons and suggestions for the future. These include the necessity for good government, the value of education and empowerment, and the role of the international community in supporting Cameroon's growth. The author underlines that although external help is crucial, the fundamental duty for transformation rests with the Cameroonians themselves.

## Personal Reflections

The author provides personal observations and experiences that have impacted their perception of Cameroon. These observations provide a human touch to the conclusion, making it not simply an intellectual critique but a genuine cry for change and advancement. The author's personal connection to the tales and themes explored throughout the book enhances the genuineness and emotion behind the story.

## Final Thoughts

In the last words, the author reiterates the significance of remembering the past while looking towards the future. The end is a striking reminder that the scream of the Cameroonians is not simply a cry of despair, but also a call for justice, dignity, and a brighter future. The book finishes on a tone of hope, with the idea that with joint work and unshakable dedication,

Cameroon can overcome its obstacles and reach a better future.

**Summary**

The conclusion of "The Cry of Cameroonians" is a complete compilation that draws together the historical, cultural, and socio-political storylines discussed throughout the book. It promotes solidarity, resilience, and optimism, while also giving practical ideas for the future. The conclusion serves as a compelling call to action, calling Cameroonians and the world community to work together towards a better and more fair Cameroon.

# APPENDICES

**11.1 Statistical Data**
"The Cry of Cameroonians" is a thorough and extensive analysis of the socio-political and economic problems experienced by the people of Cameroon. The book dives into historical antecedents, present challenges, and the ambitions of Cameroonians, giving a detailed portrait of their quest for justice, fairness, and improved living circumstances. One significant component of this book is the appendices, notably the subsection 11.1, which gives thorough statistical data to support the narrative and arguments offered throughout the text.

**Importance of Statistical Data**
Statistical data in "The Cry of Cameroonians" serves three significant purposes:

**1. Validation of Arguments:** By offering specific data, the book justifies its talks on themes such as poverty, education, health, and political repression. These data give a factual foundation for the author's arguments and observations.

**2. Contextual Understanding:** Numbers assist readers appreciate the scope and significance of different topics. For instance, knowing the actual literacy rate or unemployment data provides a deeper sense of the issues faced by the people.

**3. Comparative Analysis:** Statistics enable for comparison across time or between various areas within Cameroon. This assists in analyzing trends, development, or degradation in many domains.

**4. Policy Evaluation:** Data may be utilized to measure the success of governmental policies and initiatives. For example, health data may reflect the success or failure of public health efforts.

**Categories of Statistical Data**
The statistical data in the book may be grouped into six primary topics, each offering a deep look into various elements of Cameroonian life.

**1. Demographic Data:** This contains population number, age distribution, gender ratio, urban vs rural population, and ethnic mix. Understanding the demographic mix is vital for appreciating the social dynamics and possible areas of conflict or collaboration.

**2. Economic Indicators:** Data on GDP, income distribution, employment rates, inflation, and poverty levels give a picture of the economic situation in Cameroon. This section could also contain information about important industries, overseas commerce, and investment trends.

**3. Education Statistics:** Literacy rates, school enrollment figures, dropout rates, and education spending are essential measures. This data emphasizes the issues in the education system and the accessibility and quality of education for diverse groups of the population.

**4. Health Metrics:** Statistics on life expectancy, death rates, illness prevalence, healthcare infrastructure, and access to medical services offer an overview of the health difficulties encountered by Cameroonians. This section may also contain statistics on mother and child health, which is a crucial indication of overall development.

**5. Political and Human Rights Data:** This contains numbers on election participation, number of political prisoners, incidences of human rights abuses, and freedom of press indexes. Such data underlines the condition of democracy and civil freedoms in the nation.

**6. Social Indicators:** Data on crime rates, housing conditions, access to clean water and sanitation, and other social services give insights into the quality of life and social stability in Cameroon.

### Sources of Statistical Data

The data given in the book originates from a range of credible sources, including:

- **National Institutes and Ministries:** Official statistics from the National Institute of Statistics (NIS), Ministry of Public Health, Ministry of Education, and other governmental entities give trustworthy data.
- **International Organizations:** Reports from the United Nations, World Bank, International Monetary Fund, and World Health Organization give a worldwide perspective and comparability.
- **Non-Governmental Organizations (NGOs):** Data from NGOs operating in Cameroon, such as Amnesty International, Human Rights Watch, and local advocacy organizations, give insights into particular concerns and independent verification.
- **Academic and Research Institutions:** Studies and surveys done by universities and research centers offer depth and rigor to the statistical analysis.

### Interpretation of Statistical Data

Interpreting the statistical data demands an awareness of the larger environment in which these statistics exist. The book contains not just the raw statistics but also analysis and comments to assist readers make sense of the facts. For example, a high literacy rate may be tempered by a debate on the quality of education, while excellent GDP growth can be challenged in light of rising wealth disparity.

### Challenges in Data Collection

The book also recognizes the limitations in gathering reliable and up-to-date statistics in Cameroon. Issues such as political instability, lack of infrastructure, and governmental opacity may hamper the availability and trustworthiness of data. The author examines these problems and the possibility for contradictions or biases in the data supplied.

### Impact of Statistical Data on Advocacy

By integrating substantial statistical data, "The Cry of Cameroonians" intends to boost lobbying efforts for policy reform and foreign assistance. Solid, factual data is vital for persuading stakeholders and policymakers of the necessity for immediate action to solve the difficulties faced by Cameroonians.

**Finally**

The appendices of "The Cry of Cameroonians," notably the statistical data portion, offer a firm basis for comprehending the complex difficulties in Cameroon. Through thorough data collecting and analysis, the book not only educates readers but also prepares them with the skills essential for informed advocacy and policy creation.

**11.2 Chronology of Events**

"The Cry of Cameroonians" is an emotional and incisive analysis of the socio-political environment of Cameroon, describing the nation's journey through stormy periods and key events that have influenced its history. Chapter 11.2 of the book, titled "Chronology of Events," methodically records major milestones and turning points in Cameroon's recent history, offering a thorough chronology that assists in understanding the context of the nation's trials and accomplishments.

## Key Historical Milestones in Cameroon

**1. Pre-Colonial Era**
- **Early Civilizations and Kingdoms:** Cameroon was home to several indigenous cultures and civilizations, including the Sao civilization and the kingdoms of the Bamoun and Bamileke people.
- Arrival of European Explorers**: Portuguese explorers came in the 15th century, christening the region Rio dos Camarões (River of Prawns), which ultimately developed into Cameroon.

**2. Colonial Period**
- **German Colonization (1884-1916):** Cameroon became a German colony known as Kamerun, with the construction of governmental and economic systems.
- **World War I and Mandate System:** After Germany's defeat in World War I, Cameroon was partitioned between Britain and France under League of Nations mandates.

**3. French and British Rule (1916-1960)**
- **French Cameroon:** The bigger half was ruled by France, which established infrastructure and educational institutions while enforcing French culture and language.
- British Cameroon: Administered as part of Nigeria, British Cameroon witnessed less growth and was separated into Northern and Southern British Cameroons.

**4. Towards Independence**
- **1940s-1950s Nationalist groups:** Growing nationalist sentiments and groups, such as the Union des Populations du Cameroun (UPC), agitated for independence and reunification.
- **1954:** The UPC was outlawed by French authorities, leading to armed resistance and guerilla warfare.

**5. Independence and Reunification**
- **French Cameroon Independence (January 1, 1960):** French Cameroon obtained independence, becoming the Republic of Cameroon with Ahmadou Ahidjo as the first president.
- **British Cameroon Plebiscite (1961):** A UN-organized plebiscite resulted to the reunification of Southern British Cameroons with the Republic of Cameroon, becoming the Federal Republic of Cameroon.

**6. Post-Independence Era**
- **1966-1972:** Ahmadou Ahidjo's presidency witnessed consolidated control and persecution of dissent. The nation converted from a federal to a unitary state in 1972.

- **Paul Biya's Ascendancy (1982):** Paul Biya replaced Ahidjo, first pursuing his predecessor's programs but ultimately confronting political and economic obstacles.

## 7. Economic and Political Crises (1980s-1990s)
- **Economic Downturn:** Declining oil prices and economic mismanagement led to a serious economic crisis in the late 1980s.
- **Introduction of Multi-Party Politics (1990):** Growing internal and foreign pressure prompted the government to reestablish multi-party politics.

## 8. Recent Developments (2000s-Present)
- **Economic Reforms and Challenges:** Efforts to improve the economy and curb corruption encountered considerable challenges.
- **Anglophone Crisis (2016-Present):** Tensions between the Francophone-dominated administration and Anglophone areas evolved into a conflict, typified by aspirations for greater autonomy or independence.

## Detailed Chronology
### Pre-Independence
- **1884:** Germany established the colony of Kamerun.
- **1916:** British and French armies take over Kamerun during World War I.
- **1922:** League of Nations mandates Cameroon to Britain and France.
- **1948:** Founding of the Union des Populations du Cameroun (UPC), pushing for independence and reunification.

### Post-Independence
- **January 1, 1960:** French Cameroon obtains independence.
- **October 1, 1961:** Southern British Cameroons reunites with the Republic of Cameroon.
- **May 20, 1972:** A nationwide referendum results to the foundation of the United Republic of Cameroon.
- **November 6, 1982:** Paul Biya becomes president after Ahidjo's resignation.

### Economic and Political Evolution
- **1990*:** Reintroduction of multi-party politics despite economic collapse.
- **1992:** First multi-party presidential elections conducted; Biya wins despite claims of fraud.
- **2008:** Constitutional change eliminates presidential term limitations, letting Biya to prolong his power.

### Anglophone Crisis
- **2016:** Anglophone attorneys and teachers strike over perceived marginalization, developing into widespread demonstrations and violence.
- **2017:** Declaration of independence by Anglophone separatists, dubbing the territory "Ambazonia"; government crackdown increases.
- **2018:** Paul Biya wins re-election in a contested ballot amid continued strife.

**Analysis of Key Events**
- **Independence and Reunification:** The early years of independence were distinguished by attempts to unify the many regions and ethnic groupings within Cameroon. The transformation from federalism to a unitary state aimed at centralizing authority but also planted seeds of future dissatisfaction, especially in Anglophone areas.
- **Economic Crises and Reforms:** The economic slump in the late 1980s showed the weaknesses of Cameroon's economy, mainly dependent on oil earnings. Subsequent changes were only partly effective, with corruption and inefficiency continuing important challenges.
- **Anglophone Crisis:** The current turmoil in Anglophone areas reflects long-standing tensions about political and cultural marginalization. The situation has resulted to major human rights violations and displacement, raising international alarm and demands for discussion.

"The Cry of Cameroonians" offers a vital foundation for comprehending the complicated history and contemporary issues faced by Cameroon. By tracing the timeline of major events, the chapter helps readers appreciate the core causes of present difficulties and the continuing struggle for unity and growth in the country. The complete chronology serves as a great resource for historians, politicians, and anybody interested in the historical trajectory of Cameroon.

## 11.3 Glossary of Terms

The glossary portion of a book, especially one dealing with complicated socio-political topics like "The Cry of Cameroonians," is vital. It gives readers with precise definitions and explanations of terminology, phrases, and acronyms that are vital to comprehending the text. Below is a thorough vocabulary of terminology that could be featured in "The Cry of Cameroonians."

**A**

- **Anglophone:** Refers to English-speaking Cameroonians, particularly from the Northwest and Southwest parts of the nation.
- **Assimilation:** The process by which a person or a group's language and/or culture develop to resemble those of another group. In Cameroon, it frequently refers to the forced incorporation of Anglophone areas into Francophone administrative and cultural institutions.

**B**

- **Bilingualism:** The policy or practice of promoting and utilizing two languages. In Cameroon, this refers to the usage of both French and English as official languages.
- **Bamenda:** The capital of the Northwest Region of Cameroon, typically a focal point in talks regarding Anglophone complaints and resistance.

**C**

- **Cameroon Development Corporation (CDC):** One of the main employers in the Anglophone areas, active in agriculture and industries.
- **Centralization:** The concentration of administrative authority in a central government, frequently challenged in the context of Cameroon's governance system.
- **Colonialism:** The historical era when Cameroon was colonized by Germany, and then partitioned between Britain and France following World War I.

**D**

- **Decentralization:** The devolution of administrative authorities or duties from a central authority to local entities, touted as a solution to some of Cameroon's political challenges.
- **Douala:** The biggest city in Cameroon, a significant economic center, and part of the Francophone area.

**E**

- **Ethnic Groups:** Various ethnic groups in Cameroon, such as the Bamileke, Bassa, Bakweri, and Beti, each having different cultural identities.
- **Elders:** Respected older members of a group or culture, generally active in traditional leadership and dispute resolution.

**F**

- **Francophone:** Refers to French-speaking Cameroonians, particularly from the central and southern areas.
- **Federalism:** A suggested system of governance that incorporates numerous levels of government, each with its own powers. Many Anglophones support for a restoration to the federal structure that existed before to 1972.

**G**

- **Gendarmerie:** A military unit entrusted with policing responsibilities among civilian populations, often active in preserving order in Cameroon.
- **Grassfields:** The highland area in the Northwest, recognized for its cultural diversity and history of resistance.

**H**

- **Human Rights:** The fundamental rights and freedoms that all persons should be afforded. The book presumably explores abuses of these rights in the context of the Anglophone crisis.
- **Heritage:** The customs, cultures, and history handed down through generations, significant to both Anglophone and Francophone groups.

**I**

- **Independence:** The time when Cameroon obtained independence from colonial rule: French Cameroun in 1960 and British Southern Cameroons in 1961.
- Internally Displaced Persons (IDPs)**: People who have been forced to evacuate their homes but stay inside their country's boundaries, a big problem in Cameroon owing to persistent violence.

**J**

- **Justice:** The legal or philosophical notion by which fairness is administered. In the Cameroonian context, it frequently alludes to the perceived lack of justice for Anglophones.

**K**

- **Kumba:** A important town in the Southwest area, notable for its economic operations and as a scene of severe upheaval during the Anglophone issue.

**L**

- **Legislature:** The branch of government responsible for creating laws. The functioning and representation in Cameroon's legislature are issues of controversy.
- **Linguistic Marginalization:** The systematic exclusion or devaluation of a linguistic group, significant in the context of Anglophone and Francophone disputes.

**M**

- **Marginalization:** The process by which some people are driven to the fringe of society, economically, socially, or politically.

**N**
- **Mount Cameroon:** The tallest mountain in West Africa, situated in the Southwest area and a symbol of natural heritage.
- **National Dialogue:** Refers to attempts by the Cameroonian administration to resolve the problem via inclusive conversations with many stakeholders.
- **Ngraffi:** A name used to designate the people and culture of the Western Grassfields, typically participating in the Anglophone movement.

**O**
- **Occupation:** Military or administrative authority over a territory. In Cameroon, this word might characterize the presence of military personnel in Anglophone areas.
- **Oppression:** Prolonged severe or unfair treatment, an issue widely explored in the context of Anglophone-Francophone relations.

**P**
- **Plebiscite:** A direct vote by the people on a particular proposition, such as the 1961 plebiscite that determined the destiny of British Southern Cameroons.
- **Political Prisoners:** Individuals jailed for their political activity, a crucial subject in talks about freedom and democracy in Cameroon.

**Q**
- **Quasi-Federalism:** A phrase characterizing the administrative organization of Cameroon that purports to be federal yet works with strong central authority.

**R**
- **Repression:** The act of subduing someone or something by force. This phrase is regularly used in the book to characterize government measures against Anglophone demonstrations and movements.
- **Reunification:** The combining of British Southern Cameroons and French Cameroun in 1961, led to the foundation of the Federal Republic of Cameroon.

**S**
- **SCNC (Southern Cameroons National Council):** A political group campaigning for the independence or increased autonomy of Anglophone areas.
- **Self-Determination:** The right of a people to decide their own political status, a core demand of Anglophone campaigners.

**T**
- **Terrorism:** The illegal use of violence, typically against civilians, to accomplish political purposes. The government occasionally characterizes separatist operations as terrorism.
- **Traditional Leaders:** Chiefs and other indigenous authority who play key roles in local government and dispute resolution.

**U**
- **UN Trusteeship:** The arrangement under which British Southern Cameroons was managed by the United Kingdom on behalf of the United Nations before its plebiscite and final reunification with French Cameroun.
- **Unity:** The condition of being unified or linked as a whole, a prominent idea in national discourse but challenged by regional differences.

**V**
- **Violence:** Physical force designed to injure, damage, or kill someone or something. The book presumably discusses different sorts of violence encountered in the Anglophone areas.
- **Victimization:** The activity of singling someone out for harsh or unfair treatment, typically addressed concerns minority rights and ethnic groups.

**W**
- **West Cameroon:** Refers to the previous state within the federal system that comprised of the Anglophone regions before the unitary state was founded in 1972.
- **War Crimes:** Serious breaches of the laws and customs applicable in armed conflict, which could be examined in reference to the current war.

**Y**
- **Youth Militias:** Armed organizations formed mostly of young people, engaging in the fight either in favor of or against the government.

**Z**
- **Zone of war:** Areas undergoing continuing war, mainly the Northwest and Southwest areas of Cameroon.

This glossary contains crucial words that aid in understanding the socio-political backdrop and topics explored in "The Cry of Cameroonians," affording readers a basis for appreciating the complexity of Cameroon's Anglophone problem.

# AFTERWORD

As I bring this book, *The Cry of Cameroonians*, to a close, I reflect on the journey that inspired its creation. The words inscribed on these pages are not merely mine, but the collective voice of a people yearning for justice, peace, and a brighter future. Each chapter is a testament to the resilience of the Cameroonian spirit, an unbroken will that has endured the cyclones of political unrest, social inequality, and economic hardship.

Writing this book has been both an intellectual and emotional endeavor, influenced by my own experiences and profound connection to my homeland. Through this voyage, I have come to realize that our struggles are not isolated, nor are they unique. They reflect the broader challenges encountered by many African nations as we seek for self-determination, decent governance, and sustainable development. Yet, despite the agony and the obstacles, there is hope. The lament of Cameroonians is not one of defeat, but of determination—a call for change, a call for unity, and a call for action.

I hope that this book serves as a flame, initiating conversations and reflections not just among Cameroonians, but also among global citizens who believe in the principles of freedom, equality, and human dignity. We all have a role to play in molding the future of our nation, and it is through our collective efforts that we can create the Cameroon we dream of—a Cameroon where every voice is heard, where every life is valued, and where peace and prosperity are not just aspirations, but realities.

To all who read these words, I urge you to not let this lament fall on silent ears. Let it inspire you to engage, to act, and to stand up for the values we hold dear. The future of Cameroon is not just in the hands of its leaders, but in the hands of every citizen—at home and abroad. It is through solidarity, comprehension, and unwavering commitment that we will rise above the challenges of today to establish a better tomorrow.

With gratitude to those who continue to fight for the cause of our nation and to those who dare to dream of a brighter future, I leave you with this final thought: Cameroon is not lost. It is still wailing out, and it is up to us to answer.

Thank you.

— Dr. Therence Atabong Njuafac

# ABOUT THE AUTHOR

## Dr. Therence Atabong Njuafac

Dr. Therence Atabong Njuafac is a distinguished Cameroonian scholar and social commentator, known for his dedication to issues influencing his country and Africa at large. In his thought-provoking book *The Cry of Cameroonians*, Dr. Njuafac offers an insightful examination of the socio-political landscape of Cameroon, using his platform to emphasize urgent challenges that have long impacted his homeland.

With a foundation anchored in academia and an unwavering commitment to social justice, Dr. Njuafac has become a voice for those often unheard. His work reflects a deep-seated concern for human rights, governance, and the pursuit of equity within Cameroonian society. Drawing upon a multitude of research and personal observations, *The Cry of Cameroonians* presents not only an exposé of the hardships encountered by the Cameroonian people but also advocates for sustainable and inclusive solutions aimed at nurturing unity and progress.

Dr. Njuafac's writing is both poignant and eloquent, carefully balancing a scholarly tone with accessible language to reach a wide readership. Through his work, he aims to inspire dialogue and encourage a collective sense of responsibility, inviting readers to contemplate upon the actions required to drive meaningful change. His commitment to these themes makes *The Cry of Cameroonians* a critical and pertinent piece, imploring both Cameroonians and the international community to heed the voices advocating for peace, dignity, and reform.

# ACKNOWLEDGEMENT

Writing *The Cry of Cameroonians* has been a journey profoundly rooted in the profound experiences, challenges, and aspirations of the people of Cameroon. I am indebted to all those whose voices, fortitude, and resilience have inspired and shaped this work. This book is as much theirs as it is mine—a testament to their fortitude and an ode to their unyielding spirit.

My sincerest gratitude goes to the team at Humanity Helping Hands Cameroon (HHHC) for their unwavering support and encouragement. Their dedication to elevating the lives of Cameroonians has been a potent reminder of what community, compassion, and collaboration can achieve. I am also grateful to Apostle Mbeanang Dilland A., Falon Atabong, Awandem Terence, Assist. Prof. Filiz Katman, whose guidance has illuminated my path with wisdom and insight.

I extend profound gratitude to my friends and family, who have been a constant source of love and encouragement throughout this journey. To my readers, thank you for embarking on this journey with me. May this book serve as a reminder of the resilience and dignity of the Cameroonian people, and may it inspire a deeper understanding of our shared heritage and future.

Dr. Therence Atabong Njuafac

Milton Keynes UK
Ingram Content Group UK Ltd.
UKHW022016131124
451149UK00013B/1161